WHY BRILLIANT PEOPLE BELIEV

A PRACTICAL TEXT FOR CRITICAL ↗ THINKING

AND CREATIVE!

A Classical Discipline Meets the Digital Age

J. Steve Miller and Cherie K. Miller

Wisdom Creek Academic

Early Comments

"Why Brilliant People Believe Nonsense" should be must reading, not just for every college freshman but for anyone who wants to think clearly and rationally. As someone who taught college-level logic and critical thinking classes for more than two decades, I found the book fascinating from cover to cover and a real aid to my own understanding. By the time one finishes the book one is bound to have a far better understanding of why the leading intellects of every age have so often gotten it wrong. More importantly, the careful reader of the book will be far better equipped to guard against such blunders in his or her own thinking.

- Doug Erlandson, Ph.D., author, assistant professor of philosophy, University of Nebraska (retired)

"In this compulsively readable work J. Steve Miller and Cherie K. Miller offer an invaluable tour of critical thinking and life wisdom. Countless fascinating anecdotes keep the reader turning the pages, and every story has a lesson to teach, an insight to bestow. Why Brilliant People Believe Nonsense is an ideal handbook for wise living in the twenty-first century."

- Randal Rauser, Ph.D., philosopher, author and professor at Taylor Seminary, Alberta, Canada

With poignant examples, organized contentions, and dry wit, Miller's book is a mental rout that will turn exclamation points into question marks.

- Orin C. Davis, Ph.D., Lecturer in Critical and Creative Thinking at the University of Massachusetts, Boston

From birth, I was taught to mindlessly believe whatever the smartest and most successful people said. This book taught me to learn from everyone, but to think for myself. Often, the author tells fascinating stories to make his points, so that even deep concepts are easy to understand and remember. Do you want to learn how to think for yourself? Read this book.

- Katarina Kocsisova, college freshman

I suppose everyone will be CEO of something, whether it be a little league team, a family, or a multinational corporation. To be successful, leaders must assimilate information, weigh advice, and in short, THINK. Beyond helping us to recognize our flawed thinking, Miller provides a thorough roadmap to thinking more accurately and creatively. And fortunately for reluctant readers, he uses entertaining and insightful stories to make the subject matter come to life.

-Reade Cody, author, entrepreneur and president of AngelLink, AccountLink and Peoplink

Engaging, thought-provoking, and surprisingly…fun! Requiring students to master this book before taking my courses in law and business ethics would make my job so much easier.

- Dr. Fred Jones, professor at Louisiana College, Supreme Court attorney, author and speaker

"Brilliant! Every high school senior and college freshman should devour this book!"

- Dr. Robert McGinnis, educator and author

"High school proved that I can retain information long enough to pass tests, but with this book I have started learning how to critically think through issues and find the real truth in information."

- Nick Dodenhoff, college sophomore

"The author has a way of writing that comes across very personal, like he genuinely cares about helping his readers in their quest for wisdom. I seldom sense that degree of passion and compassion in the books I read."

- Erica Lundak, college sophomore

For corrections, book orders, professor desk copies (typically a pdf), free student pdf versions, author appearances, permissions, inquiries or interviews, contact the publisher by email or regular mail at:

Wisdom Creek Academic
(An imprint of Wisdom Creek Press, LLC)
5814 Sailboat Pointe NW, Acworth, Georgia 30101
www.wisdomcreekpress.com
info@wisdomcreekpress.com
jstevemiller@gmail.com (for direct contact with the author)
770-337-4385

Cover Illustrations by Chelsea Wilson
Cover Design and Layout by Carole Maugé-Lewis

Publisher's Cataloging-in-Publication Data

Miller, J. Steve, and Miller, Cherie K.

Why brilliant people believe nonsense: a practical text for critical and creative thinking / J. Steve Miller. -- Textbook edition.

pages cm

Includes bibliographical references and index.

ISBN 978-0-9883048-9-5

1. Critical thinking. 2. Creative thinking. I. Title.

BF441.M55 2015 153.4'2

QBI15-600106

LCCN: 2015907777

Vector drawing of "Dr. Cackler" purchased from the kbeis portfolio on istockphoto.com
"Indiana Jones" photo from the Urosh Petrovic portfolio, purchased from istockphoto.com

Dedication

To Dr. Peter Schaefer (1973-2015), former Senior Research Psychologist, Department of Defense. Your pursuit of wisdom challenged and inspired many, including myself. Your brilliance and passion will be greatly missed.

Acknowledgements

The following professors and educators gave valuable input, from recommended resources to advice on content and publishing:

Katherine Ebener, Kennesaw State University

Jon Michael Fox, Buffalo State College

Dr. Keisha Hoerrner, Kennesaw State University

Dr. Fred Jones, Louisiana College

Dr. Phillip Page, Assistant Superintendent of Schools, Cobb County, Georgia

Dr. Tammy Powell, Kennesaw State University

Dr. Gerard Puccio, Buffalo State College

Dr. Randal Rauser, Taylor University

Bob Schoenberg, University of Massachusetts, Boston

Jeremy Szteiter, University of Massachusetts, Boston

Dr. Peter Taylor, University of Massachusetts, Boston

Special thanks to those above who teach in the Master of Arts program in Critical and Creative Thinking at the University of Massachusetts, Boston, and those at the International Center for Studies in Creativity at Buffalo State College, New York. May your tribe increase! Bob Schoenberg will contribute ideas to the accompanying website on how to teach this material, drawing on his years of teaching critical and creative thinking.

Other friends and acquaintances helped with everything from brainstorming ideas, to editing, to adding insights from their fields of expertise: Dr. Ken Walker, Dr. Peter Schaefer, Dr. Robert McGinnis, Sr., and Dr. Robert McGinnis, Jr. Thanks to family friends Maxwell Orochena, Mark Hoerrner, Reade Cody, and Tim Harman.

Over 60 of my students at Kennesaw State University shared their reflections on early versions of various chapters, leading me to make helpful changes.

Family members Ann, Richard, Angela, David, Paul, and Andrew all offered candid input.

Carole Maugé-Lewis, professor and coordinator of graphic design at the School of Art and Design at Kennesaw State University always does a remarkable job with the design and layout of my book covers. On this project, she recruited Chelsea Wilson to draw the original cover illustrations.

I owe a great debt to many of my early teachers/mentors, foremost among them: Dr. William Lane Craig, Dr. Robertson McQuilkin, and Dr. Al McAllister, who challenged and equipped me to think critically during my formative college and graduate school years.

Cobb County and Kennesaw State University librarians came through securing books and articles that weren't available either locally or through digital databases.

For a list of authors who've impacted the content of this book, see the Index and End Notes. If I've said anything profound in these pages, attribute it to my great fortune to learn from those researchers, writers and teachers who went before me.

"I" in this book refers to J. Steve Miller as the primary researcher/writer. Cherie, who I'm extremely fortunate to call my wife, contributed more than enough ideas, resources, leads, connections, and edits to warrant her being listed as coauthor.

Transgressions of grammar and fact rest on me. Please alert me to corrections and ideas for improvement at jstevemiller@gmail.com. I consider this a "living" document that will hopefully grow and improve over the years. Your ideas can make a difference!

Contents

INTRODUCTION

Brilliant Nonsense: Example #1

Steve Jobs, the brilliant co-founder and CEO of Apple Inc., significantly impacted six industries: animated movies, computers, music, phones, tablet computing and digital publishing. As I write, Apple ranks as the world's most valuable company (measured by market capitalization). So whenever you use a Mac computer, iPhone, iPad, iPod, or iTunes, credit Steve Jobs and his brilliant associates.

But his decisions weren't always brilliant.

When Jobs, ever the perfectionist, aspired to build a new headquarters, he chose what he considered the top architectural firm in the world and agonized alongside the architects with every detail. After they agreed upon the drawings, he brought them home to show his family over dinner.

Far from being impressed, his son Reed joked that the aerial view looked like male genitalia. Initially, Jobs dismissed the comment as a typical product of a teen mind. But the next day, to his horror, he realized his son was right. The experts changed the design.[1]

So why did one of the top business leaders in the world, working with elite architects, fail to notice something so significant? Why couldn't the experts see, after endless dreaming and drawing, what a teen casually noticed over supper?

Brilliant Nonsense: Example #2

A band played their hearts out for years. Their fans loved them, but their manager had contacted and been rejected by every record label in the industry catalog.[2]

Why the rejection? Some industry leaders believed that the public's taste in music had shifted from groups to solo singers. Decca Records at least allowed them to audition, but rejected them, in part because groups with guitars were considered "on the way out." None could envision such a band producing significant sales.[3]

The year was 1962. The band was *The Beatles*. They were eventually signed by a small, struggling label and quickly rose to become the most popular band in history, selling over a billion units worldwide. And contrary to the industry experts, five decades down the road, bands with guitars are as popular as ever.

Smart people often form wrong opinions and make stupid decisions. This book examines the mental flaws that informed their decisions—decisions that make or break businesses, relationships, and lives.

Put more positively, I aspire to help us think more clearly and creatively, resulting in better decisions and cutting-edge innovation.

The Languishing Art of Thinking

Both IBM and Apple were driven by their mottos:

> IBM - "Think"
>
> Apple - "Think Different"

The day they forget those mottos will be the day they begin their descent into irrelevance.

Unfortunately, the science and art of thinking is often relegated to a sideshow in contemporary education. As one pundit put it, "Today's education consists of transferring a set of notes from the teacher to the student, without going through the minds of either." For many students, a decent rote memory suffices to regurgitate the facts on test day.

Thus, we memorize the Kings of England without debating the pros and cons of monarchies, failing to consider how those insights might help us to better run a business, or a country. We memorize the events of World War II, leading up to the bombing of Hiroshima and Nagasaki, but fail to grapple with the moral issues involved with a decision that obliterated 200,000 people, many of them civilians.

Was it justified? On what grounds? When a professor asked his bright graduate students these questions, some (from countries where vast rote memorization produced high test scores) responded with blank faces and a desperate plea: "Tell us the answer and we'll memorize it!"

As novelist Dorothy Sayers lamented, many students never master "the lost tools of learning," such as sound research and critical thinking. They're introduced to a short list of subjects, but graduate without the tools to master a new subject.[4]

Yet the ability to master new information and explore new fields is critical at a time when last year's knowledge may be irrelevant to solve this year's problems.[5] As philosopher Eric Hoffer put it,

> "In times of profound change, learners will inherit the earth, while the learned find themselves beautifully equipped to deal with a world that no longer exists."

What's at Stake?

If we fail to learn these skills, and neglect to sharpen them throughout our lives, we're easy prey for the schemers, the charlatans, the cult leaders, the get-rich-quick presentation that seemed brilliant at the seminar, but disastrous after the investment.

The stakes in weighing evidence are high. Do I marry her or not? Do I trust the traditional doctor or the herbalist? Will the vaccination more likely save me or kill me? Is marijuana relatively harmless, or a potentially addicting motivation killer? Should I become a plumber or a philosopher...or neither...or both?!? Life's most important questions are answered by acquiring relevant, accurate information and drawing valid conclusions from it.

The Payoff

This book intends to sharpen your thinking skills. Those who engage deeply enough to understand, internalize and apply the skills should find themselves:

- Thinking more clearly.
- Leading more effectively.
- Innovating more creatively.
- Seeing through the common deceptions of advertisers and salesmen.
- Simplifying complex and convoluted arguments.
- Managing life's decisions more confidently.
- Expressing convictions more powerfully.
- Becoming indispensable to the business community.

Why Critical* *and Creative** Thinking?

Underscoring the need for both critical and creative thinking in business, consider these challenges from two recent *Harvard Business Review* articles:

- "If you want to succeed in 21st Century business you need to become a critical thinker."[6]
- "A company's most important asset isn't raw materials, transportation systems, or political influence. It's *creative capital*—simply put, an arsenal of creative thinkers whose ideas can be turned into valuable products and services. Creative employees pioneer new technologies, birth new industries, and power economic growth. Professionals whose primary responsibilities include innovating, designing, and problem solving—the creative class—make up a third of the U.S. workforce and take home nearly half of all wages and salaries. If you want your company to succeed, these are the people you entrust it to."[7]

***Critical Thinking** = the process we use to analyze and evaluate propositions.

***Creative Thinking** = the process we use to create and develop unique ideas.

A survey of over 1,000 people who hire for various industries, conducted by the Accrediting Council for Independent Colleges and Universities, asked respondents to rank the importance of various competencies for the future. They ranked "novel and adaptive thinking" first, for both "current importance" and "future importance."[8]

Taught in isolation, critical thinking can become a rather negative, snooty enterprise. So beyond using critical thinking to reveal the flaws in a proposed solution, businesses want innovators who can use both critical *and* creative thinking to propose better solutions. As we shall see, in real life decisions, both are integrally entwined.[9]

Why Focus on the Shortcomings of the Brilliant?

Because it's both entertaining and instructive. *Entertaining* because it's quite amazing to watch brilliant people do dumb things; I suppose it makes us intellectual mortals feel better about ourselves. *Instructive* in that it helps us to see the subtlety of error. If the brilliant can be led astray, how much more vigilant should the rest of us be?

Why Me?

Having successfully navigated three diverse undergraduate schools and two graduate schools, I've picked up a few tips on how to reap the most out of formal education. But after graduation I found myself learning outside the university, zealously seeking the wisdom to navigate challenges in my shifting careers and personal life. I've dedicated my best years to equipping and inspiring young people and their leaders both nationally and internationally.

But more importantly, I'm addicted to learning! When I encounter important issues that impact me and my family, I can't rest until I've sufficiently studied them. These issues often lead me into various fields—science, philosophy, history, literature, psychology, etc. And I can't resist a biography of an interesting person, whether a political leader, innovator, business success, writer, musician or intellectual. From this wide reading, I gather relevant and entertaining examples of creativity and faulty reasoning. I hope that my lifelong enthusiasm for learning is contagious!

A Bias Toward the Practical

In raising my own children and teaching students at Kennesaw State University, I'm constantly challenged to transform the complicated and obtuse into something clear, memorable, and practical.

To succeed in life, we need to learn proper nutrition and exercise, how to make relationships work, how to run a business, how to deal with failure, how to make moral decisions, and how to vote wisely in a democracy. Yet, how do we separate fact from fiction when thousands of conflicting voices authoritatively urge us to practice nonsense?

That's the essence of this book—finding wisdom and avoiding nonsense.

I major on the practical—stuff you can actually use in daily life. And rather than just spoon-feeding simplistic answers, we'll wrestle together over important issues that challenge us to think. Often the solutions aren't so black and white and may involve as much creativity as logic.

And since no political party or worldview holds a monopoly on clear thinking, I'll try to be even handed when I critique what I deem to be nonsense. Whether I read Republicans or Democrats, traditional doctors or alternative doctors, atheists or theists, conservatives or liberals, there's plenty of nonsense to draw from, so I'll strive for balance.

Since I'm rather eclectic, I'll draw illustrations from various fields—from football to physics, from music to intellectual history. Hopefully, the variety will help produce more "Aha!" moments than yawns.

And since specifics are more enlightening (and entertaining!) than generalities, I often refer to arguments made by real people. In doing so, I don't intend to show disrespect for these individuals—merely disrespect for their arguments. I sincerely hope I've not misunderstood or misrepresented anyone. If I have, those errors will reinforce my point that we need to think for ourselves rather than put blind faith in experts, even if that "expert" is me.

(Please do let me know where I've unwittingly spouted nonsense, so that I can make corrections in future revisions. I'm at jstevemiller@gmail.com.)

The Content

In a typical chapter, I tell stories of blunders made by bright people, invite readers to reflect with me upon the causes, suggest ways to avoid them, and finally discuss ways to think more creatively in the subject area.

To help students engage their higher level thinking, I ask thought questions and recommend further paths to explore. Those wishing to expand on certain ideas might also find help in the extensive endnotes.

Teachers may wish to assign select chapters that they deem most relevant to their students and goals. (See the Table of Contents for descriptions of each chapter.) I provide teaching tips, extensive lesson plans, and presentations, all free on the accompanying website:

www.criticalcreativethinking.wordpress.com

So let's dive in and sharpen our ability to think...and think different!

J.S.M. - Kennesaw State University, Spring 2015

Tip for Students

To get the most out of this book, read a chapter long before your class and write down your takeaways. In this way, by the end of the book, you can consolidate your practical wisdom into ten or so goals, so that your reading can more easily result in life change.

Reading a chapter early allows time to reflect upon the content and apply it to life. You'll likely see the principles operating in your other classes, in conversations with friends and family, or in the dialogue of a movie or TV show. Give yourself time to reflect, and you'll find yourself thinking more critically and creativity in daily life, which is the purpose of this book.

SECTION ONE

WHY DO BRILLIANT PEOPLE BELIEVE NONSENSE? BECAUSE THEIR ATTITUDES MAKE THEM VULNERABLE

CHAPTER 1
THEY'RE OVERCONFIDENT

"And if I claim to be a wise man,
it surely means that I don't know."

— *Kansas* ("Carry on My Wayward Son")

"It's not so much what people don't know that hurts them;
it's what they do know that ain't so."

— Mark Twain

A TV Series That Couldn't Possibly Work

The top executives at Disney—drawing upon their years of experience in the entertainment industry—expressed their total disdain for a new series that their ABC network underlings were pushing. Their expert opinion?

- "This is a waste of time."
- "That's never going to work."

On a scale of one to ten, with ten being the best, the CEO graded it a two.[1]

But its creator, Lloyd Braun, against the recommendations of his superiors, moved forward with the pilot for "Lost," which became ABC's first breakout hit in years, topping all the ratings, capturing the imagination of millions of followers, winning an Emmy Award for Outstanding Drama Series and a Golden Globe for Best Drama.

Yet, even after seeing the pilot, the CEO was singularly underwhelmed. "*Lost* is terrible," he complained, "Who cares about these people on a desert island?"[2] Although millions of viewers ended up caring, Braun was fired before the series even started.

How could the experts, with their many years of experience in the field, totally miss the public appeal of this series?

I'd suggest that, with education and experience in a field, overconfidence can creep in. By losing touch with viewers, customers, and colleagues, industry leaders can subtly transform from wisdom *seekers* to wisdom *dispensers.* Whether or not this accurately explains the Disney debacle, it almost certainly explains many other top-down business and personal decisions that in retrospect look foolish.

From my experience and study, pride, overconfidence, and arrogance lead to more nonsense than failing to detect logical fallacies. These traits will come up repeatedly in this book. A quest for truth requires the humble recognition that I might be dead wrong, even in my area of expertise. The arrogant collect information, not so much to search for truth, but to reinforce their prejudices.

By contrast, the great philosopher Socrates challenges us from millennia past that his greatest intellectual achievement—that which set him apart from the masses—was his realization of how little he knew.[3] Thus, he strove to humbly follow the evidence wherever it led.[4] So before we examine common errors in research and reasoning, let's reflect upon this foundational attitude for the seeker of truth.

He Never Stopped Learning

Some mega-successes resisted the urge to become overconfident, so that they never stopped humbly learning. Consider Sam Walton.

Walton built Walmart—the world's largest retailer—from scratch, fueled by his voracious, unrelenting search for retailing wisdom. Even after he acquired an arguably unequalled knowledge of retailing, he remained more of a learner than a teacher.

- He spent many a Saturday morning at 4:00 AM sharing donuts with his truck drivers, getting their perspective on how different locations fared. This is one of my favorite mental pictures of a humble wisdom-seeker: the greatest retailing mind on the planet munching a donut across the table from his truck drivers, gleaning wisdom from those who see the inner workings of his stores from an angle he might never see.[5]

- Once a week, he met with his store managers, so that they could mutually learn from their failures and successes.[6]

- He seemed to spend as much time in competitors' stores as his own, gathering fresh ideas.[7]

- He attended seminars, read reports, and drained industry leaders of their wisdom. Note how the executive vice president of the discounters' trade association in New York City described his first meeting with Walton (another of my favorite mental pictures of Walton):

> "So in comes this short, wiry man with a deep tan and a tennis racket under his arm. He introduced himself as Sam Walton from Arkansas. I didn't know what to think. When he meets you, he looks at you—head cocked to one side, forehead slightly creased—and proceeds to extract every piece of information in your possession. He always makes little notes. And he pushes on and on. After two

> and a half hours, he left, and I was totally drained. I wasn't sure what I had just met, but I was sure we would hear more from him."[8]

Listen to Walton as he expresses his humility in passionately pursuing ideas:

- "I learned a lesson which has stuck with me all through the years: you can learn from everybody. I didn't just learn from reading every retail publication I could get my hands on, I probably learned the most from studying what John Dunham [a competitor] was doing across the street."[9]
- "Great ideas come from everywhere if you just listen and look for them. You never know who's going to have a great idea."[10]
- "I'd still say that visiting the stores and listening to our folks was one of the most valuable uses of my time as an executive. But really, our best ideas usually do come from folks in the stores. Period."[11]

Contrast Walton with managers who never ask the part-time workers for their ideas, the professor who never asks her colleagues or students for input to improve her teaching, or the physician who fails to listen to his patients. Those who stop learning make decisions based upon their whims, or warmed-over ideas from decades past, which might be as irrelevant to today's world as cassette tapes and floppy disks.

Opening the Idea Floodgates

Yesterday's great ideas can become today's nonsense. What worked last year might not work this year. That's why we need to insure a steady flow of fresh ideas. Jack Welch, one of the most successful business leaders of our time, implemented processes at General Electric to allow the free flow of ideas. These processes led to transforming a lumbering, behemoth company into an innovator that acted like a startup.

Rather than trusting in their extremely talented and educated top management to generate the best ideas, Welch encouraged everybody, from all levels of GE, to share their ideas. But a roadblock exists in many, if not most companies—a part of the company culture that stifles fresh ideas.

Welch explains:

> "I have always been a huge proponent of candor. In fact, I talked it up to GE audiences for more than twenty years. But since retiring from GE, I have come to realize that I underestimated its rarity. In fact, I would call lack of candor the biggest dirty little secret in business. What a huge problem it is. Lack of candor basically blocks smart ideas, fast action, and good people contributing all the stuff they've got. It's a killer."[12]

Why is the candid exchange of ideas so rare? Often our supervisors aren't open to new ideas, either because they're intimidated or aloof. (Isn't it intriguing how two seemingly opposite traits—insecurity and pride—can manifest themselves in precisely the same attitudes and actions?)

Welch identified this problem at GE. To overcome it, when he gathered people for training, he'd ask their managers to leave the room. With the intimidating presences safely out of earshot, people felt open to share. When the managers returned, the participants had distilled the best ideas to recommend for implementation.[13]

Consequently, GE's ordinary workers felt valued; their voices mattered. Finally free to speak his mind, a middle-aged appliance worker lamented:

> "For 25 years, you've paid for my hands when you could have had my brain as well—for nothing."[14]

How tragic! Twenty-five years relegated to silence. Yet doesn't he represent multitudes of workers and students, who seldom get asked for their candid input?[15]

The Point

Why do brilliant people believe nonsense? Some become convinced—by their grades, degrees and experience—that they don't need constant input from others. They're overconfident. By blocking or ignoring candid input, they set themselves up for dumb mistakes. By tearing down those walls, humble learners unleash a torrent of fresh ideas to keep themselves challenged, fresh, and growing.[16]

Remember, it took a child to notice that the Emperor had no clothes. It took a teen to notice that Apple's proposed headquarters looked like…well…something they certainly didn't want to be remembered for. Perhaps showing the humility to run our ideas by a spouse or roommate or child or student could save us from more nonsense than reading ten academic books on logical thinking. For this reason, I'll return to this theme in later chapters, showing how it often helps us to overcome obstacles we face on our quest for truth.

Action Points
Overcoming Overconfidence

1. Keep your pride in check.

Were you brought up like those in the fictional town of Lake Wobegon, "where all the women are strong, all the men are good looking, and all the children are above average?"[17] If so, don't be surprised if you focus on your strengths, ignore your weaknesses, and view your coworkers and fellow students as a bit slow. Most male drivers surveyed think they drive better than average.[18] Go figure.

So identify attitudes that inhibit your thinking, that block a constant flow of fresh ideas. Is it pride—the notion that you're so learned that you have little new to learn? Is it a sense of superiority that subtly tells those "beneath" you that their ideas don't count?

If you're overconfident, many top companies will sense your pride and pass on hiring you. As one executive at Google said, "We try to avoid people that have incredibly large egos that are inconsistent with their abilities or are not good at working in teams."[19]

2. Get candid input from peers and superiors.

Surround yourself with people smarter than yourself. Resist the temptation to surround yourself with "yes men" and "yes women." Most of us need two kinds of friends—positive peers to encourage us, and candid peers to keep us realistic and challenged.

Accomplished novelist Terry Kay says that he honed his craft while reporting sports for the *Atlanta Journal*. Under the leadership of sports writing legend Furman Bisher, the writers would meet as a group, read each other's columns, and critique them mercilessly.[20] What an education! Do you have people in your life who will regularly, fearlessly, tell you what they think? If not, who could you give permission to be one of those people?

3. Solicit the wisdom of "normal" people.

When brilliant film director Steven Spielberg was directing the hit film E.T., he asked seven-year-old actress Drew Barrymore what she would say if she were writing a certain line. He went with her response.[21] So if you're a young, aspiring artist, why not get your little sister's candid opinion? She just might be more objective than your mom.

As a writer, I may give chapters or entire manuscripts to thirty or more diverse people for candid input. Some are fellow writers or experts in a field; but I learn a surprising amount from young people and those who don't like to read or write. Fellow writers look for cool sentences, clever analogies and grammatical minutia. Non-writers want to know if it's interesting, useful, and makes sense. I gave an early chapter of my personal finance book to an eighth grade writing class, even though the book targeted older teens and adults. Their input was first rate.[22]

4. Reap more from your reading and classes.

By far, most of my students don't enter my classes as passionate seekers of wisdom. Instead, they focus myopically on identifying and remembering what they might need to know for a test, seemingly giving little thought to gathering wisdom for life.

By contrast, I interviewed Ajit Gupta, a Silicon Valley entrepreneur from India who's disrupting the communications industry with his novel approaches to solving communication and data sharing issues. When he studied for his master of arts degree at the University of Alabama, he went beyond reading and listening to lectures for the purpose of merely passing tests. Instead, he looked for ideas that he could use for his future business pursuits. When he came across a useful idea, he'd put it in a box. So when he graduated and moved to Silicon Valley, he arrived with more than just a degree. He arrived with seven boxes full of ideas, the most promising of which he pursued in his business ventures.

As a result, Gupta holds 12 technology patents, sold one of his companies for the stock equivalent of about $500 million and keeps innovating with his new company, recently winning "The Big Idea Award" for the most disruptive business model at the 2013 Innovator Awards.[23]

Other people collect ideas through applications such as Evernote, which can sync with their smart-phones, iPads, desk-top computers and other devices. Still others make notes in their e-books for later reference. I tend to buy used paper books, so that I can mark them as I read and index them in the back (e.g., I might write, "great idea for creativity, p. 15") for ideas I might use in the future.

Questions That Can Identify and Avert Pride-Induced Disasters

1. Who are some "normal" people who might be valuable sounding boards for my ideas?

2. Do I have an emotional stake in an issue that makes the outcome more than a matter of evidence? Who might I consult to get a bigger picture?

3. Is my level of certainty on an issue warranted by the strength of the evidence?

4. Have I read or heard out the top proponents of opposing views with an open mind?

Flex Your Neurons! Pursuing the Point of Know Return

1. What were some of your parents', friends', and associates' most disastrous decisions? How could a bit more humility, or candid input, have possibly averted these disasters?

2. Do you know people who believe a truckload of nonsense, but believe it's brilliant? Why do you think they believe it?

3. What advice would you give a friend or colleague to reveal how her pride is resulting in poor decisions?

4. What were some of your most memorable misjudgments?

5. What actions and attitudes could help prevent such beliefs and decisions in the future? Could asking others for candid input, or casting the net for ideas more widely have helped? If so, how?

6. Many of us detest the behavior of certain large corporations. I certainly don't agree with everything the leaders of Walmart and General Electric do. For this reason, some people resist learning from such organizations. How can we learn to sift the good from the bad so that we can open our minds to excellence wherever it may be found?

7. If Sam Walton and Jack Welch were working in your realm of influence (family, vocation, education, community service, etc.), how might they stifle arrogance, welcome candor, and unleash a steady flow of fresh ideas?

8. In your work, how often are you asked for input? Do you feel you have good ideas to offer, if only people would ask in the right way? How might this insight influence your style of leadership, now or in the future?

9. Do your coaches or parents or teachers or other authorities ever ask you how you would run things if you had the authority? Would regularly asking your advice be a good idea? Why or why not?

10. Are there times when candor can be harmful? If so, in what situations?

Recommended Trails
For the Incurably Curious and Adventurous

1. To see how Sam Walton started a company that encouraged ideas from all levels, read *Sam Walton: Made in America*, by Sam Walton, with John Huey (New York: Doubleday, 1992).

2. To see how Jack Welch transformed an old company that tended to rely on management for ideas, into a company that acted more like a nimble, young start-up, soliciting ideas from all levels, read *Winning,* by Jack and Suzie Welch (New York: Harper-Collins, 2005), especially chapter two on "candor." See also *Jack: Straight from the Gut*, by Jack Welch, with John A. Byrne, (Warner Business Books: New York, 2001), especially chapter 12 on transforming GE's training center into an idea factory.

3. To see how Pixar Animation and Disney Animation use a "Braintrust" to get fresh ideas in the early stages of their films, moving them "from suck to not suck," read *Creativity Inc.: Overcoming the unseen forces that stand in the way of true inspiration,* by Ed Catmull, with Amy Wallace (New York: Random House, 2014), especially chapter five, titled "Honesty and Candor."

4. This is a great article to see how successful companies encourage and manage creativity: Managing for Creativity, by Richard Florida and Jim Goodnight, *Harvard Business Review*, July 2005.

Making It More Personal
Practical Takeaways

"Our thoughts are so fleeting. No device for trapping them should be ignored."

— Henry Hazlitt

In each chapter, I include this section to help you consolidate your takeaways. It takes only a few minutes; but without taking time to do a final reflection, you'll likely finish the book with a blur of ideas that never impact your life. In the final chapter, I'll ask you to reflect back on these takeaway sections to consolidate your main thoughts and set ten of them as personal goals.

Writing takeaways requires engaging your higher level thinking, reflecting on your own personality and interests and strengths and weaknesses and life direction, and creatively deciding which ideas apply most profoundly to your own life. Use the questions to start your thinking. You don't have to answer all three questions if only one or two reveal your main takeaways.

What are one or more ideas provoked by this chapter that you can apply to help you think more critically?

____

____

____

What are one or more ideas that you can apply to help you think more creatively?

____

____

____

What else do you want to make sure you don't forget?

____

____

____

CHAPTER 2

THEY'RE UNDER CONFIDENT

Challenging Expert Opinion Through Research in a Digital Age

"*Beware of false knowledge; it is more dangerous than ignorance.*"

— George Bernard Shaw

"Blind respect for authority is the greatest enemy of truth."[1]

— Albert Einstein

In fleeing overconfidence (Chapter One), don't run to the opposite extreme—under confidence—which can prove just as frustrating in a search for truth. The under confident may fail to engage critical issues at all, reasoning:

> "Who am I to question brilliant experts who've spent their entire lives studying and reflecting? I'll just find the experts and trust their conclusions."

But trusting experts can be dangerous business, because experts spout nonsense as well as truth. Yet many continue to trust them uncritically, because after all, *they* are the experts, not us.[2]

To help break the debilitating spell that experts often cast, let's reflect upon some of their confident pronouncements that didn't turn out so well.

Music Critics

On Elvis Presley:

"You ain't goin' nowhere...son. You ought to go back to drivin' a truck." (manager of the "Grand Ole Opry," firing Elvis Presley after his first performance)[3]

On The Rolling Stones:

"The singer will have to go." (the Stones' new manager, assessing Mick Jagger in 1963)[4]

On the Future of Rock Music:

"It will be gone by June." (*Variety*, 1955)[5]

On Johann Sebastian Bach:

"[Bach's] compositions are deprived of beauty, of harmony, and of clarity of melody." (composer and music critic in *Der critische Musikus*, Hamburg, May 14, 1737)[6]

On Ludwig van Beethoven:

"Beethoven's Second Symphony is a crude monstrosity, a serpent which continues to writhe about, refusing to expire, and even when bleeding to death (Finale) still threshes around angrily and vainly with its tail." (A review written after the first Leipzig performance, in *Zeitung fur die elegante Welt*, 1828)[7]

"An orgy of vulgar noise." (Louis Spohr, violinist and composer, on Beethoven's Fifth Symphony, 1808)[8]

Literary Critics

On Charles Dickens:

"We do not believe in the permanence of his reputation.... Fifty years hence...our children will wonder what their ancestors could have meant by putting Mr. Dickens at the head of the novelists of his day." (*The Saturday Review*, London, May 8, 1858)[9]

On William Faulkner:

"The final blowup of what was once a remarkable, if minor, talent." (Review in *The New Yorker*, Oct. 31, 1936. Thirteen years later Faulkner was awarded a Nobel Prize for Literature).[10]

On Mark Twain:

"A hundred years from now it is very likely that [of Twain's works] 'The Jumping Frog' alone will be remembered." (Harry Thurston Peck, editor of *The Bookman*, Jan., 1901)[11]

On Walt Whitman:

"...Whitman is as unacquainted with art as a hog is with mathematics." (*The London Critic*, 1855)[12]

Publishers

Editor of the *San Francisco Examiner*, rejecting Rudyard Kipling's submission:

"I'm sorry, Mr. Kipling, but you just don't know how to use the English language."[13]

Film

Will the film succeed?

MGM production executive advising co-founder Louis Mayer to not bid on the rights for *Gone with the Wind* (Mayer took his advice and passed):

"Forget it, Louis, no Civil War picture ever made a nickel."

"*Gone with the Wind* is going to be the biggest flop in Hollywood history. I'm just glad it'll be Clark Gable who's falling flat on his face and not Gary Cooper." (Actor Gary Cooper commenting on his turning down the part of Rhett Butler. Adjusted for inflation, *Gone with the Wind* was the most successful film ever made.)[14]

Will the actors succeed?

MGM executive on Fred Astaire's screen test, 1928 - "Can't act. Can't sing. Balding. Can dance a little." (Astaire went on to star in 31 musical films, eventually deemed the fifth "Greatest Male Star of All Time" by the American Film Institute.)[15]

"You have no talent" - Universal Pictures executive to actor Burt Reynolds.

"You have a chip on your tooth, your Adam's apple sticks out too far, and you talk too slow." - Same executive to Clint Eastwood. (Both Reynolds and Eastwood went on to become the most profitable actors of the 1970's, still playing successful roles today.)[16]

Technology

Electric lights will never make it

"...unworthy of the attention of practical or scientific men." (Conclusion of a committee, commissioned by the British Parliament, reporting on Edison's incandescent lamp, c. 1878)[17]

"When the Paris Exhibition closes electric light will close with it and no more will be heard of it." (Erasmus Wilson, professor at Oxford University, 1878)[18]

Record players will never make it

"The phonograph...is of no commercial value." (Thomas Edison, 1880)[19]

Radio will never make it

"The radio craze...will die out in time." (Thomas Edison, 1922)[20]

"I am reported to be 'pessimistic' about broadcasting.... The truth is that I have anticipated its complete disappearance.... ...[People] will soon find a better pastime for their leisure." (British author and historian H.G. Wells, 1928)[21]

Television won't make it

"Video won't be able to hold onto any market it captures after the first six months. People will soon get tired of staring at a plywood box every night." (Darryl F. Zanuck, head of 20th Century-Fox Studios, c. 1946)[22]

Computers won't make it

"Worthless." (Sir George Bidell Airy, Astronomer Royal of Great Britain, speaking of the "analytical engine" invented by Charles Babbage, 1842.[23] Airy's opinion resulted in the British government discontinuing funding for Babbage's work in mechanical calculation. Today Babbage is considered the inventor of the computer.)

"I have travelled the length and breadth of this country, and have talked with the best people in business administration. I can assure you on the highest authority that data processing is a fad and won't last out the year." (Editor of business books at Prentice-Hall publishers, c. 1957)[24]

"There is no reason for any individual to have a computer in their home." (Ken Olson, President of Digital Equipment Corporation, at the Convention of the World Future Society in Boston, 1977).[25]

It's impossible to produce atomic energy

"There is not the slightest indication that [atomic] energy will ever be obtainable. It would mean that the atom would have to be shattered at will." (Albert Einstein, commenting sometime after 1931. The atom was first "shattered" seven years after his comment.)[26]

On smoking and cancer

"If excessive smoking actually plays a role in the production of lung cancer, it seems to be a minor one." (Dr. W.C. Heuper, National Cancer Institute, *NYT*, April 14, 1954.)[27]

On economic forecasting

These pronouncements came just before the stock market crash of 1929, which sparked The Great Depression:

"Stocks have reached what looks like a permanently high plateau." (Irving Fisher, Professor of Economics at Yale University, Oct 17, 1929, seven days before the crash.)[28]

"[1930 will be] a splendid employment year." (U.S. Department of Labor, Dec. 1929)[29]

The end of the age of invention

"Everything that can be invented has been invented." (Charles Duell, Commissioner of the U.S. Office of Patents, in trying to persuade President McKinley to abolish his office, 1899.)[30]

Reflections

Foolish quotes by experts are by no means rare. My main source for the above quotes, *The Experts Speak*, by Christopher Cerf & Victor Navasky, contains about 2,000 expert pronouncements that later proved to be nonsense. Yet, we continue to trust in and quote experts, often as slam dunk evidence to prove a point.

Why do brilliant people believe nonsense? Because they often swallow expert opinions without critically reflecting upon them.

Obviously, I'm not out to discount all experts and their opinions. Many people draw foolish conclusions by *failing* to consult experts. But it's one thing to respect them, quite another to follow them blindly. The frequency of their folly, confidently proclaimed in our most trusted publications, warns the wise against uncritical acceptance. Many bow in reverence to experts of every sort and far too many students mindlessly memorize the opinions of their professors. After all, who are we to question a PhD in her field?

Honing our Research Skills with a Contemporary, Vital Issue

None of the above quotes were recent. To discover if today's expert opinion has reached a higher plane, let's examine some contemporary pronouncements in a field that's of vital interest to all of us: medicine.

With scientific knowledge readily accessible through the Web, we'd expect today's experts to be more informed and less liable to spout nonsense, particularly in high stakes, scientifically-based fields like medicine. So let's consult trusted medical sites concerning that most common of all infectious diseases—the common cold.

The importance of accurate information concerning colds is hard to overestimate. In the United States alone, colds account for 40 percent of all absences from work, with an economic impact exceeding $20 billion per year.[31] And colds can be dangerous. It's not uncommon for colds to lead to pneumonia and even death, particularly among the elderly.

The following story is fictitious, but I gathered the quotes from authoritative medical sites in January of 2014. By patiently engaging in "Julie's" research, we can pick up a few tips to sharpen our own quest for truth. And don't merely grasp her method—catch her passion!

Level 1 Learning - Hear an Expert Opinion

Julie's daughter Jade is begging to play outside in the sandbox, but it's the first cool and breezy day of Fall. A year ago, Jade caught a cold that progressed to a harrowing bout with pneumonia, so Julie is understandably cautious. Besides, her family is flying in for Thanksgiving at the end of the week and she doesn't want illness to spoil the festivities.

Julie's mother always swore that exposure to cold can lead to colds, but Julie's know-it-all best friend, Mandy, assured her that cold weather has nothing to do with it. "Colds are caused by viruses," Mandy proclaimed smugly. "A respected doctor cleared that up for us at the 'Raise Them Right' parenting conference."

Level 2 Learning - Consult a Site or Article or Book that Summarizes Expert Opinion

But Julie's not so sure. Mandy's dead certain about almost everything, but in the end seems to strike out as often as she hits homers. Even if cold weather isn't the *immediate* cause, couldn't it be a *contributing* cause, like weakening the immune system? And no single doctor, no matter how well respected, is omniscient. Wouldn't it be wise to consult other doctors, or an authoritative medical site that consolidates their wisdom?

So Julie opens her trusty laptop on the kitchen table and asks Google, "Can cold air cause colds?" But to bypass the pop advice, she wisely adds to her search, "*WebMD*," billed as "The leading source for trustworthy and timely health and medical news and information."

"It's so easy these days," reflects Julie, "to get authoritative information through the Web!" Sure enough, with a couple of clicks, she gets her answer in 10 seconds flat. Now it's Julie's turn to feel smug.

At least for a moment.

Here's what she reads:

> "Cold weather...does not cause colds—at least not directly. Despite its name, the common cold is not caused by cold." "It doesn't have any effect at all....There's no correlation," says a cold and flu expert.

Julie's response: "Well, that's rather convoluted. The first sentence hints that there might be an *indirect* correlation* between cold weather and colds. Then the expert assures me dogmatically that it has no effect whatsoever—"no correlation."[32]

> ***Correlation** = A relationship or connection between two or more things.
> Think: "Co-Relation"
> Example: "There's typically a correlation between the height of children and the height of their parents."

"That sounds like a clear contradiction. If I cut some-one's jugular and he dies, would the same expert insist that neither I nor the knife were causes, since the "direct" cause was the loss of blood? At the very least WebMD should call it a correlation. (Jade impatiently knocks on the door with her sandbox toys.) Don't these writers know that multiple causes can be 'contributing causes,' both directly and indirectly? Either might keep me from opening the door for Jade."

Think!

If you were Julie, where would you look for more information at this point in your quest?

Level 3 Learning: Compare Other Summaries of Expert Opinion

Julie decides to consult other authoritative medical sites.

(**Note to reader**: Please resist skimming this section. Although it's a bit tedious, sound research requires dogged diligence and saintly patience. If you're reading this as an assignment, try to forget for a moment that it's school work. Instead, imagine yourself to be Indiana Jones or Sherlock Holmes, obsessing on solving a mystery where lives are at stake, which is certainly the case with this issue.)

- ***Medicalnewstoday.com*:** (This site promises to give up-to-date medical facts.): "Experts say that going out when it is cold does not have any effect on the risk of catching a cold or spreading one."[33]

  Julie's Response: "Hmm...so 'not any effect' would seem to rule out cold air as both a direct and indirect cause. But that contradicts the 'at least not directly' statement from WebMD. Also, neither of these first two articles were documented with primary sources. I'd better look further."

- ***Everyday Health*:** (Claims peer review by top medical experts at places like Harvard.) This site underscores the WebMD sentence, stating that exposure to cold weather can be an indirect contributor, but fails to tell how it might contribute.[34]

  Julie's Response: "That's not helpful, since it lacks the specifics I need. If the "indirect" cause is that more people gather inside and spread germs during cold weather, then this wouldn't impact Jade going to the sandbox."

- **The respected *Merck Manual*,** billed as the most widely used medical textbook, states: "Susceptibility to colds is not affected by exposure to cold temperature...."[35]

  Julie's Response: "Another dogmatic statement that seems to ignore indirect causes, if there are any. But this is a respected source that medical professionals use for reference!"

- ***MayoClinic.com***: (Connected with one of the most respected clinics in the world.) This site says you're more susceptible to colds in Fall or Winter *because that's when more people are indoors*.[36]

  Julie's Response: "Bingo! So that's the supposed correlation! Jade, put on your hat and jacket!"

  "But I'm losing faith in these supposedly authoritative sources. They contradict one another; some internally contradict; none so far are documenting their sources and none are very thorough. And besides, here in Atlanta people stay indoors, not just when it's cold, but when it's too hot and muggy. If "more people indoors" is the culprit, why don't colds peak during midsummer in south Georgia and Florida? Perhaps just a few more sources...."

- According to the U.S. Government sponsored ***National Institutes of Health*** **(NIH)**, "Researchers still haven't identified the causes of 20 to 30 percent of adult colds, presumed to be viral."[37]

- **Julie's Response:** "PRESUMED!?! Now *this* is demoralizing. All the other "experts" told me that colds were caused by viruses, period, which seemed to rule out getting a cold directly from exposure to cold weather. Now I'm informed that for one fifth to one third of colds, we don't really know their cause! So how can we know that exposure to cold *isn't* a contributing cause in these cases?"

- **NIH:** "Seasonal changes in relative humidity also may affect the occurrence of colds. The most common cold-causing viruses survive better when humidity is low—the colder months of the year. Cold weather also may make the inside lining of your nose drier and more vulnerable to viral infection."

  "Although a connection exists between the number of cases of the common cold and the fall and winter seasons, there is no experimental evidence that exposure to cold temperatures increases the chances that you will get a cold."[38]

  Julie's Response: "So theoretically, according to the NIH, cold weather *could* be a culprit in causing colds, but we don't yet have the experimental evidence showing it. This is a far cry from the "expert" who assured me in no uncertain terms, "It doesn't have any effect at all." Perhaps some of those earlier articles hadn't been updated by recent studies. This one was last updated in May of 2011, two and a half years ago."

- ***The Centers for Disease Control and Prevention***: The CDC is America's health protection agency. It has a section on preventing colds, which says nothing about limiting exposure to cold.[39]

  Julie: "I wonder if other countries are accessing different information or interpreting the research data differently. When I lived in Slovakia, parents were hyper about their kids getting the least bit cold. Let's check a European site." (Jade is getting hot in her coat and absently pulls at the computer cord for attention.)

- **National Health Service**: ("The NHS is one of the world's largest publicly funded health services.") According to this UK site, "The only thing that can cause a cold or flu is a cold or flu virus. Getting cold or wet won't give you a cold. However, if you are already carrying the virus in your nose, it might allow symptoms to develop."[40]

  Julie's response: "Now *that's* convoluted! The first sentence contradicts the USA's National Institute of Health, which stated that for up to a third of colds, we don't yet know the cause. If the NIH is right, the NHS statement is a presumption rather than a statement of fact, and should have been stated as such."

  "But let's assume, for the sake of argument, that the first statement *is* correct. If so, the second sentence draws a conclusion from the first statement, but equivocates* on the word "cold." In the first sentence, "cause a cold" means that the flu virus has multiplied enough to cause symptoms, which agrees with common usage and definitions. But the second sentence ("Getting cold or wet won't *give you a cold*") uses a similar phrase to mean something entirely different: "to get some cold viruses in your nose, whether or not they multiply and develop symptoms."

  ***Equivocation** = A logical fallacy in which a person uses a word to mean multiple things, while appearing to use the same meaning throughout.

  "Significantly, we've just shifted to an obscure definition, invalidating the argument. No doctor says 'You've got a cold' solely because you have 25 microscopic cold viruses lying dormant in your nose, but no symptoms. Every medical site I've read begins by defining a cold with its symptoms. Now they want to change the meaning mid article, effectively muddying the waters!"

  "If they stick with the common definition, this article should have more precisely concluded: 'Getting cold or wet won't put cold viruses into your nose. But if you're already carrying cold viruses, getting cold or wet could allow the viruses to enter the body and multiply, thus giving you what we've previously defined as a cold, complete with its symptoms.'"

  NHS: But there's more on this site, a new bit of evidence that none of the other sites mentioned. "A study at the Common Cold Centre in Cardiff found that people who chilled their feet in cold water for 20 minutes were twice as likely to develop a cold as those who didn't chill their feet." 180 students participated in the study.[41]

  Julie's response: "What the...?!? If that was a decent study, then it contradicts the Merck Manual's dogmatic statement that "Susceptibility to colds is not affected by exposure to cold temperature...." It also contradicts the National Institute of Health's statement that "there is no experimental evidence that exposure to cold temperatures increases the chances that you will get a cold."

  "Yet, this study comes from a hotbed of specialized research on the common cold. Cardiff University is one of Britain's leading universities. Its Common Cold Centre has conducted clinical trials and clinical research on the common cold for over 25 years. Dr. Eccles, who works at the Center and wrote up the study, has written or co-written 65 articles on the cold in peer-reviewed journals over the last decade."[42]

NHS: The authors suggest that some of the people with cold feet were already carrying cold viruses, although they were having no symptoms. Getting chilled caused blood vessels in the nose to constrict, affecting the defenses in the nose and making it easier for the virus to replicate.

Julie's response: "That does it for supposedly authoritative sites that try to summarize the latest evidence for me! The cold feet study was published nine years ago and should have been considered by these sites. I'll dig into the primary studies and summaries of evidence myself, reading the professional, peer-reviewed literature."

Level 4 Learning: Find Primary Sources,* Especially Documented Studies in Peer-Reviewed Literature*

Julie logs into her local library system to search vast databases of peer-reviewed journals. There she finds the primary article reporting the research on the cold feet, plus several other peer-reviewed studies in such respected journals as *The International Journal of Tuberculosis and Lung Disease*, *Acta Otolaryngologica*, the *British Journal of Hospital Medicine, and Family Practice,* all of which suggest that getting cold impacts colds beyond forcing us indoors with more people.[43]

***Primary Source =** first-hand testimony or direct evidence about a topic. Example: a researcher reports on his latest research.

***Peer Reviewed Journals =** publications in which people report findings from their original research, or summarize prior research. Experts in their fields (their "peers") decide if an article is worthy of publication. In later editions of the journal, experts may add to or challenge earlier articles.

Level 5 Learning: Reflect on and Summarize Results

Julie: "The sites I trusted to consolidate medical science failed me. Their confusing shifts in word meanings, dogmatic pronouncements, internal contradictions, lack of documentation, failure to acknowledge significant studies, and contradictions with similar sites led me astray."

"Enough research for now; I'll try to summarize what I've found. If I define a 'cold' as almost everyone commonly uses it, such as the World Health Organization, it means 'an illness with symptoms such as sneezing and a runny nose, resulting from a cold or flu virus multiplying in the body.'"[44]

Thus I conclude:

1. As the weather gets colder, by each degree Celsius, winter deaths increase. The onset of colder weather, even moderately colder in tropical climates, is correlated with more colds.

2. There is no scientific consensus as to why this happens. Perhaps there are several causes.

3. While the "more people inside" hypothesis surely explains some of the increase in colds, there's no conclusive evidence that it explains all or even most colds. In fact, some scientists note that this hypothesis, as a complete explanation, doesn't make sense and contradicts available data.

4. Competing hypotheses, such as cold air causing nasal blood vessels to constrict and inhibiting the immune response, are consistent with the available data.

5. With Jade's medical history and a family gathering around the corner, the current evidence (at least the portion I was able to find) suggests that letting Jade out in the cold, without a space suit, is a bad idea. We'll watch *Beauty and the Beast* for the 64th time instead. (Jade throws her coat on the floor and with breathless anticipation presents Julie with the treasured DVD.)

The Challenge of Consolidating Wisdom

If our brief excursion into respected medical sites is any indication, many of our most trusted sources have let us down. Why?

Think!

Before I suggest answers, use your higher level thinking to brainstorm: Why would these trusted and supposedly authoritative sites contain such confusing and contradictory data on such an important topic?

On such a critical subject (the cold), in such an important field (medicine), for the most frequented and trusted articles to be in such a deplorable state of disarray suggests that the solution to providing current, accurate medical knowledge runs deeper than updating a few articles. Perhaps their *method* of gathering and disseminating knowledge is somehow flawed. Let's look at some of the problems these sites (as well as general consolidation sources such as *Encyclopedia Britannica*[45]) face.

1. It takes knowledge of a very specialized field to identify the true experts who can write or fact-check any given article. In today's social media, hordes of pseudo-experts want to establish themselves as "thought leaders" and proclaim themselves "experts" and get quoted. Often, although some medical writers may be fairly competent in the general field of "infectious diseases," they may not be up-to-date with the more specialized issue of "causes of the common cold."

2. A successful article will likely result from a team effort. Imagine that writing an article on the common cold fell upon a single individual. She should ideally have mastery of the specialized field, a researcher's diligence, a writer's gift of lively prose, an analytical philosopher's knack for precision, a temperament of dispassionate objectivity, a judge's skill for weighing evidence, and the humility to express conclusions with the appropriate assurance/doubt. How many such people exist? If such a job description requires a team, can these organizations afford to hire competent teams to manage each specialty?

3. Many primary sources, or academic consolidations of research, aren't readily available. Online databases of peer-reviewed articles are far from complete. Older articles or articles from less popular journals are often unavailable, or available only as brief summaries. (Those with access to a university library may be able to get articles scanned into pdf documents and e-mailed from distant libraries.) Often, the most authoritative textbooks cost hundreds of dollars (such as one I found on the common cold), unless they can be borrowed through interlibrary loan.

4. Because of the constant and increasing flood of new information, articles of a medical nature need to be updated quickly as new studies impact the field. Yet, without unlimited funds, how can anyone keep articles on thousands of diseases updated?

5. The above factors mean that enormous amounts of time and money would be required to research, write, and constantly update such huge online databases, as well as medical textbooks. It's likely that, in order to stay within budget, websites of this type simply can't keep up with the ever-increasing flood of information. In other words, don't hold your breath for drastic improvement in these sites over time.

If American sites aren't yet acknowledging a nine-year-old cold feet study done by a respected university in Great Britain, how much less likely are they to consider recent research in Brazil or Burma, especially if it is published in Portuguese and Burmese?

Thus, in the early decades of the 21st century, we often find ourselves information rich, but wisdom poor. Enormous amounts of data exist, but finding the most authoritative data and summaries of that data can be challenging.

Yet, the stakes are high. Nursing home managers might read one of the above sites and conclude that saving money by turning the heat down a few degrees in the winter and putting an additional blanket on each resident is both fiscally and compassionately warranted. If their source was mistaken, they could cause much needless suffering.

How might we overcome this apparently deplorable state of consolidation? How might parents and researchers find consolidated information more effectively?

The Promise of Crowdsourcing*

One path to overcoming the above challenges would be to harness the power of crowdsourcing. After all, Julie, although not a medical specialist, thinks clearly and precisely, not to mention being a tireless researcher. If the consolidation sites she consulted offered to take input, she could point out the contradictions, overstatements, and studies they overlooked.

***Crowdsourcing** = getting input from many people, typically using the Internet.

But for site administrators to read constant input from hordes of people, some valuable and some bogus, and regularly update thousands of articles would require a huge staff of paid editors at a likely prohibitive expense to each organization.

So why couldn't someone set up a website that allows anyone to edit and update, expert or not, as long as they document their sources and state their conclusions clearly and accurately? Julie could recommend updates to the article on the common cold, complete with documentation. Experts who are passionate about the subject, such as those working at the Common Cold Centre at Cardiff University, just might volunteer as gatekeepers to minimize nonsense. Faculty and students doing research in Brazil and Burma could summarize and contribute summaries of their research in English that editors for popular consolidation sites might never find.

Such a site is called a wiki* (from a Hawaiian word meaning "fast" or "quick.")

***Wiki =** a website that allows its users to add to and edit its content.

"That'll never work," I once thought. "It will result in a veritable Pandora's Box of biased, poorly written information, worthless for serious research. It will merely give flat earth advocates a platform for their views." Yet, in the case of a common cold article produced on a wiki, I was dead wrong.

The Value of Wikipedia

While Wikipedia articles vary widely in their quality, making it inappropriate to list as an authoritative source in a serious paper, I'm finding it increasingly valuable in many subject areas as a starting place for research and a guide to important studies.

Let's imagine that Julie had begun her search on Wikipedia. Here's the relevant portion of the article on the common cold pertaining to her specific question: 46

> Some of the viruses that cause the common colds are seasonal, occurring more frequently during cold or wet weather.[26] The reason for the seasonality has not been conclusively determined.[27] This may occur due to cold induced changes in the respiratory system,[28] decreased immune response,[29] and low humidity increasing viral transmission rates, perhaps due to dry air allowing small viral droplets to disperse farther and stay in the air longer.[30] It may be due to social factors, such as people spending more time indoors, near an infected person,[28] and specifically children at school.[23][27] There is some controversy over the role of body cooling as a risk factor for the common cold; the majority of the evidence suggests that it may result in greater susceptibility to infection.[29]

Note some of the distinct advantages of this article over the earlier sites Julie consulted.

1. Unlike the other "authoritative" sources, every factual statement (in some cases, every clause) is documented, typically with authoritative, peer-reviewed sources. Julie could consult the primary sources and judge for herself whether a Wikipedia statement was warranted. If sections of articles aren't well-documented, Wikipedia administrators warn readers that the section lacks authority, thus imposing a discipline that other medical sites often lack. Significantly, this article contains 93 references to significant sources, compared to few, if any, references on many of the competing sites.

All contributors to the article, rather than pulling their expert cards and expecting people to believe on their authority, are expected to defend their statements with evidence.

2. Wikipedia gives us a much more thorough article than the other sites. Truth is often compromised through abbreviation, when editors impose word limits. This lengthy Wikipedia article will probably continue to grow over time, because servers can now affordably hold vast amounts of information. Electrons are free and silicon (the second most abundant element on earth) is cheap.

3. Wikipedia articles can be updated frequently. I'm writing this sentence the morning after Super Bowl XLVII. Overnight someone, or a team of people, updated Wikipedia's Super Bowl article to include a blow by blow summary of the game. The Wikipedia article on the common cold was updated 30 days ago. Compare this to the article on the National Institutes of Health site, which was updated two and a half years ago.

4. It can handle massive numbers of niche articles. In addition to hundreds of *common* diseases, scientists have identified (so far) about 7,000 rare diseases.[47] If it's difficult to keep articles on *common* diseases updated on traditional medical sites, how much more difficult would it be to inform and update us on every *rare* disease? Crowdsourcing offers the hope that medical specialists and articulate people impacted by such diseases will passionately keep us up with the latest research via Wikipedia articles.

As I write, Wikipedia contains about four and a half million articles, growing at a rate of about 300,000 articles per year.[46]

5. The problem of prohibitive cost was solved. All writers freely volunteer their services. Why? There may be many reasons. But surely it's significant that they're typically passionate about their subjects and want the truth about them to be available. And since the articles aren't copyrighted, contributors don't view their efforts as making someone else rich. It's quite intoxicating to many to know they are contributing to the consolidation of human knowledge in a free environment.

Checking Expert Opinion with Multiple Sources of Different Kinds

Just as articles on medical sites can fall short, Wikipedia's approach has its own weaknesses. Although administrators fight valiantly against bias, it frequently raises its ugly head, particularly on topics where people hold strong, diametrically opposed opinions. On niche topics, such as an article on a business that isn't a household name, or a rare medical condition, a single person may be responsible for the content, with the article reflecting his or her biases and limited knowledge.

For these reasons, researchers should typically consult many sources, including different *types* of sources (encyclopedias, wikis, national health sites, peer-reviewed journals, etc.). As King Solomon wisely counsels us from millennia past: "In an abundance of counselors there is safety."

Summary of Julie's Approach to Evaluating Expert Opinion

1. Hear a presentation by an expert or seemingly informed person.

- Watch a video, like a TED Talk.

- Hear a professor or pastor.
- Read an article.

As you read or listen, keep your mind open, resisting forming an immediate, firm conclusion. Remind yourself, "All I know so far is that this is what one person believes about the subject."

Ask yourself:

- "Is she a specialist in her field?"
- "Is she respected in her field?"
- "Is she representative of her field, or considered a renegade?"
- "Is there a reason she might be biased?"

2. Find a variety of summaries of current research and expert opinion.

- Sites showing authority through their connections or authoritative authors
- Traditional Encyclopedias (e.g., *Encyclopedia Britannica*)
- Specialist Encyclopedias and Reference Sources (e.g., the *Encyclopedia of Philosophy*)
- A crowd sourced resource (e.g., Wikipedia)

3. If you need to go deeper, find the primary sources, looking first for literature reviews* and consolidation articles in peer-reviewed journals.

4. Summarize your findings.

***Literature (or "Lit") Reviews =** Articles that discuss published information in a particular subject area. Sometimes they simply list the sources with minimal description, but typically they synthesize and summarize the findings/opinions of the authors they cite.

Catch Julie's Passion!

In her quest, Julie never stopped thinking. While she respected medical experts, she didn't swallow their opinions uncritically. This required moving past understanding a sentence or paragraph to pausing for reflection, asking new questions, and comparing the current paragraph to both her life experiences and other statements she'd read. Like Sherlock Holmes, her alert mind sifted evidence, sniffed out inconsistencies, and recognized clues (e.g., the "at least not directly" phrase) to discover new paths that begged to be followed.

Later chapters will help us to refine these skills; but the relentless passion for truth is foundational. Without it, we're unlikely to either fully engage in our research or continue the quest, long after our shoes have worn thin and our feet blistered.

And note Julie's motive. She was driven by her daughter's need—a benevolent, pure need—rather than pleasing a professor or making a killing off publishing her view. As we'll see in later chapters, pure motives are critical for doing objective research.

Action Points
Going beyond Expert Opinion

1. Practice healthy self-talk when reading/listening to experts. Conclude "Now I know what one expert thinks" rather than "Now I know the truth."[49]

2. Look for evidence beyond dogmatic pronouncements. Ask: "What evidence led him to this conclusion? Does that evidence look strong or weak?"

3. Learn how to fully use available resources to dig into primary sources, including search engines, your local library, a university library, etc.

4. Learn how to obtain obscure resources that might be vital to your quest. Consider interlibrary loan, or obtaining scanned copies of studies or articles from distant libraries.

Questions That Can Identify and Avert Expert-Induced Disasters

1. Why should I pay attention to this person? Does she have credentials in this area? Is she truly an expert? Is she a talented researcher who documents her sources?

2. What degree of trust can I put in this publication? Is it known for its objectivity, or does it take a position? Is it sponsored by an organization that might have reason to show bias?

3. Are there other sources I should consult?

Flex Your Neurons!
Pursuing the Point of Know Return

1. How might under confidence hinder your thinking?

2. Why do people often fail to exercise independent thought when they hear an expert or follow a cult leader?

3. Besides overconfidence and under confidence, what other attitudes (e.g., laziness, prejudice) may hinder independent thought and research?

4. How can multi-tasking while researching (e.g., checking Facebook, texting, watching TV) impact our ability to reflect deeply and critically? (Are you multi-tasking now?)

5. What keeps you from fully engaging in your research into subjects vital to you?

6. In this chapter, did the evidence presented show that (choose one);

   a) experts are typically wrong

   b) experts are often wrong

   c) experts are sometimes wrong

   Explain your answer.

Making It More Personal
Practical Takeaways

What are one or more ideas provoked by this chapter that you can apply to help you think more critically?

____

____

____

What are one or more ideas that you can apply to help you think more creatively?

____

____

____

What else do you want to make sure you don't forget?

____

____

____

Recommended Trails
For the Incurably Curious and Adventurous

1. In this book, see especially Section Three to learn to spot logical fallacies, such as equivocation, in articles and speeches and documentaries.
2. If you have access to premium online research tools/ databases (such as Galileo) through your school or local library, this is a helpful step-by-step introduction to academic research: http://www.lib.vt.edu/help/research/. (Often, your university or local library system can provide you with free access to these tools from your home.)
3. To further sharpen your research skills, Google such phrases as "how to do academic research."
4. If you're doing a long-term research project, e.g., for a company project or a master's thesis, your supervisor will surely recommend resources to guide your search. Additionally, consider a recent work on this subject by Peter J. Taylor and Jeremy Szteiter, who work with the MA degree in critical and creative thinking at The University of Massachusetts, Boston: *Taking Yourself Seriously: Processes of Research and Engagement* (Arlington, Massachusetts: The Pumping Station, 2012). I like their emphasis on getting input from peers and supervisors at every phase of the project, from writing out your proposal, to doing research, to putting your results in writing. This practice seeks to combine the humility of my first chapter (e.g., get candid input from others) with the passionate research of chapter two.[50]
5. For more stupid quotes from experts, see Christopher Cerf and Victor Navasky, *The Experts Speak: The Definitive Compendium of Authoritative Misinformation* (New York: Pantheon Books). The original version was 1984, updated by the 1998 edition.
6. To explore some of the reasons why experts are so often wrong, see Philip E. Tetlock, *Expert Political Judgment* (Princeton, New Jersey: Princeton University Press, 2005). This Berkeley professor argues—with impeccable research and evenhanded discussion—that experts in various fields who predict the future are typically less accurate than a collection of reasonably informed people. "The foxes" (who know many little things) tend to predict better than "the hedgehogs" (who know one area of expertise), although the latter are considered the experts and everybody wants to hear their opinions in the media.
7. To understand the strengths and weaknesses of Wikipedia, I enjoyed this history of Wikipedia: Andrew Lih, *The Wikipedia Revolution: How a Bunch of Nobodies Created the World's Greatest Encyclopedia*, Hachette Books, 2009.

SECTION TWO

WHY DO BRILLIANT PEOPLE BELIEVE NONSENSE? BECAUSE THEY'RE COMFORTABLE WITH EXISTING BELIEFS

CHAPTER 3

THEY'RE MARRIED TO BRANDS

"Most people are other people. Their thoughts are someone else's opinions, their lives a mimicry, their passions a quotation."

— Oscar Wilde

Imagine that someone invented a device which, when installed in your store, influenced customers to purchase your most overpriced products, even if they were lower quality, less tasty, and less needed than less expensive products? Well, wait no longer—it's here! Only it's not a device; it's a sales strategy based upon powerful psychological forces. It sways both the wise and the foolish, the informed and the uninformed. It's called "branding," and it threatens to bypass objective reasoning to separate the unaware from their money.

The Poor, Poor Lawyer

It was my first time to feel sorry for a lawyer.

As we walked toward his Lexus in the parking lot, he explained, "I felt pretty smart when I bought it. I'd completed law school, passed the bar exam, and joined a firm. It seemed natural to finance a car commensurate with my new status. Then came the recession and I was let go. Today I'm stuck with outlandish payments, no salary, and I owe far more than I could sell it for. Now I feel pretty dumb."

I never felt so smug as I hopped into the reliable used car I'd bought with $2,500 cash. (It had seemed commensurate with my status as a starving artist and wannabe intellectual. It even came pre-dented so that I wouldn't lose my cool when family members would later bang it up a bit.)

A Lexus, depending on the model, sells at a wide variety of prices. Imagine that his was median priced—about $60,000. Since he wasn't a starving artist, let's grant for a moment his premise that, as a lawyer, his clients may expect him to have a nice car, indicating that he's smart and successful.

Granted, a Lexus is incredibly reliable.[1] But why not save $30,000 by purchasing one of the more economical Lexus models, or purchasing it used to avoid losing the thousands of dollars in value the moment you drive it off the lot? (After all, once you've purchased and driven a brand new car, isn't it now "used"?) If you simply must get a brand new car, why not consider purchasing a low mileage Toyota Avalon, virtually the same luxury car as the Lexus ES350, for $7,000 less, made by the same company that makes Lexus?[2]

Or, how about a three year old Toyota Camry, one of the most reliable and popular used cars, for $12,000? Many of the lawyer's clients who read personal finance literature would see the long-term wisdom of this economical purchase. (This lawyer had plenty of good company. The recent recession found many doctors and lawyers rethinking their lifestyle and dumping their exorbitant car payments.)[3]

Why did a lawyer, presumably equipped with a high bandwidth frontal lobe, make a mistake that's so elementary to personal finance—purchasing an expensive, unnecessary, depreciating asset with credit, when we can never be certain of a healthy economy and a steady and increasing income?

What can we learn to avoid similar mistakes?

The Power of Brands*

***Brand =** An association of positive qualities with a widely recognized product. Examples: Nike or Coke.

Often, our decisions are driven largely by powers that have nothing to do with personal happiness, practicality, and successful living. Let's imagine that this lawyer had not lost his job and planned to retire in 30 years at age 60. If, in five years of heavy business travel he figured on running each car into the ground and buying or financing a new one every five years, he'd likely save $10,000 per year by purchasing a used Camry over a new Lexus. If he invested that money each year in a mutual fund that achieved an average rate of return on stocks for 30 years, he'd have almost two million dollars to retire on, *just from his savings on cars*.[4]

How can brands drive smart people to sacrifice over two million dollars for something that they don't need, and that might (in the case of job loss, illness, etc.) cause long-term misery?

Think!

Some brands are truly worthy of their following and worth the extra expense. Others aren't. So let's apply our critical thinking to our favorite brands. Write down some of the brands and services you regularly choose by default: perfume, makeup, cell phones, computers, mechanics, cars, soft drinks, coffee, food, clothing, etc.

As we continue, keep these brands in mind and try to evaluate them objectively through critical thinking. In which cases does your marriage to these brands make sense? In which cases does a similar product look more attractive? What research might inform your decisions?

How Brands Short-Circuit Critical Thinking

Brands pose special challenges to those who wish to make rational decisions. Understanding how brands influence us can weaken their grip.

1. They Harness the Power of Peer Pressure.

Even if the car salesman's pitch isn't argued with sound evidence, my lawyer acquaintance, though skilled in logic and evidence, is predisposed to believe the pitch, since owning the car might enhance his image. It's not so much that peer pressure temporarily suspends reasoning. Rather, despite having the academic intelligence to pass the dreaded bar exam, the pressure to appear successful hijacks his brain, employing his mental powers to justify an unnecessarily risky purchase.

"But the Lexus is so reliable! I'll save so much in repairs!" his mind argues. But with a bit of research he could find a survey of mechanics that found the economical Toyota Corolla to have fewer and less expensive repairs than the Lexus.[5]

When professor Thomas Stanley studied first generation, self-made millionaires, he found that one of their dominant characteristics was independent thinking, particularly on material purchases. He went to the ritzy neighborhoods to survey the wealthy, but was amazed to find that while the residents had the *appearance* of wealth (big house, cool car), they had overspent, and possessed little *real* wealth. As they say in Texas, "Big hat, no cattle."

He found those with *real* wealth in normal neighborhoods with the middle class. Their conservative tastes allowed them to accumulate wealth. Their favorite vehicle? A rather humble Ford F-150 pickup truck. Thus Sam Walton, once the wealthiest man in America, wasn't eccentric at all by driving about Bentonville in his old truck. First generation millionaires prefer *real* financial success over the *appearance* of financial success. To resist spending and accumulate wealth, they see through the ads, resist the peer pressure, and make decisions in line with their financial goals.[6]

Of course, peer pressure similarly influences smaller purchases, which add up over time. Are those $150 tennis shoes significantly better than the $40 pair? If so, where are the objective studies that provide evidence? Are you paying the extra $110 for a brand name, or for real quality?

And lest you think I'm unfairly picking on jocks and preppies, take a Goth who swears he's not impacted by peer pressure and suggest that he wear a Justin Bieber t-shirt to the upcoming death metal concert. Won't happen. For most of us, image and peer pressure drive our decisions more than practicality and function.

Think!

Reflect on your purchases. If these weren't considered cool among your peers, would you still purchase them? In these cases, is peer pressure inordinately influencing you? Granted, image can be important; it can be tied to your reputation. But are there compromises you can make with your favorite brands to preserve your image without paying exorbitant amounts for certain brands?

2. They Make You Swear They're Truly Better

One of the most fascinating and revealing business blunders of recent times was the Coca Cola company's decision to replace Coca Cola, their signature product, with the "New Coke." Here's how it unfolded.

Pepsi ran an extremely successful ad campaign in the 1980s—the "Pepsi Challenge"—in which they dared people to do a blind taste test: Coke vs. Pepsi. Those who took the challenge typically preferred Pepsi and many switched to Pepsi, resulting in panic at Coke headquarters. The charts showed that Coke was dying, so their scientists worked feverishly until they developed the "New Coke." They did their homework, spending $4 million on blind taste tests with 190,000 people to confirm that people liked New Coke better than both the old Coke and Pepsi.

So in 1985 they dropped the old Coke, replacing it with the new. Problem solved. After all, it's all about the taste, isn't it? So they thought.

The result? Coke's sales dropped to a new low. Why? Apparently they failed to consider the power of the Coke *brand*. Hordes of customers *thought* they liked the old Coke better, even if they didn't. So Coke reintroduced the old Coke as Coca-Cola classic. By 1986, New Coke held only 2.3 percent of the entire soft drink market, with Coke classic at 18.9 percent and Pepsi at 18.5 percent.

The point here is really quite astounding. The majority of the population, more than adequately tested on 190,000 people, liked the taste of New Coke better than both Pepsi and Coke classic. So why don't they buy the better tasting soft drink? Apparently the public's reasoning, and perhaps even the perception of their taste, had been supplanted by years of successful marketing.

In 1987, the *Wall Street Journal* ran its own blind taste test of Pepsi, Coke classic, and New Coke. New Coke won, underscoring Coke's earlier testing. Yet interestingly, only two of the 100 participants said that they preferred New Coke before the taste test. Seventy of the participants mistakenly thought they had picked their favorite brand. Even more interesting, some of the mistaken tasters became indignant:

- From a Coke classic drinker who chose Pepsi: "I won't lower myself to drink Pepsi. It is too preppy. Too yup...Coke is more laid back."
- From a Pepsi drinker who chose Coke: "I relate Coke with people who just go along with the status quo. I think Pepsi is a little more rebellious. And I have a little bit of rebellion in me."

Note that these comments have nothing to do with taste, which we'd think would be why people choose a soft drink. New Coke did what it was designed to do—win taste tests. What it failed to do was to wean people from their almost fanatical loyalty to the old Coke.[7]

Lesson learned: It's not just about the taste. It's what advertisers *tell us* that we should like better.

While teaching on personal finance to a group of college students, I did a blind sampling of a name brand cola to Walmart's cheaper imitation. Although the Walmart brand won out, I've got to wonder how many would change brands if bringing it to a party might cause their peers to think they were either dirt poor or boringly cheap.

Or, perhaps when they know what they're drinking, they actually *think* they like their favorite brands better. This was confirmed in a study where college students were asked to sample Pepsi and Coke. Yet, the researchers had secretly switched the products, so that they were actually drinking Coke from a Pepsi bottle and Pepsi from a Coke bottle. The result? Students were "significantly influenced by the label of the product they preferred and not by taste differences between these products." The bottom line? In the war of taste versus brands, brands prevail.[8]

Think!

So you're convinced that your brand is truly the best. Have you objectively researched the evidence? If the research isn't available, is there a way to do your own research, like a blind taste test on food and drink items?

3. The Temptation to Trust Implicitly Rather than Research Adequately

When we see a brand, we tend to trust that it's the best product rather than weighing the evidence. So writers looking for a publisher may find a company claiming "We lead the industry in helping new authors market their books." If the company throws in 50 blurbs from happily published authors, why compare with other publishers? With an unsubstantiated claim and all the blurbs they could muster, the company quickly branded itself as the safest publishing option.

I researched about 50 such publishing companies, several of which claim to "lead the publishing industry" in some way. It stands to reason that they can't all be leading. And if a wannabe author digs a bit further, like searching the name of the publisher, plus "sucks" or "complaints," she'll typically find a host of dissatisfied customers.[9]

Yet many authors think, "I've spent years writing this book. I just want somebody to print it and get it out there." Often, they're looking for an easy decision and are satisfied with the company's claims and blurbs. After publication many regret their poorly researched decision.

Publishing is one of those "Wild, Wild West" industries that's undergone radical change in the past decade. Remember, in times of rapid change, it's the learners who win, not the learned. Don't let company claims and select customer testimonies establish instant respect and short-circuit your research.

Conclusion

Why do brilliant people believe nonsense? Because they're fooled by the power of branding.

Successful brands short-circuit our thinking, or urge us to employ our reasoning to justify trusting them. Wise consumers question their attraction to brands, looking for objective evidence that the brands are worthy of their allegiance. Following are some tips, exercises, and further reading that might help.

Action Points
Break through the Brand Barrier

1. Let evidence, rather than emotions driven by ads and peer pressure, drive your decisions.

It may indeed be wise for a lawyer or doctor or realtor to drive a nice car. But how nice? And what do you and your clients define as "nice"? Some people prefer a doctor or lawyer with a modest car. I do. Otherwise, I may consider them materialistic and thus overpriced. ("I'm paying for his luxury car and fancy house with this outrageous bill!")

Do you even know what your clients expect? Have you ever studied research in your profession on the issue? Responding to the question of what lawyers drive, someone responded, "I work in an office with 52 lawyers. I am looking at the parking lot right now. I see Honda, Toyota, BMW, Ford, GM, Nissan, one ancient Mercedes, a Lexus, Jeeps." One lawyer responded that he drives a PT Cruiser; his secretary drives a Lexus.[10]

For car purchases, compare the true value of brands with *Consumer Reports*, *Kelly Blue Book*, and *Edmunds.com*. Find similar reports and review articles for other purchases.

2. Understand what you're actually paying.

In major purchases, dealers often distract us from the total cost by focusing on the upfront cost or seemingly "affordable monthly payments." But those payments often include interest, so that you may pay $5,000 extra over time for a $20,000 car. To include other cost factors, such as repairs, gas mileage, resale, etc., play with the "True Cost to Own" calculator at www.edmunds.com.

In minor, daily purchases, we often fail to consider the long-term cost. Purchasing a four dollar Latte each morning doesn't seem like a major splurge. But over time, that little habit costs $120 per month, $1,440 per year, $14,400 per decade, or $72,000 in 50 years. If that $1,440 per year had been invested for 50 years at eight percent interest, you'd end up with about $900,000. So is a daily latte worth $900,000 to you?

Seeing today's purchases in light of their future worth, if wisely invested, helped Warren Buffett to resist ads, brands and peer pressure throughout his grade school and college years. Looking at frivolous purchases beyond just $5 for a meal out, $50 for a sweater or $40,000 for a new luxury car, he foresaw what that money could grow to (future money) if invested for a lifetime. In this way, Buffett overcame the power of the brand.[11]

3. Begin to Reflect More Deeply on Your Own Reasoning Processes (Meta-cognition)*

***Metacognition = thinking about your thinking processes.**

While all of us *think*, few people seem to think very deeply about *how* they think. In this chapter, as well as the following chapters in this section, we're examining common forces (such as brands) that hijack our thinking, often without our permission or awareness.

So you absolutely *know* that Nike is the best tennis shoe on the market. But *how* do you know that? (Reflect on your thinking!) Were you subtly convinced by athletes' testimonies in the media? Have you actually done a blind test of many brands to see which feel better? Have you read objective studies of various brands that give evidence as to which are the best? By thinking about our thinking, we can often overcome the forces that seek to hijack our reasoning.

The following questions engage our meta-cognition.

Flex Your Neurons! Pursuing the Point of Know Return

1. Why do I trust my plumber, bank, grocery store, mechanic, or food label? Out of habit? Because my parents trusted them?

2. Have I shopped around recently and compared reviews on my favorite brands?

3. Do I know how to find true value for the products that most concern me?

4. What's my total cost over a lifetime for purchasing this product instead of a less expensive one?

5. Is peer pressure (opinions of my relatives/friends/neighbors/associates) unnecessarily influencing my purchases?

6. Will changing my purchasing habits impact my happiness either positively or negatively?

7. Spontaneity can be the spice of life. How can purely logical decision-making take the fun out of life? How can we find a balance that's both wise and fulfilling?

8. How do my personal values impact such decisions? After all, there's more at stake than just money and quality. One might very well say that, to her, the pleasure brought by that daily Latte is worth the cost. Another may argue that, to him, spending $20 thousand more for a car "that girls think is cool" is well worth the price, if the alternative is a reliable, but boring car, which attracts equally boring girls. How would you respond to each of them?

Making It More Personal
Practical Takeaways

What are one or more ideas provoked by this chapter that you can apply to help you think more critically?

____

____

____

What are one or more ideas that you can apply to help you think more creatively?

____

____

____

What else do you want to make sure you don't forget?

____

____

____

Recommended Trails
For the Incurably Curious and Adventurous

1. For understanding brands, see *Married to the Brand: Why Consumers Bond with Some Brands for Life,* by William J. McEwen (Gallup Press, 2005). This book can help us understand how companies build brands, so that we can both resist poor purchases and brand our own products.

2. For understanding how first generation (they earned their money, didn't inherit it) millionaires think differently about brands and status in their big purchases, such as homes and cars, see *The Millionaire Next Door: The Surprising Secrets of America's Wealthy,* by Thomas Stanley and William D. Danko (New York: Pocket Books, 1996) and *The Millionaire Mind,* by Thomas Stanley (Kansas City: Andrews McMeel, 2000).

3. A good starting point for exploring meta-cognition: http://cft.vanderbilt.edu/guides-sub-pages/metacognition/ .

CHAPTER 4

THEY'RE BLINDED BY PREJUDICES, PRECONCEPTIONS, AND BIASES

"The myth of neutrality is an effective blanket for a host of biases."

— David Byrne, *Bicycle Diaries*

"I have yet to see a piece of writing, political or non-political, that does not have a slant. All writing slants the way a writer leans, and no man is born perpendicular."

— E.B. White

A Costly Oversight

In the early days of Rock & Roll, the popular Isley Brothers band toured Europe with a young keyboard player. "A great keyboardist," remarked Ronnie Isley. "He had a briefcase of songs that he had written, and we said one day we'd listen to them. But we never did. We figured this guy with the big glasses, how could he write something that would be funky* enough for us? I regret that."

***Funky =** unconventionally stylish or cool.

No wonder he regretted it. Elton John, the "guy with the big glasses," struck out on his own, producing seven consecutive albums that hit #1. He went on to sell over 300 million records, making him one of the top five best-selling music artists ever.[1]

Why would the Isley Brothers—savvy and successful artists—let such a ludicrous bias lead them astray? Their nonsensical notion that "people who don't look cool can't produce cool music" led to an embarrassing and costly error.

A Deadly Mistake

Between the world wars, anti-Semites began to exert influence in Germany, but ran into a bit of an embarrassing quandary concerning their Jewish citizen Albert Einstein. Imagine the difficulty of spreading propaganda about the Jews being an inferior race when their most famous scientist, the very poster child for the word "genius," was teaching at one of their universities.

To deal with the Einstein issue, engineer Paul Weyland and experimental physicist Ernst Gehrcke formed the "Study Group of German Scientists for the Preservation of a Pure Science." They attacked Einstein with articles and speeches claiming that his theory of relativity was a "big hoax," being Jewish by nature. Nobel Prize winner Philipp Lenard, who would later become a committed anti-Semite and Nazi, joined the movement, attacking what he considered absurdities inherent to relativity. Adolf Hitler, not yet in power, lent his voice to the cause in a newspaper article, lamenting: "Science, once our greatest pride, is today being taught by Hebrews."[2]

As the anti-Semitic movement grew, Einstein backed out of speaking at the annual convention of German scientists because 19 scientists published a "Declaration of Protest" to bar him from the meeting. Soon thereafter, he fled to America.

It's surely one of the great ironies of history that a member of a supposedly inferior race would help to convince President Franklin Roosevelt that his theory of relativity suggested the feasibility of an atomic bomb. Had the Nazis developed it first, they might have ruled the world. As a result of Einstein's urging, America won the race to develop the weapon that would help end World War II.

Before the war, Einstein had prophetically stated, "If and when war comes, Hitler will realize the harm he has done Germany by driving out the Jewish scientists."[3]

Reflections

The first blunder I related was made by seasoned musicians, the second by brilliant scientists. Their common tie is that both made grave errors based on unfounded prejudices: people who don't look cool can't write cool music; Jews are inferior.[4]

Yet, no matter how acutely we feel the sting of prejudice when it attacks us, no matter how much we study it in school, no matter how ugly it looks when we see it in others, it's mindboggling how it keeps reappearing in different forms. For example, if any group knew the horrors of prejudice, it was the Jews during Einstein's time. Yet Einstein had to chide some of his fellow German Jews for looking down on Jews from Eastern Europe.[5]

This tendency also surfaced in America, with Jews from Western Europe looking down upon Jews from Eastern Europe.[6] And it wasn't always subtle. According to a biographer of Steven Spielberg, Cincinnati Jews from Germany "held Eastern European Jews in utter contempt."[7]

What power could be at once so pervasive and yet so irrational? How can we keep it from poisoning our thinking and influencing our decisions?

Broadening the Landscape

Before readers yawn off this tendency as a problem for others, but surely not us, let us take a few steps back to view the larger landscape. Observe your own mind sizing up people. (Again, we're practicing meta-cognition.) What unwarranted labels do you pin on people the moment you see them? Admittedly some in each category exhibit common characteristics, but why do we so quickly label *all* in a group, before getting to know them as individuals?

Do you find yourself (consciously or subconsciously) throwing people into the following categories? If so, are your preconceptions founded on sufficient evidence?

- Obese people are undisciplined.
- Skinny people are anorexic or on meth.
- White people think they're superior.
- Short people can't be taken seriously.
- Goths are evil.
- Religious people are closed minded hypocrites.
- College professors are liberal.
- Women wreck cars more than men.
- Athletes are dumb.
- Preppies are snobs.
- Other ___________________________.

Think!

What blanket judgments do you make that are supported by insufficient evidence? What led you to such beliefs? How can we fight this all-too-human tendency?

Preconceptions are Alive and Well in Academia

As we saw in the opening illustrations, smart people can fall into prejudices and preconceptions just like everybody else. Since this book puts the spotlight on brilliant people who believe nonsense, let's see how academics often size up their students.

Celia Popovic and David Green set out to discover if professors' preconceptions of their students were accurate. So they studied over 1,200 students and their professors, representing 14 subject areas, in both British and American universities. They began by asking professors to identify the characteristics of students who were typically more successful. Then, they followed the students to see if the professors' preconceptions were correct.

Their conclusion? The professors were typically wrong.

Professors thought that the following types of students would academically outperform other groups:

- certain ethnic groups (typically white)
- "independent thinkers whose parents encouraged debate"
- those with at least one parent who completed college
- those who spoke English at home
- those who came from specific states
- those who were not student athletes
- those who showed an interest in current events and politics

Yet none of these categories of students performed better than the others. Most of the faculty were dead wrong.

Think about it. These professors are professionals who have completed at least a master of arts degree, taught at the college level, read widely, exposed themselves to diverse people and ideas, worked with many students, and prided themselves on objectivity. Yet it's another case of smart people believing nonsense.[8]

The Psychology of Prejudice

Perhaps grappling with the roots of prejudice can help us to combat it.

Some people are taught from birth to look down on certain groups. Others find themselves convinced by intolerant propaganda. And it's much easier to believe such teachings if we're facing economic crises (such as Germany at the time of Hitler) or insecurity and feel compelled to assign blame somewhere.

But even those taught tolerance from birth develop unwarranted biases. David Green notes two primary theories as to how we develop preconceptions, such as those held by the above professors: [9]

1 - The Economy Model

Our minds can't process everything we experience, so we notice only the characteristics that stand out to us and quickly organize groups of people and things by characteristics. This is useful when a three-year-old burns himself on a space heater. He reasons, "That thing burnt me last night. Avoid anything that looks like it." That's useful information, but probably fails to distinguish between a space heater and a humidifier, or a heater that's on from one that's off.

Imagine a professor who knew athletes from his high school days who cared nothing for grades.

No wonder his mind automatically, to this day, throws athletes into the "unmotivated student" category. It's a quick and easy way to organize data, but often leads us astray.

2 - The Differentiation Model

This has two aspects:

a) We understand things by putting them into groups.

b) We like to raise the status of our own group.

It's easy to see how these two aspects combine to produce prejudices. We meet some PhDs and our minds automatically place them in a group. But since PhDs can make us feel dumb, we look for faults and notice that some of them are very impractical, unable to manage their money or carry on successful relationships. By noting those characteristic and assuming they describe all PhDs, we've raised the status of our own less-educated group.

Whatever may be the most accurate model, it's safe to say that our minds automatically put things in categories. It's not always a bad thing; it's a part of how we make sense of our world, and works wonderfully to help us avoid burning ourselves repeatedly on space heaters. But realizing that our minds automatically categorize data long before we've analyzed it sufficiently, we should question our assumptions and be willing to subject them to more rigorous analysis.

"The Ultimate Attribution Error"

However professors might *initially* categorize athletes, it's easy to see how they may *reinforce* their conception. Midway through a semester, an athlete falls asleep in his class, which our professor attributes to his being an athlete, probably worn out from two hours on the soccer field. But even if later in the day he grades the midterm and discovers that a jock made the highest grade on the midterm, he won't likely revise his preconception. Rather, he views the bright athlete as an exception to the rule, attributable to some extraneous factor such as having attended a superior prep school.

Psychologists call this "The Ultimate Attribution Error," and it plagues us all. When we see *good* behavior in our ingroup (a group we're a part of), we typically attribute it to innate characteristics of our group members. When we see *bad* behavior in our ingroup, we typically attribute it to other influences or circumstances. For an outgroup (a group outside our own), we attribute behaviors the opposite way. It's easy to see how this tendency fools our minds and reinforces unfounded prejudices.[10]

Breaking Free from Prejudice

So we find ourselves stuck with brains that continually reinforce a bundle of misconceptions. Obviously, this skews our reasoning, leading to unfounded prejudices and a resistance to learning from members of other groups we deem inferior. How can we fight this tendency toward prejudice?

1. Question Your Preconceptions.

Let's imagine that a female driver crashed into your family car during your childhood. You can still hear your dad mutter under his breath, "Women drivers!" In your teen years, friends complained in the locker room about women drivers, so that consciously or subconsciously, you assume women have more wrecks than men. Since then, every time you see a woman putting on makeup or texting while driving, your mind reinforces the belief.

But have you ever subjected that belief to rigorous analysis? Did you ever tally up the number of traffic accidents you've seen caused by women as opposed to men? If not, how do you know that your mind isn't playing tricks on you, reinforcing your prior belief every time you see a woman make a driving error, while ignoring the number of times you see men making driving errors?

One way to test preconceptions would be to consult relevant studies. After all, insurance companies are vitally interested in such statistics. One recent study found 80 percent of all serious accidents being caused by men. It didn't claim to know why. Perhaps men are overconfident, or there are more men than women driving, or they take more chances, or high testosterone leads to higher risks, or men drink more often than women while driving, or something else. But this jives with the fact that, on average, men pay more for car insurance than women.[11]

Hey, it's just one study. But it's a start as we try to critically examine our prejudices.

As Popov and Green concluded in their study of professors with preconceived ideas of their students, the best idea is for teachers to try their best to presume absolutely nothing about their students. Wouldn't that be a great idea for people outside academia as well? Is it really so difficult to not presume anything about women drivers if you haven't gathered sufficient data and rigorously thought it through?

So the next time you size up someone before getting to know her, ask yourself, how many instances of the expected behaviors have you actually seen? If you accumulated evidence from other sources, did you include a variety of reliable sources, or only sources tied to a niche view?

2. Get to know diverse people.

Over 500 studies, involving a quarter of a million people in 38 nations, show overwhelmingly that getting different racial or social groups together leads to less prejudice.[12] There may be many reasons for this, but three of the most tested and confirmed are:

a. We learn more about each other.
b. Our anxiety about getting together is relieved.
c. We grow in our empathy and perspective (able to view life from the other group's perspective).

Of these three, the last two appear to be the most important for diminishing prejudice.[13]

Diverse groups make the most positive impact on prejudices when they work together on common goals, such as a group project for school, building a company, or competing as an athletic team. So why not, when you're choosing a group for a project or social diversion, intentionally choose members who represent different groups from your own? Go out of your way to mingle with, work with, study with, play sports with, and play video games with people from diverse backgrounds and cultures.

The Payoff: Locally and Globally

Following-up on Elton John, it's relevant that his long-time lyricist, Bernie Taupin, is quite different from John. Among many other differences, Taupin lives on a ranch in California, raising bulls and doing outdoorsy, cowboyish things. John often lives in a high rise apartment in downtown Atlanta.

But what a collaboration! Taupin writes the lyrics; John writes the melodies. They met in 1967 when both answered an ad from a record label looking for talent. Although the label rejected them, the A&R (artists and repertoire) scout introduced them to one another and the rest is history. Taupin wrote the lyrics to *Candle in the Wind* (John's most popular single) and they have collaborated on 30 albums so far.[14]

You don't have to agree with everybody. You don't have to like everything other people do. But I have profound respect for the U.S. president who noted that he'd never met a person who wasn't his superior in some way.[15] With that attitude, he could learn from everybody he met.

The John/Taupin collaboration of two diverse people doesn't seem to be a fluke. In fact, a major reason students get a college education is to one day land a good job. If that's important to you, consider the importance of doing business across borders, which means relating to people of different colors and cultures.

In my home state of Georgia,

- We exported $36 billion worth of products in 2012.
- Companies in Georgia that export are 20 percent more likely to grow faster and are nine percent less likely to go out of business.
- Exporting to new markets expands product life cycles and brings global market intelligence to businesses.
- International trade can help diversify a business and reduce risks.
- Exports contribute to the community and state economy. According to the U.S. Department of Commerce, exports create twice as many jobs as domestic trade. For every job created in making a product, another job is created to get that product to market.

- Employees of exporting firms generally make 13 to 18 percent higher wages than those of firms that don't export.[16]

To meet the demands of an increasingly global economy, we need a labor force that's cross-cultural savvy. Those who fail to understand the subtle differences between cultures will lose customers due to embarrassing snafus.

Think Different!
Cross-Cultural Challenges Intrigue our Greatest Minds

Before moving to Slovakia, I was challenged in my cross-cultural training to think: "It's typically not about right or wrong, it's just different." Thus, when confronted with differences, rather than assume other cultures are backward or just plain wrong, first try to understand the culture.

That sounds easy, but it's deceptively difficult to engage other cultures, and fraught with opportunities for disaster. Perhaps it takes a special kind of mind—adept at patient observation, flexibility, and emotional intelligence—to see past prejudices and "the way we've always done things." No wonder our university offers a PhD in International Conflict Management!

Here are a few (we could list thousands!) examples of cross-cultural differences that trip up intelligent people.

Communication Assumptions:

- A writer for a local machine company, communicating with his headquarters in Japan, studied a technical manual when he kept coming across the strange phrase "hot rock." Eventually, he realized his Japanese counterparts had translated the American company Firestone literally, so that their translation back into English came out quite different than expected!

- You're doing business with a Slovak company and want to honor the CEO by speaking some Slovak. Your host asks if you need anything. It's quite warm in the room, so you search Google Translate on your i-Phone for "I'm warm." It translates literally "Som teplo," which you say to your host with excellent pronunciation, and a twinkle in your eye for having identified with his world. Your host hesitates a bit, not sure how to respond. Later, you discover that althought the literal, word for word translation was correct, when used as a phrase in popular Slovak lingo, it means "I'm gay."

  Tip: Literal, word for word translations often give inaccurate meanings. Even communicating in the same language with different subcultures and age groups can be challenging. For example, in today's use, the word "sucks" typically refers to something that's bad, poorly done, or a disappointing circumstance." Pretty innocent. Yet, during the 1960s and early 1970s; it had quite a different meaning. Back then, many considered it the most offensive word in the English language.

People would do well to remember this sordid history when using the term among baby boomers. The Urban Dictionary (http://www.urbandictionary.com/) can be helpful to suggest a variety of English meanings often absent from traditional dictionaries.

Social Assumptions:

Americans often tap out the rhythm to an old ditty: "Shave and a Haircut, Two Bits." (It's one tap, slight pause, four taps, longer pause, then two taps.) In America, it's totally innocent, with one person tapping the first five taps in one room and a friend answering from another room with the final two taps. Just don't do it in Mexico. It's a very offensive insult.

Aesthetic Assumptions:

In America, as I write, thin is in. While we like to imagine that we're objective in our assessment of beauty, our culture (as seen through the eyes of Hollywood) tells us what is beautiful, and we believe it. In other cultures, thin isn't in.

For example, in certain areas of Nigeria, engaged women isolate themselves for months in tents, gorging themselves to make themselves attractive and marriageable. In their culture, it's intuitively obvious that fat is beautiful and thin is ugly. (Perhaps a creative entrepreneur could set up cultural exchange programs to help match those deemed unattractive in one culture to those who seek them out in other cultures!)

Body Language Assumptions:

After the walls to Eastern Europe came down, lecturers began travelling from the West to give talks. Some made the mistake of keeping a hand in one of their pockets while speaking. In America, it communicates informality. Little did they know that in Eastern Europe, movies portrayed shady and conniving characters chatting with hands in their pockets. It's not the image speakers wanted to give!

"Weird," you may say. But remember, we seem just as weird to others when we cross their borders. In locations such as Slovakia, a small country bordering five other countries, people are used to looking for and respecting cultural differences. But in more isolated countries with large land masses such as America, people can live their entire lives isolated from other cultures. It's called provincialism, and can easily lead to dysfunction when we deal with people different from ourselves.

Travel writer Bill Bryson once said that he relished crossing borders because in each new country, he had to become a child again. He no longer knew how to do the simplest of tasks—cross a street, eat a meal, purchase groceries. Why not relish that feeling of adventure? Get to know people from different groups, trying your best to set aside all preconceptions, except for the assumption that you're probably doing something today that would look quite silly to those who grew up with a different set of cultural norms.

Conclusion
Relish Diversity and Go Global!

Increasingly, my work with collaborators and markets is global. This week, from my office in *Georgia*, I received a call from *Peru* to book me on a nationally syndicated, *Los Angeles* based radio station. An author acquaintance from *Louisiana*, whom I've never met personally but know through email, had recommended me for the interview.

Earlier this month, I received a copy of one of my books that's hot off a *German* press. Later this year, *Croatian* and *Russian* editions will hit their markets. I get international connections through my international agent who grew up in *Holland*, speaks several languages, but currently lives on America's West Coast. I rely on her because she understands cultural nuances and cultivates international contacts.

To my neighbors, I'm just a middle-aged guy in a modest neighborhood, tucked back into a cul-de-sac in the small town of Acworth. But being digitally connected from my home office to the world, my learning and my connections and my audiences are increasingly global. I don't ask the color of the researcher whose journal article I'm studying. Neither do I care whether she's a jock, prep, Goth, steam punk enthusiast or Trekkie.

I *am* concerned that my sources and partners are diverse, informed and have integrity. I need diversity. In an increasingly global world, ideas from everywhere and everybody are valued. Diverse people have different experiences and perspectives than my own. That's a part of what makes them so valuable. Thank goodness they're not all Acworthians!

Flex Your Neurons!
Pursuing the Point of Know Return

1. Why do we often shy away from getting to know people in other groups?
2. What groups do you typically avoid when choosing a seat for class? Why?
3. How might intentionally diversifying a business help it to succeed?
4. If done in the wrong way, how might intentionally diversifying a business lead to failure?
5. A friend tells you to beware of certain areas in downtown Chicago. Is this prejudice, or just common sense? How do we tell the difference?
6. If you're into online gaming with role playing games such as World of Warcraft, have you noticed how cultural differences make a difference in how people play the game? Do Chinese players seem more team oriented and Americans more individualistic? How can such insights help you in your gaming?

Making It More Personal
Practical Takeaways

What are one or more ideas provoked by this chapter that you can apply to help you think more critically?

____

____

____

What are one or more ideas that you can apply to help you think more creatively?

____

____

____

What else do you want to make sure you don't forget?

____

____

____

Recommended Trails
For the Incurably Curious and Adventurous

1. For understanding prejudice in academia, students going into teaching may want to read *Understanding Undergraduates: Challenging our preconceptions of student success,* by Celia Popovic and David Green (Routledge, 2012).

2. For those pursuing cross-cultural ventures and relationships and especially foreign policy, read the classic book, *The Ugly American*, by Eugene Burdick and William J. Lederer (W.W. Norton & Company, first published in 1958). It's a collection of about 20 fictional stories, based on the real experiences of the American authors and people they knew who were working with Asians after World War II.

3. Learn more by Googling such phrases as "the psychology of prejudice," "cross-cultural communication," or "the ultimate attribution error."

CHAPTER 5

THEY BELIEVE WHAT THEY WANT TO BELIEVE

"The moment we want to believe something, we suddenly see all the arguments for it, and become blind to the arguments against it."

— George Bernard Shaw

"If you can read only one newspaper, read the opposition's."

— anonymous[1]

What Killed Steve Jobs?

Jobs possessed many qualities and competencies that helped him to build a truly great company. His brilliance dazzled the world in several areas:

- He was passionate about his products, obsessing over every detail of their design.[2]
- He put intense energy and focus into his work, setting the pace for the Apple workforce.[3]
- He possessed remarkable marketing instincts, which allowed him to build a passionate following around his brand.[4]
- His mantra "Simplify!" insured that his products were insanely easy to operate.[5]
- He had a strong aesthetic sense, blending artistry and technology to create beautiful products.[6]

Yet, for all his great strengths, he also had profound weaknesses. One likely killed him.

Apple software engineer Bud Tribble borrowed a phrase from the *Star Trek* series to describe one of Jobs' idiosyncrasies—"the reality distortion field." Tribble explained: "In his presence, reality is malleable."

Jobs would often express his version of the truth—truth as he wanted it to be—and refuse to accept any facts to the contrary.[7] Sometimes the distortion field worked in his favor, such as setting unrealistic deadlines for seemingly impossible tasks. When people met with Jobs to discuss a project, they entered his distortion field and would typically come out convinced it could happen. And sure enough, sometimes his engineers accomplished what they first deemed impossible.

According to his close associates, the reality distortion field wasn't merely a technique he adopted to manipulate others. Rather, when Jobs wanted to believe something, he'd manipulate facts and memories to deceive *himself* into believing it was true.

Take the matter of personal hygiene.

Jobs was convinced that his vegan diet would eliminate body odor, so he passed on the deodorant and skimped on baths. No matter how much his associates told him that he stunk, he never seemed convinced. According to associate Mike Markkula, "We would have to literally put him out the door and tell him to go take a shower."[8]

So it's no shock that when a routine kidney screening found a highly treatable, slow-growing type of pancreatic cancer at a very early stage, Jobs ignored his doctor's advice and the advice of many wise and concerned associates. Removing the tumor was the obvious and only accepted medical option, but to the horror of his wife Laurene and their friends, he decided to delay treatment and try a hodgepodge of unproven herbal remedies, juice fasts, acupuncture, etc. While Jobs chose to believe what he wanted to believe, the cancer continued to grow. Nine months later he would relent to have surgery; but by then it had spread to the liver. It took his life at 56 years of age.[9]

Why do brilliant people believe nonsense? Because they believe what they want to believe.

Jobs wasn't the only person to live in a "reality distortion field." To a certain extent, we all do. Unless we learn to see through the field, the results can be just as disastrous for us.

Motivated Reasoning:* How Our Desires Impact Our Beliefs

***Motivated Reasoning** = allowing our emotions to bias our decisions and attitudes.

Our brains naturally resist changing opinions. Actually, studies show that it's even worse than resisting—we skew unwelcome data to make it bolster our opinion.

Let's say we've followed a political candidate enough to decide we like him. Then we hear some negative information about him. You'd think that, being rational people, our assessment of the candidate would go down a notch, even if it's a tiny notch. Yet, multiple studies have found that our assessment of the candidate actually tends to go *up*. How's that?

Apparently, that negative information causes a bit of anxiety, leading us to reflect upon all the reasons we liked the candidate in the first place. In this way, we find reasons to explain away the negative information and come out believing in him more strongly. This tendency has been demonstrated in regard to not only our opinions of political candidates, but other beliefs as well.[10]

Fortunately, our views don't have to be skewed forever. Other researchers found that if we keep hearing negative information, mounting anxiety can lead us to a tipping point, where we finally change our opinion.[11]

Lesson Learned

My takeaway from these studies? Without sufficient input from alternative viewpoints, we continue to reinforce our original beliefs and whitewash contrary evidence. So let's ensure that we're not limiting ourselves to that data that defends our current opinions. If we limit our input to a mere smattering of input from the other side, we'll likely reinforce our prior beliefs rather than allow them to be challenged by new data.

Yet, many people do the opposite. They either choose or naturally gravitate toward filling their minds with messages they want to hear, so that they never have their views challenged. If they're missing the truth, they're unlikely to find it by isolating themselves in a cozy silo* where everyone agrees with their opinions.

***Silo -** a business unit or academic unit that fails to interact with other units, thus limiting the cross-fertilization of ideas and overall performance. [Picture the tall cylindrical structures (silos) that store produce on farms.]

Here are a couple of areas where I see people insulating themselves from the whole truth in order to keep believing what they want to believe. The first is positive thinking taken to an extreme; the second is choosing exclusively news sources that reinforce our ideology.

How We Isolate Ourselves from Contrary Data

Many people accomplish great things when they set aside their negative thinking and start believing in themselves. We could give examples all day long, with an overwhelming amount of self-help books providing inspiring examples.

Example: Fifteen-year-old John fell in love with his guitar, playing it night and day. His Aunt Mimi, who was raising him, couldn't see the point of his obsession and would try to discourage him. She said,

> *"To me, it was just so much waste of time. I used to tell him so. 'The guitar's all very well, John, but you'll never make a living out of it.'"*

But little John Lennon didn't believe the naysayers. He kept right on playing, putting his heart into the music he loved, until he and the other Beatles established themselves as the most popular band on earth.[12]

I love illustrations like this! They inspire me to move forward after a serious setback. And there's no doubt that many people with poor self-esteem, who believe the naysayers implicitly, could use a good dose of positive thinking to bring balance.

But surely some take mind over matter too far. Read enough inspiring examples, reinforce them with some pop science and cherry-picked psychological studies, and it's easy to form the dangerous habit of hearing only what we want to hear and ignoring the rest. In Steve Job's case, it was a recipe for disaster. After all, to "believe it and receive it," according to the literature, we need to believe it totally, without a doubt. To maintain this level of belief, it's often necessary to block out naysayers (contrary data) who may introduce doubt. This can lead to self-deception. In effect, like Jobs, aren't some people setting up their own "reality distortion field," putting themselves at risk for similar disasters?

In order to see the limits of "limitless thinking," and mind over matter, I like to think of extreme examples that don't seem to fit the model.

Imagine that you want to be a pro quarterback. Here are some qualities that would not only come in handy, but are typically required:

- A rote memory sufficient to have instant recall of an ever-changing roster of up to 50 running plays and 200 passing plays, distilled into code for calling audibles at the line of scrimmage
- A profound visual memory for film study and recognizing defensive schemes at a glance
- Exceptional mobility to scramble and avoid tackles
- A strong arm for long passes
- Tall (average 6'5" to 6'7") to see the field over the offensive and defensive line.
- Large hands for ball control
- Leadership
- Excellent peripheral vision to spot attacking defenders while eyes are focused downfield to find open receivers.
- Excellent figure/ground perception to hit a rapidly moving target 50 yards downfield, while scrambling to avoid a blitz
- Excellent muscle coordination
- A profound sense of time to manage the game clock with strategic time outs, avoiding delay of game, and alternately scheming to run the clock down or get maximum yardage out of limited time

There's only one obstacle to reaching your dream of becoming a pro quarterback. You're an Oompa Loompa. Vertically challenged at three and a half feet tall, you can't see over the line. Your tiny hands can't control the football. And with such short arms, no matter how much you strengthen them, you'll never throw long distances.

My advice to Oompa Loompas? Frankly assess your present and potential strengths and look beyond quarterbacking a professional football team to make your mark. I hope I'm not going out on a limb here, but even without a detailed assessment, I'd suggest ruling out professional basketball as well.

But what if Mr. Loompa puts in the number of hours that some have determined it takes to make for success? I'm sorry to be so frank, but no matter how many hours he puts in, holding onto his aspiration would lead to a painfully frustrating life.

Success literature often ignores the solid science that supports our varying strengths and multiple intelligences. While some weaknesses can be overcome or at least strengthened; others, such as we've seen for our Mr. Loompa, have set boundaries. While it's easy to see that some physical assets and liabilities may pose limitations, we resist applying this to mental potential.

While coming to terms with our limitations is often seen as rather demoralizing, I've found it quite freeing. Surely the Oompa Loompa who convinces himself that he'll one day be the next Tom Brady has set himself up for a life of broken dreams and disillusionment. Similarly, in the mental sphere, I am colorblind and have a very poor visual memory. Put me in a warehouse where other workers effortlessly remember the locations and colors of boxes and I'd be known as the village idiot. My strengths include analytical thinking. Once I accept some of my inherent strengths and weaknesses, I'm free to concentrate on the areas in which I can more easily excel.

My point? The "unlimited potential" movement, although it may help some who need a boost to their self-esteem, can actually *limit* the potential of others by motivating them to focus myopically on what they *want* to believe and achieve rather than candidly assessing their strengths and weaknesses and interests, and setting their goals appropriately. By ignoring contradictory evidence, they may make poor decisions about their vocations, business goals, and personal goals, leading to a frustrating life.

Now I must admit that I haven't studied out this area thoroughly. So if an Oompa Loompa becomes the next Michael Jordan in basketball, please let me know. I'll purchase a ticket.

How Locking Ourselves into Silos Leads To Information Age Provincialism

According to Mark Twain,

> "A person who won't read has no advantage over one who can't read."

How true. But let's add a corollary which seems especially useful for the information age:

> "A person who won't read *widely* may have no advantage over the one who can't read."

In fact, the narrow reader who reads only writers who agree with him may be *worse* off than the illiterate, since no matter how obsessively he reads, he merely reinforces his prejudices. This leads us to another Mark Twain insight that we've already considered:

> "It's not so much what people don't know that hurts them, it's what they do know that ain't so."

In the information age, it's increasingly easy to isolate ourselves with the opinions of those who think like us and insulate ourselves against all else. If we set our news feeds to receive the views of our choice we may never have our views challenged. The narrow reader risks accumulating greater and greater amounts of spin and misinformation, leading to conclusions that can be as dangerous as they are erroneous. We have only to look as far as those who immersed themselves in Nazi propaganda to see where this can lead.

So let's explore our sources of current news and politics. Could we be exclusively listening to what we want to hear, thus reinforcing our prejudices rather than truly learning?

Think!

How do you get your news? Do your sources promote a certain political position? How can you find out? Are your sources biased or balanced?

The Challenge of Getting Objective News (Tip: It's not easy!)

How can we insure that we're accurately informed about candidates and wars and discoveries and job markets and other important news?

1. Understand where news sources stand.

Some of us are being indoctrinated without our consent, since we're unaware of the ideological bent of our sources.

Historically, America began with highly partisan newspapers that openly held competing political positions. To find the truth behind the bias, people had to read at least one paper from each viewpoint. But in the 1800s and early 1900s news sources shifted from taking positions to striving for neutrality (in part because advertisers wanted to reach a larger audience through a smaller number of papers with a wide appeal).

While this at first sounds noble, asking a journalist to always present both sides of a controversial issue isn't always the best path to objectivity. What if a journalist decides that all the facts point to one conclusion? Must she still, in the name of balance, devote a paragraph to argue for an opposing position that she deems worthless?

Dr. Jay Rosen at New York University argues that rather than putting a straightjacket on journalists, asking them to report from the unrealistic perspective of the "view from nowhere," why not let them express their viewpoint if they think it best fits the facts? In this manner, as technology commentator David Weinberger suggests, transparency becomes the new objectivity. Whether you're a convinced, diehard Democrat, or just as staunch a Republican, simply disclose your position in your bio so that readers can judge whether or not your biases are coloring your columns. If you're a business writer and a pharmaceutical company owns your newspaper, disclose it so that we'll know you may not be entirely objective when reporting on the medical industry.[13]

But while transparency helps, it doesn't solve all the objectivity issues. Here are two shortcomings of transparency.

First, news sources and their reporters don't necessarily believe they're presenting a niche viewpoint. The convinced Republican and equally convinced Democrat both believe they're presenting the objective truth. Thus, they're unlikely to openly disclose their slant to potential readers/viewers. And news sources that lean one direction or the other are unlikely to display this kind of branding:

> Fox News: A Great Place to Get a More Conservative Viewpoint
>
> MSNBC: Where Liberal Listeners Can Reinforce Their Political Opinions

Instead, below Fox News' logo on their website is the phrase "fair and balanced." They see themselves as giving the factual alternative to liberal bias. For MSNBC, I see no prominent wording to explain their position on their website. Yet, in other places they describe themselves as "News, Video and Progressive Community," with "progressive" apparently meaning "sympathetic to a liberal ideology."

Second, transparency falls short because we may receive reports, not from a single source, but from an aggregator of many sources, like the Drudge Report or Google News. Thus, we may not know where a report originated.

Especially with the advent of the Internet, news sources represent every view imaginable. In India, 81 satellite stations vie for listeners, with each typically claiming an ideology and reporting from that viewpoint. Each of Italy's three state-sponsored television stations represent a different political party.

In America, as I write (things change), my research revealed the following characteristics of popular news sources:

- CNN strives for political neutrality. It excels at breaking news.[14]
- Fox News was created to give voice to a more conservative position. Yet it also employs some distinctly liberal voices to provide helpful debate.[15]
- MSNBC has moved to a more liberal slant, seeking to provide an alternative to Fox News's conservative slant.[16]
- While the *New York Times* has high standards for both writing and research, studies find it leaning to the liberal side, although not exclusively. It also employs some conservative columnists for balance.[17]
- The *Wall Street Journal* tends to lean liberal in its news, conservative in its opinion pieces.[18]

Again, be aware that news sources keep shifting. They are constantly looking at their markets, with their fingers in the wind to see what large audiences want to hear. Thus, it's not easy to find objective reporting.

So much for transparency as a cure all. At present, the burden rests upon viewers/readers to learn the leanings of various news sources and their writers/editors. So occasionally study the recent history of a news source; keep abreast of research that sniffs out bias, and take into account the market each station is trying to reach. Concerning the latter, a public editor* for the *New York Times* explained its liberal slant as a desire to appeal to New Yorkers, who purchase about half of their papers.[19]

***Public Editor =** an employee of a newspaper who seeks to ensure a high standard of journalism ethics by bringing to light errors or omissions, and acting as a liaison to the public.

If you consult watchdog groups which report bias in the media, don't assume neutrality in the watchdog groups! For example, *Media Matters for America*, while at first glance appearing to be nonpartisan, is actually dedicated to "monitoring, analyzing, and correcting conservative misinformation in the U.S. media." Alternately, *Accuracy in Media* and the *Media Research Center* exist to disclose liberal bias in the media.[20]

Another way to detect bias is to understand and look for indicators of bias in articles/programs as you read them, which brings us to our second recommendation.

2. Learn how to detect bias in a news source.

Bias impacts reporting in many ways, and it's not always easy to detect. As you read and view the news, ask yourself the following questions to see if it's promoting a certain viewpoint.[21]

- *Do they employ spin?* The president approves a plan to allow more people to qualify for food stamps. Here are two reports, written from different perspectives:

  > "President Approves Plan to Help the Poor"
  >
  > "President Plunges Country into Deeper Debt"

  Although they're reporting the same event, the first article focuses on the benefit to the poor, while the second focuses on the potential damage to our economy. Both titles, while they may be technically accurate, spin the words to either praise or condemn the president.

- *Do they unfairly assign motives?* What motive does this title assign:

  > "State Budget Committee Unconcerned for Education: Votes Down Funding for New Technology in Schools"

  Do you think it's fair? I doubt the committee claimed they were unconcerned about education. Perhaps they felt the new technology would actually hinder education, or would take money from more needful educational projects.

- *Are they balanced?* Do they present all legitimate sides of the issue?
- *Do they cite sources that agree with their view, while excluding others?*
- *Do they fail to report news that puts their view in a bad light?*
- *Do stories favorable to their agenda receive prime placement* (e.g. early pages of a newspaper, prominent links from the home page of their website)?
- *Do they label people in order to either vilify of justify them?* "He's a liberal, just speaking the party line." "Of course he voted against the program! As a libertarian, he has no concern for the poor."

Warning! In looking for signs of bias, studies show that it's much easier to perceive bias in articles that don't agree with your position than those that support your position.[22] Psychologists call it the "hostile media effect." So look extra hard at news sources that tend to agree with your positions. They may be more biased than you think![23]

3. Choose a variety of reliable sources.

Remember, our purpose here is to save us from our tendency to believe what we want to believe. But we're very unlikely to overcome this tendency if we habitually hear what we want to hear. How can we break from that comfortable information silo that reinforces our prejudices?

Many people listen to exclusively one news source. Instead, especially on important issues, explore other sources.

But remember, sources from your country will likely, consciously or subconsciously, paint your country in a more favorable light. So consider international publications as well. During the Cold War, many Eastern Europeans listened to Western News to get another view. Many Americans like to listen to the British Broadcasting Corporation (BBC) for a view from abroad.

4. If reports disagree on an important issue, consult a nonpartisan fact check site, such as http://www.factcheck.org/.

A week or so following a presidential debate, Google "fact check presidential debate" to find how researchers compare candidates' claims to the facts.

These tips on news sources can help protect us from the danger of listening to only the news we want to hear, thereby reinforcing our biases rather than leading us to truth.

Action Points
How to Protect Ourselves from the Tyranny of Our Preferences

Moving from the news media to our more general task of seeking truth, how can we break outside our preferences to seek the truth more objectively?

1. Recognize that our desires impact our beliefs.

Surely none of us are exempt. In fact, those who claim to seek truth from a totally objective, dispassionate framework are probably deceiving themselves. Here are a couple of scholars who seem aware of their passions and consider their possible influence on their beliefs.

Dr. William Lane Craig, one of today's most popular and respected theistic philosophers, tells of his upbringing with no spiritual roots, and the adolescent angst that resulted from his secular outlook on life. In high school, he read H.G. Wells' novel *The Time Machine*, in which a time traveler journeys far into the future to discover the destiny of mankind. He discovers that all human and animal life have perished. His most astonishing sensation is the resulting silence. "All the sounds of man, the bleating of the sheep, the cries of birds, the hum of insects, the stir that makes the background of our lives—all that was over."[24] When the traveler returned to present times, he was keenly aware that everybody's rushing to and fro will ultimately come to nothing.

After reading this, young Craig was horrified. He thought. "No, no! It can't end that way!" But he concluded that if there was no God and no afterlife, then there was no ultimate purpose in life, no great importance to mankind.

Obviously, those who long for an ultimate purpose will be more open to spiritual answers than those who rarely think of such things. While Craig would go on to study religion and philosophy professionally, we can see how such longings can impact beliefs. Many religious testimonies relate initial longings that were fulfilled in their conversions.

But just as the religious should consider their longings in justifying their beliefs, so should the irreligious. Thomas Nagel, an outspoken atheist, professor of law and philosophy at New York University, once wrote:

> "I want atheism to be true and am made uneasy by the fact that some of the most intelligent and well-informed people I know are religious believers. It isn't just that I don't believe in God and, naturally, hope that I'm right in my belief. It's that I hope there is no God! I don't want there to be a God; I don't want the universe to be like that."[25]

Both Craig and Nagel hold PhDs in their fields from respected universities. Both have keen minds. Yet, as humans, they also have wants and desires. Fortunately, both are aware enough of their longings to admit them and take them into account as they search for truth.

"But scientists are much more objective than philosophers," some might object. Perhaps. But the history of science reveals similar passions at work among scientists to both aid and hinder discovery. We'll discuss that in chapter nine. Surely it's safest, in our search for truth, to examine our hearts and make sure they're leading us to an open minded search for truth, rather than to merely justify our passions.

2. Doubt yourself.

Knowing that we have a tendency to believe what we want to believe, wouldn't it be wise to routinely question our positions and hold them with a bit less dogmatism? The more I mature, the more comfortable I am with phrases like "It seems to me..." over phrases like "This is the way it is...."

3. Read widely, outside of your sympathetic silo.

Listen exclusively to Nazi propaganda if you want to believe like Nazis. Read only about alternative medicine if you want to discount traditional opinions. But if you're searching for the truth, read more widely.

It's cozy living in our comfort zone. Everything's warm and soft. Relieved of the terrible duty of objectively examining evidence, many listen exclusively to radio stations that reinforce their existing beliefs. By way of contrast, one of my favorite thinkers and theologians, Robertson McQuilkin, used to say that his intellectual enemies were often his best friends, because they challenged his beliefs.

4. Put checks and balances into effect.

At Microsoft, founding president Bill Gates expected people to stand up to him and argue their points if he disagreed with them. That's healthy. Those who surround themselves with "yes men" and "yes women" isolate themselves from a host of great ideas.

Flex Your Neurons!
Pursuing the Point of Know Return

1. When you read/listen to news, what are your sources? Read evaluations of your sources to see if they are biased toward a certain political position. How could you get a less biased take on the news?

2. Read the titles of twenty or so news headlines reporting on recent initiatives/statements by the current president. Do some of the headlines show bias? In what way?

3. W.C. Fields once said, "If at first you don't succeed, try, try again. Then quit. There's no point in being a damn fool about it." How does this relate to the "I can do whatever I put my mind to" movement? In what cases might this be good advice? When might it be poor advice?

4. In my critique of "mind over matter," did I actually disprove the theory, or did I merely use an extreme position to illustrate limits to mind over matter?

5. How could our tendency to believe what we want to believe impact the results of drug companies running clinical trials to test the effectiveness of their products? According to one source,

    > "Extensive evidence shows that industry-funded trials systematically produce more favorable outcomes than non-industry sponsored ones."[26]

6. Study how the government's recommendations for a healthy diet have shifted over time. Read this recent Wall Street Journal article to see how researchers can skew evidence to coincide with what they want to believe: Nina Teicholz, *The Questionable Link Between Saturated Fat and Heart Disease*, WDJ, updated May 6, 2014. Do you believe Teilcholz's evidence and line of argument, or do you still have remaining questions?

Making It More Personal
Practical Takeaways

What are one or more ideas provoked by this chapter that you can apply to help you think more critically?

____

____

____

What are one or more ideas that you can apply to help you think more creatively?

____

____

____

What else do you want to make sure you don't forget?

____

____

____

Recommended Trails
For the Incurably Curious and Adventurous

1. In the section on mind over matter, we talked about the need to discover our strengths. For more on how our strengths and styles of thinking should impact our decisions, see chapters 13 and 20 of this book.

2. Here are a couple of good books on the need to identify our strengths: *First, Break All the Rules*, by Marcus Buckingham and Curt Coffman (New York: Simon & Schuster, 1999) and *Next, Discover Your Strengths*, by Marcus Buckingham and Donald Clifton (New York: The Free Press, 2001).

3. For more on Steve Jobs and how his style of thinking impacted his leadership at Apple and Pixar, see *Steve Jobs*, by Walter Isaacson (New York: Simon & Schuster, 2011).

4. Google these phrases if you're interested in pursuing them further: "motivated reasoning," "media bias," and "hostile media effect."

CHAPTER 6

THEY'RE TRAPPED IN TRADITIONS

"*At the crossroads on the path that leads to the future, tradition has placed against each of us 10,000 men to guard the past.*"

— Belgian philosopher Maurice Maeterlinck

"*The past is a different country. They do things differently there.*"

— From the novel, *The Go-Between*

"Someone's got to take a stand!" the wealthy churchman must have thought. "The church should be a place of purity and holiness, separate from the world and its secular entertainment. How could good people welcome this worldly instrument into God's house?"

He did all that he could to thwart the efforts of the "misguided" group that had conceded to accept the sinister gift, beseeching them with tears and even offering to refund the entire price if someone would only dump the ill-fated cargo overboard during its transatlantic voyage.

Just what was this instrument of such vile associations and shady history? The electric guitar or drums? Hardly. The churchman's pleas were left unheeded; the instrument arrived safely in an American harbor, and the Brattle Street Church of Boston made room for the controversial instrument: the organ.[1]

Wouldn't you like to crawl inside that guy's head to try to understand what led to such backward thinking? I mean, an *organ*? Controversial? Really?

But let's give him a break. Times were different in early America. Instruments had different associations in people's minds. Had we lived during his time, sharing his experiences, we might have been devoted members of the "Destroy the Damn Organ Committee." I doubt today's civic and business leaders are immune to precisely the same tendencies that hijacked the mind of the misguided churchman.

Traditions develop so subtly and establish themselves so strongly that all of us, no matter how smart, can allow them to stifle our creativity and innovation.

Lessons from History

A study of the history of religious music reveals much about how traditions set in and how difficult they are to break out of.[2] A similar cycle could probably be found in such fields as education or business. Here's how it played out in church music.

Period #1: Authentic - People worship to musical styles that are congruent with their heart music—the tunes they sing in the shower, hum as they go to work, and listen to in their most relaxed moments. Thus, when outsiders visit their services, the music resonates with them.

Period #2: Separation - While music styles in secular society continue to morph, the church allows their styles to fossilize. After all, the older folks have fond associations with their church music and if the younger generation were spiritually attuned, surely they'd prefer it as well. The church justifies its exclusive use of older music with many arguments, such as "The church should be different from the world. Why should we bring secular music into the church?"

Period #3: Integration - Bold innovators, convinced that outdated forms are stifling heartfelt worship, experiment with styles popular among the larger culture.

Period #4: Conflict - Diehard traditionalists bitterly oppose the "secularization" of the church with "worldly" music. Churches split. Innovative pastors are ousted.

Period #1 (Reprise): Authentic - Many churches that adopt newer forms of music thrive, ushering in a time of renewal, which continues until churches refuse to adapt to the continued morphing of music in the larger culture. Thus history repeats itself.

Resulting Experimentation and Ferment

In the first half of the 1900s American churches typically played hymns set to the tunes of popular music of the 1800s. Over time, these had become the accepted music of the church. But during the social unrest of the 1960s and 1970s hippies began searching for God in what became known as "The Jesus Movement." Rather than purchasing organs for their meetings, they kept their guitars and drum sets and penned their own songs, which eventually revolutionized music in the church. Many churches that adapted to this new generation's music experienced explosive growth.[3]

Experimentation with musical styles has become one of the most salient characteristics of the modern church. Walk into a worship service at random and you may find styles from classical to traditional hymns, hip hop to rock, minimalist to full orchestration. In the language of ethnomusicology, many churches employ the music indigenous* to the local people (their "heart music") rather than impose styles that are foreign (or repugnant to) their experience.

***Indigenous =** originating in and characteristic of a particular region or country.

Applications to Business

Wise businesses and service organizations can learn from church history, as well as the history of the rise and fall of great businesses. If the preferences and culture and traditions of customers are out of sync with the culture and products promoted by the business leaders, customers will go elsewhere.

Last week, my wife Cherie and I visited a new restaurant. The food was great, but they assaulted us with loud 1980s' rock. We're more into 1970s' music and recent niche styles. While their clientele seemed mixed—older, younger, families—I'll bet their staff grew up in the '80s and considered that era of music "good music." They assumed that what sounded good to them (volume as well as style) would sound good to their customers. The atmosphere told us on a gut level that it wasn't our kind of restaurant. I doubt we'll return.

Traditions that Threatened Starbucks

Unlike church music styles, which may take a generation to set in, other traditions set in quickly, or are established from the start. Take Starbucks, one of the most successful business stories of our time. Starbucks opened its first store in Seattle in 1971. In 43 years, Starbucks has become "the premier roaster and retailer of specialty coffee in the world," serving customers in 18,000 stores in 62 countries. Not bad for a company that found incredible difficulty overcoming its early traditions.[4]

After Howard Schultz joined Starbucks in 1982, he travelled to Italy and caught a vision for bringing the Italian coffeehouse tradition back with him to the United States. He envisioned a place for conversation and community, "a third place between work and home." He also envisioned the type coffee they would be drinking—the kind of coffee that Schultz was passionate about.

As Schultz put it,

> "Starbucks stood not only for good coffee, but specifically the dark-roasted flavor profile.... That's what differentiated it and made it authentic.... You don't just give the customers what they ask for. If you offer them something they're not accustomed to, something so far superior that it takes a while to develop their palates, you can create a sense of discovery and excitement and loyalty that will bond them to you. It may take longer, but if you have a great product, you can educate your customers to like it rather than kowtowing* to mass-market appeal."[5]

***Kowtow =** to act in an excessively subservient manner.

Well, that all sounded wonderful to the leadership, being coffee connoisseurs who somehow knew what customers would like if you trained them. But what if their customers disagreed, deeming Schultz's ideas about "good coffee" as nothing more than dark roast elitist snobbery? What about the customers who didn't want to be "educated" about "real coffee," but simply wanted a medium roast decaf diluted with cream and caramel flavoring? Is that really so heretical? It was certainly unthinkable to Schultz and the rest of the leadership, and questioning Starbucks' orthodoxy was no easy matter.

In that first store, they learned that while you can bring Italy to Seattle, you can't make Seattle-ites like every aspect of it. Shultz played exclusively Italian opera. Customers got tired of it. There was no seating (In Europe, many coffee bars are stand up only.) Customers wanted to sit down. The rub with the leadership was that "integrity to the vision" thing—they were in love with their original vision and strongly resisted diluting it. They wanted Seattle to share the Italian experience. In the end, they reluctantly changed the music and brought in chairs.[6]

But the coffee was another matter.

Schultz and the other leaders were purists about their coffee and their distinction of offering the undiluted Italian experience. That is, until they hired Howard Behar. Behar didn't hold any purist notions of "great coffee." Rather, he held to strong principles about how to run a business. According to Behar, great companies listen to their customers. In fact, those who fail to listen die.

So right from the start, Behar gathered customer input by reading comment cards and talking to their baristas and customers. Their main message? They wanted nonfat milk. So Behar confronted Schultz as to why he wasn't listening. Schultz replied that coffee with nonfat milk didn't taste good.

"To whom?" asked Behar.

"To me..." replied Schultz.

"Well, read the customer cards," replied Behar.

"We will never offer nonfat milk," replied Schultz. "It's not who we are."

To Schultz and his store managers, even the mention of nonfat milk implied treason. But it was the late 1980s and people were trying to cut down on their fat intake. Behar wouldn't let go of it. According to Schultz, it was "one of the biggest debates in Starbucks' history."[7]

Early one morning, after a restless night, Schultz drove to a Seattle Starbucks, his mind struggling with the debate. He ordered a double espresso and took a seat, paying attention to the people ordering. A young woman, dressed in sweats, apparently fresh from her morning run, ordered a double tall latte with nonfat milk. The barista politely explained that they carried only whole milk. Frustrated, she said that she could get one from a nearby shop and left.

For Schultz, it was an epiphany. They tested low fat milk in a few stores, then extended it to the rest, resulting in a whopping 50 percent of lattes and cappuccinos being ordered with low-fat milk.[8]

From our vantage point, these decisions appear obvious. But at those points in Starbucks' history, they weren't clear at all. After all, businesses must differentiate themselves. If Starbucks were "just another of the scores of coffee shops in Seattle," what would set them apart, making them special? Once they branded themselves with that Italian distinction, wouldn't catering to the whims of customers eventually obliterate that distinction?

As Schultz put it,

> "In hindsight, that decision [introducing low-fat milk] looks like a no-brainer. But at the time, we weren't sure what impact it would have on our brand and our identity. When a Caffè latte is made with nonfat milk, is it still an authentic Italian drink? Most Italians wouldn't recognize it…."
>
> "We had to recognize that the customer was right. It was our responsibility to give people a choice."[9]

It's easy to see how we get set in our ways and resist change. It's not entirely irrational. The guardians of tradition always have arguments for their positions.

Why do brilliant people believe nonsense? Because they allow traditions to blind them to the truth.

And we're not just talking about restaurants, coffee shops and churches. The same principles apply to the music you play in your store, the décor in your university classroom, the culture you're trying to develop in your technology company, your style of teaching in your middle school class, and the unique musical style of your band.

Surely all of us could use an infusion of creativity to blow the traditional dust out of our organizations. How can we do it?

Action Points

Especially in today's fast-moving world, the mantra of successful businesses I study is "Innovate or die!" What's working today may not work tomorrow. How can we resist the tight grip of tradition?

1. Reexamine your roots.

What line of reasoning originally led your organization to adopt its traditions? Is that line of reasoning still valid? If so, perhaps the tradition is still of value. Don't change traditions just for the sake of change!

But often, with time, the original reasoning no longer makes sense.

I heard of a lady who was teaching her daughter how to cook a roast when her daughter asked, "Why do you cut it in half?" Mom responded, "Well, your granny always did it this way, so I assumed it had something to do with making sure it cooked thoroughly in the middle." But her curiosity got the best of her and the next time she talked to granny, she asked about it. Granny responded, "I cut it in half because my pan was too short!"

In this case, as well as others, it helps to revisit the decision making process that originally led to adopting the tradition.

In the case of church music, where did those old hymns originate? Why did they choose them?

It turns out that the old hymns were typically put to the tunes of popular secular ballads of their day. No wonder the new songs resonated with the people of their time. And no wonder they often failed to resonate with so many in later generations. This fact also helps to refine a relevant question. In light of the history of hymns, instead of asking, "Is it okay for churches to use the world's music," the more accurate question would be, "What era of the world's music should we use?"

The church examining its roots may discover that the tradition it wants to preserve is *the methodology* that led to its adopting hymns in the first place. Perhaps those churches during the times of Isaac Watts (adopting the popular poetry of his time) and the Wesleys (adopting the popular tunes of their time) succeeded, not because the music was in itself superior to the styles of other cultures and ages, but because it resonated with the specific culture they were trying to reach.

Back to business, if you own a retail store and your present product line was chosen based upon trends five years ago, have those trends changed enough to warrant tweaking your product line?

Again, don't dismiss traditions because they're traditions. Revisit your original reasoning that led to the adoption of the tradition. It just might still make good sense, or may need a good tweaking rather than trashing.

2. Periodically reexamine your vision, mission, and core values.

Does your vision need to change? In the case of Starbucks, their vision of the Italian experience was such a part of their DNA that they couldn't see outside of it. In a sense, their mission became more important than their customers.

3. Reassess your target culture, either here or abroad.

If you were starting the first Starbucks in Costa Rica, you'd naturally study Costa Ricans to fine tune your store to fit their culture. If certain symbols or colors would align the store with a certain political party, or if certain flavors that Americans love are despised there, you'd certainly want to know. Since cultural nuances are typically invisible to foreigners, your best bet would be to not only read up on culture, but to engage Costa Ricans in conversations about your store, *especially those who enter your store for the first time*, since they've yet to be acculturated into Starbucks' ways.

Ask questions such as:

- Does anything offend or annoy you about the store décor or service?
- What products appeal to you or disgust you?
- Are the products named appropriately?
- If you were to start a coffee shop, what would you do differently from us?

Much can be lost in translation. I recall a fine restaurant in Bratislava, the capital of Slovakia, that had a menu translated into English (perhaps from Slovak to German to English). One of the entrees was titled something to the effect of "Sheep Shit with Goat Cheese." Not too appealing. Apparently the translator lacked fluency in English and could have used an English-speaking informant to better appeal to his English-speaking guests!

While all this cross-cultural sensitivity may seem pretty obvious in starting a Starbucks in a foreign culture, it's often less obvious when starting one in our own culture. We assume that we know our own culture thoroughly.

We don't. Remember, Starbucks' leadership had difficulty adjusting their store to their own culture in Seattle, because they *assumed* that everyone would react the way *they* reacted to Italian coffee shops. They were wrong. They also failed to consider that Starbucks' customers in Southern California might have their own preferences, distinct from Seattleites.[10]

The goal should be to start a store that's truly indigenous to the local culture. You do that by starting conversations with the locals and listening intently, even if you consider the culture your own. Cultures change, and companies that pass the tests of time recognize and assess those changes.

4. Study the relevant data and reason from it with precision.

In other words, employ your skills in research and critical thinking.

The wealthy churchman wasn't arguing that tradition in itself was sacred. A body of evidence typically arises to protect traditions. I'm sure he could have listed many arguments for shunning organs, which needed to be tested by asking questions such as:

From Psychology: Do certain instruments/styles negatively impact our thoughts, regardless of personal associations?

From History: Were the instruments we presently use developed by the church, or imported from the world? Does it matter?

From Theology: Does "worldly" mean anything invented by and used by the world? If so, to be consistent, are the pastor's stylish clothes "worldly"?

From Ethnomusicology: Do instruments/styles carry the same meaning in different cultures and different generations?

Religious leaders, as well as leaders of innovative companies such as Microsoft, Google and Apple often find themselves embroiled in highly charged debates about changes and new directions. But the path to the future is paved with difficult decisions that require thought, study, candor, debate, new data, and still more thought before reaching decisions.

In the end, we dare not destroy traditions merely for the sake of constant innovation. Set them aside only if they no longer make sense. Many educational institutions have wonderful traditions that continue to reinforce their vision and goals. Treasure them!

5. Encourage small scale innovation before a major overhaul.

Another Starbucks debate erupted concerning their southern California shops pushing to offer something to compete with the cold, sugary, blended coffees that they saw selling briskly at competing shops in hot weather. Schultz resisted, arguing that it wasn't a true coffee drink. It would dilute their integrity.

Finally, a renegade store, without permission, bought a blender and started experimenting. They eventually got upper management on board and continued to experiment until they developed the Frappuccino, an icy blend of dark-roast coffee and milk. Schultz still thought it was a mistake, but allowed 12 stores to test it. It was a sensation. They rolled it out nationally and the first year sold $52 million worth of Frappuccinos, representing seven percent of their total revenue.[11]

As Sam Walton said of his success with Walmart:

> "I think my constant fiddling and meddling with the status quo may have been one of my biggest contributions to the later success of Walmart."[12]
>
> "After a lifetime of swimming upstream, I am convinced that one of the real secrets to Walmart's phenomenal success has been that very tendency."[13]

6. Set in place mechanisms that force you to regularly reevaluate traditions.

Someone said that the seven last words of the church were, "We never did it that way before." Those could also be the seven last words of businesses. What mechanisms might ensure that we keep innovating?

Several studies, one of them examining over 90 prominent creatives in various fields, found great ideas coming, not typically from isolated eureka moments, but from a process.[14]

Typically, innovators have been researching and thinking about a question for some time. For example, the theory of gravity didn't come to Newton in full bloom when the apple dropped from the tree (if we can trust this story). Rather, he'd been reflecting on the question of what holds the universe together for some time and had a strong background in math and science.[15]

In the same way, we're much more likely to innovate if we've ensured a constant flow of data to fuel our thoughts. If you're in business, do you read publications in your field? Edison and his team saw breakthrough after breakthrough, resulting in over 2,300 U.S. and foreign patents. But his ideas didn't come out of nowhere. He read widely, urged his staff to do the same, and kept abreast of many scientific journals. This study helped to guide their experiments.[16]

7. Beware of enthroning traditions.

Soichiro Honda revolutionized the motorcycle industry and then disrupted the automobile industry by introducing some of the most reliable, emissions-efficient, popular cars ever. He succeeded largely by thinking differently. To keep his company innovating, he outlawed the use of the word "tradition" at Honda Motors, considering it alien to the principles he'd established.[17]

8. Learn from outside your field.

We most eagerly learn from within our own field of specialty, where we feel the most comfortable and where we get so many relevant ideas. But it often pays to look outside our field.

When leaders at the Mayo Clinic wanted to improve the efficiency of their scheduling, they felt the need to look outside the medical community. If their scheduling methods could account, for example, for the fact that an elderly patient or wheel-chair bound patient would need more time to get an MRI, they could help more patients get through the process without waiting. So in the 1950s Mayo leadership learned from the Pullman Train schedulers. By the 1970s Mayo was an early adopter of computers for scheduling, adapting software used by Boeing and NASA.[18]

On Creativity
Think Different!

Apple leadership made resisting tradition a part of their DNA. Here's a marketing passage they used to describe their innovative culture.

Here's to the crazy ones.
The misfits.
The rebels.
The troublemakers.
The round pegs in square holes.
The ones who see things differently.
They're not fond of rules.
And they have no respect for the status quo.
You can quote them, disagree with them, glorify or vilify them.
About the only thing you can't do is ignore them.
Because they change things.
They push the human race forward.
And while some may see them as the crazy ones, we see genius.
Because the people who are crazy enough to think they can change the world
are the ones who do.

[Permission requested on Apple's web form Feb. 19, 2015]

(By the way, this version of the passage had been written and revised 62 times.[19] Innovation can require lots of tinkering! Yet, many students are offended when a teacher suggests that they make a second revision of their paper. As one writer noted, "Writing is rewriting.")

Flex Your Neurons!
Pursuing the Point of Know Return

1. You're teaching English as a Second Language in another country. How will you decide what kind of music to play as people enter?

2. You're starting a new restaurant. What kind of music will you use? What kind of décor? Concerning your menu: How will you keep tweaking it to make sure tradition doesn't calcify after people's tastes have evolved?

3. How would you evaluate your high school, or your department in your university? What aspects seem more based on tradition than function? In your opinion, which traditions help the goals of the school and which ones hinder the goals? Is there a system by which traditions are evaluated to see if they still serve a useful function?

4. If your business or service organization is thriving, have you set in place ongoing evaluation to make sure it doesn't get too set in its ways?

5. Are you in love with your traditions? Are you letting personal preferences interfere with getting candid input?

6. You did a study abroad to Sao Paulo, Brazil and fell in love with Brazilian steak houses. You want to replicate the experience in America with your own steakhouse. How will you decide which traditions to import and which to leave behind?

7. You cook the same meals for your family every week. Might it help to try at least one new dish every week? Is there a way you could solicit regular input from your family without it becoming a gripe session? How could you overcome the inertia that keeps you in your traditional, comfortable rut?

Making It More Personal
Practical Takeaways

What are one or more ideas provoked by this chapter that you can apply to help you think more critically?

____

____

____

What are one or more ideas that you can apply to help you think more creatively?

____

____

____

What else do you want to make sure you don't forget?

____

____

____

Recommended Trails
For the Incurably Curious and Adventurous

1. For more on creativity and innovation, I profited from reading *The Myths of Creativity: The Truth about How Innovative Companies and People Generate Great Ideas*, by David Burkus (San Francisco: Jossey-Bass, 2014.)

2. Here's a good article by Burkus on implementing creative support groups: http://99u.com/articles/21521/in-praise-of-the-creative-support-group.

3. Many writers and artists who experience writers' block have been set free by *The Artist's Way*, written by journalist and screen-writer Julia Cameron (New York: Tarcher/Putnam, 1992). In part, she recommends that blocked artists write three pages of stream-of-consciousness writing each morning, plus take an "artist's date" (you and your inner artist) each week to nurture your creativity. Could adopting (or adapting) such practices increase your creative output?

4. Other well respected books on creativity and innovation include *Uncommon Genius: How Great Ideas Are Born*, by Denise Shekerjian (Penguin Books, reissue edition 1991); and *Creators on Creating: Awakening and Cultivating the Imaginative Mind*, Barron, et. al., editors (Tarcher, 1997). The former is a study of 40 creative people to see how great ideas are born. The latter is a collection of essays by famous creative people, describing their own creativity. *Exploring the Nature of Creativity*, by Jon Michael Fox and Ronni Lea Fox (Dubuque, Iowa: Kendall/Hunt Publishing Company, 2000), gives an accessible introduction to the subject for students. Those wanting a more academic introduction to creativity, summarizing what scholars in various fields are researching and discovering about creativity, written more for academics than for creative individuals looking for inspiration, consider the *Handbook of Creativity*, by Robert J. Sternberg, editor (Cambridge University Press, 1998). If you need a more up-to-date handbook, see *The Cambridge Handbook of Creativity*, by James Kaufman and Robert Sternberg, editors (Cambridge University Press, 2010).

CHAPTER 7

THEY FAIL TO IDENTIFY HIDDEN ASSUMPTIONS

"Your assumptions are your windows on the world.
Scrub them off every once in a while, or the light won't come in."

— Isaac Asimov

Assumptions in Entertainment (or How to Fool Intellectuals)

It was talent night at Kennesaw State University. An international student took the stage and baffled both students and faculty by apparently defying the laws of time and space. He appeared on the stage, in clear view of the audience, announcing that in a moment the lights would black out for two seconds, after which he would appear elsewhere. Sure enough, after a moment of darkness, the lights returned to find he'd disappeared from the stage. But no. Someone opened a box that appeared securely chained shut and out climbed the student.

Great minds wrestled with the seeming impossibility. How could he have rushed to the box, jumped inside, and shut it so quickly? Even if he made it, it seemed securely chained. Could it have been some kind of smoke and mirrors? Perhaps he wasn't originally on the stage at all—projected as some kind of hologram. But he looked so real, so really there.

For his grand finale, he announced that in the next two seconds of darkness, he'd once again disappear from the stage and the lights would reveal him walking in the back door of the auditorium—obviously a distance that couldn't be travelled in two seconds, even if he sprinted the shortest distance, straight down the middle aisle, in complete darkness.

The lights flipped off. They flipped on. He was walking in the back door. The audience was astounded.

After the applause, he revealed his secret. Unknown to the audience, he had an identical twin brother, who joined him on the stage to take a bow.

One faculty member said he couldn't believe that it never occurred to him that the student had a twin brother. That's what happens when we unconsciously limit our thinking with unwarranted assumptions. In this case, the assumption was revealed in the very wording of people's thoughts: "How did *he* do that?" "How did *he* move so quickly?" "Was *he* really where we thought *he* was from the start?"

It wasn't *he*; it was *them*. Their very questions limited the range of possible answers.

Assumptions in Warfare: How False Assumptions Lost a War and Changed the World

The year was 1776. The setting was the North American British colonies. The big event was a rebellion against the mother country by some troublemakers who were discontent with British rule. The outcome would reshape the modern world.

The question I'd like to answer is not whether the British or the Americans were right in their cause—many American colonists sided with their mother country and fought for the British. Similarly, many British argued in their Parliament against the war. I'd like to pose a different question:

> "Why did the most powerful, well-trained army on the planet lose a war to an army that seemed inferior in every way?"

To set the stage, let's first grasp just how superior the British forces were.[1]

- The British leaders were trained in the art of warfare in the top schools of their time. None of the American leaders had been trained in military schools. They picked up what they could from reading books. General George Washington had seven or eight years of schooling by a private tutor, just enough to learn to "express himself on paper with force and clarity." General Nathanael Greene and Colonel Henry Knox would become two of his most important leaders. Green was a thirty-three year old self-educated Quaker; Colonel Henry Knox was a twenty-five year old self-educated bookseller.

- The British leaders had vast experience. Neither General Washington nor any of his leaders had ever led an army.

- The British troops were well-trained and well-disciplined. The American troops were largely young farmers, schoolteachers, shoemakers and the like, learning as they went along.

- The British were well-clothed and equipped with the best cannons and guns, not to mention having the world's dominant fleet of warships. The Americans had little artillery and were woefully short of gunpowder. Their clothing was often inadequate to the point of marching barefoot. Sickness often ravaged the camps.

- The American troops were far outnumbered. To make matters worse, large numbers of soldiers considered going home and deserting the cause. They were often miserable, missed their families, and had plenty of reasons to believe they could never defeat the

> British. And besides, many of their own countrymen were Loyalists, siding with the British.

So why didn't the British forces obliterate the American troops early in the conflict? Many reasons could be discussed, but I'd like to suggest one that stood out to me in reading David McCullough's respected book on the beginnings of the Revolutionary War, titled simply *1776*.

Here's my key observation:

> The Revolutionary War was a contest between *the learned* (the British) and *the learners* (the colonists). The British were overconfident because they far outnumbered the American army, were well-equipped, well-trained, and knew how to fight. They *assumed* they knew much more than they'd ever need to know to defeat the pitiful American army, deriding them as "the country people," "the rebels," "a preposterous parade," or a "rabble in arms."[2]

Being learned can be a great thing, but it can also lead to false assumptions.

The American leaders, by contrast, were avid learners. They in no way assumed they would win this contest against a formidable power. They knew they didn't know everything about warfare and were thus hotly pursuing whatever wisdom they could pick up from anyone and anywhere.

Here's how "the learners versus the learned" played out in a couple of critical, early battles.

The Battle for Boston, March, 1776

The British troops, under the command of General Howe, had taken Boston, fortifying it to the extent that many felt it could never be successfully attacked. Howe was one of the most respected, distinguished officers in the King's service.[3] He was fully assured that he had nothing to fear from the ragtag American army. As General Howe wrote to his superiors, "We are not under the least apprehension of an attack on this place from the rebels by surprise or otherwise."[4] The British officers lived comfortably in Boston, where the officers and their ladies were entertained by plays and balls and held feasts where they drank wine and ridiculed the pathetic American troops.[5]

The American army wasn't faring so well. It was January, miserably cold, and most lived in makeshift tents without winter clothing.[6] They had little gunpowder, inadequate money to pay the troops, and there weren't even enough guns for the new recruits.[7] Washington feared that if the British discovered their dire situation, they would attack immediately and end the war.

Fortunately for the Americans, the British failed to gather adequate intelligence. Thus, they failed to catch wind of a daring two month journey led by twenty-five year old Colonel Knox to snatch over 120,000 pounds of weapons, including mortar and cannon, from Fort Ticonderoga in Upstate New York and transport them through blizzards, over mountains and freezing lakes, to arrive just in time for an attack.[8]

The British leaders were educated in military studies, both in formal classrooms and in live combat. But they saw no need to continue their education on this field, assuming they were superior in every way. Howe took no interest in General George Washington. Typically, military leaders gather all available information on their enemies. They want to know how they think, in order to predict their next moves. But their degrees and experience made them comfortable, overconfident, and smug.[9]

By contrast, Washington and his forces were avid learners. With no assumptions of superiority, Washington gathered wise people around him, as he put it, "to have people that can think for me."[10] They decided to occupy the strategic twin hills of Dorchester, from which they could threaten both the British soldiers in Boston and their ships in the harbor. Cannons shot from the hills could reach both.

Washington learned from spies that Howe had sworn that if the American army occupied Dorchester, he would retaliate by attacking them, which is precisely what Washington wanted. Then Washington could battle from the advantageous positions of Dorchester, rather than directly attacking the fortified city of Boston.[11]

But one problem remained—a big one. If the British saw the Americans clamoring up Dorchester's hills, they'd attack before the Americans had a chance to fortify the hill. How do you fortify a hill overnight in the middle of winter? You can't even shovel frozen ground to make your fortifications.

Once again, continuing education came to the rescue, in the form of Rufus Putnam, a farmer and surveyor by trade, who read of a useful scheme in an artillery text by a British professor. Putnam showed the plan to his superiors, who in turn took him to Washington. The scheme involved building the fortifications and transporting them up the hills overnight by oxen and massive manpower, so that the next morning the British would awake to find Dorchester's hills fully fortified, occupied with 3,000 men, armed with guns and cannons.[12]

Four days prior to the attack, a spy warned the British of an impending attack from Dorchester, but nobody took the warnings seriously. They would be warned again, but to no avail—more evidence they were more learned than learners, captives of their false assumptions.[13]

So Saturday evening, March 2, the American army bombarded Boston with cannons. The British responded with cannon fire. On Sunday, the firing resumed, but it was all just a distraction, so that when the cannons roared once again on Monday night, they covered the sound of 800 oxen, hundreds of carts and wagons, heavy cannons, and fortifications moving quickly and orderly up the hills. Fortunately or providentially, they were aided by the light of a full moon, unseasonably mild weather, and a foggy haze that covered the thousands of soldiers in the low lands before they ascended.[14]

The British awoke the next morning to behold what appeared to be a miracle, or from their perspective, a nightmare. They were completely and utterly astonished. General Howe exclaimed, "My God, these fellows have done more work in one night than I could make my army do in three months." One British officer wrote that "This is, I believe, likely to prove as important a day to the British Empire as any in our annals." Referring to the fortifications, he marveled, "They were all raised during the night, with an expedition equal to that of the genie belonging to Aladdin's wonderful lamp."[15]

The British tried to attack, but were turned back by a furious storm of snow and sleet. The storm gave them time to rationally assess their dire situation. Attacking the well-fortified Americans would likely be suicidal. But remaining in Boston would make them sitting ducks. Their cannonballs couldn't reach the top of the hill. And their ships couldn't risk staying in the harbor. The weather eventually calmed, but by then panic had replaced the Redcoats' complacency. Their only choice was to tuck tail and sail, giving the American army extremely needed confidence that they could eventually defeat the British.[16]

The Attack on Trenton, December, 1776

The British didn't take this defeat lightly. In August, a British armada of 400 ships arrived at New York City, delivering 32,000 troops to Staten Island.[17] It was "the largest expeditionary force of the eighteenth century, the largest, most powerful force ever sent forth from Britain or any nation."[18]

Outmanned and outgunned, Washington decided that wisdom was the better part of valor. He and his 9,000 troops wisely sneaked out of New York City during the night and the British followed close behind.

Washington's troops grew weaker and weaker. Thirty to forty soldiers at a time defected to the British. Many had no shoes.[19] The American Congress fled Philadelphia. Two former members of Congress defected to the enemy.[20] On December 1, with the British army two hours behind, two thousand American soldiers deserted the army and returned home—their enlistment was up.[21] Washington's 9,000 troops had dwindled to about 3,000. By all reasonable calculations, the war was over.[22] How could Washington's pitiful band of 3,000 troops ever survive a battle with 32,000 seasoned soldiers? A Loyalist newspaper in New York described the American army as "the most pitiable collection of ragged, dispirited mortals that ever pretended to the name of an army…."[23]

But instead of attacking and finishing the war then and there, General Howe decided to return to New York until spring, leaving sufficient forces in Trenton, New Jersey, to hold the ground they'd gained. Since cold weather had set in and the outcome seemed inevitable, he saw no reason to subject his troops to a harsh winter campaign. That one assumption—underestimating the American army—may have ultimately lost the war for the British.[24]

General James Grant, the commander of the British holding forces in New Jersey, assumed that the troops in Trenton were as safe as if they were wintering in London.[25] But on Christmas night, during a vicious, blinding, snowstorm (two of Washington's men froze to death on the march) Washington and his troops marched on Trenton, attacking the unsuspecting troops the next morning, defeating them in a mere 45 minutes.[26]

The news of the American victory spread rapidly and had a remarkable effect.[27] Hope replaced despair; confidence replaced fear and dread—the rebels had boldly confronted the enemy and won a stunning victory. Although it would be another six and a half years before the war ended, the battle of Trenton was a decisive turning point. As one classic study of the American Revolution concluded,

> "It may be doubted whether so small a number of men ever employed so short a space of time with greater and more lasting effects upon the history of the world."

Thus, on the battlefield, false assumptions can spell doom for even highly trained and well-equipped troops; learners have strong advantages over the learned. Let's see what advantage the learners might have in business and technological innovation.

Assumptions in Technology: How False Assumptions Lost the Battle of the Search Engines

Early search engines such as Yahoo!, AltaVista, and Ask Jeeves didn't know what hit them.[28] Everybody who was anybody in technology assumed that these search engine powerhouses couldn't be unseated from their dominant positions, especially Yahoo!, which in 1998 attracted 75 percent of all web searches. The common assumption was that Yahoo! had already won the search engine wars.[29]

The mindset of Yahoo! executives reminds us of the British leadership in Boston and Trenton. Overwhelmingly dominating the world's searches, they rested confident that their search techniques were adequate. Why obsess on trying to improve them?[30] While the learned assumed the best, the learners—a couple of Stanford students—quietly but feverishly forged a search engine that would rule them all.

Larry Page and Sergey Brin aspired to take searching to where it had never gone before, "to organize and make available all the world's information," making them "the world's librarians." Yahoo! failed to notice Google's rapidly rising traffic, as Page and Brin stealthily won over influential early adopters so that the word quickly spread without bold advertising—Google offered a superior search.

Today Forbes ranks Google as the fifth most valuable brand in the world.[31] It employs almost 54,000 people and brought in $58 billion in revenues in 2013.[32]

Overcoming False Assumptions

Whether you're waging a war, running a business, or watching an illusionist, pay attention to your assumptions. They can be trickier than the traditions we discussed in the previous chapter in that we're typically less conscious of our assumptions. Like the professor watching the twins, we're often clueless that we're being fooled by the power of a false assumption. In this case, false assumptions produced entertainment on the positive side, mild embarrassment ("Can't believe I didn't see that coming!") on the negative side. But when it comes to business, warfare, or any important decision, such as choosing who to marry, assumptions can be tragic.

Why do brilliant people—including army generals and college professors—believe nonsense? Because they fail to recognize their false assumptions.

Fighting Assumptions*

So how do we learn to recognize and analyze our assumptions? And beyond guarding ourselves from costly errors, how can we free ourselves and our organizations to think beyond our assumptions and imagine innovations that revolutionize not only our businesses, but our world?

***Assumption =** something accepted as true, without sufficient evidence.
***Presupposition =** something assumed to be true at the beginning of an argument.

Think Different

1. Create cultures of candor.

Recall from chapter one Jack Welch's observation that lack of candor is a huge problem in modern businesses. Now we're beginning to see candor's value for recognizing and overcoming false assumptions.

Nobody likes criticism, and most of us avoid conflict like a plague. But I find many successful companies embracing and nurturing candid input and criticism, even when it hurts, even if it produces seemingly incessant arguments.

- General Washington created a rather flat organizational structure, so that ideas from all ranks could quickly reach the leadership.
- The British generals neither sought ideas widely nor took them seriously when they were voiced.
- Bill Gates, when running Microsoft, wanted people to argue for their ideas against his criticisms. His arguments with his co-leaders were legendary.[33]
- Steve Jobs and his colleagues at Apple argued fervently for what they believed.[34]

They argued because they cared about their decisions and wanted to get them right. By allowing people to candidly voice their concerns, many companies get all the facts on the table and make better decisions.

Fresh Leadership Stirs Up Starbucks

As we saw in the last chapter, Starbucks' leadership struggled greatly with reconciling their vision (an authentic Italian coffee shop experience) with listening to customers and giving them what they wanted. Sometimes it takes a new person with a fresh perspective to shake things up.

For Starbucks, that person was Howard Behar. According to CEO Schultz, Behar "hit Starbucks like a tornado."[35] For Behar, customers trumped the company vision. In his mind, if enough customers want their coffee diluted, sweet, caramel flavored, low fat, or on ice, who are we to deny them for the sake of some silly "commitment to the Italian experience?" I think Behar saw "The Italian Experience" as not just a tradition to be questioned, but an assumption to be tested. The assumption was that if Starbucks veered too far from "The Italian Experience," they'd lose their distinction, water down what they stood for, and lose their hard-earned customers. Behar wanted to test that assumption.

When "the tornado" hit Starbucks, he went straight to the customers. Rather than making decisions based on the leadership's vision, he wanted to see decisions based on data. That data would come from customer input and be tested in individual stores.

So he read customer comments. He talked to customers. He talked to baristas about the customers. He discovered what the customers wanted. Then he candidly took the information to the management. When they reacted and balked and stalled and argued, he argued back, until they began to listen and experiment, in the end taking Starbucks' profitability to new heights.

Behar's stubborn candor forced Starbucks to rethink their mission and their practices. He also forced them to ask deeper questions:

- What if the bottom line for the customer isn't "integrity to the Italian experience," but enjoying a cup of coffee prepared in the way she likes it?
- What if Starbucks' myopic focus on the quality of the coffee blinded them to the needs of the customer?
- What if many customers don't want to learn to appreciate dark roast coffee?
- In fact, what if many customers aren't even, on a deeper level, looking for coffee at all, but a friendly barista and a warm place in a cold world—a place where people care and listen? Thus Behar began to preach, "We're not filling bellies; we're filling souls."

Behar was confrontational. Schultz by nature avoided confrontation, and had inadvertently created a culture where store managers were reluctant to share and push for changes that the leadership might find offensive. Such a culture minimized arguments, but stifled candor. It took a tornado to clear the air and open up the company to a more candid sharing of ideas.[36]

Think!

In your family or business or creative endeavor or social work, do people feel free to express their opinions? Why or why not? Would a move toward candor likely enhance or hinder your goals?

2. Unblock the flow of ideas.

In both the battles of Boston and Trenton, the British leadership had been warned more than once about the impending attacks, but ignored them because of their assumptions. Their arrogance blocked the flow of ideas.

By contrast Washington actively sought ideas from everywhere, even if they came from an ordinary farmer named Rufus with his idea of transportable fortifications. Washington also listened to Knox's wild plan to haul guns and cannons from Upstate New York. As historian David McCullough summarized the latter:

> "That such a scheme hatched by a junior officer in his twenties who had had no experience was transmitted so directly to the supreme commander, seriously considered, and acted upon, also marked an important difference between the civilian army of the Americans and that of the British. In an army where nearly everyone was new to the tasks of soldiering and fighting a war, almost anyone's ideas deserved a hearing."[37]

From reading stories of successful companies, I find that they're typically more idea-driven than expert-driven. They take ideas wherever they can find them and encourage a culture that does the same. The leaders listen, often poking fun at their own mistakes, rather than carrying around the burden of being the sole fount of great ideas.

Think!

What hinders the flow of ideas in your home or business? Does the leadership believe that only PhDs, or only the executives, or only the managers are smart enough to generate the best ideas?

As I write, a newly established pizza business in my community is beating out the entrenched competition and spinning off franchises. I heard the leadership describe some of their best practices, one of which was to get their workers sharing their ideas. While they were encouraged to share ideas at any time, they met together once a month with the owners specifically to share their ideas, whether they be gripes, frustrations, or positive tips. It didn't seem to bother the leaders at all that they were getting advice from workers in their early 20s. In fact, perhaps their youthfulness and inexperience was an asset.

As obvious as this sounds when speaking of *other* businesses, for some reason it's not nearly so obvious to us in *our own* work. Does your church or service organization get input from newcomers and those newly acquainted with your work? (New folks haven't yet become acculturated to your way of doing things.) Does your band get regular input from your audiences? Do you get regular input from your children on your meals? (As the primary chef in my family, I allow no griping during the meal. But afterward, I ask what they liked and didn't like, so that I can keep improving.)

3. Allow people to follow their ideas.

Leaders often assume they know what's best for the company. But allowing workers to follow their own ideas pays off in many companies.

By 1994, Hewlett-Packard was selling almost $20 billion worth of computer and related products. Thirty years earlier, they didn't sell computers at all. Embarrassingly, they didn't immediately see their potential in the computer industry and plan for it. Instead, computer enthusiasts at HP took matters in their own hands.

HP started a project code-named Omega, building what would have been the first 32 bit computer, which in the early 1970s would have run at twice the speed of the fastest existing computers. But top management cancelled the project, due to concerns about expense, taking on debt, marketing, and competing with IBM.

But some of the Omega enthusiasts wouldn't take no for an answer. They kept the project alive in a back room. Later, when some key engineers and managers reversed their decision, they discovered that the secret skunk works* operation had made progress. In 1972, they rolled out their hugely successful HP3000, staking out their claim in the burgeoning computer industry.[38]

***Skunk Works®** = a small group of people who work on a project in an unconventional way, streamlining the process to minimize interference by management.

Think back to Starbucks' highly profitable Frappaccino. It was created because of a similar skunk works initiative. Upper management didn't want to pursue it, so a renegade store took it upon themselves to pursue it.

How to Design and Build Your Very First Fighter Jet in Under Five Months

In 1943, the U.S. Army approached the Lockheed Aircraft Corporation (now Lockheed-Martin) with a problem. Hitler's growing power was posing a threat through the air. We needed to develop a fighter jet...and fast.

But large organizations aren't typically good at "fast," when it comes to developing a new product. Contracts take months to make their way through law offices. Layers of management must sign off on plans. Workers have to sit through long meetings. Part orders make their way through layers of supervisors, some of whom can't make decisions until after next week's meeting of the part-ordering committee.

To build a fighter jet quickly, young engineer Kelly Johnson and his team created a way to avoid red tape and streamline urgent projects. When they were briefed on a project, they began immediately, although the legal department was four months away from delivering a signed contract. They were given space to work (in the case of the fighter jet, under a rented, camouflaged circus tent). They worked largely by their own rules and set their own hours.

The result? America's first fighter jet, the XP 80, took its first flight a mere 140 days after inception, a week ahead of schedule.

They named (and registered) their mysterious division Skunk Works®, after a Snuffy Smith comic strip reference to a moonshine operation ("Skonk Works") and the peculiar smell of the tent.[39]

Institutionalizing Skunk Works and Personal Time to Create

Some great companies, realizing the potential of a few enthusiasts working on a new idea, found ways to encourage skunk works and creative thinking outside standard assignments.

Bell Labs, from the 1920s to the 1980s, was arguably the most successful research and development lab the world has ever seen. A technological maternity ward, it oversaw the birth of transistors, communications satellites, lasers, cell phones and thousands of other astounding innovations that revolutionized the modern world. The transistor was arguably one of the top breakthroughs of the century. Concerning its importance to technology, Bill Gates once said, "My first stop on any time-travel expedition would be Bell Labs in December 1947,"[40] the month the transistor was born. Bell's breakthroughs made possible the age of computers, the Internet, and wireless communications. Our first active communications satellite contained 16 inventions patented by Bell Labs.[41]

At Bell, certain creative scientists were allowed amazing freedom to wander about and work on projects that interested them, whether or not they saw any present need or value. They were asked to document their ideas and progress in notebooks; but otherwise, they had freedom to think, explore, and create.[42]

Fast forward to Google.

"At Google, everyone is a skunk," according to Google historian Richard Brandt.[43] Google took innovative freedom to a new level when it instituted its 20 percent rule.[44] Rather than keeping employees so busy at their tasks that they have no time to dream up new ideas and pursue them, employees are encouraged to spend 20 percent of their time working on a project of their choice, even if it is outside their specialty. At Google, workers can start a project on their own, join an ongoing project, or form their own team. This results in hundreds or even thousands of projects, and regular breakthroughs.[45] For a company whose lifeblood is constant, cutting edge innovation, this makes perfect sense.

What if Starbucks, instead of instilling in their southern California managers that their goal was to replicate the stores in Seattle, had said,

> "Here's your blueprint and here's what differentiates us from other coffee shops. But Southern Californians don't think like Seattleites. A part of your duty is to innovate. Spend time in other shops to see what's selling. Listen to your customers. Let innovation be a part of your DNA."

With this mentality, don't you think they'd have rolled out the nonfat milk and Frappaccinos more quickly?

4. Brainstorm outside the box.

Brainstorming harnesses the power of a group of people saying whatever comes to their minds. Nothing's too stupid; nothing's out of line. Often, we need a good brainstorm to get us out of a rut, thinking outside our assumptions. A crazy idea just might spur thinking in a new direction that yields workable innovations.

5. Learn to uncover common assumptions in your field.

Relentlessly ask the deeper questions when others have stopped shallow. Imagine that early managers at Starbucks had kept asking deeper questions about their decisions. The Socratic Method has a long, successful record of helping us to dig beneath surface issues. Let's imagine how it might have helped early Starbucks' managers:

> Store Manager: "Should we serve coffee with nonfat milk?"
>
> Upper Management: "No, it will compromise our vision of the Italian Experience."
>
> Store Manager: "And why do we want to guard the Italian Experience?"
>
> Upper Management: "Because we can train our customers to appreciate dark roast coffee."
>
> Store Manager: "And why do we want them to appreciate dark roast coffee?"
>
> Upper Management: "So that they'll become our loyal customers and we'll have more customers and higher profits."
>
> Store Manager: "But what if serving coffee with skim milk brings in more loyal customers and higher profits? Can't we at least try it in one store?"
>
> Upper Management: "Hmmm…."

6. Ask the same, dumb, "obvious" questions at different intervals.

In the early days of Amazon.com, everybody pitched in to package hundreds of books a day on their hands and knees on a concrete floor. CEO Jeff Bezos complained that the work was backbreaking and rubbed his knees raw. He suggested to his associate Nicholas Lovejoy that perhaps they should get kneepads.

According to Bezos, Lovejoy "looked at me like I was a Martian, but I was serious. That's the solution I came up with." Lovejoy responded, "What about packing tables?" They went with the tables and experienced a dramatic improvement. What was obvious to Lovejoy wasn't obvious at all to Bezos. Bezos was plenty smart, but perhaps he had no experience packing large quantities of items.[46]

Every now and then, with increasing frequency in the information age, we need to look at the way we do things and ask, "Is this the best way?"

And if you're already successful, you're less motivated to challenge your assumptions. After all, your methods seem to be working.

According to Starbucks' Schultz,

> "When you're failing, it's easy to understand the need for self-renewal. The status quo is not working, and only radical change can fix it.
>
> But we're seldom motivated to seek self-renewal when we're successful. When things are going well, when the fans are cheering, why change a winning formula?
>
> The simple answer is this: Because the world is changing. Every year, customers' needs and tastes change. The competition heats up. Employees change. Managers change. Shareholders change. Nothing can stay the same forever, in business or in life, and counting on the status quo can only lead to grief."[47]

In the age of the Internet, I've learned that it pays to ask the same, dumb, basic questions at regular intervals. Every time I publish a new website, I Google "How to build a website," to see what might have changed. In the early 1990s webmasters coded sites from scratch in html. Then I learned Microsoft Front Page, which provided a "what you see is what you get" environment that was much easier to learn than the industry standard Dream Weaver. Later, people used the easy developer tools provided on the web servers. These days I'm using Wordpress, the industry standard blogging software, which typically works for building traditional sites as well as blogs. Every few years, there seems to be a better way, so I keep asking Google the same old question, "How do I build a website?" and I keep getting new answers.

Every time I publish a new book, I ask, "What's the best way to publish a book?" The publishing industry is rapidly changing, and I'd be foolish to assume that what worked last year is the best way to publish this year.

So challenge your assumptions. It's not only good business, but many find it quite exhilarating to live on the cutting edge of the best ideas.

Flex Your Neurons! Pursuing the Point of Know Return

1. Why do you think the British were overconfident in the Revolutionary War?

2. In what specific ways did their assumptions lead to defeat?

3. In what ways did Washington and his army keep learning?

4. We'd often like to know what the future holds for our economy when we make personal and business decisions. To do so, we consult the top economists and government reports. Our assumption is that the economy can be predicted with some degree of accuracy. Search for and read the following article, and similar articles, to test this common assumption: Prakash Loungani, *How Accurate are Private Sector Forecasts?*, (April, 2000, A Working Paper by the International Monetary Fund).

5. Many people assume they can predict the rise or fall of stocks by analyzing their past performance. Their data and analyses are often quite complex and convincing. It's called "technical analysis." But we assume that technical analysis can successfully predict the future of stocks. Read up on this and see if you agree with this assumption.

6. I used to study which companies the most respected stock pickers recommended for growth over the coming year. I assumed that the experts were more likely to choose the right companies. Then I found that it's highly debatable whether their predictions are any more likely to be right than throwing darts at a chart of stocks. Find articles on stock pickers versus the dart throwers and try to draw some tentative conclusions.

7. "Practice makes perfect!" It's assumed by many, but in what ways should this assumption be amended? (First, try to think of situations where it doesn't work. What if someone is practicing the wrong methods? If a professor teaches in a monotone voice for a straight hour, no matter how many times he repeats this, does practice make him a better teacher?)

8. We often assume that the best place to get help to accomplish something in a complex program like Photoshop or Microsoft Word is to consult the program's help files. How could you find out if this is a false assumption?

9. You want to be successful in business; thus, you decide to read stories of how the world's top CEOs made it to the top. What assumptions might you as a reader, and perhaps the author, be making?

10. You need to make more money off your products and your partner assumes that the obvious solution is to raise the prices. But is this necessarily the best and only option? Why or why not?

Making It More Personal
Practical Takeaways

What are one or more ideas provoked by this chapter that you can apply to help you think more critically?

____

____

____

What are one or more ideas that you can apply to help you think more creatively?

____

____

____

What else do you want to make sure you don't forget?

____

____

____

Recommended Trails
For the Incurably Curious and Adventurous

1. For more on the differences in assumptions and leadership during the Revolutionary War, read *1776* by David McCullough, (New York: Simon & Schuster, 2005).

2. For more on Lockheed-Martin's use of skunk works, see: *Kelly's 14 Rules and Practices* at:

   http://www.lockheedmartin.com/us/aeronautics/skunkworks/14rules.html.

3. For more on how Google allows people to run with their ideas (such as the 20 percent rule), see *The Google Guys,* by Richard L. Brandt (New York: The Penguin Group, 2011).

4. For more on how great companies solicit candid input from their customers, read how one successful company goes way beyond suggestion boxes to actually work with their customers to develop better products: "Managing for Creativity," by Richard Florida and Jim Goodnight, *Harvard Business Review* (July, 2005).

CHAPTER 8

THEY UNDERESTIMATE THE POWER OF THE PARADIGM

"Physical scientists have a healthy attitude toward the history of their subject; by and large we ignore it."

— P.J.E. Peebles, *Impact of Lemaitre's Ideas on Modern Cosmology*

"We're rushing headlong into the future with our eyes firmly glued to the rear-view mirror."

—Anonymous

" Each period [of scientific history] is dominated by a mood, with the result that most men fail to see the tyrant who rules over them." (Brackets mine)

—Albert Einstein[1]

A Scientist Resists Change

Scientists can get stuck in their ways just like the rest of us. One scientist didn't like the random behavior of subatomic particles as described by quantum physics. Although the troubling behavior had been confirmed by experiment after experiment, it just didn't sit well with him. One day he exclaimed in frustration:

> "I find the idea quite intolerable that an electron exposed to radiation should choose *of its own free will* not only its moment to jump off but also its direction. In that case, I would rather be a cobbler, or even an employee of a gaming house, than a physicist."[2]

"Ah, but that's one of those rare emotional scientists" you might object. "If you listen to the truly *great* scientists, you'd find ruthless objectivity, casting aside their own preferences to follow the evidence wherever it leads!"

I failed to mention that the above hissy fit was pitched by none other than Albert Einstein. And it wasn't a rare lapse into "But I don't *want* it to be true!" He would never reconcile himself to several aspects of quantum physics, even though his quantum theory of radiation predicted it, and subsequent experiments validated it.[3]

Why would a scientist resist the results of math and science?

The main issue for Einstein seemed to be his thoroughgoing determinism.* He believed that every event is *determined* by prior causes, so that free will is an illusion. A rock fell today *because* the soil was loosened, which happened *because* the rain fell, which happened *because* a low pressure system brought clouds, *because…because….*

***Determinism =** the belief that all events are caused entirely by things that happened before them. Thus, free will is an illusion.

Theoretically, according to determinism, a scientist knowing every physical state of a certain day could predict the future with precision. If, one hundred years ago, a scientist knew all the physical states of everything, determinism assures us that he could predict with certainty that on March 25, 2014, at 7:42 AM, the rock would fall. He could have also predicted that I'd be writing this exact sentence precisely at this time.

Determinism makes science a very tidy enterprise. Once you understand all the causes, you're well on your way to fully understanding a phenomenon. That's why Einstein couldn't reconcile himself to subatomic particles not obeying the rules of causation. In his mind, "…if all this is true then it means the end of physics."

Einstein would often declare, revealing his passion for determinism, "I don't believe God plays dice with the universe!" To which his fellow scientist Neils Bohr famously replied: "Einstein, stop telling God what to do!"[4]

Einstein saw the world through deterministic glasses, thus he resisted evidence—even strong evidence—that conflicted with his determinism. His phrase "I find it quite intolerable" seems so unbefitting of a great scientist. The same maverick who dared to question and overturn the mechanics of Newton refused to follow the evidence that led to the next scientific revolution.

As Einstein biographer Walter Isaacson put it:

> "Two decades earlier, Einstein had, with youthful insouciance, toppled many of the pillars of Newton's universe, including absolute space and time. But now he was a defender of the established order, and of Newton."[5]
>
> "In one of our planet's little ironies, Planck and Einstein would share the fate of laying the groundwork for quantum mechanics, and then both would flinch when it became clear that they undermined the concepts of strict causality and certainty they both worshipped."[6]

Thus, a prior commitment to a scientific theory or philosophical concept can cause brilliant scientists to resist new data and try to explain it away. In the case of Max Planck and Albert Einstein, some of their scientific colleagues would use the word "tragic" to describe their lifelong captivity to Newton's mechanics and stubborn resistance to the new quantum discoveries.[7]

And quantum physics wasn't the only object of Einstein's stubborn resistance to evidence.

Einstein's "Biggest Blunder"

Einstein's mathematical equations in his general theory of relativity predicted that our universe was on the move. In fact, according to Isaacson, his equations "screamed out" that the conventional idea of a static universe was wrong.[8] Yet Einstein continued to believe the then conventional scientific view that the universe was static, neither expanding nor contracting. Instead of letting his equations speak for themselves, he did what would seem unthinkable for an objective scientist. He introduced a fudge factor into his equations, a "cosmological constant" to harmonize his equations with a static universe.

And it wasn't like nobody called him on it.

In 1922, Russian mathematician Alexander Friedmann used Einstein's equations to show they pointed to an expanding universe. Einstein blew it off. Five years later, physicist Georges Lemaître confronted Einstein with his own paper confirming Friedmann's thesis. Although Einstein admitted that Lemaitre's calculations were correct, he found the implication—that the universe was expanding—"abominable". According to John Farrell's history of modern cosmology, Einstein "simply refused to even consider the idea of an expanding universe at that time."[9]

As astronomers continued to make new observations, Lemaitre's expanding universe and the Big Bang that started it all were confirmed to such an extent that they currently reign as the standard scientific view of origins. Einstein eventually relented on the expanding universe and Big Bang, regretting his earlier resistance. Had he only allowed himself to question the status quo view of a static universe; had he only allowed his equations to speak for themselves rather than trying to harmonize them with prevailing views, he would have predicted an expanding universe ten years before the decisive evidence came in. According to Farrell, "This would have been the greatest single prediction in the history of science."[10]

No wonder Einstein would years later reflect back and call the fudge factor his "biggest blunder" and speak of having a "bad conscious" about it.[11]

Other Top Scientists Resist the Big Bang

Was Einstein's resistance to the expanding universe an odd quirk in an otherwise objective scientific community? History would suggest otherwise. Many great scientists, in the face of mounting evidence for a beginning to the universe simply refused to accept it, although the "Big Bang Theory" continued to be validated in observations over the following decades.[12]

From Farrell's research, "...the history of modern cosmology is one of constant doubt, second-guessing, obstinacy, missed opportunities, distraction, and outright denial."[13] Here are some scientists expressing their early aversion to the Big Bang:

- "The notion of a beginning is repugnant to me...the expanding Universe is preposterous...incredible...it leaves me cold."[14] (British physicist, astronomer and mathematician Sir Arthur Eddington).
- "To deny the infinite duration of time would be to betray the very foundations of science." (German chemist Walter Nernst)[15]
- "It is not a point in support of this theory [steady state theory proposed against the Big Bang theory] that it contains conclusions for which we might happen to have an emotional preference." (Astrophysicist Fred Hoyle, stating his emotional preference for a theory that didn't involve a beginning to the universe.)[16]

Physicist and astronomer Robert Jastrow summarizes the history of astronomers' resistance to the Big Bang Theory:

> "Their reactions provide an interesting demonstration of the response of the scientific mind—supposedly a very objective mind—when evidence uncovered by science itself leads to a conflict with the articles of faith in our profession. It turns out that the scientist behaves the way the rest of us do when our beliefs are in conflict with the evidence. We become irritated, we pretend the conflict does not exist, or we paper it over with meaningless phrases."[17]

Nevertheless, as I write, the Big Bang reigns as the standard scientific view of origins. And despite the concerns of scientists like Einstein and Nernst, science seems to putter along pretty well without the "foundation" of an "infinite duration of time."

But perhaps questioning the static, eternal universe was a special case. Surely, when testing other established theories, scientists are typically more objective and scientific progress is steadily made as new data arrives.

Do scientists' preconceptions impact their science beyond quantum physics and cosmology?

Thomas Kuhn, then Professor of Philosophy and History of Science at Princeton, in his highly influential book,[18] *The Structure of Scientific Revolutions*, argued that when new evidence supports a major shift in scientific thinking—what Kuhn called a "paradigm shift"—scientists often, perhaps even *typically*, respond much like teenagers being told they can't stay out past midnight. They argue, get defensive, and try to explain away the evidence.

Kuhn isn't saying that scientists, as a matter of course, resist believing the results of their experiments. As long as the experiments don't conflict with the reigning theories of their disciplines, they may make discovery after discovery. But if an experiment conflicts with the overarching paradigm, such as the standard cosmology of the time (static universe versus expanding universe) or the standard view of the solar system (geocentric versus heliocentric)[19] scientists often put up a fuss. And sometimes, as in the case of Einstein with quantum physics, they can resist for a lifetime. In such cases, as Max Planck has been paraphrased, "science advances one funeral at a time."[20]

Kuhn's book is one of those books I read in graduate school that I keep coming back to and reflecting upon in many contexts outside of science. It's counterintuitive, yet well documented and well written. While it's been challenged in certain respects,[21] it helped me to see that if scientists, who pride themselves at objectively searching for the truth, often hold tenaciously to their old ways of thinking, how much more should educators and businessmen and artists and community leaders be aware of this tendency?

It's a tendency that causes brilliant people, even those as brilliant as Einstein, to believe nonsense.

While Kuhn spoke of paradigms in terms of the larger, overarching scientific theories, as we move to the practical outcomes we'll apply this concept more broadly to the mini paradigms that often blind us to new ways of running a business or a school or an art studio.

How to Overcome our Paradigms And Live on the Cutting Edge of Innovation

Had Einstein dreamed up relativity and immediately died, we might have considered him to have the ideal personality for innovation—a maverick who relished questioning authorities and tradition. But Einstein didn't die young, and demonstrated that the great *agent* of change could also be the great *resistor* of change.[22]

So even the most objective and daring of us are subject to getting stuck in old paradigms and resisting the latest useful innovations. Sometimes, those most resistant to recent innovations are those who participated in earlier innovations.[23] So what can we do to resist the petrifying effect of the paradigm?

A problem with paradigms is that they've become so much a part of us that we can no longer see them clearly. In fact, perhaps it's better to say that we typically see *through* them, like a pair of tinted glasses. At some point, we stop thinking about the glasses and fail to realize how they color our world. As the sun sets, we wonder why it's so difficult to see.

That's why we often need others to challenge our paradigms. We're typically in a poor position to challenge them alone.

1. Challenge paradigms with the power of two.

We tend to think of Einstein hatching his original ideas while deep in lonely thought. In fact, he spent a great deal of time hashing out his thoughts with others, often one-on-one. Einstein's big breakthrough that led to his theory of relativity came to him in a conversation with his best friend

Michael Besso, an engineer he met in college.

Einstein called Besso his "sounding board."[24] When he wrote his most famous paper describing his breakthrough, his only acknowledgement was to Besso:

> "Let me note that my friend and colleague M. Besso steadfastly stood by me in my work on the problem discussed here, and that I am indebted to him for several valuable suggestions."[25]

Throughout his life, Einstein brought on sounding boards to work with him one-on-one, especially to help him with his math. Marcel Grossman helped him work through the math of his relativity equations. Biographer Isaacson describes Grossman as Einstein's "mathematical caddie."[26]

Golf Institutionalizes the Power of Two

Imagine you're watching a golf tournament for the first time. At first, the caddie seems to function merely as a modern day beast of burden, carrying the bag for the golfer. "That looks like a pretty easy job," you say to a fellow spectator. "I wonder how much they earn." She responds, "That's Steve Williams caddying for Adam Scott. In his 12 years of caddying for Tiger Woods, he averaged earning a million dollars a year."[27] Obviously, the caddy's doing far more than carrying a bag. A closer look reveals the golfer and the caddie chatting a lot, especially just before each shot.

For those new to golf, the thinking part of the game looks pretty obvious—"Do you see the flag? Hit it as close to it as you can." But innumerable details make each shot unique, so that a poor decision based upon an overlooked detail can be the difference of $1 million or more in prize money.

A caddy might note,

- "Do you see the top of those trees blowing in the wind near the green? You can't feel it here, but since you're hitting a high approach shot, that wind will likely pull your ball twenty-five feet to the left, putting you in the lake, if you fail to allow for it."
- "Yesterday, I saw Phil Michelson miss a putt from that exact place. It breaks surprisingly strong to the left, about 14 inches, starting about 10 feet before the hole."

In overcoming our entrenched ways of thinking, thank goodness for caddies—in physics, golf and beyond.

Famous Twosomes

Think of several of the innumerable successful twosomes:

- The world's greatest investor, Warren Buffett, runs all his investing decisions by his lifelong friend Charlie Munger.[28]
- Bill Hewlett and David Packard founded Hewlett-Packard. Beyond their own collaboration, they encouraged their engineers to first run their ideas by the worker next to them—what they dubbed the "next bench" syndrome—to see if the ideas had broader appeal.[29]
- Larry Page and Sergey Brin founded Google and still hash through all the most important decisions.[30]
- Steve Jobs and Steve Wozniak founded Apple.
- Isaac Newton met Nicholas Wickham in college and they would work together closely for over 30 years.[31]
- Husband and wife writing team Will and Ariel Durant were two of the most popular historians of the 1900s.
- Engineering wizard Soichiro Honda and shrewd businessman Takeo Fujisawa, by meshing their different temperaments and different skills, built the Honda Motor Company.[32]
- Songwriting duos such as John Lennon and Paul McCartney, or Elton John and Bernie Taupin, found a creative chemistry that has charmed audiences around the globe for a half a century, and shows no signs of demise.
- Writers/scholars C.S. Lewis (*The Chronicles of Narnia*, etc.) and J.R.R. Tolkien (*Lord of the Rings*, *The Hobbit*, etc.) were personal friends, intellectual sounding boards and mutual encouragers before they became bestselling authors. According to Tolkien, "Only from him [Lewis] did I ever get the idea that my 'stuff' could be more than a private hobby."[33]

"Two heads are better than one," the old saying goes. And in science or golf or writing or investing or leading a company, it's proven every day by those who take advantage of it. You might ask, why not three or more? Another old saying suggests that while "two's company, three's a crowd." If two work well together, a third can sometimes be a bother.

But there's certainly a place for moving beyond one-on-one to the small group for inspiration, problem solving, innovation, and breaking us out of our paradigms. Even those who rely on that special person on a day-to-day basis tend to draw from larger groups as well.

Think!

Is there a person who serves as your sounding board for personal or business matters? If not, where might you find one? What type of personality and mutual interests might be most advantageous?

2. Challenge paradigms with the power of small groups.

Pixar's Braintrust

Pixar Animation Studios has produced an unheard of 14 box-office hits in a row. Yet, Ed Catmull, president of both Pixar and Walt Disney Animation, says that "at some point, all our movies suck." Taking them "from suck to not suck" is a challenge Pixar solved by getting candid input from creative people during the suck stage. Here's how it works.

The writer/director starts with a great idea. Yet, in developing that idea, he becomes so absorbed with the story that he loses perspective, and can't see the flaws that hold the film back. He finds himself stuck in a mini paradigm that he can't see outside of.

At that point, he needs fresh, candid input from other creative storytellers (the Braintrust) who watch the initial, sucky footage and say what they think. One person might say, "I really *ought* to care for that character, but I don't. What could you reveal about her that would have me pulling for her...no, *dying* for her to win?"

The director doesn't have to take the advice. It's just candid input. But that input takes the film from ordinary to extraordinary.

The Braintrust developed from the creative quintet behind the super successful film, *Toy Story*. According to Catmull, "They were funny, focused, smart, and relentlessly candid when arguing with each other."[34] Implementing this process in subsequent films, Catmull put together a variety of people—"directors, writers and heads of story"—all of whom have "a knack for storytelling," to give input during an early phase of the film's development.[35]

"Creativity has to start somewhere," explains Catmull, "and we are true believers in the power of bracing, candid feedback and the iterative process—reworking, reworking, and reworking again, until a flawed story finds its through line or a hollow character finds its soul."[36]

Other Small Groups Worthy of Study

- Google is "obsessive about having very small groups working on projects. Five or six people are generally sufficient to handle a major project."[37]

- After college, while Einstein worked in the Swiss Patent Office, he met regularly with a couple of bright people dubbed the *Olympia Academy,* named to make light of some of the more pompous scholarly societies. Maurice Solovine was a Romanian philosophy student at the University of Bern. Conrad Habicht had studied math at Zurich Polytechnic.

  Their conversations were informal, meeting at one of their homes or hiking in the mountains. They read books and discussed them, ranging from great philosophers to scientists to *Don Quixote*. Their readings and discussions of David Hume and Ernst Mach led them to question the concepts of absolute time and space, which would be critical to developing Einstein's theory of relativity.[38]

- Benjamin Franklin met regularly with *Junto*, a small group which met each Friday for "mutual improvement." Each member was responsible to "produce one or more queries on any point of morals, politics, or natural philosophy, to be discussed by the company." Additionally, once every three months, each member was required to "produce and read an essay of his own writing, on any subject he pleased." Ensuing debates were to be carried out "without fondness for dispute, or desire for victory."

  Junto's members were a diverse group of ordinary folks: a copier of deeds, a surveyor, a shoemaker, a mechanic, a clerk. Yet, they were united by their passion to continue learning. The club continued for almost four decades and was, according to Franklin, "the best school of philosophy, morality, and politics that then existed in the province...." And you couldn't beat the free tuition![39]

- C.S. Lewis and J.R.R. Tolkien met on Tuesday mornings (in a pub) and Thursday nights (in Lewis' sitting room) with an informal group called *The Inklings*. They would typically read their recent writings to the group, invite criticism, then talk or argue about whatever topics came to mind.[40]

3. Challenge paradigms beyond the small group.

Einstein published his ideas on relativity in professional journals and attended professional conferences, which kept his ideas out in the open for public debate. Peer review has an established history of successful crowdsourcing. It allowed those whose paradigms were rattled by his theories to offer counter arguments and challenges, which were in turn challenged by others in the field.

Even in the areas most impacted by Einstein's own paradigms, such as the expansion of the universe and quantum theory, he carried on extensive conversations and friendships with the primary theorists, such as Neils Bohr, hashing things out with the greatest minds in the fields. Lemaître felt that Einstein resisted the expansion of the universe in part because he wasn't familiar with the latest observations in the field of astronomy. Thus, Einstein allowed Lemaître to update him in his field of expertise.[41]

Thus, because of his open interaction with others, Einstein's resistance to the new ideas wasn't a mindless resistance. This would seem to be the healthiest way to have our own paradigms challenged—interacting with the best minds of opposing views rather than throwing stones from afar.

Paradigms are a challenge—a persistent and ominous challenge—to wise decision-making. The foolish ignore them to their peril.

Are You Caught in a Paradigm?

You might be stuck in a paradigm if (check each that applies to you):

__ You seldom say, "This is the way I think, but who knows, I might be wrong."

__ You strongly don't want to believe the other side, regardless of the evidence.

__ You seldom question the assertions of people who agree with you.

__ You hold a firm opinion, but haven't read the strongest adherents of other views.

__ You don't read people who disagree with you.

__ You don't even know if intelligent people argue for the opposing position.

__ You wouldn't be able to intelligently argue for the other side of a controversial issue, because you've never looked at their data.

__ When somebody presents an opposing viewpoint, rather than sincerely listening, you formulate your next argument.

__ When somebody presents an opposing viewpoint, all you can think of are counterexamples.

__ When you read opposing views, you look for flaws; when you read those who agree with you, you look for reasons to believe.

__ When you hear debates, you always think your side wins.

__ You can find no weaknesses whatsoever for your favorite theory. (All theories typically contain anomalies—data that doesn't fit.)

Flex Your Neurons! Pursuing the Point of Know Return

1. **If you are stuck in a paradigm with your ideas for investing, family life, business or pleasure, how will you ever realize it?** Do you have one or more people in your life who have your permission to point out your shortcomings and challenge your ideas? What practical steps could help you to remedy the situation?

2. **Are existing small groups available to keep you challenged in your field(s) of interest?** Since it's often difficult for me to get out and meet people (I have care giving responsibilities), I've found niche online discussion groups to be a great source of challenge.

3. **If you like meeting face to face, like *The Inklings* or *Junto* or the *Olympia Academy*, what are some existing groups on your local campus or in your local community?** Consider local Meetup groups (www.meetup.com) that exist on almost every topic imaginable. Check your library for local reading groups that read select books and discuss them. If you can't find a group you like, start one!

4. **Are you afraid of committing yourself long term to a group?** Can't some groups be short-term, for a current project, and then disband? What are the pros and cons of temporary groups?

5. **How can a company's board function as a protector against petrified thinking?** What hinders many boards from functioning in this way?

6. **Since old paradigms are typically supported by a scaffolding of facts and arguments, at what point do we allow new data to challenge these paradigms?**

Making It More Personal
Practical Takeaways

What are one or more ideas provoked by this chapter that you can apply to help you think more critically?

What are one or more ideas that you can apply to help you think more creatively?

What else do you want to make sure you don't forget?

Recommended Trails For the Incurably Curious and Adventurous

1. The book that first popularized the notion of paradigms in science (which subsequently spread to business, religion, and other fields), was Thomas S. Kuhn, *The Structure of Scientific Revolutions* (Chicago: The University of Chicago Press, 1962, enlarged second edition in 1970). It's often required reading in Philosophy of Science classes.

2. For popularly written works showing the susceptibility of scientists to paradigms concerning Big Bang cosmology, see Robert Jastrow, *God and the Astronomers* (New York: W.W. Norton & Company, 1978) and John Farrell, *The Day Without Yesterday* (New York: Thunder's Mouth Press, 2005). For more on Einstein introducing his "fudge factor" in resisting the Big Bang and his later resistance to quantum theory, see Walter Isaacson, *Einstein* (New York: Simon & Schuster, 2007). For those who want much more historical detail on the controversy among scientists concerning the Big Bang, see Helge Kragh, *Cosmology and Controversy: The historical development of two theories of the universe* (Princeton, NJ: Princeton University Press, 1996).

3. On using small groups to burst out of the smaller paradigms that hold back businesses, see Ed Catmull, with Amy Wallace, *Creativity, Inc.: Overcoming the unseen forces that stand in the way of true inspiration* (New York: Random House, 2014). I love how Catmull presents the process in all its messiness, so that readers understand the challenges rather than adopting often-meaningless platitudes such as "Just trust the process!" Chapter 5, titled "Honesty and Candor," describes the development of the Brain Trust and is worth the price of the book. Read a free excerpt from the chapter here: Ed Catmull, "Inside the Pixar Braintrust," *Fast Company*, March 12, 2014,

   http://www.fastcompany.com/3027135/lessons-learned/inside-the-pixar-braintrust.

4. Study the relationships of golfers to their caddies and instructors, or writers to their writer's groups and editors, to get ideas for bursting through paradigms in your field of interest.

CHAPTER 9

THEY FAIL TO ACCOUNT FOR WORLDVIEWS

"Every person carries in his head a mental model of the world— a subjective representation of external reality."

— Alvin Toffler, *Future Shock*

"The unexamined life is not worth living."

— Socrates

Imagine a Better Future

You're hanging out with a college buddy in a coffee shop one drizzly Saturday morning. John Lennon's "Imagine" plays in the background, putting both of you in a reflective mood as you assess the state of society and try to dream up a better world.

Here's how your reasoning goes:

Something's wrong. The rich get richer and the poor get poorer. Greedy corporations shower upper management with millions of dollars, earned on the backs of poor, part-time workers who struggle to feed their children. Although the workers can vote for their political leaders, how can they ever change policies when corporations spend millions on lobbyists to ensure their pet policies remain in force?

Something's got to fundamentally change. If things get bad enough, perhaps the workers should just say, "Enough is enough!" and take over, not only their corporations, but the entire government, to ensure that everyone gets his or her fair share for their labor.

After the revolution, we'd have to appoint a benevolent dictator to enforce equality, since our governmental checks and balances don't seem to be working. The dictator could enforce equal pay for equal labor: "from each according to his abilities, to each according to his needs." After the dictator gets the country on track and everybody sees how well it works, the dictator would no longer be needed. He could step down to allow some form of minimalist government to maintain order.

How "Imagine" Worked Out in Real Life

Those who know their history recognize this line of thought. Similar utopian theories have been hatched, particularly in the 20th century, and they can look very cool on paper. But the version Leon Trotsky, Vladimir Lenin, and Joseph Stalin put into place after the Russian Revolution ran into more than a few hiccups, often due to big picture issues. It's a good illustration of the importance of worldviews.*

Each of us hold a worldview—our big picture view of the world—whether we give it much thought or not. Our worldview tells us what life's all about, what's important and what's not, what's right and what's wrong.

***Worldview** = how people view the world; their big picture philosophy of life.

***Marxism =** a theory, based on the teachings of Karl Marx, that the struggle between social classes is a major force in history and that we should work toward a classless society.

So let's look at a few aspects of the Marxist* worldview and how it panned out in Russia and the resulting super power, the Soviet Union, which in the 1900s comprised about one sixth of the entire earth's surface.

On Determining Right and Wrong

For these early Russian leaders, there were no objective, universally binding morals, such as "Do not lie" or "Do not steal" or "Do not murder." Rather, they adopted a utilitarian* ethic, defining "good" as "whatever it takes to achieve our good ends." Thus their end (a future utopia) justified any means (e.g., stealing, lying, murder). For example, they took grain from the peasants (stealing), published propaganda through state controlled news (lying), and killed all who got in their way (murder)—all justified as necessary means to achieve their envisioned glorious ends.[1]

***Utilitarianism =** a theory of ethics that determines the right course of action by weighing and comparing the utility of each option. "Utility" is typically viewed as maximizing happiness and minimizing suffering for the greatest number of people.

On What Really Matters

For these leaders, influenced by the writings of Karl Marx and Friedrich Engels, the materialistic economic progress of history was what mattered. Everything revolved around obtaining future economic and material success. Presumably, this material success would lead to happiness for the greatest number of people.

Success consisted, not in establishing such ideals as freedom of thought, freedom of the press, freedom of religion, or relief for today's poor. Rather, religion was seen as "the opium of the people"—a distraction encouraged by greedy capitalists to keep the poor content in their poverty as they anticipated rewards in the next life. Thus, religion had to go. Other freedoms, such freedom of the press and freedom of expression were suppressed as well, in order to keep dissenters from gaining power.

On Human Nature

For these leaders, people were the products of the society that produced them. Period. "Once we get society right," they reasoned, "people will be smart and productive. They'll whistle while they work, work hard even when they don't have to, do what's in the best interest of their neighbors and society as a whole, etc. The dictator, once he realizes that he's no longer needed, will voluntarily step down."

On the Value of Human Life

Trotsky and Lenin didn't believe that all humans had inherent worth, which would have implied that all people should be treated fairly and humanely. (Contrast this with America's founding documents, which grounded people's "inalienable rights," in their being "created equal.")

Instead, people were viewed as pawns to be moved or executed or starved in whatever ways best served the long-term agenda. As Stalin put it, "Death solves all problems. No man, no problem."[2]

Early on, Trotsky stated, "We must put an end once and for all to the papist-Quaker babble about the sanctity of human life."[3] As a result, under Lenin, the "value of human life collapsed."[4]

The Resulting Loss of Freedoms

Lenin and Stalin suppressed freedom of speech, freedom of the press, the right to assemble, freedom of religion, and even the right for people to eat their own produce. The peasants' crops were often seized and shipped to the cities or sold overseas to finance upgrading their factories and buying machinery.

"But at least," some readers might think, "science would progress unhindered under a totally secular* government. Free from the influence of religious worldviews, science should flourish unhindered by people's worldviews."

***Secular =** attitudes, activities, and teachings that have no religious or spiritual basis.

Yet, these statements fail to realize that secularism doesn't necessarily constitute freedom *from* a worldview. It can be a worldview in itself. Thus, under Marxism, any scientific theory that seemed to conflict with a naturalistic, secular, materialistic, atheist worldview wasn't allowed.

Two scientific theories that Marxism/Communism repressed were the Big Bang Theory* and the Second Law of Thermodynamics.* Both taught or implied a beginning to the universe, which in turn implied to many people a creation by a God, since something coming from nothing, by purely natural means, seemed quite unlikely to them. The secular Marxists wanted a universe that had always existed, extending infinitely into the past and infinitely into the future.

Helge Kragh, in his detailed history of scientific theories of origins, *Cosmology and Controversy*, summed up the official position of the Soviet Union as:

> "Astronomers should serve the [Communist] party by providing anti-clerical propaganda and exposing the idealistic cosmological views of the West, in particular those which implied a creation of the world."[5]

Thus, "cosmological models with a finite time scale had to be rejected because of their theistic implications."[6] When Soviet astronomers met in Leningrad in 1948, they confirmed a resolution to fight the Big Bang Theory, since it spoke of a beginning of the universe in the finite past and could aid religious causes.[7]

The Second Law of Thermodynamics didn't fit snugly into the Marxist worldview, first because it implied that the universe must have had an initial infusion of energy to get started. If the universe was running down, how did it get wound up at the start? Where did that initial energy come from? And if this process toward randomness had been going on from eternity past, why had the universe not already reached a state of heat death?

As physicist Paul Davies put it,

> "The universe cannot have existed forever, otherwise it would have reached its equilibrium end state an infinite time ago. Conclusion: the universe did not always exist."[8]

***The Big Bang Theory =** Today's reigning model (among scientists) of how everything in the universe came to be. According to the standard theory, before the "bang" the entire universe was once compressed into a single point—a "primeval atom"—before which the universe—including time and space—did not exist.

***The Second Law of Thermo-dynamics =** a physical law stating that in a closed system (such as the universe), usable energy decreases over time. This implies that there was a beginning to the universe (having maximum usable energy) and that it will one day end (no usable energy).

Another problem for Marxists was their belief that man and society were ever progressing. Yet according to the Second Law of Thermodynamics, since everything is proceeding from high organization toward randomness, energy will one day be equally distributed, resulting in the stars (including our sun) eventually burning out and the universe no longer being able to sustain life. This descent into oblivion didn't sit well with the Marxists' materialistic view of history and their economic view, which held that society was ever progressing, and would always progress.[9]

As Kragh put it in his book on the history of entropy,

> "According to the ideology of Soviet communism, as it was formulated in the late 1930s, cosmological models with a heat death, and hence a finite upper time scale, had to be

rejected because of their theistic implications."[10]

Had you attended high school in East Germany as late as the 1970s you'd have likely been taught, as one of their textbooks put it with great assurance, "The universe has no beginning in time, and no end, and matter exists eternally."[11] Of course this teaching ignores the evidence for the Big Bang and the Second Law of Thermodynamics, but it serves well to show that worldviews often color the way we view the evidence.

The Death Toll of a Worldview

Those who caused trouble, spoke against the government, taught theories inconsistent with the government, or were considered inconvenient to the advance of society were deported, exiled, or killed. The infamous Gulags (work/death camps) were considered, as Solzhenitsyn put it, "sewage disposal."[12]

The total tally?

- "Church records show that 2,691 priests, 1,962 monks and 3,447 nuns were killed" in one year alone.[13]
- About three million children died in the government induced "Terror Famine" of 1933.[14]
- Upwards of 20 million people were killed during those early regimes.[15]
- Stalin's casual attitude toward such a large-scale extermination of human life was well summed up in his statement: "One death is a tragedy, a million is a statistic."[16]

And what about that glorious anticipated utopia that was supposed to make all the atrocities and great sacrifices worth it? It never appeared. When Stalin took over after Lenin, power became more centralized than ever. His rule was total and complete. And over the long haul, when people realized that they made the same amount of money no matter how hard they worked, incentive to work hard all but died, resulting in second rate products, poor production, and a poor economy.

Summary

Having lived in the former Soviet Union shortly after the revolution, I had a chance to see for myself how a Marxist/Communist worldview had taken its toll on people and the economy.[17]

My conclusion? Worldviews matter. They dare not go unexamined.

Yet Lenin was a bright person. He graduated college with the equivalent of a first-class degree with honors. He read widely. He wrote well. But his research and conclusions were often flawed and his moral compass typically pointed the wrong direction.

Why do brilliant people believe nonsense? Because sometimes they hold ill-conceived worldviews. And these large scale views of the world have very practical consequences for our freedoms and pursuit of happiness.

Worldviews Impact Our Everyday Decisions

We dare not leave the big picture issues to the philosophers and political leaders, because someone needs to keep them accountable. Besides, our smaller, practical, everyday decisions are typically related to our larger, overarching philosophies of life.

- Will you spend whatever it takes to drive the latest sports car? Then perhaps you're a materialist in philosophy and an ethical egoist in ethics.
- Will you spend every Saturday morning getting your nails done and reading fashion magazines? Then perhaps you value outward appearance over developing inner qualities.
- Are you passionate about serving others and helping those who can't help themselves? Then perhaps you value compassion as the ultimate motivation and service to humanity as what really matters.

So whether we're deciding how to vote, how to act, or how to run a business or family, our worldviews often provide our compasses.

What Is a Worldview?

A worldview is essentially our big picture view of the world—the philosophical glasses through which we interpret everything we see. You may also find it called by its German name, Weltanschauung. Examples of worldviews (grossly oversimplified; some overlap) include:

Agnosticism - There isn't enough evidence to warrant either belief or disbelief in God.

Atheism - There is no God.

Christianity - God revealed Himself and His will through Jesus Christ and the Christian Scriptures. The most important commands are to love God and love people.

Hinduism - People go through a cycle of reincarnations until we liberate ourselves (find/experience Nirvana) through following Hindu teachings.

Materialism - All that exists or matters is material.

Nihilism - There's no objective truth, especially in religion or morals. Life has no meaning.

Naturalism - Nothing spiritual or supernatural exists. All that exists is natural.

Spiritualism - In addition to this physical world, a spiritual world exists. It's possible to communicate between worlds.

Theism - There is a God.

Fleshing out a Worldview: Specifics and Implications

A recent example of a philosopher laying out his worldview in detail would be Alex Rosenberg, who chairs the Philosophy Department at Duke University. In his book *The Atheist's Guide to Reality*, he prefers the more positive name "Scientism" (meaning science is the only reliable guide to knowledge) to the more negative "atheism." He argues that science leads us inexorably to the following conclusions:

- There is no God.
- The world came about by purely natural, random causes.
- There is no purpose the universe. It will one day die and nobody will care that it ever existed.
- There is no meaning of life.
- We're here because of "dumb luck."
- There's no soul, no immortality.
- Free will is an illusion. Every move you make, every thought you think was pre-determined by a chain of naturalistic events operating by inviolable laws.
- There's no difference between right and wrong.
- Is anything forbidden, like abortion, euthanasia, or suicide? Nope. Anything goes.
- Does history have meaning or purpose or lessons? No.[18]
- Consciousness is an illusion. There is no mind separate from the brain.
- We have no natural rights. Clumps of matter don't have rights.[19]
- Individual human life is "without ultimate moral value."[20]

Think!

Which aspects of Rosenberg's worldview do you agree or disagree with? Do you agree that the only way to knowledge is through the methods of science (scientism)? Do you agree that science inexorably leads us to these conclusions? If everyone held Rosenberg's worldview, do you think the world would be better, or worse? If you lived consistently with this worldview and your teenage daughter asked your advice as to whether or not to start taking drugs or to date a creep or to become a prostitute, what would you say?

I hope it's becoming clear from this brief overview that worldviews are important. They impact everything about our lives, telling us what's important and what's not, what's right and what's wrong, how to treat people and animals and our environment. The worldview of Lenin, Trotsky and Stalin convinced them that killing millions of innocent people wasn't merely justified, but the right thing to do. A person whose worldview includes the doctrine of Jihad might consider destroying New York's twin towers (and almost three thousand people) a selfless act of heroism.

We'd do well to think through our worldviews carefully.

What is Your Worldview?

Everybody has a worldview. Some have given it extensive thought. Others developed theirs rather subconsciously, so that they're hardly even aware of it, even though it greatly impacts their thoughts and actions. To clarify your own worldview, answer the following questions. The more clearly you can answer them (and other big picture questions), the more clearly your own worldview will come into focus.

- Where, ultimately, did we and our world come from? Do we have an ultimate purpose or purposes? If so, what are those purposes? ______________________________

  ____

- Are people valuable in themselves, worthy of respect, or are they simply accidents of natural history, practically worthless in the grand scheme of things? ____________

  ____

- Is there a God (or gods)? If so, what can we know about God and His will for us? Is He good, personal, and worthy of respect?

  ____

- Is there such a thing as objective right and wrong? (For example, if you can say, "Whatever anybody else thinks, Hitler was wrong in killing so many innocent people!", then you believe in objective right and wrong, at least in that one case.) If so, how do we determine right from wrong?

  ____

- How can we know things? For example: Is all true knowledge obtained by the scientific method; or do we additionally know some things intuitively, or through pure reason, or by spiritual means, or by other means?______________________________

  ____

- Is there an afterlife, or is this life all there is? How does that impact your decisions and lifestyle?______________________________________

  ____

- Do our decisions make a difference, or is everything determined (by God or by nature)?

  ____

  ____

As you continue to learn and grow, your worldview may change a bit, perhaps a lot. But at the very least we should be aware of our own worldview and why we hold to it. Again quoting Socrates: "The unexamined life is not worth living."

Assessing Your Worldview

Many would argue that the early Russian leaders, although intellectually bright, held a poorly conceived worldview that led them to commit atrocities. What might have helped them reassess their views, and perhaps save millions of lives? And how can we insure that the naïve and dangerous aspects of our own worldviews don't go unchecked and unexamined? Here are some suggestions.

A. Be aware of how worldviews appeal to and are influenced by our passions.

These revolutionaries most likely thought of the development of their worldviews as purely an intellectual exercise in searching for the truth. But for Karl Marx and his followers, surely emotional factors lay largely unnoticed to them, impacting their research and conclusions.

- Stalin's beatings as a child by his harsh and brutal father probably bred in him a hatred for authority, a desire to rule, and little empathy. A materialist philosophy of life that involved violent revolution would have an obvious appeal to him.[21]

- Karl Marx, in his personal character, demonstrated a "taste for violence," "appetite for power," "bad money habits" (leading to crippling personal debt to capitalists), and

> a "tendency to exploit those around him." Surely these personal traits impacted his research and informed his political views.[22]

As we've seen in previous chapters, what we *want* to believe impacts how we evaluate evidence. Without honestly evaluating our passions, it's difficult to decide if we believe a line of reasoning because it's truly valid, or because it simply resonates with our prejudices/passions.

B. Look beyond your own culture and time.

We're all to a certain extent captives of our times. Before the Russian Revolution, the wealthy were taking advantage of the poor, the Czars ruled cruelly, and the religious system was often more a part of the problem than the solution. In such an atmosphere, making a clean sweep of everything that went before seemed quite attractive. In that society, it was easy to see Capitalism as corrupt, making Marxism look attractive as an alternative.

Yet, focusing myopically on our own recent history can lead to forming a worldview more out of reaction than a sound assessment of historical and economic facts. Stalin hated the religious leaders in his school. Lenin despised religion as he saw it. Surely their personal history enhanced the appeal of materialistic worldviews that recommended wiping out religion.

C. Seek more to understand than to be understood.

These leaders were very dogmatic about their views, seemingly unable to stomach criticism, take an honest look at contrary evidence, or to appreciate the views of other bright people. Both Lenin and Stalin persecuted intellectuals. Lenin called them "shit." Stalin appointed only "yes men" to positions of authority. Colleagues quickly learned to either agree with Stalin or die.

Contrast this approach with two other influential leaders of the 1900s—Nelson Mandela and Martin Luther King Jr.

In fighting the despicable injustices of Apartheid (segregation and unequal treatment based upon race) in South Africa, Mandela listened carefully to the arguments both for and against Marxism as a solution. He had friends on both sides of the issue. He studied their literature and had many friendly arguments and conversations with both those opposed and who supported Communism.

Although some aspects of Communism appealed to him, and he would eventually allow Communists to have a place in his movement, he didn't feel that Communism was the right path for his country. Throughout his life, Mandela didn't allow himself to study and formulate opinions without listening to all sides and having productive conversations/debates with those who held various views. Surely this practice saved him from drifting toward extreme views.[23]

Martin Luther King Jr. fought prejudice and racism in America. He could have easily taken a Marxist view and blamed the economic inequalities for blacks on capitalism. But like Mandela, he too studied the primary sources for Marxism, seeking to understand. While he felt that Marx and his followers brought to light many important issues with capitalism, he rejected several of

Marx's foundational tenets:

1. He rejected his secular and materialistic view of history, believing rather that a personal God impacted history as well.

2. He rejected Marx's ethical relativism, which he felt could be used to justify anything.

3. He rejected the totalitarianism of the state, which could turn people into impersonal cogs in service to the state.[24]

D. Put systems in place that allow your views to be challenged.

Again, Mandela seemed wise in this regard, retaining friends who disagreed with him and listening sincerely to their criticisms. Martin Luther King, Jr., was humble enough to listen to others, work with existing organizations and committees, and consider their advice.[25]

E. Look unflinchingly at problems with your worldview.

Lenin and Stalin should have been asking themselves hard questions, such as,

- "Will people continue to work hard in a system where they know they'll receive the same payment no matter how hard they work?"
- "Will a dictator really step down, after he's no longer needed?"
- "What evidence do we have that our methods will one day usher in our envisioned utopia?

How could they have known with any degree of certainty the answers to these questions, since they had no historical precedent?

Of course, Democracy has its issues as well. As Winston Churchill once said,

> "Many forms of Government have been tried, and will be tried in this world of sin and woe. No one pretends that democracy is perfect or all-wise. Indeed, it has been said that democracy is the worst form of Government except all those other forms that have been tried from time to time.[26]

Here's a specific weakness that someone pointed out concerning democracies:

> "A democracy cannot exist as a permanent form of government. It can only exist until the majority discovers it can vote itself largess out of the public treasury. After that, the majority always votes for the candidate promising the most benefits with the result the democracy collapses because of the loose fiscal policy…."[27]

Thus, administrations are inclined to push for new programs, but find it too unpopular to cut back on existing programs. No wonder it's so easy for democracies to plunge further and further into debt!

So try to look objectively at the shortcomings of your world views and governmental systems. What are their strengths? What are their weaknesses?

F. Rigorously check the accuracy of your facts and the precision of your arguments.

While this seems obvious, the number of big decisions made on poor data and argumentation are quite astounding. Make sure you've thought through your worldview!

Flex Your Neurons!
Pursuing the Point of Know Return

1. Let's now take up the important task of *recognizing* worldviews. Whether you're reading a newspaper columnist, watching a documentary, listening to an advertisement, reading a novel, watching a movie, or talking to a friend, worldviews lurk beneath the surface, expressing themselves in subtle and not-so-subtle ways.

   We can't truly understand people's motivations and actions if we don't understand their worldviews. Example: Your boyfriend works hard at his job. Perhaps that's a good sign—he wants to make an honest living and have enough left at the end of the week to give to worthy causes. On the other hand, perhaps he's a materialist, thinking only of himself and the toys he can buy with that money.

   Typically commercials and novels and people aren't explicit about their worldviews, so we must pay attention and ask insightful questions. So apply your mental floss to the following popular quotes, ads, and sayings. Take ten of them and answer these questions:

   What worldviews might they be assuming or promoting? (Either use a worldview discussed above or put the worldview in practical terms, such as "appearance is everything," "money is all that matters," "this world is all that matters," etc.)

   Do you agree or disagree with them?

   a. You only go around once in life. Go for all the gusto you can get.

   b. He who dies with the most toys wins.

   c. All is fair in love and war.

   d. Life's a sport. Drink it up!

   e. You are in a beauty contest every day of your life. - Camay soap

   f. When you've got it, flaunt it. - Braniff Airlines

   g. Live today. Tomorrow will cost more. - Pan American World Airways

   h. People First - Saturn

   i. Be Like Mike [Michael Jordan]. Drink Gatorade.

   j. The right relationship is everything. - J.P. Morgan Chase

   k. I'd Like to Buy the World A Coke. - Coca Cola 1971

   l. Live the moment - Harry Winston

m. Go Full Throttle or go home - Full Throttle

n. Like a good neighbor, State Farm is there - State Farm Insurance Company

o. Find Your Own Road - Saab

p. Live Richly - Citibank

q. Let desire lead you - JLo Deseo

r. Live like a King - Drawbridge Inn Hotel

s. "Everything Counts, Everyone Matters" - W.R. Berkley

t. To serve, not to be served - AARP

u. A Business of Caring - Cigna

v. Computers help people help people - IBM

w. No compassion, No peace; Know Compassion, Know Peace

x. Winning isn't everything, it's the only thing

2. This week, as you watch movies, read books, view commercials and billboards, reflect on what worldviews they represent, and bring some back to class to discuss. And don't just look at the words—notice the accompanying artwork, pictures and music.

3. Notice the characters in your favorite TV shows. What worldviews might each of them represent?

4. We saw in this chapter how one irreligious worldview impacted society. But how can religious (e.g. Christian, Muslim or Hindu) worldviews impact society, both for good and for ill? What about secular governments that try to remain neutral in their worldviews?

5. If you were Rosenberg, whose worldview we laid out above, how would you answer the following practical questions?

- If everything has already been determined, then why "try harder" to get ahead or to "make something of my life" or to write a book? In his worldview, does trying to change the world or change one person's life or even change my own life seem futile?

- If "nothing really matters," as Queen sang in *Bohemian Rhapsody*, then why not kill people who irritate me or hold me back, as long as I can get away with it? Couldn't I justify killing irritating or backward people as helping future generations by eliminating morons from the gene pool?

- If there's no meaning in life, if humans have no special value or natural rights, if there's neither right nor wrong, and no afterlife, then in what sense is not killing an innocent victim superior to killing?
- If there's neither right nor wrong, then can we in any meaningful way say that Hitler was wrong in killing millions of innocent people?

Making It More Personal
Practical Takeaways

What are one or more ideas provoked by this chapter that you can apply to help you think more critically?

____

____

____

What are one or more ideas that you can apply to help you think more creatively?

____

____

____

What else do you want to make sure you don't forget?

____

____

____

Recommended Trails
For the Incurably Curious and Adventurous

1. See the recent debate between two scholarly adherents of two opposing worldviews: William Craig (Theist) and Alex Rosenberg (Atheistic Scientism) at Purdue University.

   https://www.youtube.com/watch?v=uBTPH51-FoU

2. Read a history of Marxism or a biography of Marx, Engels, or one of the early leaders in Russia after the Russian Revolution. How did they develop their worldview? How did their worldview impact their writings, policies and actions?

3. We talked some about the resistance of Marxists to the second law of thermodynamics. For a very detailed and scholarly history of controversies concerning the second law, see Helge S. Kragh, *Entropic Creation: Religious Contexts of Thermodynamics and Cosmology* (Burlington, Vermont: Ashgate Publishing, 2008).

INTERMISSION
Meet Dr. Cackler

"The value of a college education is not the learning of many facts but the training of the mind to think."

— Albert Einstein (Explaining to a reporter why he didn't know facts like the speed of sound.)[1]

So far, we've seen how brilliant people such as Steve Jobs or Albert Einstein, great companies and even great countries, made serious and costly mental errors. We've also thought through the causes of these errors and looked at ways to think more rationally and creatively.

But we cover so much ground in this book that you'll never likely remember it all. Even if you have a photographic memory, although you may be able to repeat back the material on a test, you're unlikely to be able to *use* the information to run a business, evaluate an argument, or decide how to invest your income, unless I provide a memorable way to apply these skills.

That's where Dr. Cackler comes in.

Imagine that you live next door to a brilliant doctor with a loud, distinctive laugh, nicknamed Dr. Cackler. He's the best analytical thinker you know, so that when you need to think through something, you run it by him over your fence. In helping you work through a difficult issue, he often leads you through a checklist with the letters of his name.

"My name says it all," cackles the good doctor.

"First, break your evidence down into two parts. Just as my first two letters state my credentials—DR.—so the credentials of an argument can be analyzed in two parts with the same initials: the **D**ata and the **R**easoning concerning that data."

"As Warren Buffett's intellectual mentor wrote concerning investing, 'You are neither right nor wrong because the crowd disagrees with you.

You are right because your **data** and **reasoning** are right.'"[2]

"Some people offer tons of relevant facts (data), but still draw erroneous conclusions because of their faulty *reasoning*. Others reason well, but fail to take into account all the relevant *data*. In fact, **if you remember nothing else from this acrostic, always remember to examine the quality of the *data* and *reasoning* for any argument in a presentation, article, or chapter you read."**

"Consult me (or at least my name!) and you should have more success seeing through the nonsense that people expect you to swallow."

So here's the full acrostic:

D.R. C.A.C.K.L.E.R.

Data - Have you collected the relevant data/information/facts? (See especially chapters two and thirteen.)

Reasoning - Are you drawing conclusions from the data with precision? (See section three.)

With the rest of my name, let's think about some of the specific characteristics of good data and sound reasoning.

Is your argument:

Clear? Murky language often hides sloppy thinking. Recall how imprecise language obscured the causes of the common cold in chapter two.

Accurate? How were your facts derived? Do others dispute those findings? Do they jive with your personal experience and the experiences of those you know? (In section five we challenge the accuracy of certain statistics.)

Comprehensive? Are you sure you gathered *all* (or at least *enough*) of the relevant data? Did you ask all the relevant questions? In chapter two, Julie found her way to the primary sources to get more accurate data on the common cold. Starbucks' leaders tended to ignore certain data from customers. Fortunately, they hired a person who passionately argued the customers' point of view. (In chapter 13 we discuss the need for sufficient evidence.)

Knowledge-based? Do you know enough about the subject to understand and interpret the data? Innovative companies like Bell Labs, Google, and General Electric hired many specialists who could understand the data and theory behind various fields. (In chapter 25 we find people pontificating outside their fields of specialty, seemingly oblivious to their lack of expertise.)

Logical/Sensible? Have you employed logical fallacies in your reasoning? (See section three.) Have people strong in "common sense" informed your line of argument with their opinions? (See chapter 25.)

Emotionally Intelligent? Does your conclusion make sense in the light of how people feel and behave? Marx, Lenin, Trotsky, and Stalin seemed to fall short in this respect. Nelson Mandela and Martin Luther King Jr. found ways to include emotional intelligence in their reasoning. (We'll talk more about this in chapter 25.)

Reviewed? What do other knowledgeable people think of your argument? Einstein added his "fudge factor," not because his calculations demanded it, but to harmonize his equations with his preexisting view of a static universe. Fortunately, since his findings were published, other mathematicians and scientists could challenge Einstein. Google allows all their engineers to review everyone else's projects, and even spend one day a week working on a different project of their choice, so that fresh ideas keep circulating. (See especially chapters one and eight.)

But let's move from *critical* thinking into *creative* thinking, which can lead to innovation. When Dr. Cackler thinks innovatively, he:

C.R.E.A.T.E.S.

Crowdsource ideas. Jack Welch and Sam Walton developed ways to encourage a steady flow of fresh ideas from all levels of their organizations. (See chapter one.)

Run the best ideas by a friend or a group, rather than letting pride convince you that your pet ideas are the best. (See chapter eight.)

Engage your enemies and/or those who hold competing ideas. Starbucks resisted for some time talking seriously to customers who wanted products that didn't fit with their vision. (See chapter eight.)

Assume nothing. Ask the questions nobody else asks. General Howe lost strategic battles due to false assumptions. Einstein had the audacity to ask, "What if time is relative?" "What if space curves?" (See chapters seven and eight.)

Test accurately and broadly. When Starbucks allowed select stores to try selling Frappacinos, they discovered a top seller. (See chapter six.)

Explore extremes. Exploring the very fast (relativity), the very small (quantum physics), and the most distant past (Big Bang cosmology) revolutionized our understanding of matter and the universe. Reflecting upon those with extremely strong and weak mental functions can help us to understand our own mental strengths and weaknesses. (See chapters eight and twenty.)

Search outside your field. Einstein learned to question absolute time from reading philosophy. The Mayo Clinic sharpened their scheduling by learning from NASA. (See chapters six and eight.)

In our lesson plans, we'll rejoin Dr. Cackler periodically, to help summarize our sections and practice this useful tool for critical and creative thinking.

SECTION THREE

WHY DO BRILLIANT PEOPLE BELIEVE NONSENSE? BECAUSE THEY FAIL TO RECOGNIZE WEAK AND INVALID ARGUMENTS

CHAPTER 10

THEY CONTRADICT, LEAVE OUT VALID OPTIONS AND KNOCK DOWN STRAW MEN

"Anyone who denies the law of non-contradiction should be beaten and burned until he admits that to be beaten is not the same as not to be beaten, and to be burned is not the same as not to be burned."

— Avicenna

Those Who Question Logic

To the mind that's yet to be "enhanced" by some strains of modern thought, the above quote probably comes across as amusing, but useless. After all, who would deny something as basic as the law of non-contradiction or the basic laws of logic? If saying "My roommate annoys me" is no different than saying "My roommate doesn't annoy me," then how can we ever say anything meaningful? Moreover, the very act of denying non-contradiction assumes the law to be true.

Yet, some argue that our brains, like our opposable thumbs and other body parts, evolved not to perfect our logic, but to optimize our survival. According to these thinkers, when early man moved up in the world from hunter-gatherers to the African Delta, survival of the fittest favored those who learned to cooperate to grow crops, raise families, and breed domestic animals. Thus, our brains evolved to foster domesticity, rather than think through logically rigorous legal or scientific or philosophical arguments.[1]

(Digression: Surely it's equally plausible, even when reflecting upon recent history, that evolution should favor brains that are ruthless and conniving; employing a logic that's better suited to achieve selfish ends than to seek truth. When dispassionately objective intellectuals taught ideas that displeased Stalin, he removed them from the gene pool by the thousands. Thus, a large portion of 20th century man, under such regimes as Lenin, Stalin, Mao, Hitler and Pol Pot, survived by *suppressing* their creativity and independent thought and perfecting a "don't piss off the morons in charge" type of thinking. In my mind, it would be difficult to prove that long ago, living in small communities on the Delta, brilliant misfits would have survived any better.)

Thus, following this naturalistic line of argument, our brains developed primarily for primitive survival, not to reflect accurately on the great scientific theories of cosmology or macroeconomics or to develop rigorous rules of logic. Those who walked about the early Delta with their minds distracted by such matters were almost certainly eliminated from the gene pool by animals higher up on the food chain. Rather than being equipped for higher level thinking, according to this theory, we find our brains uniquely suited to think in ways that enhance our self-confidence, enable us to compete, socialize, and convince the opposite sex to mate with us.

As a result, today's brains should resonate more with *Glamour Magazine*, *Playboy* and *Sports Illustrated*, than *Physics Today* or *Philosophy Now*. In its favor, this theory successfully predicts the type and quality of magazines available for purchase at service station check-out counters.

Such academics as Psychologist Susan Blackmore and Philosopher Alex Rosenberg similarly argue that our brains, in their present state of evolution, deceive us in many ways and can't be trusted. Why then should we trust in the ability of our empirical investigations or logical argumentation to help us find truth?[2]

Without recounting the intricate details, I should also mention that eighteenth century philosopher David Hume argued, with breathtaking influence on modern thought, that taking empiricism to its logical conclusion leads to skepticism concerning any certain knowledge. His works, and many who built upon his foundation, have led some contemporary intellectuals to a thoroughgoing despair of finding truth through science or logic or any other means.[3]

This is all to say that if you read widely, you'll run across many who teach that all truth is relative and a search for truth is futile. Rather than set forth a defense of our ability to find truth, or at the very least that we have the ability to weed through nonsense in order to get *closer* to the truth, I'll just note that I've never found a thoroughgoing skeptic who lives consistently with his skepticism.

As soon as he opens his mouth or wields his pen, he begins making statements that depend upon the very laws of logic he denies. When Blackmore argues that our minds deceive us and can't be trusted, why does she go on to write the next chapter? If *she* really believes what she wrote, she can't trust *her* reasoning. If *I* believe what she wrote, I can't trust in either the accuracy of her writings or my ability to interpret them. So why keep reading?

After a professor teaches his students that we can't know truth, no sooner has he left the classroom and met his department chair than he engages her in an argument, based upon the facts and logic he denies in class, about his deplorable salary. And he certainly won't be satisfied if his boss responds that the argument is pointless because all truth is relative.

In the end, whether you claim to be a thoroughgoing skeptic or a believer in our ability to find truth, logic would seem useful, at least in arguing for a raise. So since this isn't a book on epistemology, let's proceed as if logic is indeed useful, and try to sharpen our ability to use it.

The Syllogism* as a Useful Starting Point

***Syllogism =** a type of argument that begins with two or more premises and draws a conclusion.

Increasingly, I find myself putting complex, convoluted, or long-winded arguments into the form of syllogisms in order to evaluate them. The value of this process was demonstrated to me at a recent philosophical conference. I was astonished to hear a philosopher attack a 450 page book by reducing the author's line of argument to a simple, three-line syllogism. If the philosopher succeeded, then no matter how many studies the author quoted, no matter how much data he accumulated, no matter how many more pages he wrote; if his line of argument was illogical, his conclusion wasn't warranted.

Here's the classic example of a simple, correctly formulated logical syllogism:

> **Premise 1:** All men are mortal.
> **Premise 2:** Socrates is a man.
> **Therefore:** Socrates is mortal.

The beauty of a correctly formulated syllogism is that if we agree with the premises, then we must agree with the conclusion. Do you agree that all men are mortal? Do you agree that Socrates is a man? If so, then you *must* believe that Socrates is mortal. It's a logically air tight argument.

To evaluate someone's argument, try to put it in a syllogistic format and focus on two questions:

1. Do you agree with the premises? (Are they either intuitively obvious or well-supported by evidence?)

2. Does the conclusion logically follow from the premises?

Of course, arguments can get quite complicated, requiring complicated syllogisms to replicate them in logical form. If you're interested in exploring the more complex forms, study deductive logic. But I find that basic syllogisms suffice to evaluate the vast majority of meaningful arguments, even when evaluating chapters or entire books.

Let's Analyze an Argument!

Let's start with an argument proposed by a bright person and analyze it. Here are a couple of formulations of an argument put forth by Richard Dawkins, a popular science writer who once taught at Oxford University.

In his book, *The God Delusion*, Dawkins seeks to establish atheism, primarily by attacking theism. But he does present one positive argument for atheism, which he claims demonstrates that there is almost certainly no God. Dawkins believes the argument is devastating to theism—"an unrebuttable refutation."[4] It makes for a good argument to examine, since Dawkins states it in a few sentences rather than arguing it extensively.

Here's how he puts it:

> "...any creative intelligence, of sufficient complexity to design anything, comes into existence only as the end product of an extended process of gradual evolution. Creative intelligences, being evolved, necessarily arrive late in the universe, and therefore cannot be responsible for designing it."[5]

Later in the book, he puts it this way:

> "The whole argument turns on the familiar question 'Who made God?', which most thinking people discover for themselves. A designer God cannot be used to explain organized complexity because any God capable of designing anything would have to be complex enough to demand the same kind of explanation in his own right. God presents an infinite regress from which he cannot help us to escape."[6]

Think!

Before reading any further, try your own hand at responding to Dawkins. He says that he has "yet to hear...a convincing answer" to his argument.[7] Do you think it's irrefutable? If the argument seems rather muddled to you, start by reading one sentence at a time and asking yourself, "Do I agree or disagree with this statement, and why?" Perhaps trying to put it in syllogistic format would help, or trying to express it as a line of argument. (Caution: Try not to let your personal worldview interfere with your reasoning. The question I'm asking is not "Is there a God?" but rather "Is Dawkins' argument irrefutable?")

Using a Line of Argument* and Syllogism to Clear Muddy Waters

***Line of Argument =** a simplified form of a long or convoluted argument, summarized as a series of sentences.

If I understand Dawkins correctly, here's his line of argument:

> There are only two possible ways that God's existence could be accounted for:
>
> **1) He was created by another being.** But that explanation doesn't really help because then we have to ask, "Who made *that* designer, and the one who made him?" which leads to an infinite regress of questions which we can never fully

answer.

2) He slowly evolved through time. But if He evolved, He would not have developed His incredible intelligence and power until *the end* of a long process of evolution. Yet, in order to create the universe, He needed this intelligence and power *at the beginning*. Thus, He couldn't have created the universe. Besides, what are the odds that such a complex being could evolve through purely naturalistic causes?

Dawkins thus concludes that since both of these scenarios are highly unlikely, it's highly unlikely that God exists.[8]

Put in a syllogism, it might read like this:

Premise 1: If God exists, he must have come into existence by either being created by another being or evolving slowly through time.

Premise 2: It's highly unlikely that God came into existence by either being created by another being or evolving slowly through time.

Conclusion: It's highly unlikely that God exists.

Think!

Does laying it out as a line of argument and as a syllogism help? Do you think I did it accurately? Now think through the line of argument and syllogism. Do you agree with each of the premises? (Is it sound?*) Did Dawkins argue correctly from these premises? (Is it valid?*)[6]

As we continue with this chapter, we'll introduce some logical fallacies and apply them to both Dawkins' argument and the introductory discussion.

Sound* **Syllogism = the premises are true *and* the form of the argument is valid.

Valid* **Syllogism = the form of the argument is correct, whether or not the premises or conclusion are true.

Fallacy #1: Bifurcation

Dawkins' argument seems to be a good example of a fallacy called bifurcation, whereby the argument assumes that only two (note the prefix "bi", meaning "two") possibilities exist, whereas there are actually more. This fallacy is particularly pernicious because it seems to contain an element of sleight of hand. If it is presented by a person we respect or agree with, we tend to assume that his premises represent all possibilities and we focus on the validity of the argument rather than the accuracy of the premises.

So here's how Dawkins' argument appears to be guilty of bifurcation.

He assumes that there are two and only two possible explanations for the proposed existence of God:

1 - He was either created by another being, or

2 - He evolved by natural means slowly over time.

To justify limiting the existence of God to these two options, Dawkins should have eliminated a third, seemingly viable option: that God could have simply existed from eternity past. After all, until well into the 20th century, the majority of scientists saw no problem in believing that *matter* existed from eternity past. Why then could *God* not have existed from eternity past? Is there evidence (either empirical or logical) that if God exists, He could not have existed from eternity past (or, alternately, could not exist outside of time and space)? If there is such evidence, then Dawkins should forward it. Otherwise, his premises are misleading and inaccurate in that they unnecessarily ignore this option.[9]

To put it another way, Dawkins claims that there are two and only two ways the existence of God could be explained. By explaining those two away, he claims to have explained away the existence of God. Yet, he's ignored (or deflected his readers from) a third possibility which he needs to explain away as well: that God existed from eternity past. By overlooking this third option, his argument fails, falling to the fallacy of bifurcation.[10]

Other Examples of Bifurcation

- *"The Atlanta Falcons' loss to the New England Patriots was due to either inept play or poor coaching."*

  But aren't there more options than two? Perhaps they lost primarily because of a brilliant strategy by the opposing coaching staff, or the Patriots' quarterback was on a roll, or the injury to the Falcon running back caused the Falcons to resort to "Plan B" rather than "Plan A", or any number of other possibilities that the armchair critic needs to rule out.

- *"The president must be either insane or stupid to make that decision."*

  What other factors may explain the decision? Isn't it possible that the president was privy to facts we weren't aware of, or had made a wise political bargain that required that decision, or any number of other factors?

- *"What a despicable child! He obviously either inherited bad genes or has inept parents."*

  What are some other possible contributing factors to the child's behavior? Perhaps he's sick or tired or teething.

Tip: Bifurcation becomes easier to spot once you're aware of it. When someone presents two options as if they're the *only* two options, I immediately ask myself, "Are there more options than he's presenting?" Ask the same question if someone presents three or more options as if they're the only ones. We could call it "trifurcation," etc.

Fallacy #2: The Straw Man

I'm dealing in this chapter with arguments that are very common. Familiarize yourself with them and you'll begin to see them everywhere—in articles, news broadcasts, Facebook discussions—everywhere!

The Straw Man fallacy presents a weak form of an opposing argument so that it's easy to destroy it and declare victory. The writer or speaker never actually attacks the opponent's arguments. Instead, he avoids the opponent's arguments by "knocking down a straw man."

Dawkins seems to have erected and knocked down a straw man in the argument we considered above. In brief, he argued that it's very unlikely that an evolved or created God exists. But the vast majority of theistic theologians and philosophers of the Western world would likely agree with this statement. In fact, I don't believe I've ever met a theist who believes in a created or evolved God. So arguing against this kind of a God says nothing about the existence of the eternal God that most of Dawkins' opponents believe in.

Thus, Dawkins has set up an irrelevant straw man (or in this instance, a Straw God), and tried to disprove His existence. If successful, he merely succeeds in knocking down a position that his opponents never held. The philosophers and theologians he's attacking overwhelmingly define God as one who existed from eternity past (or exists outside time and space). Dawkins should have attacked the position held by those he attacks.

Michael Ruse, Professor of Philosophy at Florida State University, himself an atheist, criticizes Dawkins' argument in part for this very reason. He concludes:

> "...I want to extend to Christians the courtesy of arguing against what they actually believe, rather than begin and end with the polemical parody of what Dawkins calls "the God delusion."[11]

Another Example of Arguing against a Straw Man

A friend remarks to you: "The last three winters have been colder than average. So much for the theory of Global Warming!"

Your friend assumes that Global Warming advocates argue in this manner: "If temperatures are truly rising, *every year* and *every geographical location* should show increased warmth." But nobody argues this. It's arguing against a straw man. Global Warming advocates actually argue that *over long periods of time* the average temperature is increasing. Those who argue against global warming should argue against this rather than a straw man.

Fallacy #3: The Law of Non Contradiction

"Man has been accustomed, ever since he was a boy,
to having a dozen incompatible philosophies dancing about together inside his head.
He doesn't think of doctrines as primarily "true" or "false," but as "academic" or "practical," "outworn" or "contemporary," "conventional" or "ruthless.""[12]

— C.S. Lewis

In Chapter 9, I mentioned philosopher Alex Rosenberg's recent book. In it he argues, among other things, that:

> **1 - There's no free will.**[13] Thus, according to Rosenberg, we think only what we've been determined to think (by our genetics, etc.) How we think is determined by evolutionary processes that often have nothing to do with producing logical thinking. I can't direct my own thinking because there's no "I" outside my brain to direct my thinking. Our brains are just advanced computers, and computers can't think "about" things. Consciousness is thus an illusion.[14]
>
> **2 - Our thinking is flawed.** "Mother Nature built our minds for purposes other than understanding reality."[15]
>
> **3 - We can learn nothing from history or people's life stories.**[16]

With that background, here's where I see contradictions piling up.

- **On changing people's opinions** - In his preface Rosenberg states that he wrote the book to help people discover the real answers to such questions as "Why am I here?" or "What is the meaning of life?" But if there's no free will, and all of our beliefs were therefore predetermined, how can he possibly hope to change anybody's opinion about anything? If evolution absolutely determines everyone's thought processes and beliefs, then how can he possibly trust his own mental processes or hope to change other people's thinking?

- **On urging life change** - Why does he keep urging us to action, if everything's determined and his urgings are therefore worthless? Rosenberg preaches, "We need continually to fight the temptation to think that we can learn much of anything from someone else's story of how they beat an addiction, kept to a diet…." But what does it mean to "continually fight" a temptation if we're already destined to fight or not fight, to either beat the temptation or fall for it?

- **On recommending a course of action** - By the end of the book he's recommending that we adopt the philosophical nihilism of Epicurus, not take ourselves so seriously, and take Prozac if you're unhappy that life has no meaning.[17] Can't he see that if we believed what he said earlier about that we can't learn anything from other people's life stories, we can also learn nothing from his own experiences and recommendations?

- **On learning from history** - He says we can learn nothing from history: "History, even when corrected by science, is still bunk."[18] But then he recounts history to make his points.[19] For example, how can we know if Prozac works, unless we accept the testimonies of other patients and rely on their stated medical histories?

Thus, it seems evident to me that Rosenberg's book is riddled with internal contradictions. Now perhaps if I asked Rosenberg personally about the apparent contradictions, he could clear them up. But in the present state of his book, they seem flagrant, leading me to question many of his conclusions.

Sometimes contradictions are not so obvious. For example, a central tenet of Logical Positivists, whose views were very influential in the early 1900s (not only in philosophy, but also psychology and other sciences), expounded the verification principle, which can be stated as: "the only meaningful statements are those that we can verify through observation." Yet, their critics pointed out that this very statement (the verification principle) can't be verified through observation, making it self-contradictory, or self-defeating. In other words, they couldn't verify the verification principle with the verification principle, making it (to be consistent with Logical Positivism) a meaningless statement.

Well, that was rather embarrassing to Logical Positivists. This insight, in part, led to Logical Positivism's demise in the latter 1900s.[20]

Summary

The arguments we've examined in this chapter were put forth by bright people with topnotch education credentials—often PhDs holding prestigious positions. If *they* are subject to falling for logical fallacies, how much more the rest of us?

Why do brilliant people believe nonsense? Because they fail to sufficiently check their beliefs against logical fallacies. How can we guard ourselves from similar errors in thinking?

Action Points
How to Spot Logical Fallacies...and Keep from Using Them in Our Own Communications

1. Take time to think through arguments that are important to you.

Most don't. In fact, they barely even pay attention. Philosopher and scientist Francis Bacon once wrote: "Some books should be tasted, some devoured, but only a few should be chewed and digested thoroughly." For the latter books, articles or lectures, if the argumentation is complicated or unclear, I often summarize it with a line of argument, sometimes chapter by chapter. It takes a bit of time, but it keeps me from ending the book in a mental fog.

2. Don't be intimidated by credentials and claims.

Surely this is, in part, why people take nonsense promoted by well-credentialed people at face value. Never listen to anyone without engaging your critical thinking.

3. Beware of the tendency to uncritically accept the arguments of those you agree with, or arguments that have an agreeable conclusion.

Professor H. Allen Orr, in the *New York Review of Books*, reflected on Dawkins' argument and his way of arguing. According to Orr:

> "Indeed he suffers from several problems when attempting to reason philosophically. The most obvious is that he has a preordained set of conclusions at which he's determined to arrive. Consequently, Dawkins uses any argument, however feeble, that seems to get him there and the merit of various arguments appears judged largely by where they lead."[21]

4. Ask yourself, "Are there facts or personal experiences that don't fit with either the premises or the conclusion?"

When I read Rosenberg's argument that we can't learn anything from history or life stories, I couldn't help but reflect on the wealth of valuable lessons I've learned from observing people's lives and reading great biographies. For example, by watching people make wise and poor financial and health decisions, I've learned much from their successes and failures. My personal experience represents one strike against his conclusion, causing me to look more critically at his argumentation.

5. Put it in a syllogism (or line of argument) and ask yourself two questions:

- Are the premises supported by sufficient evidence?
- Does the conclusion follow logically from the premises?

(To remember this point, reflect back on the **D**. **R**. of Dr. Cackler. Is the **d**ata complete and accurate? Is the **r**easoning from that data clear and accurate?)

6. Have others look at the argument.

Learn from Hewlett Packard's practice of running an idea by the person next to you. If the idea is important to you, discuss it with others. We all think a bit differently and it's very likely that others will see aspects of the issue that you don't see.

For example, Einstein once observed that scientists are typically poor philosophers. Whether he's right or not, psychologists do find people typically having strong and weak areas of reasoning. If a scientist is trying to reason philosophically, he might be wise to run his arguments by a philosopher. It's often wise to run important arguments by people who think differently from you.

7. See how others in the field respond.

Dawkins' argument is philosophical and the field of philosophy has a rich history of arguments concerning the existence of God. It would seem unlikely, though not impossible, that an expert in animal behavior (Dawkins) would dream up a slam dunk argument than never occurred to any great philosophical thinker from Plato to Immanuel Kant to Bertrand Russell. If Dawkins' argument were truly original and significant, I'd expect a loud chorus of respected philosophers to be hailing this argument's arrival.

Yet, the responses I've seen by philosophers and academics have been underwhelming at best. Philosopher William Craig went so far as to declare it "the worst atheistic argument in the history of Western thought."[22] Academic biologist H. Allen Orr noted that the argument was "shredded by reviewers."[23]

For example, some attack the argument by noting that an explanation doesn't typically require an explanation of the explanation (responding to Dawkins' contention that theists must forward an explanation as to where God came from). In other words, if we were to visit the dark side of the moon and find an advanced, but long-abandoned (at least a century old, deduced from its state of natural aging) mining operation, where all the inscriptions were in a non-human language, wouldn't we be justified in positing that alien intelligences were behind it, *even if we had no idea how the aliens came to be or where they were from*?

And it's not just theistic philosophers who find Dawkins' argument lacking.

Atheist Michael Ruse attacks Dawkins' argument in this way:

> "Like every first-year undergraduate in philosophy, Dawkins thinks he can put to rest the causal argument for God's existence. If God caused the world, then what caused God? Of course the great philosophers, Anselm and Aquinas particularly, are way ahead of him here. They know that the only way to stop the regression is by making God something that needs no cause. He must be a necessary being. This means that God is not part of the regular causal chain but in some sense orthogonal to it. He is what keeps the whole business going, past, present and future, and is the explanation of why there is something rather than nothing."[24]

Surely such rejoinders are legitimate challenges that Dawkins should respond to. Had he run his argument by some philosophers prior to publishing, perhaps he could have responded to their objections.[25]

Think Different (Creative Thinking)

One of philosopher Immanuel Kant's most valuable contributions to practical human thought was his insight that we don't experience things entirely as they are. While some people insist that seeing is *believing*, we all know that seeing can also be *deceiving*. For example, Kant notes that we don't see objects directly. Rather, we're a step removed in that we see reflections of objects on our retinas. We take another step back from real objects when our brains bring our own interpreting mechanisms to those objects, such as "quality" or "cause and effect."

Modern psychology confirms and extends Kant's insight. We don't "see" the reflections on our retinas in the same way. While *you* may see a green object on your retina, *I* may see it as brown, since I'm color-blind to certain greens. And we're well aware of common optical illusions and misperceptions. That's why eye-witness testimony is often contradictory, even when the witnesses are honest. Often, what we see shouldn't be believed.

Example: You've probably seen illustrations such as this, where our minds fool us. How many "F"s do you see in this passage?

**FINISHED FILES ARE THE RE
SULT OF YEARS OF SCIENTI
FIC STUDY COMBINED WITH
THE EXPERIENCE OF YEARS.**

Most people see only three. That's all I saw the first two times I read it. Actually, there are six. (Look slowly at each letter and count again, perhaps starting at the end.) This is similar to the problem drivers have spotting motorcycles on streets where they are rare. We're watching for cars and trucks and may not see the motorcycles at all.

Example: Are the horizontal lines below curved or straight? Use a ruler or straight edge to see.

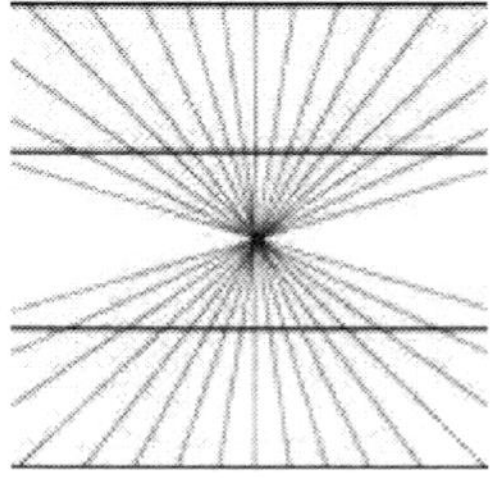

Fallacies such as bifurcation, like a good magician or an illusion, play on our brains' tendencies to see certain things incorrectly or to be distracted from crucial details. How can creativity help us to overcome distractions and wrong directions in order to innovate productively?

1. Broaden your range of input.

Who would you prefer to edit your writing?

a) A dyslexic, who struggles to read well?

b) Slow readers?

c) An autistic who often misses the big picture?

d) A top academic who teaches grammar and literature?

e) A person so proficient at reading that she can polish off an entire novel in an evening?

Intuitively, most authors seem to seek out exclusively d) and e) types, and I agree that their input has a place. After all, shouldn't avid readers and top grammarians have valuable input?

But I'm increasing seeking editorial input from a wider range of people. True, autistics often miss the big picture because they're fascinated with the details. But this attention to detail makes them more likely to see the "F"s in the above illusion. Proficient readers hardly see the word "of," and may miss a broad range of errors in my manuscripts. Higher functioning autistics may see all those little details that most of us miss.

While fast readers may excel at telling you if your story is interesting and flows well, the slow reader may be better for thinking through your line of argument, spotting places that need more documentation, or helping you with the rhythm produced by combinations of long and short sentences.

Literature professors tend to love clever analogies and brilliant descriptions, whereas the average reader may see these as distractions from the story line. That's why I like input from both.

Academics have a high tolerance for detailed argumentation and theory. While I'll get their input on this book, I can't quite trust their verdict if they tell me it's interesting. If I'm writing, not primarily for professors, but for their students and the broader public, I treasure input from those who aren't naturally interested in my subject matter. I'm blessed with dyslexic twins, and love their input. That's one reason I use lots of white space, bullet points, and illustrations. Dyslexics cringe when they see a page full of unbroken words. I've found that if I can hold the attention of struggling readers, I'm more likely to captivate a broad range of readers, and in the end delight academics as well.

2. At times, ignore the current theory that drives your research, and allow non-experts to offer ideas; or just throw a bunch of stuff against the wall to see what sticks.

Sometimes our theories and methods keep us from trying potentially fruitful experiments. Since we seldom recognize that the ruling theory may have deflected us onto a side road, it sometimes helps to toss it and try something new.

Isn't this the way inventor Thomas Edison often proceeded? I still picture him in his later years, stopping beside the road to sample plants that might be used as a substitute for the rubber used to make tires, which was in short supply during World War II.

- A thirteen year old, Jack Andraka, took an intense interest in trying to cure pancreatic cancer, after it killed a family friend. Being new to the field, he took a different direction from the standard research, resulting in his inventing a simple, cheap test to detect pancreatic cancer early, when it can be successfully treated.[26]

- Don Valencia, a cellular biologist who developed tests to diagnose autoimmune diseases, had worked on isolating molecules in human cells without destroying them. It occurred to him that this technique might work for making a concentrated extract of coffee that could capture its flavor more successfully than other extracts. He experimented with it in his kitchen, trying out different flavors on his neighbors. Once perfected, he took it to Starbucks. They eventually hired him and used the technology to expand their product line to coffee ice cream, bottled beverages, etc.[27]

3. Employ higher levels of reasoning.

Bloom's Taxonomy (most refer to the "revised" taxonomy), distinguishes different types of thinking, suggesting ways for us to move past rote memory. Unfortunately, many students seem to seldom move past merely identifying and memorizing the important parts (what might be on the test) of texts and lectures.

Yet, to succeed in real life, we must go further than recognition or rote memorization (see Level 1 in the below graphic.). We need to develop the skills of comprehending (Level 2), applying (Level 3), analyzing (Level 4), synthesizing (Level 5) and evaluating (Level 6). Search "Bloom's Taxonomy" in Google and you'll find many lists of specific characteristics of each level of thinking. Referring to such lists when working through an issue can suggest new ways to approach it.

For example, in our discussion of Richard Dawkins' argument, I first stated it (Level One) and several times put it in my own words to try to clarify it (Level Two). We skipped application, but analyzed it (Level Four) by putting it in a line of argument and syllogism, so that we could identify and examine the premises. We did a bit of synthesis (Level Five) when we brought in outside ideas of how theists conceive of the eternal existence of God, and how other thinkers have responded to the argument. Finally, evaluation (Level Six) came to play when we noted that there seems to be an element of smoke and mirrors involved in the fallacy of bifurcation.

So if you're evaluating an argument or a proposal, consider running it through Bloom's Taxonomy to expand your ways of looking at the issue. Note how several levels involve creativity.

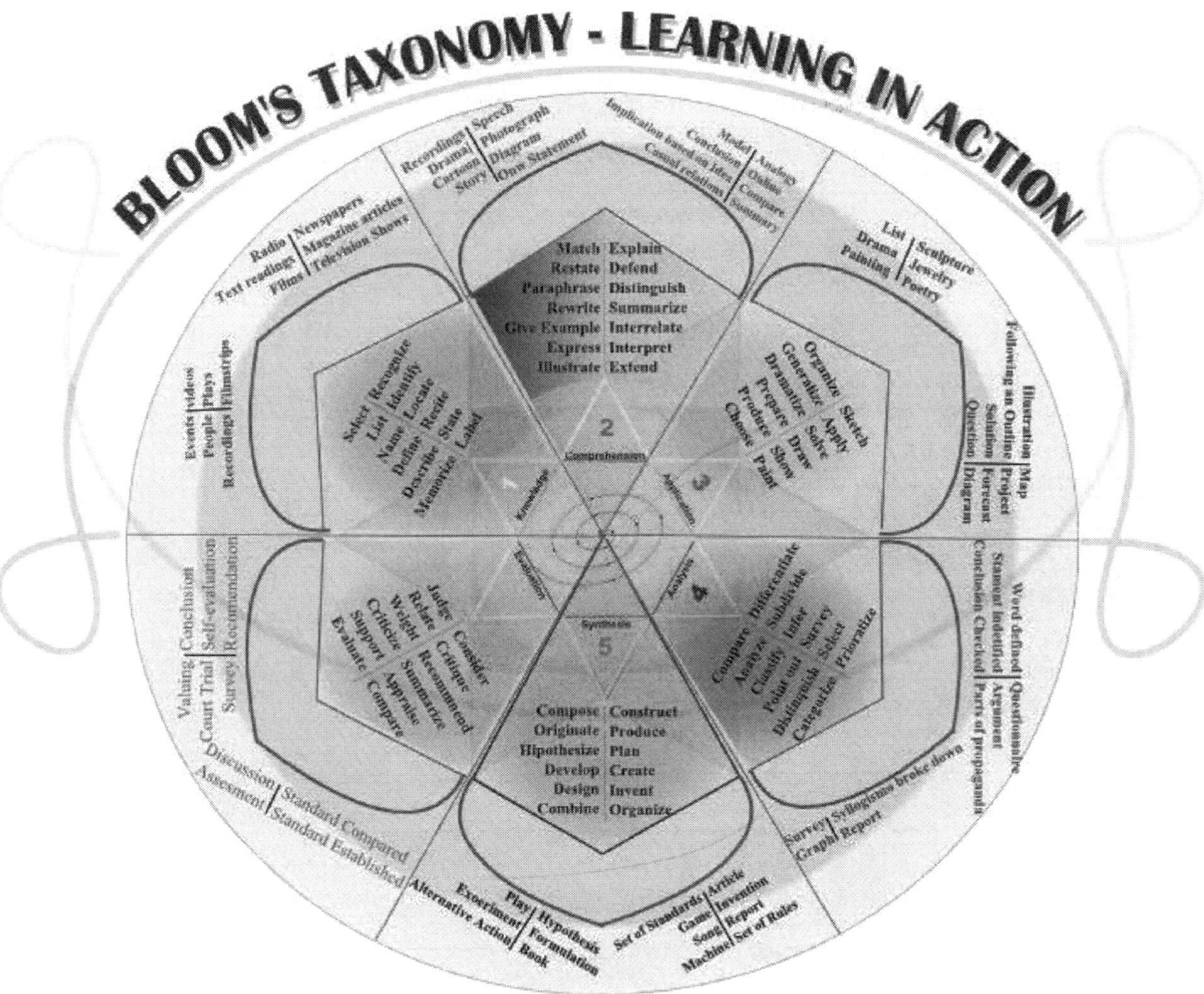
BLOOM'S TAXONOMY - LEARNING IN ACTION
Match Explain
Restate Defend
Paraphrase Distinguish
Rewrite Summarize
Give Example Interrelate
Express Interpret
Illustrate Extend
Compose Construct
Originate Produce
Hipothesize Plan
Develop Create
Design Invent
Combine Organize
Valuing Conclusion
Court Trial Self-evaluation
Survey Recomendation
Discussion Standard Compared
Assesment Standard Established

Flex Your Neurons!
Pursuing the Point of Know Return

1. Write your own example of a "straw man" argument.
2. Write your own example of a "bifurcation" argument.
3. If you agree that Dawkins' argument makes no sense, why do you think such a smart person would forward such a nonsensical argument? If you believe that the argument could make sense if reformulated, how would you change it to overcome the difficulties scholars have brought forth?
4. How could you use Bloom's Revised Taxonomy as a practical tool for thinking more critically about issues you study and write about?
5. How could you use Bloom's Revised Taxonomy to think more creatively?
6. Since our brains often deceive us, how can we protect ourselves against such deceptions?

Making It More Personal
Practical Takeaways

What are one or more ideas provoked by this chapter that you can apply to help you think more critically?

____

____

____

What are one or more ideas that you can apply to help you think more creatively?

____

____

____

What else do you want to make sure you don't forget?

____

____

____

Recommended Trails
For the Incurably Curious and Adventurous

1. To more fully understand a fallacy, it's often helpful to read other people's explanations and examples. To do this, Google "bifurcation" or "straw man."

2. Learn more about "Bloom's Taxonomy." This Wikipedia article is a good starting point to introduce it, discover the main controversies, and find other resources:

   http://en.wikipedia.org/wiki/Bloom%27s_taxonomy

3. Here's a TED talk of Jack Andraka talking about his development of a test for pancreatic cancer. Why do you think a young teen was able to develop such a test, when the experts had failed?

   http://www.ted.com/talks/jack_andraka_a_promising_test_for_pancreatic_cancer_from_a_teenager?language=en

CHAPTER 11

THEY FALL FOR COMMON FALLACIES

"The dull mind, once arriving at an inference that flatters the desire, is rarely able to retain the impression that the notion from which the inference started was purely problematic."

— George Eliot, in *Silas Marner*

In the last chapter we discussed passages where bright individuals with PhDs violated common fallacies. Even the brightest among us fall for them. As a result, we should be ever vigilant to keep our critical guard up, looking for fallacious reasoning in lectures, reading, viewing, and especially in our own writing. None of us are immune to falling for fallacies.

Until doctors come up with an inoculation against fallacies, I suppose the next best thing is to thoroughly acquaint ourselves with the most common fallacies. I chose the following fallacies by comparing a dozen or so university sites that list what they consider the most common fallacies that trip up students.[1]

Snoozer Alert!

Sorry, but this chapter and the next don't contain fascinating stories and intriguing intellectual puzzles. But please resist the temptation to skim to the following section. To think critically, we simply must familiarize ourselves with logical fallacies. Otherwise, we're fair game for all sorts of nonsense.

Think of it like math. While the formulas themselves might be boring, we learn them in order to hopefully use them for something practical in the future. You'll assuredly find many of the below fallacies used in conversations and articles.

So learn these well. Reflect upon them. Look for them in the media. Familiarizing yourself with errant reasoning goes a long way toward helping you to write, reason, speak, and listen with more critical precision.

Tip: If some of my definitions and examples don't sufficiently clarify, look up the fallacy in Wikipedia or other sources for alternate explanations.

Below this list of fallacies, I'll give you a bit of practice by asking you to connect a fallacy with an errant argument. Finally, I'll give a few tips on checking your own argumentation (particularly in writing and speeches) for fallacies.

Twenty-Seven Common Fallacies

Ad Hominem **-** translated into English: "against the person", aka "damning the source," the "genetic fallacy," "poisoning the well," related to "*tu quoque*" ("you, too!"). Defined as attacking the person (e.g. - can't be trusted, is a moron, etc.) rather than the argument.

> **Example:** "I don't believe anything he says because he's a biased political liberal." Yet, shouldn't we assess his arguments based upon his evidence and argumentation, rather than solely because of his political label?
>
> **Caution:** Sometimes a person has indeed been shown to be untrustworthy. Cautioning readers that he has been repeatedly caught in flagrant lies isn't an ad hominem fallacy. Noting a person's lack of integrity can be valid, if his argument requires us to trust him.
>
> **Tip:** If the person's character is either irrelevant to the argument or unknown, focus on the facts and arguments.

Affirming the Consequent - aka "converse error" or "fallacy of the converse." This is a formal fallacy (the *form* of the argument isn't valid) that assumes if the argument is valid going one direction, it's also valid when run the opposite direction.

Example:

> **Premise 1:** If I get the flu, I'll be nauseated.
> **Premise 2:** I'm nauseated.
> **Conclusion:** Therefore, I have the flu.

This is invalid because while it may be true that if you get the flu, you'll get nauseated, the converse isn't always true. You can be nauseated and yet not have the flu. Perhaps you have a hangover, or are pregnant.

Tip: If you see an argument in the following form, it's affirming the consequent:

> **Premise 1:** If P, then Q
> **Premise 2:** Q
> **Conclusion:** P

Appealing to Extremes - taking an assertion to an extreme, even though the arguer may never take it to that extreme.

Example: "Avid health advocates blow out their knees by their 50s by running marathons. Therefore, don't prioritize regular exercise." But not *all* avid health advocates run long distances as their primary exercise. It's an extreme statement.

Argument From Authority - aka "*argumentum ab auctoritate,*" "appeal to authority." Claiming that a position is true because an authority says it's true.

Even when the referenced authority is a true authority in the field, arguments should ultimately be based upon facts and reasoning rather than quoting authorities. Also beware of people quoting false authorities, like football stars or models selling insurance or technology.

Example: "We know global warming is true because a number of great scientists assure us it's true."

Caution: Sometimes citing authorities can be a valid part of an argument. For example, if a hefty percentage of respected scientists who specialize in a related field are all warning us about the dangers of global warming, this in itself provides evidence that global warming is at the very least a viable theory that needs to be seriously considered. Alternately, if no respectable scientists took global warming seriously, then this would surely be a strike against it, even though ultimately we're looking for hard evidence rather than numbers of testimonies.

Tip: Ask yourself,

- Are these truly experts in the field I'm discussing? Would some view them as either biased or holding to fringe views on the subject?
- Have I explained clearly how I'm using these authorities as evidence, within the larger scope of my argument?
- Would it be relevant to explain the evidence that led the authorities to come to their position on the subject?
- Are you using their testimonies as helpful resources, quoting them as a part of a larger argument, or quoting them as a slam dunk argument to make your case? Make sure you're not saying something like: "Dr. Authority believes x, so we should believe x as well."

Argument from Ignorance - aka "appeal to ignorance," "*argumentum ad ignorantium,*" related to "non-testable hypothesis." Assuming that a claim is true because it has not been or cannot be proven false (or vice versa, assuming that a claim is false because it has not been or cannot be proven true.)

Example: Nobody can prove that my client was at the scene of the crime, therefore he's innocent. (Of course, he may be in fact guilty. We may just lack sufficient evidence that he was there.)

Caution: While some would say "absence of evidence is not evidence of absence," this isn't true in every case. For example, if I walk outside and see no evidence of rainfall (no puddles, the streets aren't wet), I'm justified in taking this as evidence that it hasn't rained recently. In this case, the absence of evidence for rain is indeed evidence for the absence of rain.

Band Wagon - aka "*ad populum* fallacy," "appeal to widespread belief," "appeal to the majority," "appeal to the people." If a large number of people believe it, it must be true. It appeals to our desire to fit in.

Example: "Most people use Microsoft products, so they must be the best."

Example: "Everybody I know uses Meth, so it can't be that bad."

Caution: Some people naturally despise majority opinion and relish holding contrarian positions.[2] Those who disagree with opinions held by a majority of intelligent people should at least make sure they understand the reasons informed people give to justify their beliefs.

Tip: Remember that popular opinion is often wrong, and what's cool today may seem foolish tomorrow. In fact, it's often those who stand against the crowd who change the world. As Apple, Inc. said it in their motto: "Think different."

Begging (Evading) the Question - aka "circular argument," *"petitio principii," translated* "assuming the initial point." The conclusion is assumed in a premise.

This typically isn't as obvious as it first sounds.

Example: The Writing Center at the University of North Carolina gives a good example.

> “Active euthanasia is morally acceptable. It is a decent, ethical thing to help another human being escape suffering through death.”

At first read, it may seem pretty straightforward. But let's examine it as a premise and conclusion:

> **Premise:** It is a decent, ethical thing to help another human being escape suffering through death.
>
> **Conclusion:** Active euthanasia is morally acceptable.

Look closely at these two sentences and you'll discover that they actually do nothing more than state the same thing twice; the conclusion merely dresses up the premise in different words. "Decent, ethical" in the premise is worded "morally acceptable" in the conclusion. "...to help another human being escape suffering through death" in the premise becomes "active euthanasia" in the conclusion.

Thus, the argument doesn't tell us much, if anything, about *why* euthanasia is morally acceptable. It leaves us asking the implied question over again, "But *why* is it acceptable?", showing that the premise and conclusion merely begged (i.e., evaded) the question.

> **Tip:** Typically, rewriting the argument in the form of premises and a conclusion reveals when a question is being begged. Do you agree with the premises? Are there gaps in the line of argument? Does the conclusion say nothing more than the premises already stated?

Bifurcation - aka "false dichotomy," "black-or-white fallacy," the "either-or fallacy," related to a "false dilemma." The argument makes it appear that there are only two possible answers, but there are actually more.

> **Example:** We discussed examples in the last chapter.

> **Tip:** Ask yourself, are there really two and only two options? If not, are any of the other options viable? Have all other options been sufficiently ruled out?

Dogmatism - Not even considering an opponent's argument, because of overconfidence in one's own position.

> **Statement:** "Mercedes makes the best car ever."

> **Retort:** "But according to *Consumer Reports*…."

> **Dogmatic Defense: "**I don't care what those studies say; I *know*! Mercedes is the best."

Emotional Appeals - An appeal to emotion that is irrelevant (or largely irrelevant) to the argument.

> **Example:** "The death penalty can't be right. Have you seen a person die in an electric chair?"

> **Caution:** Emotion can often be a legitimate part of an argument. Example: "Look at these poor birds dying from an oil spill. This demonstrates one reason we should take great precautions to avoid such mishaps."

Equivocation - related to "semantics," "playing with words." Using the same word with more than one meaning, thereby invalidating the argument.

> **Example:** "Of all the animals, only man is rational. No woman is a man. Therefore, no woman is rational." In the first instance, "man" means "mankind," whereas in the second instance, "man" means "the male gender." This change in meaning invalidates the argument.

> **Tip**: Look carefully at the argument's important words. Are they used in a consistent way, or do they shift meanings?

Fallacy of Exclusion - Focusing on one group's behavior as if the behavior is exclusive to that group.

Example: "Watch those women drivers. They're always thinking of something other than their driving." But are male drivers any better? Shouldn't this statement be based on psychological studies and statistics of accidents rather than personal observations of one sex?

False Dilemma - aka "false dichotomy," "either/or," "black/white," "excluded middle." A form of bifurcation, this fallacy allows for only two extreme positions, although a legitimate middle ground might be arguable. Sometimes they paint one side as so extreme that nobody could ever agree with it.

Example: "You either support Israelis in Palestine or you're an anti-Semite."

Example: "Are you for George Bush or are you for the terrorists?"

Tip: When only two extreme alternatives are given, look for middle ground.

Faulty Analogy - aka "weak analogy." Comparing two similar things to make a point, but the analogy breaks down because of one or more significant dissimilarities.

Example: "The war in Afghanistan is nothing more than a modern day Vietnam war."

Tip: Is the analogy truly alike in all relevant respects?

Glittering Generality - aka "Weasel Words." Using words in such a broad way that almost everyone resonates with them in the same way, thus lending credence to the argument. Thus, those who argue that their position is really about "freedom," "love," "human rights," etc., can gain a following, even though the words may mean different things to different people, or are being used in such a vague way as to be essentially meaningless.

Example: "Allowing this controversial artwork in our place of business is really about guaranteeing our freedoms, in this case our freedom of expression." Perhaps, but what if the artwork trivializes or misrepresents your business, or disgusts and demoralizes your employees? Framing it as solely an issue of freedom seems to make it a glittering generality.

Hasty Generalization - related to "non-representative sample," "fallacy of insufficient statistics," "fallacy of insufficient sample," "fallacy of the lonely fact," "leaping to a conclusion," "hasty induction," "*secundum quid* (converse accident). A conclusion was reached via inadequate evidence, such as when a sample cited was inadequate (e.g., atypical or too small) to warrant a generalized conclusion.

Example: "Most Hollywood stars have terrible marriages. Just read the tabloids." Their conclusion may or may not be true, but reading tabloids is no way to decide the issue. News sources by their very nature select what's "newsy." Since a nasty divorce is more newsy than a stable marriage, the former gets the press, giving the impression that most Hollywood stars can't hold a marriage together.

Example: "I'll never fly again. I read about too many accidents and hijackings." Again, you don't hear about the thousands of flights with no incidents. Thus, you're judging from the news you hear, which is both an atypical and small sampling. The National Safety Council calculated the odds of dying in a motor vehicle accident as one chance in 98 over a lifetime. The odds for dying in air travel (including private flights) was one chance in 7,178.[3]

Tip: Notice the sample size and where it's drawn from. Is it adequate to warrant the conclusion? Is the conclusion stated in terms that are too general and sweeping?

Inconsistency - aka "non contradiction." The argument contradicts itself. (See the previous chapter for a more thorough explanation.)

Example: "Only statements that can be justified with scientific experiments can be believed." Yet, this statement itself can't be justified by scientific experiments.

Example: "Our brains developed, not to think logically, but for survival in an agrarian society. Therefore, we can't trust our reasoning." This statement uses logical reasoning, although it's claiming logical reasoning is not to be trusted.

Moral Equivalency - arguing incorrectly that two moral issues are sufficiently similar to warrant the same treatment. It often compares lesser misdeeds to major atrocities.

Example: "Killing in war is legalized murder." In some instances, this may be true. But in all instances?

Example: "Our local police act like Nazis—they have no respect for my human right to drive my car like I want."

***Non Sequitur* -** translated: "it does not follow." A general category that includes "hasty generalization," "slippery slope," "affirming the consequent," "missing the point," etc.) The conclusion does not follow from the premises.

Example: "Patrick always smiled at me and was so respectful. He couldn't have burned down the gym." Is there some absolute law of nature that states that respectful, smiling people never burn down gyms? While Patrick's character in relation to you can be a relevant piece of evidence to be considered, it's a *non sequitur* to say that it proves he could have never burned down a gym.

Tips: 1. Forget the conclusion for a moment. Looking solely at the premises, ask yourself what can be concluded from the premises. 2. Now look at your conclusion. Ask yourself what kind and amount of evidence you'd need to support this conclusion. Do the premises provide that kind of evidence? 3. Is your conclusion too extreme? Would it be closer to the truth if it weren't overstated?

Failing Occam's Razor - Prefer a simpler explanation (or hypothesis) to a more convoluted or complicated one.

Example: Your best friend Ralph flunked Calculus. Possible reasons:

1. If we were to run a psychological profile of both Ralph and his professor, we might find that they have diametrically opposed learning styles, thus making communication extremely difficult.

2. Aliens kept Ralph up all night before both the midterm and final exam, questioning him and keeping him from adequate rest and preparation.

3. Ralph admitted to never doing his homework and seldom attending lectures.

Occam's Razor would prefer the third, more simple and obvious explanation.

Warning: Occam's Razor doesn't decide all cases, since many explanations that end up being proven over time are indeed more complicated than their disproven counterparts. Typically, when choosing between competing scientific theories, the best fit with the observable data trumps simplicity. So it's wise to consider Occam's Razor a "rule of thumb" rather than a hard and fast rule.

***Post Hoc Ergo Propter Hoc* -** translated "after this, therefore because of this." Often shortened to "*post hoc,"* also called "faulty causality," "faulty cause," "false cause," or "correlation vs. causation"). Correlation and causation are confused in that one event follows another and the former is falsely assumed to be the cause of the latter.

Example: "Ever since his trip to India, Alfred's been sick. Obviously, he caught something in India that our doctors can't diagnose."

Tips: 1. When one event is claimed as the cause of another, look for other possible causes. In the above example, perhaps Alfred caught something the day he arrived back home, or already had an illness before going to India, but never developed symptoms until he returned. **2.** Give evidence beyond "this happened after that," to support your claim. For example, you might discover that Alfred consulted with seven American diagnostic specialists, who all agreed that it was a malady they'd never before seen. This would lend credence to the "he caught it in India" theory.

Red Herring - Deflecting an argument by *chasing a rabbit* (an irrelevant topic.) The name "red herring" was originally used in fox hunting, when a herring (type of fish) was dragged across a trail to throw the dogs off the scent of the fox.

Example: After Harry's wife caught him gambling away his paycheck and asked for an explanation, he responded, "At least with gambling I have a chance to get my money back. What about your weekly purchase of clothes that ends up in a bag for Goodwill? And why isn't your recent raise helping us to pay our debts?" Harry's arguments deflect from the immediate issue: he gambled away his paycheck.

Example: "Sure, the mercury found in seafood is often unsafe, but fishermen have to make a living like everyone else."

Tip: If you're not sure, write the argument out as a line of argument. This typically shows clearly where the argument got off track.

Reductionism - aka "oversimplifying," "sloganeering." Reducing large, complex problems to one or a few simplistic causes or solutions.

Example: "The problem with our economy can be reduced to two words: trade imbalance." What about other relevant issues, such as the drain of a huge national debt?

Tip: Ask yourself, "What other factors may contribute to this problem, or be a part of the solution?"

Slippery Slope - aka "snowball argument," "domino theory," "absurd extrapolation," "thin edge of the wedge," "camel's nose." Arguing that one change or event will inevitably lead to another, eventually landing them at a place they never wanted to go.

Example: "If we allow more restrictions on purchasing guns, this will be followed by further restrictions and eventually the government will confiscate all our guns."

Caution: Slippery slopes do exist. The question is, just how slippery is the slope? Is it slippery enough to make the slide to the bottom inevitable?

Tip: Look closely at your argument for each link in the chain of consequences. Is there adequate evidence to conclude that each progression is either inevitable or fairly certain? Are there abundant historical precedents that back up the claim? Are there historical precedents that provide contrary evidence?

Stacking the Deck - aka "cherry picking." Listing the arguments (or evidence) that support one's claim while ignoring the ones that don't.

Example: "Capitalism inevitably leads to a violent revolution by the proletariat. Here are fifty examples from history."

Tip: Ask yourself, "Are there counterexamples that the arguer is ignoring, or is he simply pulling out examples that support his theory?

Straw Man - presents a weak form of an opposing argument, then knocks it down to claim victory.

Example: Jack emailed his professor that he missed class due to a bad case of the flu and that he would bring a doctor's note. The next day, the professor announced in class that he would not excuse Jack's absence because his excuse was that he didn't feel like coming (not mentioning the flu or the note). Since the professor put Jack's argument in such a weak form, he was arguing against a straw man rather than Jack's actual defense.

Tip: Do you know the strongest arguments of your opponents? If so, are those the arguments you're arguing against?

Sweeping Generalization - aka *dicto simpliciter.* Assumes that what is true of the whole will also be true of the part, or that what is true in most instances will be true in all instances.

> **Example:** "All the preppies I know are materialists. Since Shawn dresses preppie, he must be a materialist."
>
> **Tip:** Particularly when arguers use all inclusive words like "all," "always," "never," "nobody," or "everybody," ask yourself if the premises and/or conclusions should have been presented in less stark terms. Do you know people who dress preppie who don't appear to be materialistic? If so, then perhaps Shawn is a part of the subset of non-materialistic preppies.

Action Points
A Checklist for Spotting Your Own Fallacies

(Ask these questions before turning in a paper, making a speech, or arguing with friends.)

- ✓ **How would your opponents respond to your argument?** What parts would they likely attack? Have you actually read the strongest arguments of your opponents and considered their side? Is there a way to strengthen your weak arguments?

- ✓ **How would your argument look as a syllogism or line of argument?** Do you have adequate evidence for your premises? Does your conclusion flow logically from your premises?

- ✓ **Is your conclusion presented with the degree of certitude that's warranted by the evidence?** (Be especially cautious if you use all-encompassing words like "always," "never," "everyone," etc.)

- ✓ **Are there certain types of fallacies that you often fall for?** (Consider how professors responded to your earlier papers or speeches, and how your friends respond to your arguments.)

Flex Your Neurons!
Pursuing the Point of Know Return
Can You Connect an Argument with Its Fallacy?

(Each page is self-contained, so don't try to connect between pages. Connect to more than one argument or fallacy if you feel they legitimately connect.)

Fallacies	Arguments
Ad Hominem	"Avid health advocates blow out their knees by their 50s by running marathons."
Affirming the Consequent	"I don't believe anything he says because he's a biased political liberal."
Appealing to Extremes	"We know global warming is true because a number of great scientists assure us it's true."
Argument From Authority	**Premise 1:** If I get the flu, I'll be nauseated. **Premise 2:** I'm nauseated. **Conclusion:** Therefore, I have the flu.
Argument from Ignorance	"Active euthanasia is morally acceptable. It is a decent, ethical thing to help another human being escape suffering through death."
Band Wagon	"Everybody I know uses Meth, so it can't be that bad."
Begging the Question	"The death penalty can't be right. Have you seen a person die in an electric chair?"
Bifurcation	"Nobody can prove that my client was at the scene of the crime, therefore he's innocent."
Emotional Appeals	"Of all the animals, only man is rational. No woman is a man. Therefore, no woman is rational."
Equivocation	"The president must be either stupid or misinformed to make that decision."

Fallacy of Exclusion	"You either support Israelis in Palestine, or you're an anti-Semite."
False Dilemma	"Allowing this controversial artwork in our place of business is really about guaranteeing our freedoms, in this case our freedom of expression."
Faulty Analogy	"Killing in war is legalized murder."
Glittering Generality	You flunked Calculus. Possible reasons: 1. A psychological profile of both you and your professor might find that you have diametrically opposed learning styles. 2. Aliens kept you from sleeping before the final exam, questioning you incessantly. 3. You admit to never doing your homework and seldom attending lectures. ______ _____ would prefer the third, more simple and obvious explanation.
Hasty Generalization	"Watch those women drivers. From my observations, they're always thinking of something other than their driving."
Inconsistency	"The war in Afghanistan is nothing more than a modern day Vietnam war."
Moral Equivalency	"Our brains developed, not to think logically, but for survival in an agrarian society. Therefore, we can't trust our reasoning."
Non Sequitur	"Most Hollywood stars have terrible marriages. Just read the tabloids."
Failing Occam's Razor	"Patrick always smiled at me and was so respectful. He couldn't have burned down the gym. "

Post Hoc Ergo Propter Hoc	"If we allow more restrictions on purchasing guns, this will be followed by further restrictions and eventually the government will confiscate all our guns."
Red Herring	"Jack emailed his professor that he missed class due to a bad case of the flu and that he would bring a doctor's note. The next day, the professor announced in class that he would not excuse Jack's absence because his excuse was that he didn't feel like coming" (not mentioning the flu or the note).
Reductionism	"The problem with our economy can be reduced to two words: trade imbalance."
Slippery Slope	"Ever since his trip to India, Alfred's been sick. Obviously, he caught something in India that our doctors can't diagnose."
Stacking the Deck	"All the preppies I've ever met are materialists. Since Shawn dresses preppie, he must be a materialist."
Straw Man	"Sure, the mercury found in seafood is often unsafe, but fishermen have to make a living like everyone else."
Sweeping Generalization	"Capitalism inevitably leads to a violent revolution by the proletariat. These fifty examples from history prove it."

Making It More Personal
Practical Takeaways

What are one or more ideas provoked by this chapter that you can apply to help you think more critically?

____

____

____

What are one or more ideas that you can apply to help you think more creatively?

____

____

____

What else do you want to make sure you don't forget?

____

____

____

Recommended Trails
For the Incurably Curious and Adventurous

1. For each fallacy that's still unclear to you, search it on Google to find more explanations and illustrations.

2. Watch or read some advertisements. Write out their lines of argument or put them in syllogisms. Do any of them fall for one of the above fallacies?

CHAPTER 12

THEY EITHER FAIL TO RECOGNIZE FALLACIES, OR MISAPPLY THE ONES THEY KNOW

"Read not to contradict and confute; nor to believe and take for granted; nor to find talk and discourse, but to weigh and consider."

— Francis Bacon, *Of Studies*

WARNING: Learning fallacies can be fatal to your argumentation and detrimental to your relationships. For these reasons, I teach logical fallacies with a great deal of hesitation. It's a bit like selling firearms to a person with no training in how to use them. I'd hate to be known as one who arms Internet trolls.*

***Troll =** a participant in social media who delights in haughtily slamming other people's positions before fully understanding either their position or the context of the discussion.

So before I present a large list of fallacies, I'll acquaint you with a particularly pernicious type of fallacious reasoning that's running rampant on the Internet, but which is strangely absent from lists of fallacies. I call it "The Fallacy Fallacy."

The Fallacy Fallacy: Debunking Debunking

I often read comments on blog posts or articles or Facebook discussions which accuse the writer of committing a specific logical fallacy and thus declaring the argument thoroughly debunked, typically with an air of arrogant finality. While the debunker may feel quite smug, intelligent participants consider him quite sophomoric.* In reality, he's typically failed to even remotely understand the argument, much less apply the fallacy in a way that's relevant to the discussion.

***Sophomoric =** a statement that is immature and poorly informed, but is spoken with overconfidence and conceit. The word is a composite of two Greek words meaning "wise" and "fool."

Surely this fallacy deserves a proper name and should be listed with other fallacies. Thus I'll define "The Fallacy Fallacy" as "Improperly connecting a fallacy with an argument, so that the argument is errantly presumed to be debunked."[1]

Don't be a troll. Here are a few ways people misapply fallacies, thus committing "The Fallacy Fallacy":

1. They misunderstand the fallacy.

"YOU'RE ALWAYS ARGUING WITH JAMIE, WHICH IS OBVIOUSLY *AD HOMINEM*." (Trolls delight in using all caps, confusing *louder* with *smarter*.) If the person was actually arguing against Jamie's arguments, rather than putting Jamie down as a person, then the arguments weren't *ad hominem* at all.

2. They fail to appreciate nuance. (They understand the fallacy, but apply it errantly.)

Someone quotes Albert Einstein to bolster his argument. "THAT'S AN APPEAL TO AUTHORITY!" shouts the troll. But citing authorities isn't always fallacious. If a person cites Einstein concerning a question of relativity theory, then Einstein is a legitimate authority. Thus, quoting him can be a legitimate part of an argument, although it's typically not a slam dunk in itself. While arguments concerning establishing facts should be argued on the basis of the evidence, in many cases citing authorities can help to substantiate the evidence.[2]

3. They assume a thorough debunking when there's typically more to the argument.

While trolls are celebrating their "brilliant" comments with a victory dance and a handful of Skittles, their opponents are often typing a clarification that makes the Trolls' comments irrelevant. We simply must take the time to thoroughly understand the arguments we're evaluating.

Making Arguments More Fruitful

For those who sincerely want to learn from one another by hashing out issues, consider this: Trolls "flame" opponents by either calling them morons or presenting their arguments dogmatically, as if they have crushed their opponents. If you're concerned about the truth, seek more to understand than to demonstrate your brilliance. To accomplish this, *suggest* rather than *slam*; express tentativeness rather than dogmatic finality; ask questions rather than accuse.

Does it in any way weaken a counterargument to word it in a cautious, humble manner, such as: "At first glance your argument appears to be an unwarranted appeal to authority. Are you really saying that your position is correct solely because Einstein believes it as well?"

In this way, the opponent is more likely to respond in a reasonable manner and you save face in case you took the comment out of context or otherwise misunderstood it.

Benjamin Franklin on Fruitful Argumentation

Franklin was one of the most influential people in American history. He learned a lesson early in life which he considered of such significance that he discussed it at some length in his autobiography. He describes learning Socratic argumentation, which he delighted to use in humiliating his opponents. (As an annoying ass during this phase of a few years, he was a predecessor to the modern day Internet troll.)

But over time, he realized that this method failed to either persuade others or to help him learn from them. Rather, it disgusted people. So he changed his method of argumentation.

In Franklin's own words, he discovered the value of:

> "never using, when I advanced anything that may possibly be disputed, the words *certainly*, *undoubtedly*, or any other that give the air of positiveness [meaning "dogmatism"] to an opinion; but rather say, *I conceive or apprehend a thing to be so and so*; *it appears to me*, or *I should think it so or so*, for such and such reasons; or *I imagine it to be so*; or *it is so, if I am not mistaken*. This habit, I believe, has been of great advantage to me when I have had occasion to inculcate my opinions, and persuade men into measures that I have been from time to time engaged in promoting…." (italics his; brackets mine)[3]

As a result, Franklin became a skilled negotiator and persuader, allowing him to help start America's library system, organize firefighters, run a successful printing business, improve our postal service, negotiate with the French to aid us in the Revolutionary War, and assist in finalizing and adopting the Declaration of Independence, just to name a few of an astonishing array of accomplishments.[4]

Some Helpful Ways to Organize Fallacies

The plethora of known fallacies can be quite unwieldy, so let's first of all look at some helpful ways of classifying them. In this way, when you sense an argument is invalid but can't remember the name of the specific fallacy, at least you might be able to identify the category in order to better evaluate or research it. (Example: "That sounds like a fallacy of definition.")

Although no single categorization scheme has become standard, you'll find some of the categories (such as "formal" and "informal") used widely.[5]

Aristotle

Aristotle was perhaps the first to categorize logical fallacies in his *De Sophisticis Elenchis* (*Sophistical Refutations*). He lists 13 fallacies under two categories: **Verbal** (those depending on language) and **Material** (those not depending on language). In modern times, those building on

Aristotle's two divisions often add a third: **Logical or Formal**—fallacies that violate the formal rules of the syllogism.

Philosopher J. L. Mackie

Mackie divided fallacies into:

Fallacies in a Strict Sense - invalid forms of deductive reasoning; the conclusion doesn't logically follow from the premises.

Formal Fallacies - The conclusion is invalid because of the argument's form. Example: Exerting the consequent—If there are too many cooks, there's chaos in the kitchen. There's chaos in the kitchen, therefore there are too many cooks. (If p then q. q, therefore p)

Informal Fallacies - The conclusion is invalid for reasons other than its form. (Example: Using vague or ambiguous terms.)

Fallacies in Nondeductive Reasoning and in Observation - errors in inductively reasoning from evidence to a conclusion or hypothesis.

Induction and Confirmation - example: *post hoc ergo propter hoc* - the fact that event "b" followed event "a" doesn't absolutely prove that event "a" *caused* event "b".

Analogy - A weak analogy, one that has few or trivial points of resemblance, may have no evidential value at all.

Classification - Example: A company may argue that all people classified as autistic are unemployable. Yet, autistic people vary greatly in their skills, so that highly functioning autistics, or those wrongly categorized, may be overlooked.

Statistics - Example: If students from City High School outperform students from County High School on standardized tests, this doesn't necessarily imply City High School has better teachers. Perhaps administrators skew the scores, or one district has more high risk students.

Probability - Example: Although the probability of flipping a coin five times and getting heads every time is low, that doesn't mean that if you got heads four times in a row, it's very unlikely that you'll get heads in the next flip. The odds are still 50/50.

Observation - Example: Often what we observe is skewed by what we want or expect to observe.

Fallacies in Discourse - The argument fails because of some reason other than invalid deductive reasoning or arguing from evidence.

Inconsistency - You can't have it both ways.

"*Petitio Principii*" - Including your conclusion in your premises (aka begging the question or arguing in a circle).

***A Priori* Fallacies** - Bringing to the argument unfounded preconceptions that influence the conclusion.

"*Ignoratio Elenchi*" - Missing the point: An argument concerning something that was never meant, in the context of the argument, to be proven.

Fallacies of Interrogation - Demanding a narrow and specific answer to questions that demand broader answers. Example: "Answer yes or no: Have you stopped beating your wife?"

Fallacies in Explanation and Definition - Example: using the same word in two different ways in an argument, thus invalidating the argument.[6]

Historian David Hackett Fischer

In Fischer's instructive and delightful book, *Historians' Fallacies,*[7] he discusses 112 fallacies under 11 categories. Note that these apply far beyond professional historians. Whenever we blog about an event, summarize our family vacation on Facebook, or write that first high school paper on "What I Did for My Summer Vacation," we're telling history, and risk committing these fallacies. Here are Fischer's categories:

Question-framing - Historians begin their research by asking one or more questions. If these questions are vague or ill-conceived, they will yield the wrong answers. Example: asking a complex question and expecting a simple answer.

Factual Verification - Failure to rigorously employ the best methods for verifying historical data.

Factual Significance - Historians can't report every fact from a period of history; they must be selective. If they select based on the wrong criteria, their conclusions will likely be wrong as well.

Generalization - Improper statistical reasoning from historical data. Example: Drawing a general conclusion from an insufficient sampling of data.

Narration - Historians gather threads of historical data and weave them into stories. Yet, "nothing but the facts" is often at odds with great storytelling, which assigns feelings and even time sequences that may not be warranted by the historical data.

Causation - Example: The reductive fallacy reduces a complex historical cause to a simplistic one.

Motivation - Historians often assign motives without sufficient evidence; for example, assuming that a Roman Emperor thinks, reacts, and is motivated by the same things that motivate a middle-aged academic historian at Berkeley.

Composition - Historians tend to study and write about groups, or individuals as part of groups, whether the groups be social, religious, national, ideological, cliques, castes or economic. One fallacy of composition is assuming that the character of one member is shared by the rest of the group.

False Analogy - Example: People often reason from a partial analogy to declare there's an exact correspondence; but in reality, analogies are seldom exactly parallel.

Semantical Distortion - Problems with unclear or imprecise prose. For example, the failure to clarify definitions of terms.

Substantive Distraction - The argument shifts the reader's attention to issues that are irrelevant to the discussion.

While categorization schemes are helpful for getting an overview of types of fallacies, none seem to be without their downsides. For example, some fallacies seem to fit snugly into multiple categories.

A Great Big List of Fallacies

In my first Appendix, I list a great number of fallacies. I don't recommend trying to memorize them. Rather, familiarize yourself with each of them so that in the future, when you run across an argument that doesn't sound quite right, you can return to the list to search for a fallacy that might apply. If you're reading this for a class, your teacher or professor may single out certain fallacies that they deem the most important or the most frequently abused in literature and the media.

Conclusion

There are many ways to go wrong in our arguments. Some are a bit technical. But by familiarizing ourselves with fallacies, learning to apply them correctly, and discussing disagreements in a civil and humble manner, we can learn from each other and mutually come closer to the truth.

Flex Your Neurons!
Pursuing the Point of Know Return

1. What do you think motivates trolls to flame people in social media or to start arguments in social settings?

2. How do trolls hinder the process of finding truth?

3. How can we keep from behaving like trolls?

4. Write your own examples (lines of reasoning that contain the fallacy) of five fallacies (from the list in the appendix) that especially interest you.

Making It More Personal
Practical Takeaways

What are one or more ideas provoked by this chapter that you can apply to help you think more critically?

___

___

___

What are one or more ideas that you can apply to help you think more creatively?

___

___

___

What else do you want to make sure you don't forget?

___

___

___

Recommended Trail
For the Incurably Curious and Adventurous

For any fallacies that seem unclear or are of special interest to you, Google them to find other explanations and illustrations.

SECTION FOUR

WHY DO BRILLIANT PEOPLE BELIEVE NONSENSE? BECAUSE THEY JUMP TO CONCLUSIONS

CHAPTER 13

THEY DRAW CONCLUSIONS FROM INADEQUATE EVIDENCE

"To act without clear understanding, to form habits without investigation, to follow a path all one's life without knowing where it really leads—such is the behavior of the multitude."

— Mencius

"I fully believe that more than one-half of the failures in diagnosis are due to hasty or unmethodical examinations. Say to yourselves that you will not jump at a conclusion, but in each instance will make a thorough and painstaking physical examination, free from prejudice, and your success is assured."[1]

— Dr. William Mayo, one of the founders of the Mayo Clinic

Kicked Out, Homeless, But Taken In

Last year I read a bittersweet story that resonated with many and prompted an outpouring of love that restores people's faith in humanity. According to the news, an 18-year-old boy admitted to his parents that he was bisexual. They responded by heartlessly kicking him out of the house, taking his car, and confiscating his life savings. They even called the police to make sure there was no trouble.

Where would he live? Without money, how would he continue college? Without a car, how would he get to work?

Fortunately, a concerned couple welcomed him into their home and set up an online account for people to donate money. Over the next few days, over four hundred people, the vast majority almost certainly strangers, donated over ten thousand dollars. Over the following months, donations grew to over twenty-five thousand dollars.

Yet, a few things struck me as odd about the story as reported in a popular online news source; so I marked it to return for potential updates. First, the only two sources were apparently the young man and the couple who took him in. Yet, it was reported as if it were established fact (e.g., "A boy was thrown out" rather than "A boy claimed he was thrown out.") There was no indication that anyone had interviewed the policeman, read the police report, talked to neighbors, or talked to the young man's family. (Perhaps I was a bit skeptical because our family has on occasion taken in "homeless" teens with gut-wrenching stories, only to find that a phone call to the parents can yield a much different story.)

Yet, despite the paucity of evidence, the comments below the article (over 1,500 of them) virtually all accepted the report at face value. In addition to reassuring the young man of their support, readers viciously ripped apart the parents, horrified that anyone could treat their own flesh and blood in such a heartless manner. They referred to the parents as "low lifes", "pathetic haters," "monsters," and the "parents from hell." Some sought contact information so that they could directly give them a piece of their minds.

So why were readers judging the parents without hearing their side? And there was money involved—lots of money—giving incentive to possibly skew or hide facts to appeal to people's emotions.

The article was picked up by many other news sources, both nationally and internationally, but some reported it more tentatively, as "according to a teen" rather than reporting it as established fact.

Later, additional information surfaced. Under one of the secondary reports, a neighbor wrote in anonymously (explaining he wanted to guard the parents' location and privacy) to say he had seen the entire event and that the son's report was largely fabricated. According to the neighbor, the event wasn't about the child's sexual preference at all. The parents were laid-back people who had known for years that their son was bisexual and tried hard to love and make wise decisions regarding their son. The neighbor painted a picture of an angry, out-of-control teen who had been given every imaginable chance to act responsibly at work and at home, but refused to cooperate.

Months later, the original article was updated with a report claiming to be from the young man's father, who again gave a completely different take on the event than the son. According to him, he'd know that his son was bisexual for years. That wasn't the issue. The argument was over such issues as the son's drinking and driving, his issues at work, and his posting inappropriate content on the web that could jeopardize his future employment. Things had gotten so bad that they instituted some restrictions about driving and the Internet that he refused to follow. He pitched a fit. They didn't kick him out; he chose to leave. They didn't take away his transportation; he threw the keys at them. He assaulted his stepmom and the policeman suggested that she could press charges, but she didn't want to hurt his future job opportunities.[2]

So now we know the truth…or do we?

Imagine that you're on a jury, trying to decide what happened in this case. So far, here's our evidence:

- A young man claimed he was taken advantage of.

- A couple took him in, who said they believed his story.
- Someone claiming to be a neighbor said it didn't happen that way.
- Someone claiming to be the father said that the original story was largely lies.

My Conclusion?

It's a family squabble. I don't even remotely know the family members. I don't personally know anyone who saw the events. I know nothing about their history or character. I've never seen the police report. I have no decent evidence to help me decide who to believe, if any of them.

Yet, most readers of the original report apparently naively assumed that the first version of the story was true, on the basis of virtually no evidence, and many acted on that assumption, publically condemning the parents and enriching the son. In this case, a large segment of people drew conclusions from insufficient evidence.

How can we move from naïve to wise in our evaluation of people's claims? Here are some clues from this story.

From Naïve to Wise by Focusing on the Evidence

1. Read and listen with a healthy dose of skepticism.

Those who've taken the time to get to know at least a dozen people in their lifetimes are aware that people skew events for all kinds of reasons. Perhaps the young man has anger issues and skewed the events to get revenge or to get a place to stay or to get money. Perhaps the parents skewed the events to help them save face. Perhaps the neighbor was pushed by the parents to write an anonymous reply, or held a grudge against the teen. The fact is, we simply don't know. In this case, we have insufficient evidence to draw not only a firm conclusion, but even a tentative conclusion.

So why did 1500+ people confidently write responses that condemn the parents and support the child? Why are people giving money when there's so little evidence as to what happened? It seems that in many cases, even bright, literate people allow themselves to be swayed before the evidence is in. We're especially vulnerable if we identify with someone's plight and our emotions hijack our reasoning.

The wisdom of Solomon warn us: "The fool believes everything, but the sensible man considers his steps."

So when you initially read a report or hear a friend relate an event, don't be naïve and accept it unthinkingly.

- Even if it comes from a trusted friend, run it through your thinker. Could she have been mistaken? Could she have misunderstood her sources?
- Even if it's reported in the *New York Times*, run it through your thinker. Did the reporter use good sources? Did he get input from all relevant sides?

Think!

a. Imagine that this case was brought to court and you were hired to investigate. Who would you interview? What other evidence might you gather?

b. Imagine that you're the senior editor at the news source that first ran the article. The reporter hands you the article for editing. How would you respond? What would you tell the reporter about fact checking and integrity in journalism? What guidelines would you suggest to set a higher standard for factual reporting?

For some people, the cost of jumping to a conclusion results in the loss of a twenty dollar donation or a few wasted moments writing a comment. For others, it leads to investing their life savings with a con artist, joining a cult, or marrying a scoundrel. So don't naively take everything at face value. Consider the evidence.

2. Demand a sufficient number of cases or witnesses.

The news story above was based upon insufficient testimony. A young man told a heartwrenching story; a couple apparently believed it, and their testimonies provided the sole foundation for the article.

So how many testimonies do we need to provide sufficient evidence to believe a report? How many studies do we need to confirm a theory? Well, this very much depends upon the events or theories being verified. The question "How much evidence is sufficient evidence?" is often debated in various fields of study. This is yet another reason to bring along a healthy bit of skepticism to each lecture we hear, each video we watch, each article or study we read.

Sometimes, one confirmed experiment or observation provides sufficient evidence to overturn an established theory. In this regard, scientists and philosophers speak of Black Swans, a term which has an interesting history. In 16th century London, Europeans had seen only white swans. Since hundreds and thousands of white swans had been observed, they concluded that black swans didn't exist. So when speaking of something that could never happen, they'd say it was "like a black swan," meaning impossible.

"Have you ever met an honest politician?" a Londoner might ask an acquaintance. She might sarcastically reply, "They're about as common as a black swan."

But when Dutch explorer Willem de Vlamingh visited Western Australia in 1697, he was amazed to find black swans. In this case, one confirmed observation was enough to overturn an established theory.[3]

In the case of the Black Swan, an absolute negative was being claimed—"There are no black swans." In such a case, all you need to verify is one black swan to topple the theory. But in other cases, we need more or different types of evidence.

Before we look at other principles of sifting evidence, let's look at another example.

How Many Hours of Practice Yields Peak Performance?

In the *SF Gate*, the Pulitzer Prize Winning site that accompanies the San Francisco Chronicle, an acclaimed photographer suggested to up-and-coming artists:

> "Always remember what Malcolm Gladwell said: 'Anybody can be a master of anything if they put in 10,000 hours.'"[4]

This advice has been repeated over and over in recent years, by educators to their students, by coaches to their athletes, by parents to their children. It has astounding implications. If accurate, it has a huge appeal to teachers, parents and overachievers:

- It simplifies **teachers'** responsibilities, putting the onus of responsibility on the student. If it's true that any student can learn most anything, then a teacher can say to a failing student: "Your poor grade in math is your own fault. You simply need to put in the hours of study."
- It gives competitive **parents** a vision and a game plan for training an exceptional child. "If we chain her to the piano starting at age five and get her into an elite music school, she might play Carnegie Hall by age 20!"
- It gives **high achievers** a road map for success: "If I want to be a tennis star or golf pro or astrophysicist, I simply have to put in the hours of practice. I think I'll start today!"

On the negative side, if this claim is inaccurate, much harm could result.

- Parents may infuriate and alienate their children by imposing unrealistic expectations. If some children simply can't learn Algebra, e.g., because of some innate disability, yet parents force them to study it for hours a day, children will understandably become discouraged.
- Adults who catch a passion for a sport or hope to develop a skill might assume they've missed their chance to put in sufficient hours. Many people want to become writers in their adult years. But if they've got a full-time job and family responsibilities, can they really hope to put in 10,000 hours of practice?

- Students who have a poor aptitude for certain subjects may find themselves marginalized. If influential educators believe that "the future belongs to technology," they might require everyone to achieve an unrealistic mastery of math and science, assuming that anyone who puts in the hours can achieve such mastery. Those who flunk would be dismissed as lazy—unwilling to put in the hours.

In my life's work, it's been extremely important to know whether I can master any skill I choose, or whether I need to continually assess my strengths and weaknesses and put my time into developing the skills I have the most potential to both enjoy and master. These two life strategies can lead to very different paths, which can result in either frustration or fulfillment, depending on which is correct:

> **Life Path #1** - Decide what I want to do (choose anything) and put in the hours of preparation.
>
> **Life Path #2** - Evaluate my strengths and passions, using them to narrow down my life goals.

With its importance in mind, let's take a closer look at that statement that advice-givers have been handing out so freely of late:

> "Anybody can be a master of anything if they put in 10,000 hours."

First, we should note that Gladwell probably never said those exact words. He certainly didn't say it in the book that popularized it—*Outliers*. He discusses "The 10,000 - Hour Rule" in chapter two. Since this issue is important to all of us, especially to the little girl who's been chained to her piano by her overachieving mom, let's try to understand exactly what Gladwell said and evaluate the evidence he presents.

> **Tip**
>
> As you read the following, think through it yourself. After all, this is an important topic. Do you agree or disagree with each point? Does it jive with your life experiences and the life experiences of your friends and family?

Gladwell's Evidence in Chapter Two of *Outliers*

Exhibit 1: Several people achieved extraordinary success through a lot of practice.

Bill Joy was one of the most important movers and shakers in the computer revolution. A math whiz (he aced the math portion of the S.A.T.), he entered the University of Michigan at age 16 and fell hopelessly in love with computer programming. Fortunately, the school had one of the world's foremost computer science programs, complete with a unique setup to allow students to practice their programming. (People didn't have personal computers in those days, making it difficult to practice programming, since students had to share time connecting remotely with huge, million dollar mainframe computers.) He entered the computer industry at just the right time, put in an estimated 10,000 hours of programming, became a fabulous programmer, and the rest is history.

Gladwell reinforces this story with the stories of super-successful people such as Bill Gates, The Beatles and Mozart.

Gladwell's Conclusion: Bill Joy succeeded by taking 1) his raw ability and 2) unique opportunity and 3) practicing for an insane number of hours.[5] The stories of Bill Gates, Mozart, and others reinforce this pattern.

Reflections on Exhibit 1: This is an extremely small sampling to draw a general conclusion from (think: the fallacy of "overgeneralization" from our previous section). Yet he sees the examples as more than mere illustrations of a truth. He proposes that his stories of the Beatles and Bill Gates are "tests" of the idea that "the ten-thousand-hour rule" is "a general rule of success."[6]

Note that the cases cited were all people who seemed to have an extraordinary interest in and innate ability to master their fields. Granted, they may well illustrate that, even if you're gifted, you'd be wise to practice for tons of hours to become truly great in certain fields.

But what does this tell us about people who, after a few years of pursuing music, seem to be rather ordinary in their potential? And what of those who have disabilities associated with music? Is it wise for a tone deaf, rhythm-challenged, clumsy-fingered five-year-old to aspire to Carnegie Hall by age 20, committing herself to putting in her 10,000 hours to make it happen? Or should the parents, after a year of frustration and dismal progress, unchain her from the piano and allow her to explore some of the thousands of other potential strengths and interests?

Perhaps in this case the parents should consider W.C. Fields' advice (mentioned earlier in the book):

> "If at first you don't succeed, try, try again. Then quit. There's no point in being a damn fool about it."

But many of us cringe at Fields' advice. It seems so un-American. We want to believe that anybody can do anything she aspires to. But what if the evidence simply doesn't bear this out?

So how does Gladwell address this critical issue: the importance of innate talent?

Exhibit 2: The more psychologists study the careers of the gifted, "the smaller the role innate talent seems to play and the bigger the role of preparation seems to play."

Here Gladwell cites a study. Psychologist K. Anders Ericsson and a couple of his colleagues studied violinists at Berlin's elite Academy of Music. They divided students into three groups: 1) The stars (elites who might become world-class soloists) 2) Those who were "good," but not great 3) The not-so-good, who should probably shoot for teaching music in public schools rather than performing.

They then asked each group how much they practiced. All started playing at about the age of five. In their earliest years, they all practiced about the same amount: two to three hours per week. But around age eight, the eventual stars separated themselves from the pack by increasing their hours per week:

- Age Nine: six hours
- Age Twelve: eight hours
- Age Fourteen: sixteen hours
- Age Twenty: over thirty hours per week

Thus, by age twenty, the stars had practiced ten thousand hours, the good students eight thousand hours, the not-quite-so-good just over four thousand hours.

The researchers then studied professional pianists and found the same pattern, accumulating ten thousand hours by the age of twenty.

Significantly, there were no "naturals" who made it to the top without massive practice. Nor did they find students who put in the hours but failed to achieve mastery.[7]

Gladwell's Conclusion:

> "...performing a complex task requires a critical minimum level of practice.... In fact, researchers have settled on what they believe is the magic number for true expertise: ten thousand hours."[8]

While innate talent has its place, according to Gladwell, its role is less than we once thought, with research arguing against "the primacy of talent."[9]

Exhibit 3: Gladwell quotes Daniel Levitin, a neurologist, to reinforce this view:

> "The emerging picture from such studies is that ten thousand hours of practice is required to achieve the level of mastery associated with being a world-class expert—in anything." "In study after study, of composers, basketball players, fiction writers, ice skaters, concert pianists, chess players, master criminals, and what have you, this number comes up again and again."
>
> "...no one has yet found a case in which true world-class expertise was accomplished in less time. It seems that it takes the brain this long to assimilate all that it needs to know to achieve true mastery."[10]

My Positive Reflections

First of all, for the positive. I love Malcolm Gladwell's writing style! If academics would study his style of writing and learn from his ability to put obtuse studies into prose that non-academics delight to read, more academics would be directly impacting the public.

Second, we need generalists like Gladwell, who can take studies from various fields and show how they impact us. The studies he cites and the points he makes, even those I disagree with, never fail to stimulate my thinking. Too many academics, in my opinion, are captives of their specialty, unable to relate their specialized knowledge to the typical problems we face, which often requires drawing from several areas of specialization.

Third, I think his main point is well-taken. (Let's not fall for the fallacy of throwing out the baby with the bathwater.) Here's my take away from Gladwell's chapter, as I might express it to my students:

> "If you want to become great at something, put in the hours. Nobody plays electric guitar like Yngwie Malmsteen or acoustic guitar like Tommy Emmanuel without practicing obsessively. Don't think for a minute that coasting through English classes, relying on your innate talent, will make you a great writer. If you want to be a truly great writer, scientist, nurse, musician, or business leader, put in the hours!"

Two Questionable Conclusions

Yet, I question two of Gladwell's conclusions. He states the first quite clearly. The second he presents more guardedly; but some of his readers have shouted it from the housetops.

> **Conclusion #1** - "Ten thousand hours is the magic number of greatness."[11]
>
> **Conclusion #2** - Raw talent isn't so important. It's the number of hours you put into it. (He doesn't put it exactly this way, but implies it. He writes "…the closer psychologists look at the careers of the gifted, the smaller the role innate talent seems to play…."[12] He also refers approvingly to those researchers who "argue against the primacy of talent."[13])

Recall that in this chapter I'm showing how smart people draw conclusions based upon inadequate evidence. In my opinion, those bright coaches and educators and parents who routinely repeat these claims have built their recommendations on a shaky foundation. Here are several of my problems with Gladwell's conclusions, each of which serve to elucidate how to spot insufficient evidence. Compare them to your own evaluation.

Think!

Some people turn off their brains when someone critiques another view, assuming a thorough debunking is in progress. Instead, critique my critique! You might agree with some of my contentions and disagree with others. Perhaps I'm guilty of the "fallacy fallacy," whereby I accuse someone else of fallacious reasoning, but argue fallaciously myself.

Questions for Evaluating the Amount and Quality of Evidence

1. Does the line of evidence warrant the conclusions?

Here's how his argument seems to line up:

1. Two studies found that talented musicians who practiced more outperformed talented musicians who practiced less.

2. According to the two studies, 10,000 hours was the magic number of hours that the top musicians devoted to practice.

3. A neurologist stated that this magic number has turned up in many fields (basketball, chess, etc.).

4. The neurologist claims there are no exceptions to the 10,000 hour rule.

5. Gladwell states that research is leading us to see innate talent as less and less of a differentiator.

6. Stories of several highly successful people show that they achieved mastery in their fields by massive amounts of experience.

Conclusion: If you want to master a complex skill, put in the 10,000 hours. Raw potential is overrated.

Laying this out as a line of evidence reveals significant weaknesses. Most dramatically, two studies aren't typically enough to draw a conclusion in this subject area. It isn't as simple as disproving that all swans are white. To draw any general conclusions about the 10,000 hours, I'd expect Gladwell to cite a host of studies and show me some significant literature reviews (studies that summarize the results of the relevant studies).

After all, surely hundreds—perhaps thousands—of studies have examined what differentiates the best students from mediocre students, top quarterbacks from average ones, top fighter pilots from lesser ones, how disabilities impact students, how practice impacts various types of students, etc. Do those studies unanimously conclude that it's only (or even primarily) the amount of hours that makes the difference? Are there truly no exceptions to the rule?

The paucity of studies cited makes his research appear to be cherry-picking (picking the studies that agree with your thesis and ignoring the rest.) When he speaks of a developing consensus, and the neurologist speaks of the 10,000 hours being proven out in many fields, we have to simply trust them. He points us to no research that supports such a consensus. As for the dramatic quote from the neurologist, as we saw in chapter two, we can find quotes from "experts" to support almost anything. Show us the research behind the quote if you want to convince us.

2. Do the conclusions jive with my experience?

One way to engage our higher level thinking is to reflect upon what we read and compare it with our own experiences. Our life experiences, although they may at first appear rather lame compared to professional, peer-reviewed research, often offer significant data that can help us evaluate scientific theories. When I read Gladwell's chapter, I first compared it to some of my own experiences.

First, reflections on my personal academic strengths and weaknesses don't jive with either of Gladwell's conclusions. I'm strong in my analytic and communication skills. Thus, skills such as exegesis, hermeneutics, deductive logic, math, and research come easily to me. Show me the principle once and I tend to quickly understand it and retain it. For other students, it may take twice as long to comprehend such subjects, and they may still find difficulty understanding, retaining and using them. Thus, it's conceivable that if it took me 5,000 hours to master a field related to my strengths, it might take another student 10,000 hours.

Reflecting on my academic *weaknesses*, I have a deplorable rote memory in certain disciplines. For example, foreign languages have been a particular struggle. In college, I studied well over three hours outside of class for each hour in class to memorize Greek paradigms and word lists. My accursed roommate, who apparently had a near photographic memory, could make A's by paying attention in class and reviewing for a few minutes after class. Imagine the difference in time it would take for each of us to master a language. If it took my roommate 5,000 hours to achieve fluency in Greek, it would in all likelihood take me 20,000 hours. In this case, the hours required to master a complex field differ wildly between me and my roommate. The 10,000 hour rule doesn't seem to apply at all.

At this point, defenders of the rule that "we can do anything that we practice for 10,000 hours" may admit that there are, of course, extremes which make exceptions to the rule. For example, we must take into account mental disabilities and profound academic strengths and weaknesses. And in sports, don't expect a three foot tall Oompa Loompa, even if he put in 10,000 hours, to become a professional basketball player.

But in admitting these extremes, aren't we saying that, at least in some cases, raw potential does indeed matter a lot? A legally blind person won't become an NFL referee, even if he puts in the 10,000 hours of practice.

So let's move beyond the extremes. Don't all of us fall somewhere on a spectrum between the extremes of photographic memory vs. hopelessly forgetful, social butterfly vs. social moron, tall vs. short, fast vs. slow, coordinated vs. clumsy? If the 10,000 hour rule doesn't work for a three foot tall Oompa Loompa training to play pro basketball, what about a four footer, or five footer or even six footer? (Those playing the forward position are almost always 6' 6" or taller.) And if we keep making exceptions, then doesn't the "rule" become meaningless, dying the death of a thousand qualifications?

3. Was the study well-designed to rule out alternative explanations?

Let's imagine that I wanted to design a study to test the hypothesis that innate talent isn't that important for piano players; rather, it's the hours of practice that matter. I might pick a totally random group of 100 five-year-olds who've never seen a piano and offer them piano lessons by the same teacher. Then I'd ask them to practice the same number of hours per week—no more, no less. If, after one, five and ten year evaluations, they all showed the same level of skill, this would support the theory that innate potential doesn't matter that much.

Comparing this imagined study to one of the studies cited by Gladwell, we realize that Gladwell's study was ill-designed to prove that innate talent isn't a strong differentiator.

One problem with the study is that it had to assume that the students all started with the same innate potential, so that the amount of practice would be the sole differentiator between the elite and non-elite players. Certainly all had potential, or they wouldn't have progressed as far as they did before their acceptance into the elite music school. But how could researchers know up front that all these started the school with the *same* potential, and that the differences in potential were not impacting their progress?

The researchers claimed that the *only* difference between the elites and the non-elites was the amount of time they put into practice. *But what if innate talent was impacting the number of hours they put into practice?*

Imagine that you practiced piano and did very well at the beginning stages—well enough to get you into a recognized music school. But as you were handed increasingly difficult pieces and were expected to not only get the notes right and memorize them, but to express emotion through your playing, it just didn't happen like it did for many others. No matter how much you practiced, others seemed to blossom while you fell behind. Your parents and teachers were also aware of your lack of progress, leading to less encouragement by them to pursue a solo career. In such a case, wouldn't you be tempted to do the minimum amount of practice and shoot for a teaching career rather than a solo career?

And if the opposite happened—the more difficult the pieces, the more you excelled beyond the others—don't you think that you might fall ever more in love with the piano, responding to the positive strokes by your teachers and parents and the applause at recitals, so that you begin to practice more and more?

In other words, the question of *why* they practiced more was never addressed by the study.

Without controlling for this critical question, we have no reason to conclude that, had the worst students simply upped their practice to equal that of the elite students, they would have been elite as well. Without answering this crucial question, the study would seem to tell us nothing about the impact of raw talent on superior performance.[14]

4. Did they consider other explanatory hypotheses?

Gladwell seems to assume that the cited studies keep repeating the "magic number" because it's the precise number of hours that the brain/muscles need.

Yet, perhaps there's another, equally reasonable explanation for the "magic number"—*there's only so much time you can put into a sport or hobby or skill before you reach the age of 20.* Even if you love something and obsess on it, you've only got so much time to obsess once you eat, sleep, sit in school for six hours a day, do enough homework to pass, take family vacations, visit Aunt Eleanor on Sunday afternoon, and do chores.

So you're 14 years old and practice football for a couple of hours after school each day. On weekends, you throw the ball with your friends for about four hours. That's about 14 hours per week. During the summer you take in a football camp and get more hours to play on your average day, which brings up the average to about 16 hours per week. How much will you have practiced by the age of 20? Multiply it out and you've practiced 10,000 hours, precisely the amount of time that the excellent violinists practiced.

There are also physical limitations. Even if I'm obsessed with the piano, my fingers need time to rest and my muscles need time to repair. The same goes for weightlifting, tennis, football, or hockey.

Thus, there are only so many hours available to obsess on something before age 20, even if we absolutely love it. If that number is around 10,000 hours, then perhaps "the magic number" is merely telling us how many hours people who are in love with something obsess on it, rather than how many hours are required to master a field.

5. Did the subjects of the study well-represent the populations to which the conclusions are being applied?

No. Gladwell concluded that 10,000 hours is the magic number, implying that it works its magic for everyone. But the subjects of the studies all showed exceptional innate talent from the start. His personal examples included Bill Gates, The Beatles, and Bill Joy, all of whom, Gladwell admits, began with exceptional raw talent in their fields. The study he cites dealt with piano players who were good enough to be accepted into an elite music school,[15] again indicating potential that others might not have.

In other words, the studies may tell us nothing about how a person with normal potential in the field, or a person with learning disabilities, or an Oompa Loompa trying to make the basketball team, would progress with 10,000 hours of practice. Nobody tested them.

6. Does further research yield different conclusions?

- **Research into counterexamples**

Gladwell gives the example of the Beatles gaining massive experience during their time performing in Hamburg. By putting in their hours playing as a group, they gelled and were able to perform at the level that made them one of the most successful bands in history.

Yet, their drummer during those Hamburg days was Pete Best. Even after all that practice, George Martin at their record label decided that they needed a new drummer. The other members of the Beatles agreed. According to them, Pete wasn't good enough. They replaced him with Ringo Starr.[16]

So if it's the hours that matter, and not so much the talent, why wasn't Pete Best good enough after putting in all the hours at Hamburg?

Joshua Foer considered himself to have an average memory, but spent a year improving his memory under competitive memorizers and a memory researchers. One expert said that if he devoted an hour a day, six days a week to studying memory techniques, he could place in the top three of the U.S. memory championship in a year. He took the challenge and won the event a year later. That's 365 hours of practice, far less than 10,000 hours.[17]

- **Research on strengths**

Studies of over two million people in the workplace by the Gallup Organization found that people vary greatly in their potential. These studies indicate that a major key to success is to discover our strengths, develop them, and find meaningful work that utilizes our strengths. Since our greatest potential for improvement is in our area of strength (according to strength advocates), they don't recommend knocking yourself out trying to master a field that's in an area of weakness. It's not just about practice, according to Gallup's research; it's about practicing in those areas where you have the greatest potential.[18]

- **Research on weaknesses**

Research indicates that while some have inherent weaknesses serious enough to be labeled "disabilities," many if not most of us find ourselves far enough on a spectrum to be considered weak.[19] My problems with rote memory jive with this research. Although I've never been diagnosed with a disability, I'm far enough over in the spectrum for poor rote memory to realize I don't need spend my life trying to achieve fluency in multiple foreign languages. Putting 10,000 hours per language into trying to achieve fluency would likely be frustrating and fruitless for me.

Conclusion

We have a tendency to jump to quick, obvious conclusions. We read about a boy being kicked out by his parents. We conclude: "His parents are heartless morons." Five of our students are flunking algebra. We conclude, "They're obviously not studying enough. If they put in the hours, they'd be mastering the subject."

But truth isn't always so obvious, and it often can't be wrapped up in the tidy packages that appeal to us. So don't be naïve. Think. Reflect on the evidence. If it's an important topic, think long and hard; discuss it with friends, and dig into the research. It just might make the difference between success and failure, fulfillment and frustration.

Think Different
Tips on Achieving High Performance

Studies of high performing people[20] find that while the amount of time practicing is indeed a factor, other recommendations include:

1) **Get immediate feedback on your performance.** Study great golfers. Typically, they're still getting regular input from top golf coaches. Don't trust your own judgment; get input from great teachers. Professional quarterbacks get regular input from their quarterback coaches to help them reach the next level.

2) **After discovering specific areas of weakness in an area you wish to master, concentrate on them.** Top figure skaters don't just practice figure skating in general; they discover their weak points and concentrate on improving them. Once typists reach a certain speed, they tend to stagnate and stop improving, no matter how much they type. Those who make it to the next level of typing work on their sticking points (often discovered by trying to type faster and noting where they mess up).

3) **Study the best.** Chess masters don't just play more than others, they study the games of the great players.

4) **Approach it like a scientist.** Reflect on what helps and hinders your progress. Keep records to follow your progress. Do little experiments along the way to personalize and tweak your training.

In what area would you like to achieve expertise? How might you pursue it?

Flex Your Neurons!
Pursuing the Point of Know Return

1. When you read a moving story, such as the one on the boy who was kicked out by his parents, do you tend to believe it implicitly, or question its veracity? How can we strike a balance between being naïve on one hand, and cynical on the other?

2. When did you believe someone, but later were disappointed to discover he was either mistaken or lying? What could you learn from that experience to keep from being deceived in the future? (Example: "Fool me once, shame on you. Fool me twice, shame on me.")

3. You hear an authority in a field give a riveting TED talk. Which responses are typically most appropriate for motivated learners who value the truth:

   a. "Now I know the truth!"

   b. "Now I know what one scholar thinks about this issue."

   c. "That was interesting. I wonder if other scholars in the field might disagree?"

   d. "That was some darn good evidence she presented. I think I'll tentatively adopt her position unless I see strong evidence to the contrary."

   e. "Anyone who disagrees with her isn't thinking!"

4. Do you agree that 10,000 hours of practice yields peak performance? Why or why not? Are there exceptions? If so, how can you know if you are an exception?

5. How can we determine how much evidence is enough to warrant adopting a position? Can we ever say we're "certain," or can we do no better than conclude, "the weight of the evidence at this point favors believing this"?

Making It More Personal
Practical Takeaways

What are one or more ideas provoked by this chapter that you can apply to help you think more critically?

____

____

____

What are one or more ideas that you can apply to help you think more creatively?

____

____

____

What else do you want to make sure you don't forget?

____

____

____

Recommended Trails
For the Incurably Curious and Adventurous

1. To understand Gladwell's case for 10,000 hours leading to peak performance, read *Outliers: The Story of Success,* by Malcolm Gladwell (New York: Little, Brown and Company).

2. Study the "Woozle Effect," a term taken from a chapter of A. A. Milne's classic tales, in which Winnie the Pooh and Piglet followed footprints in the snow, which they deemed to have been left by a Woozle. As the tracks multiplied, they discovered that they were actually going in a circle, following their own tracks. Researchers use this term to describe a supposedly growing body of evidence, which turns out to be a bunch of scholars quoting each other, with no solid evidence to back up their claims.

3. For more study on innate and/or developed strengths, and how they impact our potential, see *Now, Discover Your Strengths*, by Marcus Buckingham and Donald Clifton (Pocket Books, 2001). The authors believe that, based on their research, our greatest potential for growth lies in our areas of strength, rather than our areas of weakness.

4. To understand more of how our minds differ, thus giving us more potential to develop in some areas than others, read *Frames of Mind: The Theory of Multiple Intelligences*, by Howard Gardner (BasicBooks, 1983).

5. Search YouTube for presentations by Malcolm Gladwell on "outliers" and by Marcus Buckingham on "strengths." Compare and contrast their approaches to developing full potential.

6. For those interested in health care, particularly those going into medical professions, introduce yourself to the concept of "Evidence-Based Medicine." At first, it seems like a no brainer—hold doctors accountable to make medical decisions based on the best evidence. But like most good ideas, there are drawbacks as well. Here's a good article to get you started:

   http://en.wikipedia.org/wiki/Evidence-based_medicine#Limitations_and_criticism.

CHAPTER 14

THEY'RE SNOWED BY SUCCESS BIAS

"If you spend your life only learning from survivors, buying books about successful people and poring over the history of companies that shook the planet, your knowledge of the world will be strongly biased and enormously incomplete."

— journalist and author David McRaney

The Cure for Wimps

In middle school I was the stereotypical "98 pound weakling." Make that 120 pounds—I was also short and pudgy—everything a guy didn't want to be. I tried football for a day, but my fall allergies made running any distance impossible. I wheezed so loudly that coaches surely envisioned lawsuits if I were to drop dead on the second lap. If we'd had inhalers in 1969, I'd have carried one.

It all came to a head in gym class when each student, in full view of the class, was instructed to jump up to a bar and see how many pull-ups he could do. I managed to jump to the bar (no small feat), but could do no better than hang on. "Stevie Miller - Zero," the coach probably noted on his clipboard.

That was it. Something had to give.

Fortunately, ads in comics offered a solution: Charles Atlas products. His ads were legendary—typically a short comic strip showing a 98-pound-weakling getting sand kicked in his face by a bully at the beach. The wimp's girlfriend makes an insulting remark about his being a "little boy." Thoroughly humiliated, he sends off for the Charles Atlas course, so that next time at the beach he decks the bully, impresses the girl, and is proclaimed "Hero of the Beach." Beside the ad stands Charles Atlas himself, wearing Tarzanesque shorts to accentuate his wasp-thin waist and muscular physique. Under him were etched the words: "Awarded the Title of 'The World's Most Perfectly Developed Man.'"

It was corny for sure, but appealing to a pudgy middle schooler. Next time I looked in the mirror, I desperately wanted to see Charles Atlas.

I don't remember which products I started with, but soon I'd begun hitting the weights and saw immediate improvement. My brother and I asked for new equipment every Christmas until our basement became a gym. For inspiration and instruction in our mutual quest for manliness, we subscribed to magazines such as *Strength and Health* and *Muscular Development*. We consumed the protein shakes and supplements they recommended.

The magazines provided the insider information we needed: the work-out routines and special diets that produced top body builders such as Arnold Schwarzenegger and Sergio Olivia. Duplicate their diets and workouts—put in those Gladwell hours—and we should look like them.

And of course there were the women—fabulous-looking women—sitting on their shoulders and feeling their biceps, with facial expressions indicating a state of perpetual worship for these demigods. This was obviously the way to impress girls.

But the original promise of Charles Atlas never fully materialized. I never looked like him and certainly was never voted "Dalton High's Most Perfectly Developed Man." That award, had it been offered, would have probably gone to one of my best friends—Dee Hodge. While I hit the weights, ate health food and took vitamins, Dee sat at home playing his guitar and drinking two liter Cokes. Yet he was a natural—broad shoulders, thin waist, large frame, naturally muscular. Had he put in my hours of weightlifting, he might have become a world-class bodybuilder. But the magazines didn't talk about inherent limitations such as body types. Neither did they mention that while I was swallowing vitamins, the most muscular bodybuilders were consuming steroids. They just kept feeding me success stories, and I kept buying their products.

The Nature of Success Bias

My work-out buddies and I had fallen for success bias—the fallacy of looking only to successful people to learn how to be successful. It's a form of cherry-picking—studying only the most successful rather than considering a random or representative sample. The magazines we read told exclusively success stories, e.g., how top body builders built their bodies. I never once read of a person who emulated their workouts and drank their protein shakes but failed to gain magnificent muscle mass.

In retrospect, reading *Strength and Health* and working out was a valuable pursuit for my teen years—much healthier than my contemporaries who read Timothy Leary and experimented with psychedelic drugs. I lost the baby fat, gained confidence, grew stronger, felt better, and looked better. The habit of weekly strength and cardio-vascular training has lasted into my 50s.

I was also pleased to discover that the magazines' visual suggestion that girls go for the guys with the largest biceps and most impressive dead lift was largely fiction. My high school girlfriends never once showed the least interest in how much weight I could lift.

(A word to the wise: Don't be fooled by the models who pose for today's hunting and muscle car magazines. Shocking as it may be to some, they're *paid* to wear bikinis while drooling over powerful engines and ecstatically showing off dead fish. But I digress....)

Thus, in my case, falling for success bias did me little harm. I was fortunate. But that's not always the case.

Success Bias beyond Bodybuilding

We love to read about successful people. We want to know how Warren Buffett made his billions, how Bill Gates and Steve Jobs built successful technology companies, how May Kay built her cosmetics company, how the Beatles produced Beatlemania, how Tom Brady became an outstanding quarterback, how Ernest Hemingway learned to write, and how Martin Luther King Jr. successfully fought for human rights. I've read about all these people and many more, with great profit.

The problems come when we draw conclusions too quickly—such as reading a few success stories and mindlessly concluding that we've discovered a pattern that anybody can follow to similar success. The appeal of success bias is powerful, charming even the brightest among us. How can we sift through the hype to find the gold nuggets often lie beneath the surface?

Think!
Seeing through Success Bias

The next time an article or documentary or book or professor urges you to follow the path of a successful person, consider some of the following points.

1. What could we learn from those who followed the same path, but failed?

The Biased Nature of Magazines, Conferences, etc.

Magazines are typically "for profit" businesses. Without a profit, they fold. How do body building magazines make money? Largely from those who place ads in their magazines—typically selling exercise equipment and food supplements. So imagine you're a writer submitting an article to a body building magazine on how many people in your gym *failed* to develop great physiques, even though they faithfully took the supplements and followed the most respected exercise routines. Would the magazine publish it? Probably not.

Their advertisers pay for the ads that sell the supplements and equipment. Why risk offending the advertisers? And why risk discouraging the readers, who may not subscribe next year? For this reason, magazines and popular websites are treasure troves of success bias. The same goes for many conferences and seminars. Attend a financial seminar or an Amway or Shacklee or Mary Kay conference. You'll hear from a veritable parade of winners who became rich following their principles of selling the products.

So ask yourself, "What about all those losers who followed the principles and didn't succeed? How large a group are they and why didn't they succeed?"

Learning from Losers

Imagine that the year is 1855. You're a Kentucky farmer and have become, like everyone else, enamored with stories of people striking it rich in California's Gold Rush. In fact, you subscribed to the *Goldrush Times*, which tells the stories of those who struck it rich.

You're asking the question, "Should I sell the farm, uproot my family, and make the arduous journey across the country?" The data you'd need to make the decision was probably not available to you. Whether you read stories of 10 people or 1,000 who struck it rich, you're lacking critical data. What you really need to know is:

> "Of the hundreds of thousands of people who are looking for gold, what percentage are actually getting rich? If eight out of 10 are getting rich, I'll consider going; if one out of 100, I'll keep the farm."

History tells us that only a tiny percentage of people made it rich. Some of the early arrivals in 1848 made it big quickly, picking up nuggets that lay on top of the ground. Within the next seven years it became increasingly difficult for individuals to succeed. Yet the success stories continued to circulate and an astounding 300,000 people risked great hardships to travel to California in hopes of cashing in.[1]

Isn't this precisely our situation when evaluating a job opportunity, an exercise routine, a new diet, or whether to pursue a master of arts degree? Don't just feed me success story after success story. Instead, compare the successes and failures and give me some odds that this gamble will pay off.

Should You Borrow Large Sums of Money to Start a Business?

Imagine that you've just watched a documentary on how Sam Walton started Walmart. You wrote down everything he did, including the fact that he secured huge loans from banks to build new stores. You read up on several other successful businesses and see that they too borrowed large sums of money. So you go to your local bank to ask for a loan to start your dream business.

Yet, you made the decision based upon examining only a few successes. What about those businesses that borrow money and fail? Some studies find 71 percent of business startups failing within the first decade.[2]

Wouldn't it be wise to do some research into why they fail, including the pitfalls of borrowing large sums of money?[3]

And What about the Other Bands Playing Hamburg?

Let's look at a success-biased argument expressed as a syllogism, which shows it pretty clearly to be a form of cherry-picking and overgeneralization.

> **Premise One:** If the Beatles succeeded by playing together for an extraordinary number

of hours, then other bands who put in the hours will become very successful as well.

Premise Two: My Polka band plays for an extraordinary number of hours.

Therefore: We will become very successful.

If the first premise stands, it seems like a valid argument (the conclusion logically follows from the premises). But is it sound? Just how strong is that first premise? What if your band has no talent? What if there's only a tiny market for your style? What if you write songs that nobody likes?

Without studying the bands that put in the hours and never saw great success, we've failed to account for significant data. What about all those other bands who played Hamburg at the time of the Beatles? How many went on to significant success? How many didn't? What made the difference? These are the questions that take us beyond success bias.

2. Are there instructive counter-examples who succeeded without following the success principles?

According to Gladwell, the Beatles performed twelve hundred times before they became successful. From this, we might draw a tentative principle:

> A band must put in significant time playing together before they're good enough to succeed.

But keep the principle tentative and read other successes. *Led Zeppelin* was another extremely popular band out of England. Did they have to put in their twelve hundred performances as a group before they were good enough?

Hardly.

Lead guitarist Jimmy Page and Bass player John Paul Jones had both done extensive studio work. Singer Robert Plant and drummer John Bonham came with much experience as well. Each of the members had put in their personal practice through the years and played with other bands. When they came together for their first jam, everything simply clicked. According to Page, "It was magical. Everything just came together."

After a few days (not years) of rehearsal time, they hit the road for a mini tour of Scandinavia. That was mid-September. When they returned, Page insisted they were ready to cut an album. So in October, they rented Olympic Studios in South London and produced their first album, *Led Zeppelin*, in a mere thirty hours of studio time.[4]

It was a raging success. As recently as 2003, *Rolling Stone Magazine* ranked the album 29th in their lineup of the 500 greatest albums of all time.

So with this counter-example, we can revise the principle we drew from the Beatles:

> Put in your time—*individually, with other bands, or with your current band*—in order to pursue success.

Comparing the stories of many other successful bands might lead us to tweak the principle further, or abandon it altogether.

3. Consider extreme examples, then work your way back to "normal."

Temple Grandin is autistic. Examine her brain scans and you'll find that her neurons (brain cells) are connected in ways that enhance her ability to understand and remember things visually. But if neurons connect in a way that gives an unfair advantage in one area, they can't optimize other areas. For example, she can't remember faces or understand Algebra. She's plenty smart. She teaches at Colorado State University. But because of the way she's wired, she'll always excel in some areas and struggle in others.

Grandin suggests that looking at her brain as an extreme case, we can better understand our own wiring, which is likely somewhere else on the spectrum. So if Grandin studied the paths that 20 people took to acing Algebra, it might not help her at all, since she's wired differently.[5]

Tip: Ask yourself when evaluating success stories: "Is there anyone I know who could have followed the same path but would have probably not succeeded? If so, what others might this path not work for?"

4. Do the winners have unfair advantages?

- Gladwell mentions timing as a major factor in great financial successes.[6] That's a great point. Bill Gates and Steve Jobs were born at the perfect time to take advantage of the personal computer revolution. Had they been born five years earlier or later, they may have achieved little success. Led Zeppelin toured America when many were looking for the next big band from Europe.[6] Study Walmart and Quick Trip and many other companies to find similar advantages to their timing.[7]
- For personal sales and pyramid strategies such as Amway, Mary Kay, Tupperware or Shacklee products, surely the size and quality of a person's existing web of trusting relationships would give a huge advantage. Also, surely those with delightful personalities, strong social skills, and natural leadership would have a significant advantage over those who lacked such strengths.

So when the testimonies of the successful begin, look for unfair advantages that might accompany the super successful.

5. Did you consider related factors such as opportunity cost?

During the early years of the Web, businesses simply put their brochures up on a website to establish a web presence—a way for their customers to find and contact them. But then along came Web 2.0—unleashing "the power of us" by allowing people to interact on the Web. With such tools as blogs, forums, Facebook, Twitter, and LinkedIn, people began connecting with one another, opening opportunities for marketing our products and businesses.

For almost a decade, I've followed developments with social media networking. As a writer, I'm well aware that publishers don't just look for writers who can write good books; they want writers who can *market* their books. To many in the publishing industry, web-based social networking solved many problems for authors. It offered the opportunity to connect with existing readers and draw new readers. Through social networking, authors could establishing themselves as thought leaders and build followings. It seemed to be the answer to the talented writer who lacked a platform to sell her books.

Quickly, social media established itself as "the thing" that all authors needed to pursue. Thus, when an author sent a book proposal to a literary agent or publisher, she might be asked, "But who is likely to buy your books? Do you have a blog? If so, how many followers do you have? How many comments do you get on your posts? How many people follow you on Twitter? How many Facebook 'friends' do you interact with?"

If the author's response was vague, or if she merely reemphasized, "But it's really a good book!" the agent or publisher might respond, "Come back to me when you've got a successful blog and a thousand Facebook followers."

Yet, it seemed to me that this advice was based on success bias—stories of select authors and select business people who had done well with social media. The critical question they failed to address was: What's the evidence that this approach should work for everyone?

One of the problems was the vast amount of time it took to build a successful blog (one with a significant active following) and to retain hordes of active Facebook followers. Social media gurus recommended spending vast amounts of time to build a significant social media following.

- Chris Brogan: minimum of 2 hours daily.[8]
- Web Worker Daily: minimum of 2 hours, 13 minutes daily.[9]
- Miller Finch Media: four and a half hours daily.[10]
- Nonprofits and Social Media: 60 hours per week.[11]

Yet, very few authors write full time. Some teach. J.R.R. Tolkien taught at Oxford during the day, hung out with his family when he got home, and wrote in the evening after the children were in bed. Had social media existed in his time and he'd spent two hours each evening blogging and hanging out on Facebook, we'd have likely never read *Lord of the Rings* or *The Hobbit*.

It seemed to me that the advice-givers weren't taking into account opportunity costs (see the Broken Window Fallacy), whereby they assumed that authors, in addition to working, raising families, writing, and exercising, had two free hours floating around each day to develop social media.

Besides, there are hundreds of ways to market books. See marketing guru John Kremer's book, *1001 Ways to Market Your Books*. With 1000+ ways to market books, who has ever proven that social networking on the web is the most effective method for every author and every book? Nobody that I can find. Yet, if we spend all our marketing time doing social media, we can't spend that time with other marketing initiatives.

Social media experts never seemed to address the issue of limited time. Instead, they just told us success stories of authors who'd built significant social media followings and urged us to follow their examples. They were trying to convince us, and were probably convinced themselves, with success bias.

6. Consider conducting a study that might back up or refute the claims.

As an author, it was critical to decide how to best use social media, such as blogs. Three informal studies helped. First, I visited the websites and blogs of the presenters at a well-attended social media conference. Overwhelmingly, I found very little interaction (comments, etc.) on their blogs. If they were the gurus, why weren't significant hordes interacting with them? Something seemed amiss. The few who had a good number of active followers had unfair advantages. For example, one ran a blog that supported his software. Obviously, users would return to the blog to report problems with the software. This success told me nothing about the potential of a low-profile author for gathering a significant following.

Second, I studied low-profile authors who'd sold a lot of books. I found that they used a variety of marketing approaches that worked well for them. While I knew a few authors whose sales seemed to come primarily from social media, my broader study of successful authors showed me that social networking was far from the only marketing game in town.

Third, I asked on a publishing forum (think: crowdsourcing) what was working for authors in marketing books. If they said that they used blogging and Twitter, I'd ask, "But how many book sales can you definitely attribute to this method?" Typically it was very few.

With this informal research, I concluded that successful book marketing looked different for different authors. Some did well with social media while others used different methods to achieve success. Their choice of marketing methods often depended on the nature of their books and their personal strengths and interests.

Tip: Ask yourself, what kind of research would it take to support or refute the claims being made based upon people's successes?

7. Question, question, question.

From the film, *The Matrix*:

> **Trinity:** It's the *question* that drives us, Neo. It's the question that brought you here. You know the question, just as I did.
>
> **Neo:** What is the Matrix?

> **Trinity:** The answer is out there, Neo, and it's looking for you, and it will find you if you want it to.

For those in search of The Matrix, *the question* drove them. Unfortunately, most people these days don't seem to be driven by questions. Perhaps they're used to uncritically reading textbooks and memorizing the main points for tests. Perhaps they're naturally naïve, taking most everything at face value. Or perhaps reading this text while listening to music, texting on your phone, and keeping abreast of Facebook friends doesn't allow enough random access memory in your brain for critical thinking.

Whatever the case, if we want to stop jumping to conclusions and resist success bias, we'd better start by asking more and better questions.

In the case of social networking for authors, this was an important issue for me. Respected publishers, literary agents and social media gurus confidently instructed me that authors needed to build significant social media followings to build their author platforms. But if I were to follow their time consuming advice, when would I find the time to write my books?

Think!

Imagine that you plan to start a coffee shop or motorcycle repair shop or _____(name a business or social agency that interests you). If a marketing professional gave you the same advice concerning social media as they were giving me as an author, what questions would you like to clarify?

Rather than blindly follow their advice, I began asking questions—lots of questions:

1. How many low-profile authors succeed at building significant followings with this strategy?

2. How many fail, and for what reasons?

3. Why would people follow blogs written by authors who don't already have a high profile? Wouldn't people more likely follow the blogs of authors who were already successful?

4. How much time does this take?

5. Do I have that much time?

6. Do we have evidence that our limited marketing time is better spent with this strategy than the hundreds of other strategies?

7. Does building interactive followings work better in some industries than others? Is there solid evidence that it works in my industry?

8. What if some people don't enjoy spending hours a day on Facebook and blogging? Won't that lack of enthusiasm impact the quality of their work?

9. How much time in research would it take to become a legitimate thought leader in my field?

10. Do I really want to become a thought leader? If I were to become one, wouldn't I have gobs of emails to go through every day from people asking me questions and wanting a bit of my platform?

11. In order to build my blog following, will I end up spending more time marketing my blog than marketing my book?

12. Won't I lose friends when I start trying to sell them my products on Facebook, even if a sales pitch is only one out of 100 entries?

13. If my blog is about writing and publishing, won't I be attracting fellow *authors* rather than potential *readers*?

14. Do people in my target group actually subscribe to blogs of my type and follow them passionately? How many?

15. Is there enough relevant, interesting, practical information on my topic to blog about it for years on end?

Researching these questions led me to indeed use blogs and forums and other social media, but in ways much different from trying to build a following around myself. In this way, I utilize the power of social media without having to spend vast amounts of time blogging and interacting on Facebook. (Rather than digress, I'll just mention that I lay out these thoughts in my books on book publishing and marketing.)[12]

Like Neo and Trinity, it's *the question* that drives seeking minds. It's *the question* that drives us far deeper than the off-the-cuff responses on Ask.com or a line-up of success stories at a conference.

I can't tell you the specific questions you need to be asking to get the answers you seek, since formulating good questions is as much an art as a science, and the questions differ from issue to issue. And don't be discouraged if each answer you find spawns ten new questions. That's progress, since without critical questions driving us, what will motivate us to keep passionately learning?

Think Different!

Some might argue that once we see the problems with success bias, we should stop listening to success stories. Like Rosenberg, they may argue that since our brains often trick us and history can be interpreted so many ways, we should give up trying to learn from history, including the history of people's successes.

But I strongly disagree.

For me, the best way to keep from falling for success bias is to read *more* people stories, not less. For in reading many stories, I gather data to compare and am less likely to believe that the testimony at the conference represents the only true path to success. By reading about both the *Beatles* and *Led Zeppelin*, I learn more about the music industry and have real life examples (data) by which to evaluate other people's claims.

Thus, although I sometimes disagree with Malcolm Gladwell, I love to read him and wrestle with his ideas. He never fails to provide provocative food for thought. Although my muscle magazines contained success bias, they also had a lot of great ideas. I had to learn to separate the wheat from the chaff; but in doing so, I learned much about health and fitness which benefited me throughout life. While I disagree with much of today's advice about social networking for authors, I've learned enough to adapt social media to my specific needs.

Reaping More from Biography and Success Stories

As you read people stories and business stories, be aware that it's not always obvious what actions contributed to their success and what hindered their success. It's easy to fall for the fallacy of *post hoc ergo propter hoc*—assuming that the success that followed was a result of each decision made previously. For example, Steve Jobs could obsess endlessly on the details of his products, sometimes exasperating his associates. Was this quality a part of what made him successful, or did it hold him back, or was it sometimes positive and sometimes negative?

It's a subjective judgment, but I lean toward the latter.

I read that Harvard Business School encourages teaching business by telling business stories. Some of the benefits are clear:

- We remember stories better than lists of facts.
- We engage our critical thinking by comparing one company to another and drawing out the principles ourselves, as opposed to memorizing keys to successful business.
- Stories inspire as they teach.
- We can use the stories to teach and inspire others.

That's why I never tire or reading biographies and stories of businesses. That's why I often quote from great biographies in this book. The history of Bell Labs teaches me about innovation and the contributions that unique (and often strange) people can make. Benjamin Franklin challenges me to seek wisdom and keep practical. Albert Einstein and quantum theorists teach me the importance of imagination and to not assume what seems obvious. Paul Orphalea's success at Kinko's shows me how a dyslexic, A.D.D., nonreader can start and run a fabulous business. *Led Zeppelin* and the *Beatles* have much to teach us about collaboration, hard work, and passion.

Biographies do more than teach me about success. They disrupt my all-too-human tendency toward inside-the-box thinking and provincialism. Reading of Ghandi or Jesus transports me from my little cul-de-sac in metro Atlanta to foreign lands, challenging my culture's pull toward materialism and consumerism. Reading Paul Johnson's provocative description of influential intellectuals warns me of the pitfalls of the life of thought and research and publishing.

And especially in the older biographies, I've noticed a significant pattern—they all die. It's the darndest thing. Whether they invented the airplane or atomic bomb, developed the first transistor, ruled the Roman Empire or hit a baseball like nobody before or since, they always die. And typically, they exit life with more of a whimper than a bang.

Generally, I grieve a bit after that final chapter; I feel like I knew them. Then I reflect on the total impact of their lives, positive and negative, and compare it to my own. So Sam Walton obsessed his entire adult life building the largest retailing outfit on the planet. Why didn't he stop with one successful store, or two, then go do something else with his life? Did he spend enough time with his family? Did he feel in some sense destined or called to complete this task?

What keeps Warren Buffett going to work each day into his 80's, even though for decades he's already established himself as one of the most successful businessmen/investors alive? In part, he looks at his portfolio of investments as a work of art:

> "I am painting this painting that is Berkshire Hathaway; the canvas is an unlimited size."

This is the life Buffett has carved out for himself, but is it the one I want? Is that the painting that I want to gaze upon at the end of my life and feel satisfied that I used my allotted years to complete it? What do I want to be known for?

Some seem to blitz through life "full of sound and fury," yet wonder at the end if it "signified nothing."

So biographies tell me more than how to be successful—they force me to reflect more deeply on what "success" really means to me. In my view, it's more about helping others and leaving the world a better place; but study interesting people for yourself and see what you conclude.

For these reasons, I carry books with me wherever I go, reading them while waiting for a child at school or getting my car fixed. Interestingly, I've found that getting small bits each day may be more profitable than reading huge chunks at a sitting, since my mind needs time to reflect on new thoughts. So I read a few pages about the Beatles at Hamburg and have to stop when my children get in the car. While driving home from school, I reflect on the passage or discuss it with my children. That's where I engage my critical thinking and transform knowledge into wisdom.

As I encounter interesting thoughts, I index them in the back of each book. Some people may be able to do this just as well in an e-reader such as a Kindle—highlighting and adding notes. But for me, marking up paper books still works better. I've gathered a couple of hundred books into my office that I keep referring to as I write this book. Thousands of others are available to me on shelves in other rooms. The ones I've read, I've marked up with extensive notes on the final blank pages, referring to pages with insights and quotes that may one day prove valuable:

- "pp. 62, 221, 320 on motivation"
- "p. 3 on wisdom"
- "chpt. 2 on the power of caring"

I look especially for the fascinating, the interesting, the practical, and the counterintuitive, like Bubba Watson establishing himself as one of today's top golfers, without ever taking a golf lesson. Now *that's* interesting, and may apply to any number of topics of interest to me.

And don't neglect books on great failures. Reading *The Smartest Guys in the Room* about the rise and fall of Enron taught me more about running a business than many books of business successes.

As a result of voracious reading and marking up books, when I write or speak on a topic, I have plenty of material to draw from, and can easily document it. When my writing or latest business project requires new research, I order new books and mark them up. If they're too expensive, I check them out from the library or order them through interlibrary loan and take notes on legal pads, which I place beside my books. You may find a better way to read and reap from biography, but this way works for me.

And besides all the *profit* in wisdom, it's so incredibly *fun*! So go find a great biography about somebody you admire and see what all the excitement's about!

Flex Your Neurons!
Pursuing the Point of Know Return

1. Before your next class, look for examples of success bias. Listen to commercials; reflect on ads in magazines. Think back to times when you've been persuaded, for good or for ill, by success bias. Bring your ideas back to class for discussion.
2. How can we learn from successes while being aware of the pitfalls of success bias?
3. How do lotteries use success bias to their advantage?
4. Would you have likely moved across the country to pursue fortune during the gold rush? Why or why not?
5. What part may social media play in your area of business interest, or your passion for social activism? How can it be used? How might it be abused?
6. What people inspire you? How can you learn from them, without falling for success bias?

Making It More Personal
Practical Takeaways

What are one or more ideas provoked by this chapter that you can apply to help you think more critically?

____

____

____

What are one or more ideas that you can apply to help you think more creatively?

____

____

____

What else do you want to make sure you don't forget?

____

____

____

Recommended Trails
For the Incurably Curious and Adventurous

1. In learning to be successful in business, I profited from a book by a young man who created a successful business, sold it in his 20s, then interviewed 100 highly accomplished leaders in diverse fields—actors, CEOs, senators, scientists, heads of nonprofits—to find the secrets to their success. He concentrated on their early years, which makes it especially valuable to those in their teens and 20s. While we must certainly beware of success bias, the author did a great job of simply letting people speak for themselves, rather than trying to force everyone into a tidy package of "20 keys to success." Thus, many of their approaches contradicted one another, showing the variety of ways people find success, or how success finds them. Here's the book: *Nobodies to Somebodies*: *How 100 great careers got their start,* by Peter Han (New York: The Penguin Group, 2005).

2. Success books often try to gather principles that can make anyone a success, while ignoring people for whom the principles may not apply. That's why I like to look long and hard at people who don't seem to fit the norm. Consider these: Temple Grandin is autistic but puts her mind to great use as a researcher and professor. She argues that it's too simplistic to think that some people have autism and others don't. Instead, people find themselves somewhere on a spectrum between the extremes. If this is true, then it says a lot about our need to find niches in which we can be successful, given where our brains fit on various spectrums. *The Autistic Brain: Thinking Across the Spectrum,* by Temple Grandin, with Richard Panek (New York: Houghton Mifflin Harcourt, 2013).

3. Paul Orphalea started the extremely successful printing company, Kinko's (later sold to FedEx). The way he started and ran his company was very unique because of his disabilities. For example, he couldn't read. *Copy This! Lessons from a Hyperactive Dyslexic Who Turned a Bright Idea into One of America's Best Companies*, by Paul Orphalea, with Ann Marsh (Workman Publishing Company: 2007).

4. For a quick read of what's happening in today's top businesses, from entertainment to technology to the restaurant business, subscribe to the award-winning magazine Fast Company. You'll get the scoop on the latest in innovative thinking and making it in an ever-changing business climate. The more articles you read, the more you can compare business stories. What advice contradicts? How does success in one industry differ from another industry? How do people with different strengths and personalities lead in different ways? Why do some great companies eventually fail? It's not all cut and dried, and a regular dose of business stories can keep us from swallowing trite and shallow success advice.

5. Do further research by searching terms such as "success bias," "survival bias," "survivorship bias."

CHAPTER 15

THEY DISCOVER MEANINGLESS PATTERNS

"It is necessary to know the power and the infirmity of our nature, before we can determine what reason can do in restraining the emotions, and what is beyond her power."

— Benedict de Spinoza

Would You Trade Your House for a Tulip Bulb?

Had you lived in seventeenth century Holland, you might have. The Dutch named the phenomenon *tulpenwoede*, translated "tulip fury." English speakers call it tulip mania. Some just call it crazy.

Here's the background.

The Dutch began growing tulips in 1590. The flowers and their bulbs eventually became extremely popular and prized across borders. Of course, many people bought them simply because they were beautiful, but one characteristic made them especially appealing to speculators. The cultivated bulbs they acquired from Constantinople, when planted, might change or "break" into a different variety. Yet part of the original might be retained as "streaks, feathers, or 'flames.'" Plant the baby bulbs and they hardly ever return to the original coloring. In this manner, people could develop never-before-seen versions of the tulip.

As a result, a few bulbs from a tulip deemed especially unique and beautiful might be considered the only ones of their kind and bring a great price. After all, the parent bulbs would produce new bulbs and the owner could continue to sell this rare and beautiful breed. Different types of tulips were given important names like "Admiral," "General," or "Augustus."

Much like a unique painting by a famous artist, it's difficult to assign monetary worth to a rare bulb. Neither bulbs nor paintings serve an especially valuable practical function or have great intrinsic value. After all, the Mona Lisa is just dried paint on a sheet of paper. What gives it worth is that we consider it beautiful and rare (the only one) and it is a da Vinci. Thus, its worth could be considered "whatever people are willing to pay for it." In this sense, it's much like a bulb from a tulip that's rare, beautiful, and comes from a type named "da Vinci."

With this background, here's how tulip mania broke out in the second decade of the 1600s.

Tulips became extremely popular in France, but the demand outpaced the supply, and you can't double or quadruple the supply of tulips overnight. Thus, the prices increased dramatically. At the wedding of Louis XIII tulips were said to be as valuable as diamonds. Then it got even weirder. Bulbs kept commanding ever higher prices over time until "A mill was exchanged for one tulip bulb; a brewery for another."[1]

Back in Holland, feverish speculation hijacked the minds of bright people as they saw their friends getting filthy rich trading bulbs.

> "By June 1636 many varieties had tripled in price and more. A comparison of prices at that time with certain bulbs sold in December 1634 shows increases from 15 guilders to 175 guilders; 40 to 350, and 800 to 2,200."[2]

Let's try to calculate a very rough exchange of seventeenth century guilders into today's dollars in order to comprehend the magnitude of this increase. The average skilled laborer in Holland made approximately 1563 guilders per year. In 2012 America, the average carpenter made $39,940 per year.[3] From this, let's estimate that one guilder in seventeenth century Holland was worth roughly twenty five dollars in contemporary America. This translates to one bulb selling for $55,000 at the height of the tulip craze!

Imagine You Were There

So imagine that you lived in Holland during this time period. In June of 1636, your buddies at the pub hand you a chart from the *Amsterdam Business Weekly* indicating that tulip bulbs have tripled in value over a brief span of time.

You wisely caution: "That's way too much to pay for a flower bulb!"

They reply: "But many of these tulips are extremely rare. Far-sighted people want to cultivate them to make money in the future. After all, tulips have become the rage in France and soon it will hit other countries as well. We want to get in on the ground floor of this growth industry. You should join us!"

You reply: "I don't have enough money to invest."

They reply: "But you don't even have to invest in a whole bulb. Even the poor can invest in small portions, by weight. It's like buying a small amount of stock in a company. Besides, banks will loan you the money. Obviously they consider it a safe bet."

You thought that this was surely an economic "bubble," which would eventually burst, but you read financial experts who argued that tulips weren't overvalued at all. In fact, according to them, the increase might continue almost indefinitely, since many other countries would almost certainly catch tulip fever and want a piece of the action.

You resist for months, painfully watching your friends' bulbs increase in value month by month, so that your buddy who borrowed and invested $1,000 (40 guilders) in June sold it for $8,750 (350 guilders) in December. Finally, you cave in and borrow $5,000 to invest.

Unfortunately (or in your case, *tragically*), like all economic bubbles, it burst.

In a little over a month after you bought it, your bulb would be almost worthless, and you'd be stuck making payments on the $5,000 you borrowed. It's unclear exactly how it all unraveled historically, but it must have happened quite suddenly. On the first day of February traders were still urging people to buy and still offering eight-day guarantees against losses. Three days later it was reported that nobody wanted to purchase tulips. Your spouse now thinks you're an idiot for not investing earlier and selling out by December, reminding you of your folly every month you make a payment on that wretched $5,000 loan.[4]

Think!

Had you lived through tulip mania, do you think you'd have invested? If so, what would have pulled you in?

- Smart economists writing that the increase in price was only just beginning?
- Seeing your friends get rich?
- Your spouse reminding you that you're the only one in your social circle who was dumb enough to miss out on the opportunity of a lifetime?
- The temptation to "get rich quick?"

Our Attraction to Economic Bubbles

Our first reaction to tulip mania might be to assume that people back then must have been really stupid. I mean, thousands of dollars for a tulip bulb? Really?

Actually, among the Europeans, the Dutch had a strong reputation for their serious character and business savvy. They were smart enough to lead Europe in commerce during that era. To protect their trade, they built a navy twice the size of the British and French fleets combined.[5] So they can't be easily dismissed as morons. It seems to be yet another case of smart people believing nonsense. It's like some strange power takes over and deceives otherwise reasonable people.

More Flower Bubbles, and Beyond

To make matters worse, history keeps repeating itself. "Surely not!" you might object. "With that dramatic period of lunacy behind us, surely people learned to beware of economic bubbles and to nip them in the bud. Surely nobody since the original Tulip Mania would invest in a business or industry just because the charts show its going up in value—especially if it involved plants!"

But alas, it's difficult for bright minds to resist the power of perceived patterns. Less than a century later tulip mania hit Turkey, to the point that a single bulb from Persia was sold for a thousand gold pieces.[6] A century after Holland's tulip mania, as if to commemorate that period of economic folly, the Dutch experienced a similar mania with hyacinth plants, with certain specimens selling for 4,900 guilders.[7] The eighteenth century French experienced their own déjà vu of tulip mania with their dahlia craze. One dahlia was traded for a rare diamond. A well cultivated dahlia bed was sold for today's equivalent of $280,000.[8]

But surely practical, down-to-earth Americans wouldn't involve themselves in such nonsense.

Unfortunately, recent history tells a much different story. To name a few bubbles:[9]

- During the 1920's **Florida land boom,** the rapid growth of Florida land values convinced wealthy investors that Florida was a paradise just waiting to be developed. A huge billboard in New York's Times Square proclaimed to frozen New York investors that "It's June in Miami." Developers feverishly built neighborhoods and even entire cities; trains couldn't carry enough supplies; and at its fever pitch the same properties were bought and sold at auction as many as ten times in a single day. Of course, the bubble eventually burst and much of the development became ghost towns.

- During the **Roaring Twenties** (1920s), the stock market seemed to grow endlessly. As we mentioned in chapter two, up until the crash, great economic thinkers were predicting a rosy economic future: "Stocks have reached what looks like a permanently high plateau." (Irving Fisher, Professor of Economics at Yale University, seven days before the crash.) "1930 will be a splendid employment year." (U.S. Department of Labor, Dec. 1929). Thus, people kept feverishly buying and selling stocks until the great stock market crash at the end of 1929, ushering in the Great Depression.

- The **technology (dot-com) bubble** of the late 1990s found investors speculating on the rise of technology companies, many of which had yet to even turn a profit. Yet, "smart" investors reasoned that the future lay in computers, harnessing the power of the Web, and virtually anything that had a ".com" attached to it. So speculators poured money into tech companies and tech mutual funds, driving the prices ever higher until it burst in 2000-2001.

- In the 2000s, we experienced the **housing boom and bust.** Although many complicated factors contributed to this crisis, a part of the bubble involved investors and individual homeowners seeing the rapid increase in real estate values, giving them the confidence to borrow beyond their means to purchase properties they felt certain would keep rapidly increasing in value. Banks lent money for builders to build way ahead of the market and to speculate on new developments in areas such as Panama City, Florida. (Déjà vu the Florida Land Boom?) When it busted, homeowners and investors found themselves owing way more than their homes were worth. Many lost their homes. Even banks faltered.

This happens so often that it's tragically amusing. One researcher found American real estate since the year 1800 becoming overpriced and speculators getting over-exuberant about every eighteen years, before it all goes bust.[10]

So why do we keep making the same mistakes? How can we keep from losing our shirts in the next economic bust?

Why This is Important

I hope you can see that we're not just talking about lessons for big-time investors. It involves all of us. In order to know whether to rent an apartment or buy a condo, we need to know something about where our often irrational economy currently stands. All who are saving for retirement need to know something about investments. All who are looking for jobs need to assess the job market, which is often related to booms and busts.

Also, the problem with patterns extends well beyond economics. Remember one of the reasons we mentioned that record labels rejected the Beatles? They perceived a pattern that they mistakenly thought would extend. They saw people buying records by solo performers and saw guitars as becoming less important. By extending this "pattern" into the future, they determined that the Beatles wouldn't fly. If we fail to resist our tendency to find false patterns, we'll make poor decisions as well.

How to Resist Latching onto Patterns

1. Understand how our brains can fool us.

Much study has been done on the psychology of investing. The more aware we are about how our brains work with patterns, the better we should be able to think through our decisions. Here are some tendencies we should all be aware of:

- **When our brains are stimulated twice concerning something, like a stock going up twice or more, our brains unconsciously tell us to expect it to go up again.** It's almost irresistible. We think we've discovered a pattern, even if it's a random event.[11]

- According to investment journalist Jason Zweig, **"the neural activity of someone whose investments are making money is indistinguishable from that of someone who is high on cocaine or morphine."**[12] Doesn't that explain a lot about tulip mania and human behavior during economic bubbles?

- **We tend to remember our wins and forget our losses.**[13] A study of 80 investors found that 88 percent of them overestimated their returns.[14]

Thus, it's easy to imagine we're excellent stock pickers, when we're actually losing money. We remember the times we won money with the lottery, but fail to add up the amount we lost over time to win that money.

If we're conscious of the ways our brains fool us, we're more likely to question our brains when they're "discovering" false patterns.

2. Don't buy stuff just because it's going up in value.

Often stocks and houses and lands and guns and gold increase in value for ludicrous reasons.

> "*The dumbest reason in the world to buy a stock is because it's going up.*" – Warren Buffett[15]
>
> "*Your chances of selecting the top-performing [mutual] funds of the future on the basis of their returns in the past are about as high as the odds that Bigfoot and the Abominable Snowman will both show up in pink ballet slippers at your next cocktail party.*" – Jason Zweig[16]

3. Discover the longer history of the relevant subject.

During the most recent real estate bubble, a top real estate investor was asked if he thought we were in a bubble. He responded that he'd never seen a real estate bubble. What ignorance! I wonder how much he lost when the bubble burst.

When investment advisors tout certain stocks or mutual funds, showing their past five year or ten year performance, look up the longer term performance. Often you'll see a far different picture.

4. Be prepared for the rational explanations that justify investing during a bubble.

As writer Joseph Bulgatz described the tulip craze:

> "A feeling had come over the country that the tulip trade would never end, that all of Europe would participate, and that all the money from it would come to the Netherlands. And indeed it is possible to see how the phenomenon seemed to have an irresistible growth, crossing class lines and national boundaries, reaching out to include ever cheaper kinds of bulbs, and always pushing prices ever upward."[17]

Reflect upon that. The continued growth of the tulip market seemed "irresistible." Just substitute "Florida land" or "tech stocks" for "tulip trade" in the above quote and you'll see how people justify joining in the irrational exuberance. During the tech stock bubble, experts argued that far from being a bubble, we had entered a "new economy" based upon exploiting the web, cell phones, computers and other new technology. When real estate prices begin to rise wildly, people will argue, "They're not making any more land, you know. It's got to keep going up!"

5. Understand how the power of chance inevitably produces "brilliant" winners.

One statistics professor likes to ask a student to flip a coin for a period of time and record the series of heads and tails. Then, she asks the rest of the class to *imagine* they are flipping coins and record the results. She then leaves the room, returns after a designated time, and asks the students to turn in their records.

Amazingly, the professor can tell, looking at the papers, which paper recorded the actual coin-flipping. How? The person actually flipping the coin records longer series of heads and tails than the others would have imagined. Who would guess, for example, that there might be a series of ten heads in a row?

This is a significant insight for evaluating stock pickers and economic forecasters. Today, investors can choose from over 7,000 different mutual funds, which are combinations of stocks, bonds and cash equivalents. From our little coin flipping experiment, we can predict that, even if all the fund managers were morons, 10 percent of the funds would end up in the top 10 percent, simply because of dumb luck.

This is why wise investment strategists recommend NOT investing in a fund simply because it has the best return for the last year, or even the last ten or twenty years. It's next to impossible to know if the fund came out on top because the managers were brilliant, or because the economy cooperated with their strategy for a brief time, or because of pure luck.[18]

The same goes for the investment strategist who claims that he beat the market for the past decade, or predicted the last five economic downturns. Perhaps he did; but can we know that it wasn't just dumb luck? How can we know for certain that the strategy he used to predict the last market upturn or downturn will predict the next big change?

After all, *correlation doesn't always imply causation*. This can be shown by all kinds of ridiculous examples.

- Money manager David Leinweber studied various economic statistics to discover what might correlate most closely to predicting the U.S. stock market performance for the years 1981-1993. He discovered that if a person had bought a total stock market index fund based each year on the amount of butter produced each year in Bangladesh, they could have predicted the market with a 75 percent accuracy. Had he further refined his forecasting model by taking into account the total number of sheep in America and other irrelevant stats, he could have predicted returns with a 99 percent accuracy.[19]

- *Money* magazine editors found that companies whose stock exchange symbols had no repeating letters beat the market significantly.[20]

My point? While butter production in Bangladesh and a company's stock market symbols may *correlate* with past stock market successes, don't assume that those ridiculous factors *caused* stocks to rise, and especially don't assume they can be used to predict the future of the market. Similarly, if a bright economist notes a historical correlation of top-performing stocks with such factors as "dividing the dividend yield by the square root of the stock price," it's typically found to have no relation whatsoever to *future* yields.[21]

6. Resist the wisdom of crowds, even crowds of experts.

Remember one of our lessons from chapter two: don't allow expert opinion to shut down your own thinking. Just because you see smart people making lots of money building houses, selling carpet, selling computers, or selling coffee, don't assume you've discovered a pattern that's the cusp of the future. It may grind to a halt tomorrow, perhaps due to some out-of-the-blue trigger, such as a war nobody saw coming, a recession in Europe, or a terrorist attack.

An acquaintance was building decks for houses during the housing boom, raking in tons of money. Had he followed the crowd, he'd have used that money to move to a nicer neighborhood, since interest rates were low and banks were eager to lend. Instead, since he never assumed the boom would last, he went against the crowd and used his extra money to pay off his modest house.

After the boom went bust, nobody wanted a new deck, so he became a mechanic. Because of his low overhead (no house payments), he was nimble enough to quickly find a niche in another industry. Those builders who overextended by borrowing themselves into nicer neighborhoods likely lost their ritzy homes during the bust.[22]

7. Look more to the intrinsic value of a company than to the behavior of stocks.

When stocks in general are going up, most investors (and their friends) think they're geniuses for picking the right stocks. But as Warren Buffett says, "...you only find out who's been swimming naked when the tide goes out."[23]

Rather than following the investing crowd, Buffet goes against the flow. He's bold (buying) when others are scared (selling) and scared when others are buying. Basically, he studies companies to find out which ones have the greatest intrinsic worth and potential for long-term growth. Then, he buys them when they're underpriced—when everybody else is selling.

8. Understand what you're getting into.

We've talked about overconfidence in chapter one; but applied to money management, it's especially a killer. According to Zweig, "One of the most fundamental characteristics of human nature is to think we're better than we really are."[24]

Someone asked almost 3,000 entrepreneurs to estimate their odds of succeeding. 81 percent estimated at least a seven out of ten chance. An incredible 33 percent said there was zero percent chance of failure! Yet, when they were asked what they thought of the *typical* person starting a business in their field, they estimated that only 39 percent would succeed. This degree of overconfidence is quite astounding, which can easily lead to a lax attitude about seeing the need to master your field. Rather than humbly asking people for advice, we "have a terrible time admitting that we don't know something." Even worse, we probably have no clue how much we don't know.[25]

So don't become intoxicated with perceived patterns and mindlessly following the crowd, like lemmings, off the next economic cliff. Benjamin Graham's statement on investing deserves repeating:

> "You're neither right nor wrong because other people agree with you. You're right because your facts are right and your reasoning is right—and that's the only thing that makes you right. And if your facts and reasoning are right, you don't have to worry about anybody else."[26]

Think Different
Sometimes Patterns are Real!

So now that you're prepared to resist all patterns, let's make things a bit more complicated. Sometimes, patterns are worth noting. You'll need wisdom to discern between real (patterns that will continue) and imagined patterns.

Moore's Law and the Computer Revolution

When Steve Wozniak built the first Apple computer, he first offered it to Hewlett-Packard, since he was working for HP and felt it was the ethical thing to do. Happily for Wozniak and his partner Steve Jobs, HP turned it down, seeing personal computers more as a toy for hobbyists.[27]

But visionaries such as Steve Jobs and Bill Gates saw the potential of computers. At Microsoft, Gates envisioned "A computer on every desk and in every home." They saw the day when homemakers would routinely look up recipes for dinner on their computers. But why could Jobs and Gates conjure up the future when others couldn't?

I think a part of it was a pattern, discovered by Gordon Moore in 1965. Moore's Law stated that, because of the increasing number of transistors that could be placed on a computer chip, the power of computers to process information should double approximately every two years, making it less and less expensive to accomplish more and more on a computer. Although Moore's Law will inevitably slow down, it has proven true to this day.[28]

A part of the problem in comprehending the power of Moore's Law comes from the fact that it *doubles* rather than *adds*. We have a difficult time envisioning exponential growth, since it starts so small but ends up unimaginably large.

Imagine a checkerboard with 64 squares. In the first square you drop a grain of wheat. In the second you drop two, in the third four, in the fourth eight. Do you know how many grains of wheat you'd have by the 64th square? Enough to cover the entire country of India 50 feet in grain![29] That's the incredible power of repeated doublings.

Thus, rather than focusing on the limitations of the early computers, which were so pitifully slow as to be of hardly any practical use, Jobs and Gates envisioned a future where the doubling of storage capacity and speed, and corresponding lowering of prices, would quickly lead to personal computers and devices with almost unimaginable potential. Because of understanding the power of multiplication as a part of Moore's law, they could foresee average people using computers to create graphics, watch videos, collaborate globally, do their homework, do research, and do their taxes.

The Pattern of Multiplication through Investing

Warren Buffett fully comprehended the power of multiplication in investing. He understood a pattern that was well-established and proven by math, but that few people seem to have to the capacity to grasp regarding their investments.

Money invested at ten percent interest doubles approximately every seven years. Money invested at seven percent interest doubles approximately every ten years. It's called "The Law of Tens and Sevens." Buffett could multiply money even faster by achieving rates of return far beyond ten percent.

But even doubling every seven years multiplies money in shocking ways. Invest just $20 a week (about three dollars a day), starting at age 20, at an annual average return of ten percent interest per year (the average return of stocks for the past 80 or so years), and you'll be a millionaire in your 60s. Run the numbers on an online interest calculator. It's like magic!

So some patterns hold while others don't. The former can make us successful while the latter can fool us and break us. To tell the difference between the two, run decisions through the principles we listed above.

Flex Your Neurons!
Pursuing the Point of Know Return

1. When Cherie worked at a Chicago bank, the teller next to her was robbed. Although the teller repeatedly pushed the hidden emergency button, the security officer didn't arrive at the scene until after the robber had left. The officer walked in complaining, "Will somebody please stop pushing their emergency button?" Why do you think he ignored the alert and how does it relate to this chapter?

2. It's difficult for the human mind to grasp the power of multiplication with investments. To understand the powerful pattern, Google "interest calculator" and find one that provides fields for monthly investments. To check out the "$3 per day" or "$20 per week" investment plan, put in an initial investment of "0", a monthly investment of $80, an interest rate of 10 percent (the average return on stocks) and the time of investment as 48 years (the 20-year-old would have become 68). How much money would you have for retirement if you simply understood and took advantage of this pattern? (Note: We're *assuming* that the long-term pattern of stock returns will continue to hold, and that a crash won't happen late in your investment!)

3. An economist predicted the last two economic crises in America. Does this mean I should believe him in his prediction of the next economic crisis? Why or why not?

4. Do you think you would have bought extremely expensive tulip bulbs during Holland's "tulip mania"? Why or why not?

5. Are housing prices going up in your area? If so, does this make it a no brainer to invest in real estate? Why or why not?

6. Investor extraordinaire Warren Buffett says that, regarding buying stocks, he's scared when others are greedy, and greedy when others are scared. What do you think he means by this, and why has it been a good strategy for him? How does this relate to making decisions from perceived patterns?

7. How do you plan on guarding yourself from making poor decisions based upon meaningless patterns?

Making It More Personal
Practical Takeaways

What are one or more ideas provoked by this chapter that you can apply to help you think more critically?

____

____

____

What are one or more ideas that you can apply to help you think more creatively?

____

____

____

What else do you want to make sure you don't forget?

____

____

____

Recommended Trails For the Incurably Curious and Adventurous

1. Study "Extrapolation" and see how it dovetails with this chapter.

2. For more on tulip mania, real estate bubbles, and other examples of the insanity of crowds, see Charles Mackay's 1841 classic, *Extraordinary Popular Delusions and the Madness of Crowds*, which is still often recommended by those teaching investing. More recently, Joseph Bulgatz wrote a similar, updated volume on the same topic titled *Ponzi Schemes, Invaders from Mars & More Extraordinary Popular Delusions and the Madness of Crowds* (New York: Harmony Books, 1992).

3. For psychological factors that impact our investing, including our proclivity for finding patterns, see *Your Money and Your Brain: How the New Science of Neuroeconomics Can Help Make You Rich,* by Jason Zweig (Simon & Schuster, reprint edition, 2008).

4. Google "economic bubbles in America" to see how economic ups and downs regularly occur, fooling investors and causing people to make foolish decisions in the light of perceived patterns that fail to pan out.

SECTION FIVE

WHY DO BRILLIANT PEOPLE BELIEVE NONSENSE?

BECAUSE THEY BELIEVE "LIES, DAMN LIES, AND STATISTICS" (With credit to Mark Twain)

CHAPTER 16

THEY FAIL TO CLOSELY EXAMINE STATISTICS

"They've done studies, you know. Sixty percent of the time it works every time."

— From the Film "Anchorman"

A Crisis We Must Avert

According to the US Department of Education, we've got a crisis on our hands. I'll let the below U.S. government web page explain.[1]

The United States has become a global leader, in large part, through the genius and hard work of its scientists, engineers and innovators. Yet today, that position is threatened as comparatively few American students pursue expertise in the fields of science, technology, engineering and mathematics (STEM)—and by an inadequate pipeline of teachers skilled in those subjects. President Obama has set a priority of increasing the number of students and teachers who are proficient in these vital fields.

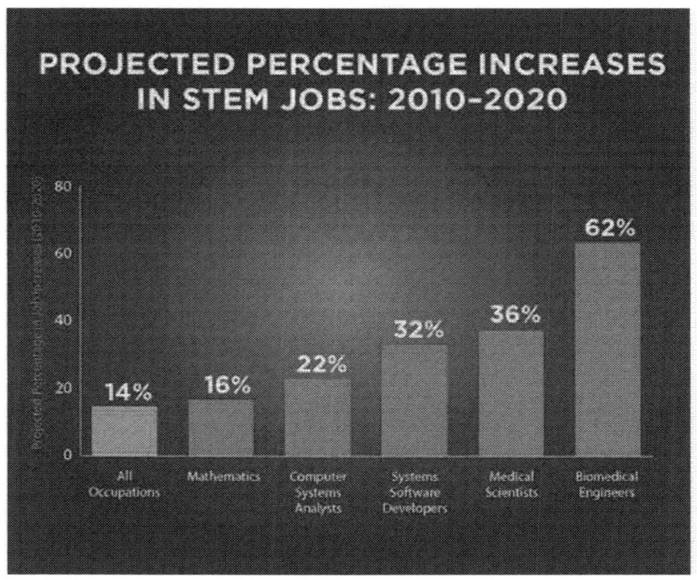

The need

Only 16 percent of American high school seniors are proficient in mathematics and interested in a STEM career. [expand/collapse]

Think!

In your own words, state what these statistics are telling us. Second, state what they're *not* telling us. What further information would you like in order to better analyze the problem and dream up possible solutions?

It's difficult to overestimate the importance of this issue. Those who act on these statistics make decisions and implement policies that impact all of us.

- The government plans to allocate hundreds of millions of our tax dollars (340 million dollars budgeted for 2015) into initiatives that will help to churn out more and better STEM teachers and students.[2]
- We urge our children to pursue these fields, in order to save America and take advantage of a huge growth industry, even if their interests and innate talents may suggest other fields.
- We must necessarily deemphasize certain skills and subjects (less diversity of high school course offerings, less time put into other subjects) in order to prioritize the crying need of the day.

With this background, it's no wonder that when CNN surveyed the job market in 2012, they chose Biomedical Engineering as #1 in the list of the "Best Jobs in America."[3]

A Deeper Look at the Crisis

There's no doubt that we want to produce great scientists and offer the best opportunities in science to our students. I love science and enjoy math! And nobody doubts that we should always pursue ways that we can tweak our education to inspire the next generation of scientists.

But statistics can be confusing, leading us to make poor decisions. In order to better understand this chart and the looming crisis, let's dig a bit deeper into the data that forms the foundation for these claims. This will serve as an example case in examining statistics.

1. Understand exactly what the chart is measuring.

In this case, note that *the percentage increase* doesn't tell us *how many jobs will be available in this field.*

Look back at the chart, focusing on biomedical engineers, since it's the most dramatic stat. A cursory glance tells us that 62 percent *of all jobs* in 2020 will be biomedical jobs. Compare that to only 16 percent of high school grads interested in a STEM career and the outlook seems bleak indeed. Surely we need to motivate tons of students to study biomed!

But that's a misreading of the chart.

One tip-off that we've misread it is that if we add up all those percentages, they come to well over 100 percent, showing that the chart must not be talking about percentages of available jobs at all. In fact, the graphic tells us in the title that it's charting the *percentage increase*, not *the number of jobs*.

Think of percentage increase in this way. If there were only one biotechnical engineer in 2010, and authorities told us that we needed a total of two biotechnical engineers in 2020, our chart would show that we needed a 100 percent increase in biotechnical engineers. While the 100 percent would seem very dramatic on a chart, compared to the growth in other fields, surely we wouldn't tweak our entire educational system to gain one more engineer over a ten year period. So it's important for us to know just how large this field is.

Obviously, this chart doesn't give us the information that we need.

2. Discover How Many Biotech Engineers We Actually Need

At this point, I began searching for the information I lacked. On a United States Department of Labor site I discovered that "because it [biotech] is a small occupation, the fast growth will result in only about 5,200 new jobs over the 10-year period."[4]

Thus, America as a nation needs to graduate 520 biomedical majors *per year*, during the ten year time period, to meet the demand for 5,200 new jobs.

3. Discover if Our Current Masters and PhD students Are Likely to Supply the Demand

America has over 550 *graduate* school programs related to biotech. Thus, if each of them graduates only one student per year, this could supply the demand. This isn't even considering all the *undergraduate* programs that offer biotech degrees. Nor is it considering the foreign techies that we grant temporary work visas to when we have a sudden or overwhelming demand in a field. Neither is it considering that almost half of those employed in STEM vocations don't even *have* or *need* STEM degrees. (The field needs a variety of specialists from various fields, not just biotech majors.)[5]

So where's the impending shortfall—the "comparatively few American students" pursuing "expertise in the fields of science, technology, engineering and mathematics?"

4. What Percentage of Students Do We Need to Push to Pursue Biomed Careers?

Over 15 million students are currently studying in America's four-year colleges, who will graduate with either undergraduate or graduate degrees (I subtracted the students who likely won't graduate.)[6] Thus, the 5,200 total (not per year, but for the decade) biomed specialists we need is merely .03 percent of the current student population. In other words, we desperately need, not three out of 100 students, not three out of 1,000 students, but three out of every 10,000 college students to major in biomed or a related field.

But let's give ourselves a bit of a cushion, since some may change majors or get a job in a different field. So let's say we need 10 out of every 10,000 (or 1 out of 1,000) college students to study for a biomed career. Surely, if we need so few students, we could offer incentives such as scholarships if we're falling behind.

So how many students does my local high school need to motivate into biomed?

The local high school my children attended has about 2,000 students. Assuming that they all graduate, how many students do we need to motivate to go into biotech to meet the need? If we need one out of 1000 students, that comes to about…two.

Actually, not all high school students go to college and some, once they get there, drop out, so let's be generous and say we need eight, which would be less than one graduate per graduating class over a ten year period.

So we're changing our curriculum and deemphasizing other career paths in order to get one graduate from each high school class to choose biomed? Do we really need to motivate more students to go into a field that seems to already have an overabundance of qualified workers? This is beginning to sound very odd.

But perhaps we're being unfair. We've obsessed on biomed students, without taking into account other STEM fields.

5. Ask, "Beyond Biomed, How Many STEM Workers Do We Need?"

According to the Department for Professional Employees, "In 2011, STEM jobs made up 5.2 percent of the total workforce nationwide."[7] Compare this with the above chart and accompanying information. A part of the "crisis" they identified was that only 16 percent of high school grads were interested in a STEM career. Yet, if we already have 16 percent of our students (according to the above chart) heading for five percent of the jobs, why are we desperately pushing for more? Perhaps we should be redirecting some of them to other careers.

Again, according to this department, "The supply of new STEM graduates is robust." Just how robust?

> In academic year 2011-12, 141,000 bachelor's degrees were conferred to graduates in natural sciences and mathematics and 146,000 bachelor's degrees were awarded to students in computer sciences and engineering. Also in academic year 2011-12, 26,000 master's degrees were awarded in natural sciences and mathematics and 66,000 degrees were awarded in computer sciences and engineering. Nearly 25,000 doctor's degrees were awarded to students in natural sciences, mathematics, computer sciences, and engineering in academic year 2011-12.[8]

That sounds like a lot, but is it enough to meet the current needs?

6. Study the Current Job Market for STEM Careers.[9]

The projected growth in the chart was for the years 2010 to 2020, which means we're well into this decade. Surely, if there's a crisis, we should see lots of unfilled job openings and extremely low unemployment in the field. So I Googled "finding a job in biomed" and "finding a job in STEM."

Here's what I found:

- A 2012 Washington Times article claimed that, while we keep pushing for more scientists, "the jobs aren't there."[10]
- Only 14 percent of PhDs in biology and life sciences are finding positions to teach and research through our colleges within five years. "The supply of scientists has grown far faster than the number of academic positions."[11]
- The pharmaceutical industry, one of the largest employers of STEM graduates, has downsized. "Largely because of drug industry cuts, the unemployment rate among chemists now stands at its highest mark in 40 years."[12]
- A panel at the National Institutes of Health, another big employer of STEM grads, noted that a "glut of trainees and a dearth of academic positions in the United States is creating a dysfunctional biomedical research system, particularly biomedical students...."[13]
- According to Jim Austin, at ScienceCareers, "...it seems awfully hard for people to find a job. Anyone who goes into science expecting employers to clamor for their services will be deeply disappointed."[14]
- A 2011 study from Georgetown University found that "10 years after receiving a STEM degree, 58 percent of STEM graduates had left the field."[15]

How Accurately Are We Able to Forecast Future Job Needs?

A 2012 National Science Foundation report, before giving their predictions of the growth in STEM jobs, admits that "Projections of employment growth are plagued by uncertain assumptions and are notoriously difficult to make."[16]

They list such unknowns as how much the government and corporations will spend on research and development, how much research will be outsourced overseas, and the difficulty of predicting new products and industries that may emerge. Also, we can't predict economic crises, either domestic or global, that impact hiring.

Thus, the NSF report concludes, "The reader is cautioned that the assumptions underlying projections such as those that follow, which rely on past empirical relationships, may no longer be valid."[17]

By contrast to the chart at the top of this chapter, a 2014 report of the National Science Foundation predicts that the biological sciences will grow 20 percent for the years 2010-2020. That's still a hefty increase, but less than a third of the earlier prediction of 62 percent.[18]

Since we're well into the decade, surely it's relevant to look at the present state of this much-anticipated surge of growth. According to the Bureau of Labor Statistics, here's the state of STEM occupations through 2013.[19]

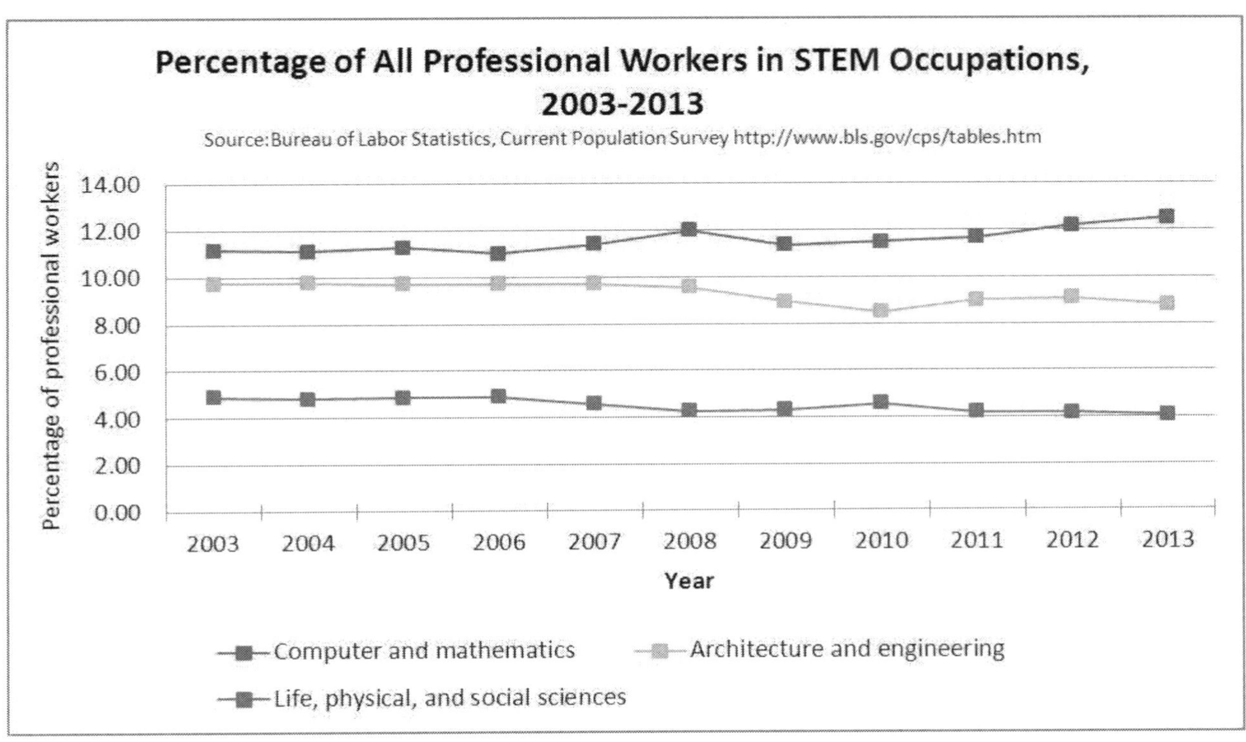

Well, that's rather disappointing. If these figures can be trusted, from the years 2010 to 2013 computer and math occupations have grown (as a percentage of all professional occupations) by about one percent, architecture and engineering less than one percent, and the life, physical, and social sciences have *decreased* by less than a percent. (In fact, during the entire period from 2003 to 2013, the percentage of people working in the "life, physical, and social sciences" has decreased.) In the first third of the 2010 to 2020 decade, although we've graduated an abundance of STEM majors, we've yet to see signs of the huge projected increase of jobs.

How could economists have been so far off? Perhaps the boom will come in the last half of the decade. Yet technology, like other industries, doesn't just keep growing forever. Instead, it goes through times of boom and bust. "There will be times when employers find it difficult to find technology workers, and times when technology workers are laid off en masse." And like other booms and busts in the economy, they're terribly difficult to predict.[20]

Should You Go into Biotech?

If you're studying biotech, you may be panicking about now. Don't. If you think I'm telling people to leave the field, you've missed my point. The point is, we can't put our full confidence in government statistics and projections. We must think them through for ourselves.

If you're passionate about biotech, don't just study biotech; study the biotech *industry* to see where the jobs are and to understand the current opportunities and challenges.

By the time you read this, my stats will have grown cold and we may be experiencing a boom in biotech. Check the latest stats. Talk to people in the industry. Some suggest that getting a more general engineering degree would allow more nimbleness to pursue the growth industries in science after you graduate, and to change careers if those areas later fade. Read articles in the industry. Also read the comments of real, live engineers, scientists and mathematicians who comment below the articles, sharing their real life experiences.

Tips from this study:

1) Always look closely at statistics and charts, whether they're coming from respected experts, Harvard University, or huge government surveys. Understand exactly what they're purporting to show.

2) Consider the potential for bias in presentations. Would the organizations supplying or presenting the information be more likely to receive government grants if the statistics were dramatic?

3) Ask good questions, such as,

- How were these statistics gathered?
- Are there alternate ways to interpret them?
- Could they be charted (displayed) a different way to give a different impression?

4) Find other relevant data that might either confirm or call into question the original stats.

Conclusion

Why do brilliant people believe nonsense? Because they base their beliefs on faulty or misleading statistics. So pay attention to statistics and their accompanying charts. Challenge their assumptions. Question their conclusions. Consider the agendas they may represent.

And NEVER STOP THINKING!

Think Different!

Using Google with More Finesse

My research for this chapter was done largely through using Google, not the specialized databases available only through universities and libraries. Learning to use Google effectively can pay rich dividends as we think our way through life and try to see through nonsense. Here are a few tips to using Google more effectively.

1. Start by asking the right questions.

When I first looked at the statistic on the growth of STEM occupations, I realized that the stats weren't giving me the information I needed. They only gave me the percentage increase. These are some of the questions that first came to mind:

- Where did this stat come from? A respected organization? It didn't tell.
- What is the evidence that we'll have a huge lack of workers?
- Do other estimates of percentage increase differ?
- How many people are currently working in STEM jobs?
- If this is indeed a growth industry, how many slots do we need to fill?
- How many people are currently being trained for these slots?
- What are other ways these slots can be filled? (International work visas, people trained in other areas, one year certificates, two year degrees, etc.)
- Are we currently seeing a dearth of workers in these areas?
- Are there reasons for bias that might impact the formulation and presentation of these statistics?

2. Search Google with key terms.

Keep trying different combinations of words until you find the data you need, for example: "STEM jobs," "Percentage of STEM jobs," "Statistics on STEM jobs," "Careers in STEM jobs," etc.

3. Keep organized!

For this study, as I gathered large amounts of data, I copied and pasted information into a Microsoft Word document under headings for each of the questions/sections.

4. With each article or resource you read, note the terms and references that are just begging to be followed.

Think like Sherlock Holmes; you're gathering clues for further research as you're going along. One article may reference a study that becomes the key to unlock the rest of your research. If it looks promising, highlight it and mark it for future snooping.

5. Learn to search within articles and books.

So you find an online book that you've been told contains a study on the growth of STEM occupations. The table of contents doesn't help. At that point, search the document by clicking Ctrl/F on your keyboard (or whatever your operating system uses to search a document) and typing STEM into the box to find all references. To search within a pdf, use the search provided by Adobe.

6. Learn how to narrow your searches.

For example, if you want to search for government statistics on STEM related subjects, type "STEM .gov" into Google, which prioritizes information about STEM on government sites.

Flex Your Neurons!
Pursuing the Point of Know Return

1. Try to find solid information on career prospects that might match your strengths and interests. Search terms/phrases such as “careers” and “best jobs” and “average pay for jobs” to try to find the best (most accurate, up-to-date, thorough and useful) career sites. Bring your results back to class for discussion.

2. What harm might come when we unnecessarily prioritize spending and weight curricula toward pushing huge numbers of students toward a narrow set of occupations? For example, many predict a coming shortage of physicians. Since physicians aren't typically counted as STEM workers, might we contribute to a shortage of physicians by not financing and emphasizing them as much as STEM professions?

3. A doctor recommended that my dad start taking a blood thinner, which would cut his possibility of having a stroke in half. What questions would you like to ask the doctor before making this decision? (Think particularly about what we just learned about "percentage *increase*" and apply it to "percentage *decrease*." Teachers can look to the online teacher resources to find my answer.)

4. When a politician says that during his term he "lowered the national deficit," does he mean that he lowered the national debt, or that he merely reduced the amount that the debt was increasing (percentage decrease)?

5. Collect some statistics that you see in various advertisements. What questions would you like to ask to determine if the stats truly prove what they claim to prove? (Example: 100 percent of dentists surveyed prefer ____ toothpaste. But how many dentists were surveyed? How were the dentists chosen? Do other surveys of dentists show the same preference?)

Making It More Personal
Practical Takeaways

What are one or more ideas provoked by this chapter that you can apply to help you think more critically?

____

____

____

What are one or more ideas that you can apply to help you think more creatively?

____

____

____

What else do you want to make sure you don't forget?

____

____

____

Recommended Trails
For the Incurably Curious and Adventurous

1. To do further assessment of the future of STEM jobs, read some of the articles that I referenced in the endnotes for this chapter.
2. If you're pursuing STEM vocations (or any specific vocational area), find the most authoritative sources to track the types of jobs available, unemployment stats for various sectors, who's hiring and where, etc. If a Google search fails to uncover the best sources, ask your librarians...they live for moments like this!
3. Seek out people in your field of interest to ask about job prospects (what people actually do during an average work day, where jobs are available, is it fun and fulfilling?) Job fairs often put you in contact with such people. Also, look for specialized online communities.
4. To learn more about tricks and tips to use Google more effectively, see the appendix on this topic in the accompanying website:

   www.criticalcreativethinking.wordpress.com.

CHAPTER 17

THEY MAKE COMMON STATISTICAL BLUNDERS

"Eighty percent of statistics are made up on the spot."

— Anonymous

Everybody's Having Sex!

Most teens are strongly driven by peer pressure. If they believe that their friends are all taking drugs, they're more likely to take drugs. If they believe all their classmates are having sex, they feel strong pressure to not miss out.

That's why it's important for us to know how many young people are actually having sex. If your 15-year-old sister feels that she's the only virgin left in her age-group, she's more vulnerable to yield to the pressure of her 18-year-old boyfriend. "After all," insists her boyfriend, "everybody's doing it. Don't be a prude."

Unfortunately, the media and educators and government agencies often *increase* that pressure by relying on and quoting misleading statistics, apparently to call attention to issues they feel need to be addressed.

Ever since the 1960s we've been strongly influenced by the sexual revolution. Everyone except recluses living in caves seem to know that everybody's having sex with everybody, unless there's something wrong with you. Thus, in an episode of the popular TV series *House*, the awe-inspiring diagnostician, in considering a sexually transmitted disease as a possible cause of the troubling symptoms of a young boy, says something to the effect of, "We all know that 110 percent of all 16-year-old boys are having sex."

So imagine that you're a 16-year-old virgin watching this episode. You feel humiliated, out-of-touch, unpopular. The next day at school your respected health teacher begins a section on sex ed. "I'm not so out of touch as to imagine that you're not having sex. I just want to teach you have to have it more safely." Once again, you feel the flush of embarrassment at being a virgin when everybody else has already experienced sex.

In assuming that "everyone's doing it," aren't teachers encouraging—even prodding—peer-driven teens to start sex early? I recall a substitute teacher who addressed a sex education class of 15-year-old girls and suggested that they should put off sex till they find someone they want to spend the rest of their lives with. Girls came up after class and said, with huge expressions of relief, "You mean it's okay to say no to sex?" Apparently, their regular teacher had, either implicitly or explicitly, communicated that 15-year-old sex was expected and inevitable, thus putting strong pressure on her students to join the crowd.

Think!

What percentage of 15-year-old girls do you estimate are regularly having sex? How many do you think have had sex only once? How many not at all?

So What Do the Stats Really Say?

I researched this issue in some depth in the late 1980s and early 1990s while I assisted a public school system with their sex education program. The media, health authorities, government agencies, and popular music converged to tell us that most young people were having sex. But in order to think through our approach to teaching sex education, I needed to start with accurate statistics. After all, one survey found that the greatest pressure to have early sex is neither love nor lust, but peer pressure.[1] And with millions of teens acquiring sexually transmitted diseases each year,[2] along with increased emotional anguish and the risk of pregnancy, the stakes were indeed high.

"Everybody's doing it" was based upon a statistic claiming that most teens are "sexually active." Thus, the regular teacher of the 15-year-old girls' health class likely started with this assumption and expressed it to her class as "I know most of you are having sex...." But this statement makes several assumptions, making it a good example of how statistics can lead us astray.

1. Older teens are more likely to have had sex than younger teens.

Since most 18 to 19-year-olds are out of high school, graduates shouldn't be included in statistics that claim to assess high school students. Some older teens are even married. When we limit our study to only high school students, I found that most high school students had not experienced sexual intercourse, not even once.

But the health teacher was speaking to a specific subset of high school students—15-year-old girls. The most comprehensive surveys found that 70 percent of them had never had sex. And if you subtract from that 70 percent those whose only sexual experience was involuntary (rape), then 80 percent of that age group had never had voluntary sex.

It's beginning to look like, among 15-year-old girls, the great majority are *not* doing it.[3]

2. The term "sexually active" is misleading, seemingly designed more to arrest public attention and heighten the sense of urgency than to paint an accurate picture of high school sex.

Remarkably, to the researchers and agencies feeding the information to the public and our schools, "sexually active" meant "have had sex at least once." Yet it was seldom defined in popular media and gave the impression that every youth who was "sexually active" was "sleeping around" or "having sex most every weekend."

Yet, surely we wouldn't consider a person "*physically* active" if he had walked around the block once in his lifetime. We'd expect him to be getting regular exercise, at the very least once a week. It certainly confuses the issue to label someone "sexually active" when her sole sexual experience was a rape at the age of 14, or one voluntary act of sex that she later regretted.

(As an example of how confusing this phrase can be, when one girl was asked if she was sexually active, she responded, "No, I just kind of lie there.")

As a result of these confusing statistics, agencies and educators and journalists gave the impression that most high school students were sleeping around. So how many are actually "active" in the sense of either having sex regularly or sleeping around? One study found that 20 percent of the teens categorized as "sexually active" had experienced sex only once."[4] Another study found that only 14 percent of high school girls had accumulated four or more sexual partners.

In fact, one survey found 84 percent of teen girls saying that what they most wanted to know about sex was how to say no without hurting the other person's feelings.[5]

So much for "all high school students are sleeping around." So why are so many high school students feeling such pressure to start having regular, early sex? Why do they *think* everybody's doing it? Sure, Hollywood must take part of the blame, but sensational news reporting, sensational reports by respected agencies, and naïve educators should shoulder part of the blame as well.

Why do brilliant people believe nonsense? Because they fail to look deeply enough into the statistics that impact their decisions and their teaching.

I hope that this look at the statistics of sex and how people use them gets you a bit angry. After all, we're talking about people here: our little brothers and sisters, our friends. When we allow people to pass on misinformation, we hurt people.

My point? Statistics are important. Interpreting them incorrectly impacts not only us, but the people we love.

Frequent Statistical Blunders

Familiarize yourself with the most common statistical fallacies and you'll be more likely to spot them in your reading and viewing.

Look Carefully at How Charts Display Data

Failure to Maintain Consistency

In 1976, a respected science foundation posted a graph purporting to show an astonishing drop in the number of Nobel Prizes in science that were awarded to U.S. citizens.[6]

> **Think!**
>
> Look carefully at the chart below before reading my explanation. Can you see what's potentially misleading?

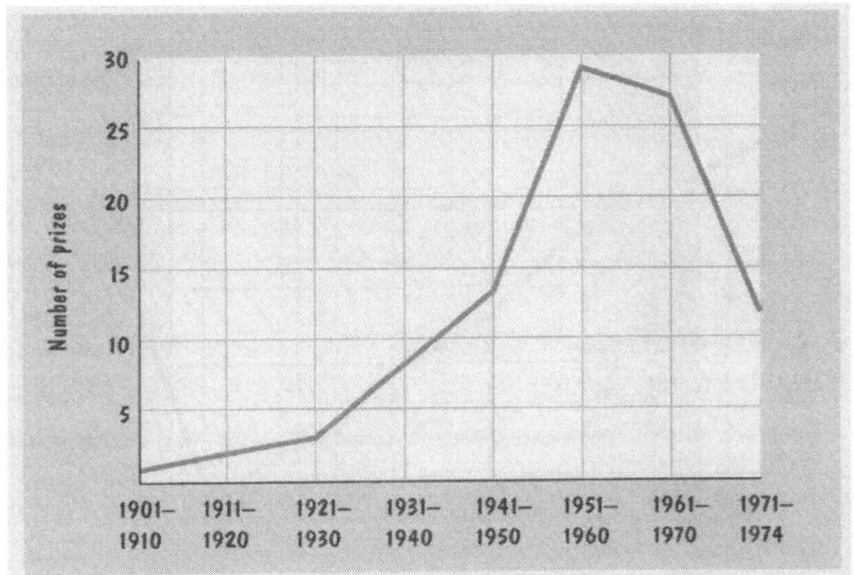

The problem? Each period of years represents a decade, *except for the last one*, which is for only four years. No wonder we see a huge drop in Nobel Prizes! We would expect the period of four years to show less than half of the winners for the typical ten year period. That's exactly what we find. But graphing it in this way gives the strong (but wrong) impression that we've lost our scientific edge.

So let's take a longer view, showing the rest of the decade after the chart was published.

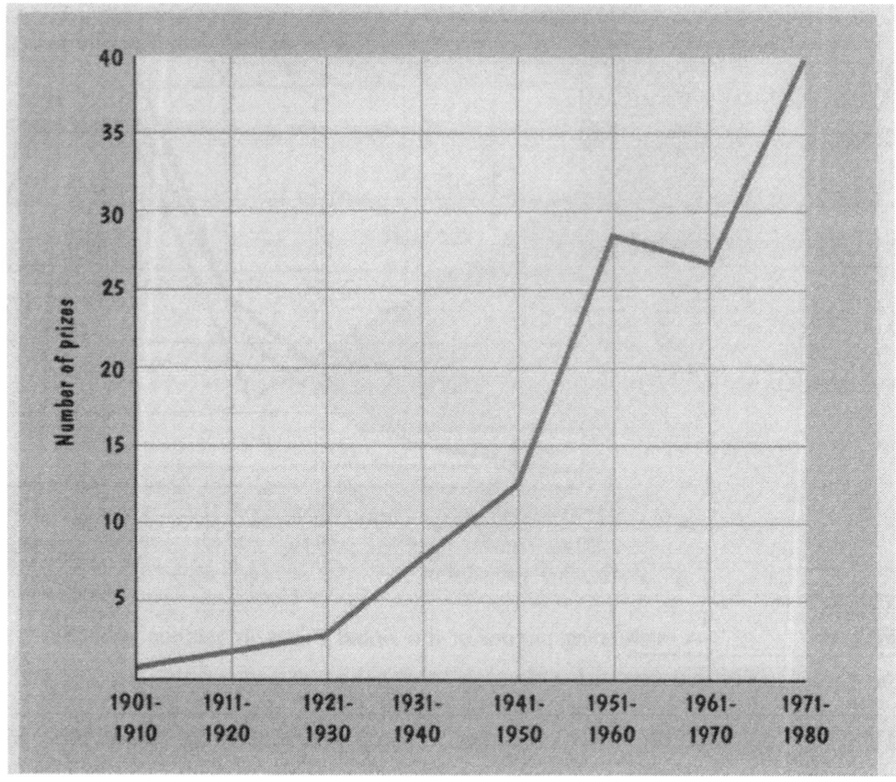

Now *that's* more like it! America's back in the Nobel Prize ball game! Whatever their reasons to publish such nonsense, it well demonstrates how charts can be manipulated to conform to someone's agenda.

The moral of the story? Always make sure that charts maintain consistency in the spaces allotted for periods of time or any numbers.

Omitting Origins

Some of you would like to teach—perhaps in a school or seminars or a service organization or a summer camp. All communicators should be interested in the claims we're about to assess.

Imagine that you want to hone your teaching skills, so you look up some articles on teaching and find this vital information, presented on the website of one of our most respected institutions of higher learning.[9]

> "Research on student attention in lectures has demonstrated that attention levels naturally vary during lectures in predictable ways. In fact, attention is high during the first minutes, then it falls down and stays flat for the rest of the lecture. Toward the end of the lecture, attention picks up again, with some fluctuation, according to the following graph. (Bligh 2000)":

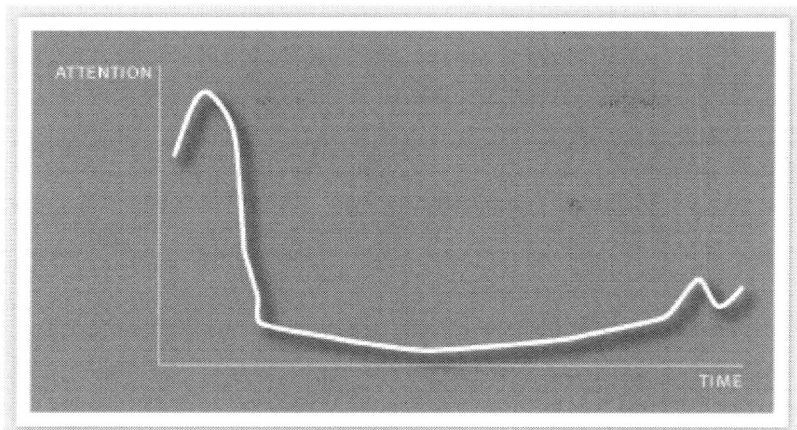

Study as Posted (as of 2015) on a Leading Research University Site

Think!

From your first impression of this chart, what can we learn about communication?

At first glance, it tells me that students listen attentively for the first couple of minutes, then they quickly fall into a near comatose state, remaining there till the last few minutes of the lecture, where they regain just enough consciousness to close their notebooks in preparation for their next classes.

My takeaway? If I want to say anything important, I'd better say it in the first couple of minutes, since the rest of my lecture is pretty much a waste of time.

Although I find this graph in many authoritative articles and presentations, the more I thought about it, the more I smelled a rat.

Think More Deeply!

What's lacking from this chart? Does the chart jive with your personal experience and your observations of fellow students during lectures, even if they're interesting?

Here's how I dug a bit deeper and what I discovered.

1. I first noticed the lack of numbers and labels on the x and y axes.

Without numbers, the chart is almost meaningless. Note two ways the chart could be presented, depending on the numbers that informed the chart and their meaning.

Presentation One - The most natural way to read this graph is to assume it's measuring students' attention, with zero attention (comatose) at the bottom and maximum attention (students fully dosed on Ritalin/Adderall) at the top. From left to right, we'd see the timeline of a typical one hour lecture. (See chart with my wording below.) Is that how you interpreted the original chart?

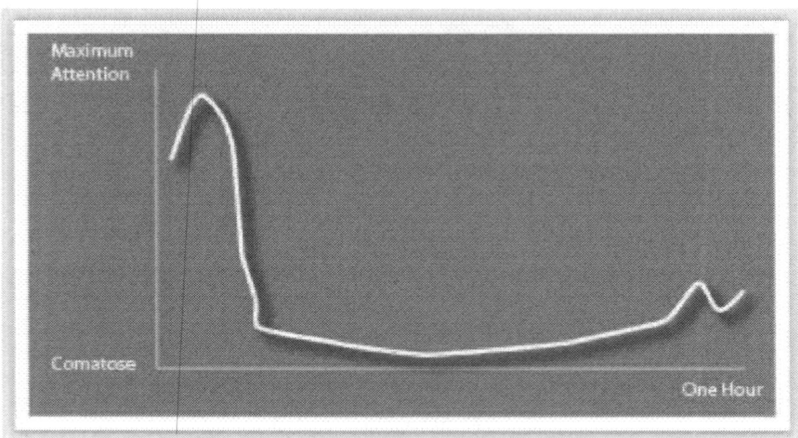

Study Labeled as I Interpreted It

Presentation Two - An alternate way to look at this data would be to assume that the above graphic omitted the origins (doesn't begin with zero attention), making the drop in attention appear much more dramatic. If so, then by reinstating the origins, we would see the wane of student attention in a much less dramatic light. Note how wildly different this looks (see chart below), compared to the graph that started with zero!

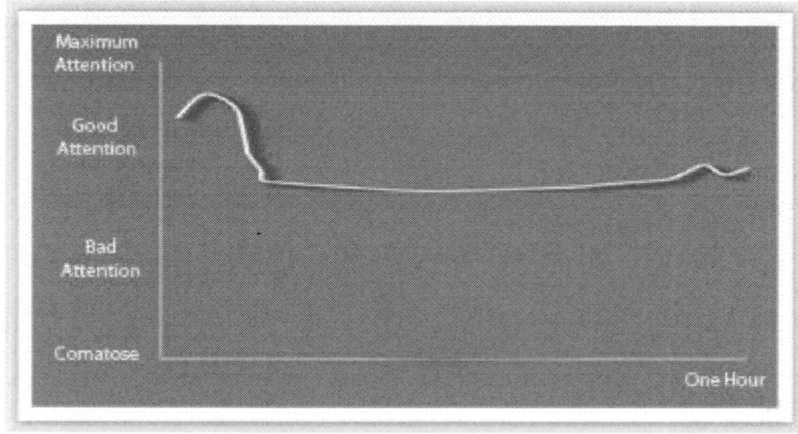

Another Way the Study Could Be Interpreted, Reinstating Origins

So which of these two (or something between these extremes), represents the truth behind the chart? Without further snooping, we have no way of knowing, since nobody's giving us any numbers to graph.

2. My second suspicion arose when I activated my higher level thinking enough to compare it to my own experience.

"How does my own attention fluctuate when I attend a lecture?" I asked myself. Of course, my attention varies significantly according to the content of the lecture (relevant versus useless) and the quality of the speaker (riveting versus a hopeless bore). Yet I don't see anything in the chart allowing for such extremes of relevance and quality.

In general, I do admit that I'm probably a bit more alert at the start of a one hour lecture than 40 minutes into it. Yet, I'm still paying at least enough attention to continue taking notes. I'm not comatose. If she's a decent communicator on a tolerable subject, and 30 minutes into the lecture she shares an entertaining illustration or a piece of new information that is especially relevant, I'm all ears. If 40 minutes into the lecture she tells a hilarious life experience or joke, I often laugh and look around to find the rest of the audience laughing as well. They certainly don't seem comatose.

3. My suspicions were confirmed when I dug up the source.

The above university webpage cited the source of the chart as "Bligh, 2000," in a book titled *What's the Use of Lectures?*[8] I pulled up a free digital version of the book through my university library and found the original chart, which I discovered had somehow evolved significantly over time. [See below. Note the much milder downward curve and how the last jolt of attention comes much closer to the original level of attention/performance (see below) than in the more recent drawing of the graph (see above)].

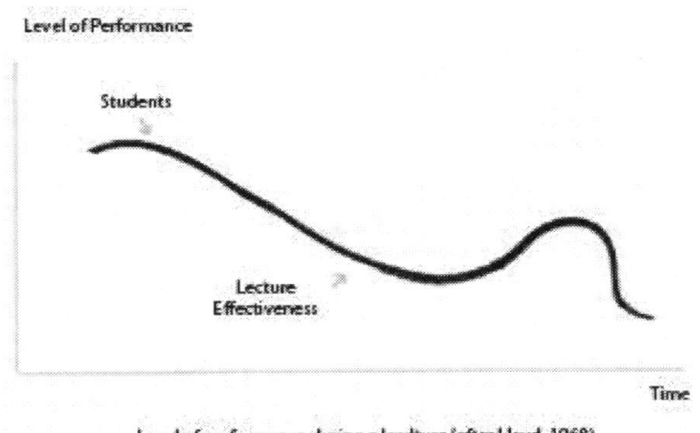

Same Study as Presented by Bligh in the Year 2000 in His Text

One difference I notice is that this chart says it's measuring "Level of Performance" instead of "attention." In the accompanying text, Bligh explains that Lloyd had observed the frequency of students taking notes, assuming that more note taking correlated with more learning. So in reality the chart merely tells us at what points in the lecture his students took the most notes. From that bit of data he hypothesized that taking more notes indicates better attention and leads to better performance.

But wouldn't an equally viable hypothesis be that almost all students take notes during the opening of the lecture to write down the title of the lecture and briefly explain the topic of the day? As the lecture proceeds, students probably write much less—only the points they think will be relevant to the test. At the end of the lecture, if the teacher summarizes his main points, wise students jot down those main points, since they may be on the midterm. Thus, if this hypothesis proves consistent with note-taking behavior, the study found precisely what we'd expect, even if it had no correlation whatsoever to attention or performance. In other words, this study may say little to nothing about waning attention during lectures.[9]

Bligh notes the inadequacies of Lloyd's study and after comparing other studies concludes, not that all lectures are largely ineffective after the first five minutes, but that "...the first 20-30 minutes of a lecture are different from the remainder. The remainder is probably less effective and less efficient."[10] This is a vastly different impression than I got from viewing that original chart.

Although Bligh's description of Lloyd's study helped me to understand what the study was about (note taking), it didn't help me to put numbers on the graph, in order to see just how dramatic the dip in note taking was. For this I had to order Lloyd's original study through interlibrary loan.

Here is Lloyd's original chart:

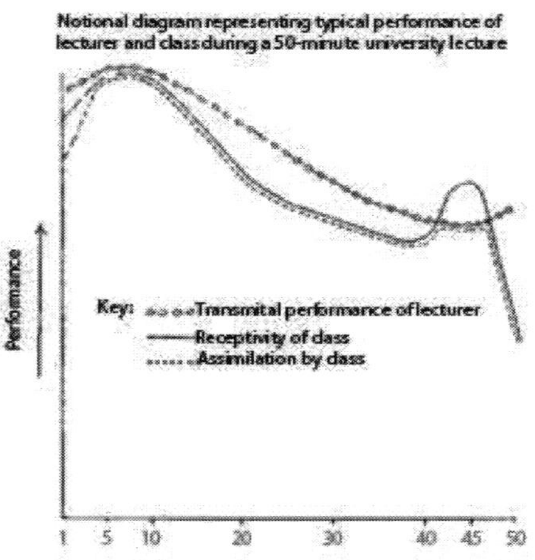

The Chart that Started It All
Same Study as Originally Published by Lloyd in 1968

My first observation is that each of the "copies" of this chart, as used by later studies, was redrawn, and not to the original scale. I sincerely hope people weren't skewing the chart in order to make their points more dramatic. Let's assume the best: perhaps scholars were working from a faded original and a limited budget, so they gave it to a first grade child with crayons to redraw to scale for publication.

My second observation is the lack of numbers on the "Performance" axis. Reading the original "study" explains the omission. The author tells us that there was very little (if any) scientific study behind the chart:

"The conclusions which follow do not represent the results of an experiment or even

> those of a formally organized enquiry. They are basically a synthesis of personal judgments arrived at, some subjectively, some more objectively, over the years."[11]

In brief, Lloyd observed his biology classes (less than riveting subject matter, I might guess) through the years, talked to his colleagues about their impressions of student performance during different points of the lecture, and finally took two of his biology lectures and looked over the notes from 19 of his students. He found that they took more notes at the beginning of class, dropped off sharply after 10 minutes, then experienced a small upsurge in note taking late in the class. From this he *assumed* that their attention waned after the first 10 minutes. Since he didn't pretend to know *how much* their attention waned, he didn't put numbers on it. Perhaps this is why later scholars felt free to redraw the chart to suit their needs.

My third observation is that Lloyd drew his bottom line much farther up on the vertical axis, giving the impression that although he thought students' attention declined after the first ten minutes, they didn't go anywhere near completely comatose. (More precisely, concerning what he was measuring, they didn't completely stop taking notes during the middle of the lecture.)

4. I gained further confirmation of my suspicions by finding more recent studies relevant to attention spans.

Lloyd published his original "study" in 1968. What relevant research has emerged since then?

A more recent study actually tested how much students were *retaining* from each segment of a lecture. No differences in retention were found, indicating that attention must have remained at levels at least adequate to retain the content until the end of the lecture.[12]

In another study students used clickers to indicate when they had a lapse in attention. Throughout the class time, with the first spike being at about 30 seconds into the lecture, students reported lapses (mind wandering) of mostly a minute or less. The numbers of lapses increased over the course of the lecture, but attention was much better when teachers interspersed active learning.[13]

What We Learn from these Studies

Lectures aren't futile, as the original chart seemed to indicate. Instead,

> "...a good lecture, one that is well crafted and expertly delivered, can surpass instructional media not only in cultivating so-called higher levels of learning, such as critical thinking, analysis and problem-solving skills, but also in the transmission of factual information" (Figlio, Ruish & Lin, 2010).[14]

But students *do* indeed get distracted, and more so as the lecture goes on. So in addition to learning to lecture well, in many contexts teachers would do well to avoid speaking nonstop for more than 15 to 20 minutes at a time. Instead, they would be wise to break up lectures with active learning such as student discussions to maximize student learning.[15]

Thus, regarding statistics, we see how the original chart didn't provide a clear origin, and subsequent drawings cut the origins even more, giving the impression that attention decline was far more drastic.

How Those with Agendas Can Manipulate Statistical Charts

Omitting origins allows people to take relatively minor differences and make them look huge.

(Isn't this fun? We're learning to think like many political statisticians!)

So let's look at one more example of omitting origins to demonstrate how agendas can influence presentations of statistics. Imagine that you're a politician and a major part of your platform is to improve education. You're preparing a PowerPoint presentation and have asked your statistician to prepare a chart showing how America compares to other countries in test scores.[16] Follow the conversation:

Statistician: I've got stats on science testing for 34 primarily prosperous, first world countries. Since test scores are heavily influenced by poverty rates, I figured that the rest of the world (about 162 other countries) would typically score worse than us, which puts us in the top 10 percent. According to this chart, we're looking pretty good!

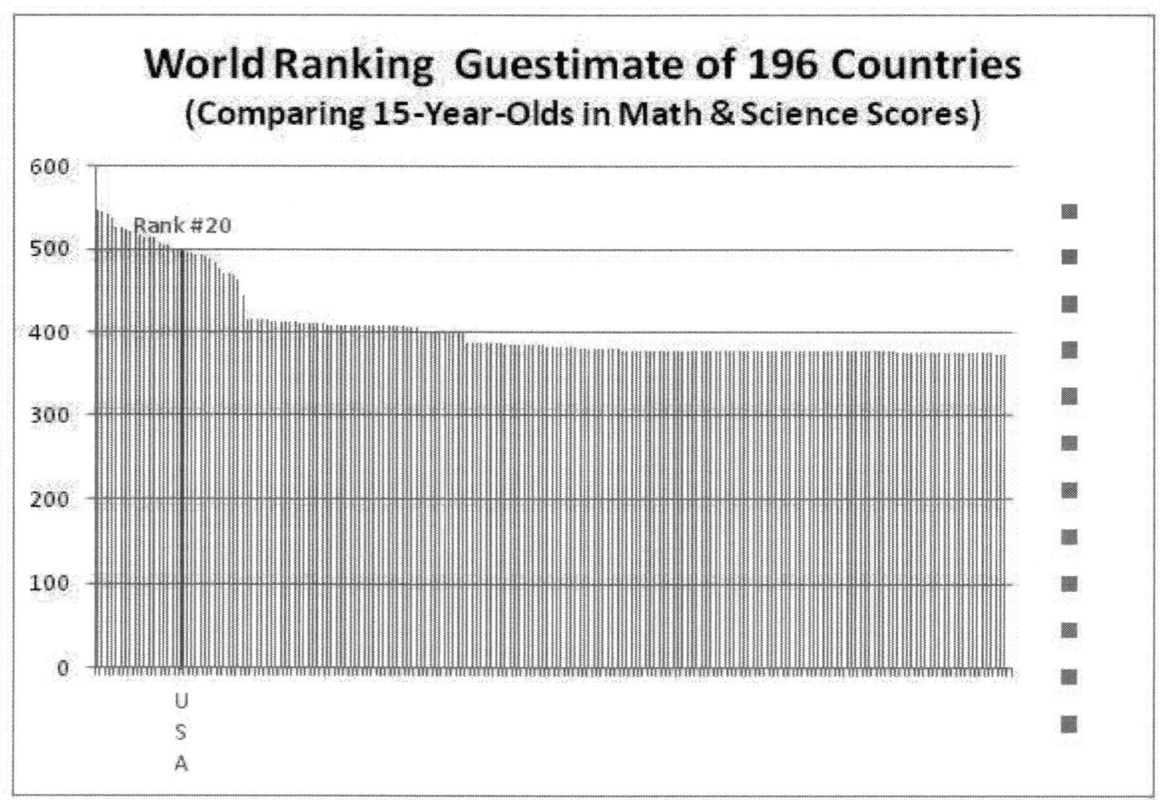

Politician: Well, I think you're having to guess too much. Surely many more of those countries are out-educating us. Besides, this chart makes us look too good. Let's cut out the rest of the world and just compare ourselves to some of the first world countries.

Statistician: Okay. So the PISA test was given to 34 OECD countries, which are almost all developed, first world countries. We were close to average, which might not be so bad when you consider America's demographics, including large pockets of poverty and large numbers of students who are still learning English, which is extremely different from so many of the largely homogeneous cultures that beat us on testing.

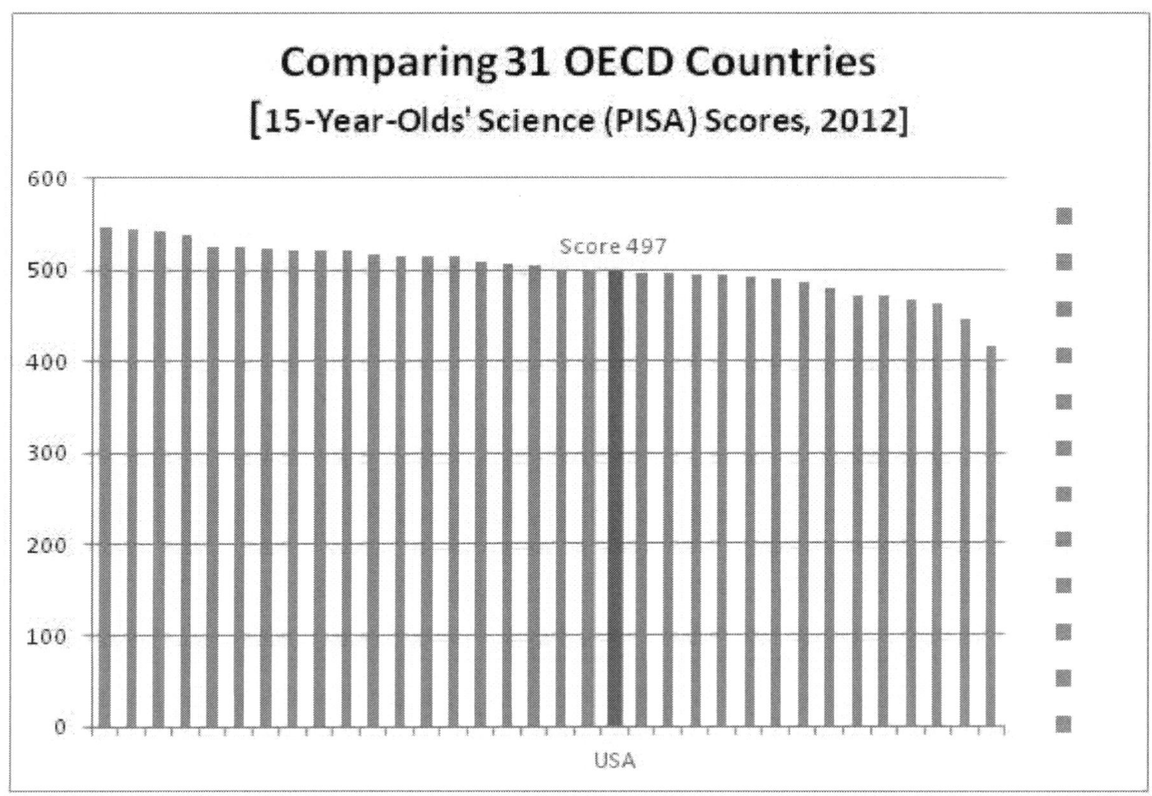

Politician: That won't do at all! The chart suggests that there's not that much difference between us and other developed countries. With bars that long, it looks like the difference between our scores and those above us might be the difference of just a few questions on the test. Can't you make it look like we're further behind the top countries? For goodness' sake, a big part of my platform is education. I need to convince people that we've got a crisis on our hands!

Statistician: Right...now I get it! You want me to "torture the data until it confesses what you want it to say." So let's hide all those lower numbers on the bottom of the chart and focus on the higher ones by eliminating the origins, so that the difference looks more dramatic. How about this?

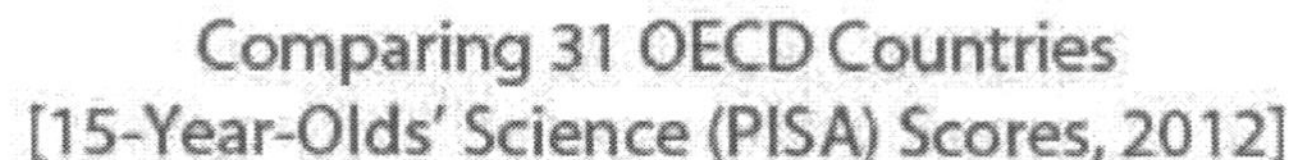

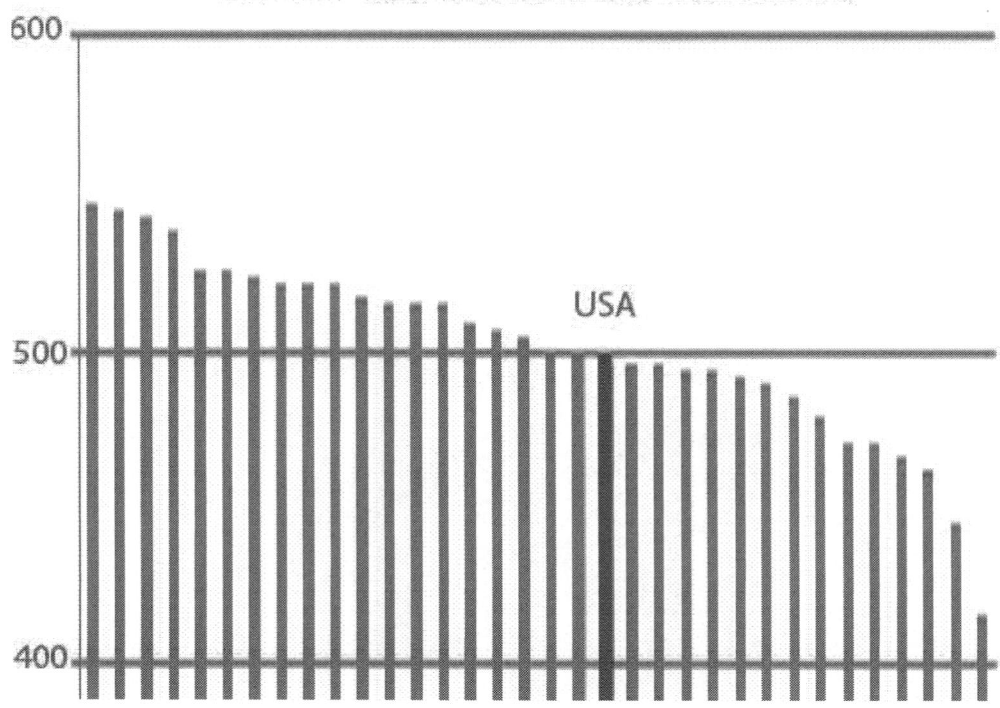

Politician: Much improved! But those countries that lag behind us still make us look better in comparison to them. Can't we do something about that? When I give my presentation, I need people to gasp, to moan, to feel like we're in a desperate mess.

Statistician: I think I'm catching on…how about this?

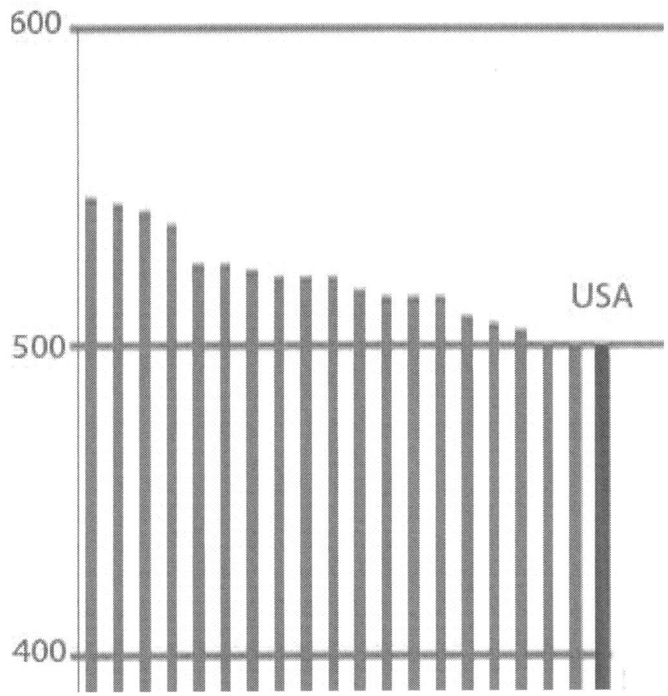

Politician: That's it! But is it accurate? What will the fact checkers say?

Statistician: Oh, it's completely accurate. Since we knew that the USA came in about average among the developed countries tested, and that we were ranked at #20, we just lopped off the rest of the bunch and compared solely the top 20. That puts us dead last!"[17]

Tip: To critique statistics, it's often helpful to put yourself in the shoes of the people presenting the statistics. Ask, "Might they have reasons to present data in a way that fits their personal agendas?" Sadly, the final graph is closer to the way we typically see these stats presented, since presenters often want to use the data to shock their audiences and move them to action.

Erroneous Extrapolation

In 1940, each car on a highway carried an average of 3.2 people. Fast forward to 1960 and the average was 1.4. This was a drop of 1.8 people in two decades. Extrapolate this out and by 1980 we should have had an average of less than 0 people per car! Of course, this is absurd. Yet it demonstrates the folly of assuming that past trends will continue indefinitely into the future.[18]

Especially beware of extrapolations concerning investments and the economy. Financial advisors often show charts of past performances to encourage us to invest in a certain stock or mutual fund or industry.

Imagine that you want to invest $10,000 so that it can grow into a substantial down payment for a house. It's January of the year 2000. Tech stocks (as represented by the NASDAQ stock exchange) have been growing rapidly and the NASDAQ is close to reaching 5000.

Your financial advisor shows you the graph below, extrapolating that tech stocks can only keep going upward. "After all, this is 'the new economy,'" proclaims your advisor, "based on the explosive growth of technology and particularly the Web. Had you invested your $10,000 four years ago, you'd have almost $50,000 by now. The Web and technology are our future—they aren't going away. They can only keep going up!"[19]

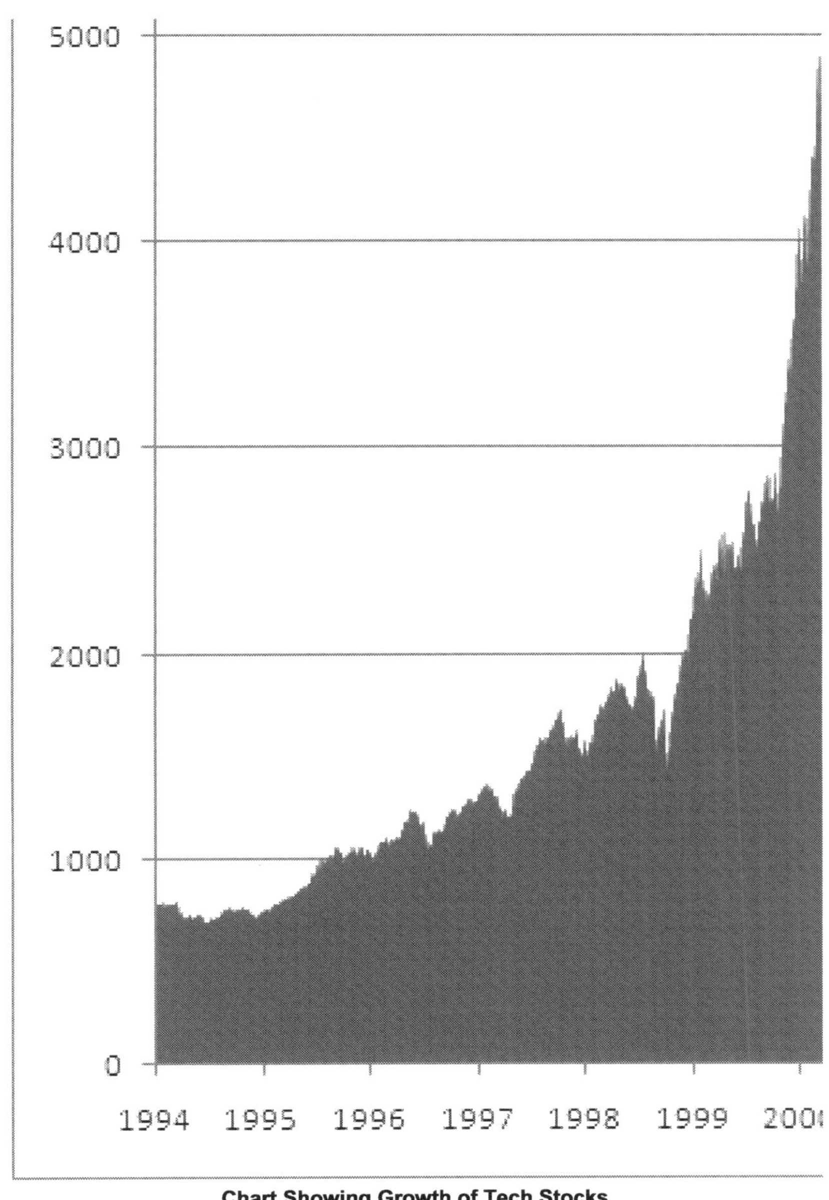

Chart Showing Growth of Tech Stocks
At the Time You Talked to Your Advisor

He seemed like a nice enough guy, and he was always reading up on technology and investing, so you put your $10,000 into a fund that indexes (seeks to mimic) the tech-heavy NASDAQ. The following chart shows what happened to your money over the following eight years.

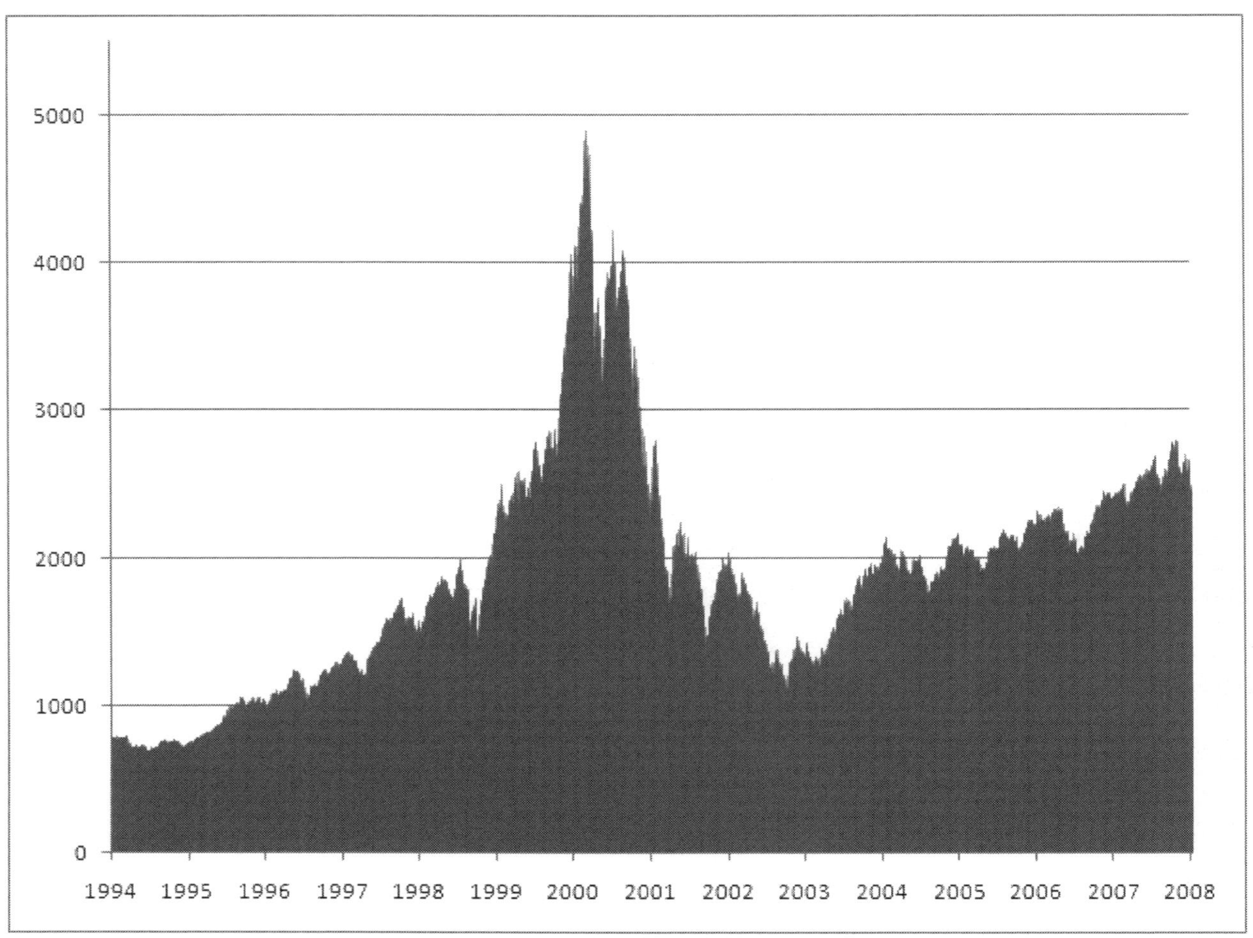

Chart Showing the Drop in Tech Stocks
In the Years Following Your Investment

In simple terms, a few months after you invested, the bottom dropped out of tech stocks. It was a bubble. (Economic bubbles are so obvious *after* they burst.) The extrapolation into the future looked nothing like what actually happened. Eight years after buying in, your $10,000 worth of tech stocks are worth about $5,000. You'd have likely done better buying a $10,000 bass boat. At least you could have brought home something for supper.

So much for "the new economy."

Our tendency to use past stock market data to extrapolate into the future is so pronounced, and so often wrong, that reputable investment companies post a warning beneath all of their reports of returns:

> "Past performance is no guarantee of future results."

It's just another way of saying:

> "People often get into trouble when they extrapolate charts into the future. It's risky

> behavior that has lost many a fortune."

Cherry Picking

This was another deceptive factor in the above investment advice. The advisor failed to show us a long-term chart of the behavior of tech stocks, which would have shown times of growth and decline, bubble and bust. By cherry picking only the most current period of growth, I had no way to consider the bigger picture.

Presenters are notorious for choosing a period of time that supports their position.

Failure to Understand Primary Sources And How the Data Was Derived

To evaluate the claims about student attention, I dug up the primary sources. It's truly amazing how many authorities keep quoting statistics and passing along charts without ever checking the data they're based upon.

Concerning evaluations of education in America, it's often reported that our test scores have been plummeting through the years. Bob Wise, president of the Alliance for Excellent Education and former governor of West Virginia, referred to our education being in a "free-fall." According to an article in Newsweek, "U.S. students, who once led the world, currently rank 21st in the world in science and 25th in math."[21]

So just when were these golden years in American education when we "led the world?" I can't find them. According to Brookings Institution scholar Tom Loveless, a noted expert on international testing, we *never* led the world in scoring. According to him, the first test comparing us to other countries was performed in 1964. Our 13-year-olds came in next to last compared to the other 11 countries tested.[22]

According to Loveless,

> "The United States never led the world. It was never number one and has never been close to number one on international math tests. Or on science tests, for that matter. It is more accurate to say that the United States has always trailed the world on math tests."[23]

So who do we believe, Wise or Loveless? If this issue is important to you, dig into the data for yourself. If writers/speakers fail to document their sources, they may be repeating nonsense, no matter how great their credentials are.

Poor Arguments from Accurate Data

I love following the Atlanta Falcons, learning a bit more each season about the intricacies of professional football. A few years ago, when running back Michael Turner was having an outstanding season, I read the following comment by a fan or sports analyst: "Whenever the

Falcons run Michael Turner enough to churn out over 200 yards, the Falcons win. So, it's obvious what we need to do going forward. Run Michael Turner!"

To put this into a syllogism:

Premise 1: "If Michael Turner ran over 200 yards per game in every winning game so far, then coaches should always prioritize running Turner."

Premise 2: "Turner ran for over 200 yards per winning game so far this season."

Therefore: "Prioritize running Turner."

Think!

Budding football analysts, what problems do you see with this argument?

My problems are with the first premise.

- What if the coaches prioritize running Turner only in games where the opponents don't excel at stopping the run?
- What if the next team we play stinks at defending the pass, but excels at stopping the run? Shouldn't we prioritize our passing game instead of running Michael Turner?
- What if the two offensive linemen who open up holes in the defensive line for Turner are currently on injured reserve?
- What if, since the next team we face is also looking at these statistics, they double team Turner?

If any of these four scenarios bear out, we'd be wise to *not* run Turner full out every game.

Football, to the casual observer, consists of a bunch of burly fellows trying to get a ball across a line. To the sophisticated analyst, it's an extremely complicated game of chess, where no two pieces (players) are exactly alike, the pieces constantly change (injuries and substitutions) and strategies often change midgame to exploit a perceived weakness or to counter the opponent's strategy.

Thus, to truly understand how a statistic may apply to running an NFL team, we need to understand more than logic. We need to understand football.

Conclusion

H.G. Wells wrote long ago, "Statistical thinking will one day be as necessary for efficient citizenship as the ability to read and write." That day has arrived! Every day, the media delivers statistics concerning sports, investments, education, health, the job market, and business. Those who don't know how to evaluate statistics are at the mercy of those who spin them to support their agendas.

Flex Your Neurons!
Pursuing the Point of Know Return

1. Are fatty diets really a major health risk? One recent researcher claims that the original researchers cherry-picked the countries studied, purposely choosing countries that fit their hypothesis. Read the article and see if you agree. Nina Teicholz, "The Questionable Link Between Saturated Fat and Heart Disease," Wall Street Journal, April 22, 2015; http://online.wsj.com/news/article_email/SB10001424052702303678404579533760481486-lMyQjAxMTA0MDEwMzExNDMyWj

2. How much water should we drink each day for optimum health? Is the evidence for eight cups a day sufficient? Here's an article to begin your search: http://www.blogofherbs.com/advice/squashing-the-8-cups-of-water-a-day-myth

3. During the "Cold War" between the Western World and the Soviet Union, I heard of a one-on-one athletic event between a Russian and an American, with the American winning. The Russian press release read, "Russia Places Second, America Next to Last." Perhaps it was only a joke, but it well demonstrates how titles can skew data. This week, look for illustrations of how titles of articles show bias in reporting studies.

4. Freshmen in college often perceive that "everybody's drinking" alcohol, putting pressure on them to "grow up" and join the crowd. One study found college students estimating that only five percent of their fellow students are not drinking. But are their estimates highly inflated? Try to find some well-done, recent statistics on how many college freshmen are actually drinking on a regular basis. Bring your results to class for discussion.

Making It More Personal
Practical Takeaways

What are one or more ideas provoked by this chapter that you can apply to help you think more critically?

____

____

____

What are one or more ideas that you can apply to help you think more creatively?

____

____

____

What else do you want to make sure you don't forget?

____

____

____

Recommended Trails For the Incurably Curious and Adventurous

For a good introductory text on statistics, especially for those who are scared of math and statistics, I like Gary Smith's *Introduction to Statistical Reasoning* (New York: WCB/McGraw-Hill,1998. Older editions are more affordable). It uses lots of practical, clear, interesting, real-life examples. It also concentrates on critical thinking and problem-solving skills rather than memorization and plugging in formulas. Like the present book, Smith chose to begin chapters with interesting dilemmas rather than begin with a formula followed by examples—a great way to engage interest and higher level thinking.

SECTION SIX

WHY DO BRILLIANT PEOPLE BELIEVE NONSENSE? BECAUSE THEY BOTCH HISTORY

CHAPTER 18

THEY FAIL TO LEARN FROM HISTORY

"*Those who cannot remember the past are condemned to repeat it.*"

— Santayana

They say you can learn a lot about people by the books they read. If so, those who peruse my personal library would likely conclude first of all that I've fallen hopelessly in love with reading. Second, they'd conclude that I'm especially addicted to history in the form of biographies and business stories.

Why?

Primarily because I'm very practical. While I certainly value learning from personal experience, I see its limitations—I can only experience so much. Thus, I much prefer learning from the vast personal experiences of others. Besides, floundering around trying out this and that results in tons of costly mistakes. I learn so much about successful relationships, my spiritual life, writing, teaching, business, and health by reading how others succeeded and failed.

Thus I read Anthony Bordain or Julia Child to learn from the lives of successful chefs, Eric Clapton and *The Beatles* to learn about perfecting skills and the price of success, Albert Einstein and Isaac Newton on lessons from science and scientists, Nelson Mandela and Martin Luther King Jr. and Mahatma Gandhi on how to impact people and society, Jack Welch and Warren Buffett on business and investing.

In this way, as I make personal and business decisions, I can make them not only in the context of my personal ethics and belief system, but also in the context of how hosts of others fared by making similar decisions. Because of my wide reading, I can ask myself, "If Jack Welch were running my business, what would he change? And how might Warren Buffett or Michael Dell or Steve Jobs put their personal spins on it?"

(I personally prefer reading over watching documentaries because I can cover so much more ground in less time, and can more easily make notes for future reference. Others may find good documentaries and select video presentations and personal interviews more useful.)

Let's take a personal life decision. Many people smoke cigarettes and seem to enjoy them. Should I start smoking? Well, I could either learn by my own experience (take up smoking and discover over time if it was a good decision) or by learning from the personal experiences (histories) of others. I might ask, "Of people who've smoked for a couple of decades, what percentage are glad they started and highly recommend it to those they love?" If the percentage is quite low, I've just learned something valuable from history.

Naysayers

Admittedly, some smart people beg to differ, agreeing with Hegel's pessimistic assessment that the only thing we learn from history is that we can learn nothing from history.[1] But surely that's a huge overstatement that nobody can live with consistently.[2]

If you decide that smoking crystal meth is a bad idea, didn't you draw that conclusion, at least in part, from the overwhelming testimonies of meth addicts, demonstrating that those who start using meth have a terrible time giving it up, and that those who fail to stop ruin their most important relationships, their jobs, their life savings, and develop complexions ideal for casting in Zombie movies? If we admit that we learn such a valuable lesson from the lives of meth users, then we're admitting that we can learn from history.

Learning from History

Surely we'd be foolish to ignore the history of drug abuse and repeat that sad history in our own lives. As I tell my children,

> "If you want to destroy your lives, at least find a new way of doing it. Don't destroy yourselves in same ways people have done it for thousands of years. A life spent repeating the known follies of the past isn't just tragic, it's embarrassing."

Smart People Who Failed to Learn from History

History is replete with tragic stories of bright people who failed to learn from her. Yet, today's bright people often continue to ignore it.

- **History tells us that risky sex (e.g., jumping from partner to partner) is emotionally and physically dangerous.** Thus, the influential intellectual Rousseau produced child after child, complicating his relationships and helping to fill the local hospital with orphans, who likely died there.[3] Philosopher Bertrand Russell's pattern of chasing skirts caused terrible emotional anguish to his wives and children, not to mention himself.[4] Famous Russian writer Tolstoy frequented brothels and acquired STDs that tormented him throughout his life.[5] These weren't rare occurrences. In some areas of Europe in the 19th century, one out of every ten men had syphilis.[6]

  Surely this would be an important historical lesson to learn; but amazingly, many people today prefer to learn from personal experience. Thus, in the UK in the first decade of the 21st century, we've seen syphilis surge by 1,000 percent. And it's not just risk-taking teens. One third of the cases are middle aged men.[7]

- **Here's a historically established formula for entrepreneurial failure:[8]**

  1 - Start your business in a hurry
  2 - In a field you know nothing about
  3 - With borrowed money

  Now read the rise and fall of the Enron corporation to see history repeat itself in one of the most tragic and costly business failures of all time. The leaders were undoubtedly brilliant people, but were too arrogant to consider some of the lessons of history. Thus, they made quick deals, purchasing companies in industries they knew little about, borrowing billions of dollars to bet on their future success.[9]

Why do brilliant people believe nonsense? Because they fail to learn from history.

How to Learn from History

1. Get a general overview.

Hopefully, a good formal education provided this for you. But we look at history through different eyes as adults. For this reason, although I'm well into my 50s and an "Instructor in Philosophy," I'm reading some shorter histories of philosophy (such as Will and Ariel Durant's popular *Story of Philosophy*) and plan to read a larger history of civilization and several books of lessons from history (such as the Durant's volume, *The Lessons of History*.)

Why the overview? It's easy to get so fascinated with the trees that we miss the forest. By getting the bigger picture first, or going back to remind ourselves of the larger context, it's easier to understand more specific histories in their context.

2. Read history with a critical eye.

We'll talk more about this in the next chapter. But suffice it to say that even the best historians must pick and choose from billions of historical events. Which are the most important to write about? They typically choose what they believe to be the most important or interesting events, which is naturally impacted by their personal interests, biases, and worldviews. So think as you read.

And before you purchase a book or documentary, do a bit of research. Before I read a book, I want to know up front if it's worth my investment of time and money. Do I have reason trust its research? Will I be able to quote from it with authority in the future? Some are so biased or poorly researched or so blended with fiction that they're worth little for those seeking real history.

Example: When films are "based upon real events," how do we know what's real and what's made up? Perhaps the "real events" in a television special on Elvis are that he became famous, gained weight and died in his bathroom. They get these three facts correct, but skew everything else for dramatic effect and justify it with "artistic license." To sift the truth from the Hollywood spin in Spielberg's *Lincoln*, search Google for the Lincoln scholars who fact checked it.[10]

3. Read histories of people and topics that fascinate you.

Do you love cars? Read articles or books or watch documentaries on the history of those cars. I'm currently reading Masaaki Sato's history of Honda. By reading about something of interest to me, I not only glean business ideas on such topics such as breaking into an established industry, innovation, marketing, producing quality products, and taking chances versus risk management; I also learn much about Japanese history and culture.

Some who would be bored to tears with reading a history of the 1960s in America might learn and retain more of that history by reading a good history of their favorite '60s' bands or a biography of a key figure in the civil rights movement.

4. Prioritize the history that's most relevant to you.

If you're fascinated with wars, generals, presidents and changes in borders, you'll delight in works of general history. But if you're interested in succeeding in a vocation, pursuing a talent, learning wise money management, or improving your personal relationship skills, you'll likely find little help in a general history book. Instead, find specialist histories.

To better understand the impact of paradigms, I read histories of both the Big Bang Theory and the laws of thermodynamics. I wasn't just naturally drawn to these topics (point #3), but I felt I needed the background to write chapters eight and nine.

So you may not be naturally inclined to study economic history or the stories of people who managed their money wisely or poorly. But if you need help with your personal finances, such a study might help. Start with some authoritative articles (respected scholars in their fields, writing in respected publications.) If you need more, read a book like Burton Malkiel's *A Random Walk Down Wall Street*. Learning elements of the history of stocks and the history of successful businesses could save investors from much heartache and investing folly.

What do you imagine golf sensation Tiger Woods studied in college? Health? Sports therapy? Wrong. Those might have been more inherently interesting to him, but knowing how many successful sports figures either mismanage their finances or allow others to mismanage them, he studied economics at Stanford.

To learn more about personal finances, consider reading parts of an authoritative biography of Warren Buffett, such as Roger Lowenstein's *Buffett: The Making of An American Capitalist*, or Alice Schroeder's more recent *The Snowball*. While most people seem interested in how he invests his money to achieve such a high rate of return, very few people would seem to have the type of mind and personality to pull that one off.[11]

But we *can* all benefit from learning how Buffett earned and saved and invested his money from elementary school through high school. Read that portion of his biography (skipping the rest, if it's not relevant to you) and you'll learn how he worked normal jobs that anyone could work (paper routes, finding and selling golf balls, caddying, etc.), and invested it wisely so that by high school he was earning more than his teachers. Follow this up by reading Benjamin Franklin's *Autobiography* and you're well on your way to understanding personal finance.

If you aspire to be a writer, don't just study texts on how to write. Study writers to understand the great variety in their approaches to writing, marketing, managing the writing life, and navigating the business of writing. Madeleine L'Engle had a terrible time finding a publisher for *A Wrinkle in Time*. A chance encounter with a publisher at a social event, after she'd given up on it, allowed this classic to be published.[12] Novelist Fannie Flagg has difficulty mapping out her novels, so she stretches a clothes line down her hallway and attaches pages of the book to visualize the order of events.[13]

Reading a biography never fails to give me more and different wisdom than I was expecting. Example: I'm always amazed and intrigued by successful people's quirks. Read *The Idea Factory* on the history of Bell Labs and you'll find one of their most brilliant scientists riding up and down the company halls on his unicycle, while juggling. He'd hang up his phone on his colleagues mid-conversation for seemingly no reason. But he was far from the only one with quirks. How all these diverse personalities worked together to make many of the most important scientific discoveries of modern times gave me insights into management and understanding people. (As one author titled his book, *Everybody's Normal Till You Get to Know Them*.)

If you struggle with disabilities, read Paul Orfalea's autobiographical history of his successful print shop chain, Kinko's (later acquired by FedEx). Its subtitle says it all: *Lessons from a Hyperactive Dyslexic Who Turned a Bright Idea into One of America's Best Companies*.

Much wisdom lies waiting to be mined from the biographies of both successes and failures in fields relevant to your personal success.

5. Plan for, reflect upon, and value personal experiences.

A valuable part of your personal history is your experience. While I love learning from the experiences of others, there's often no substitute for personal experience.

Planning for Experience

If you're interested in running a restaurant, don't just study restaurant management, work at a restaurant! There's so much to learn from experienced waiters, chefs, prep chefs and managers that's difficult to pick up from a book. The more personal experience you accrue, the better you can draw upon your rich personal history.

Peter Han interviewed 100 extremely successful people in diverse fields to discover the secrets of their success. He found that many of them made vocational changes, in part, because of what they felt they could learn from the new job.[14]

Reflecting upon Experience

In an age of constant communication, with texting and Facebook constantly distracting us, it's easy to neglect the fine art of introspection.

So you hate your job. Ask yourself, in fine detail, what *exactly* you hate about it. Do you hate working with people in general, or just hate working with *those* people? Is the job too mundane, too challenging, or requires skills you lack? Does *anyone* love that kind of job, or is it just crappy all the way through? Do you love or hate direct contact with customers?

By thoroughly reflecting upon that recent history—what you love and hate about your present job—you prepare yourself to seek out increasingly fulfilling jobs in the future.

Valuing Experience

The leaders at Enron failed to value business experience. Instead, they tended to deprecate experience in their hiring, choosing top students soon after college, assuming they were smart enough to figure things out. The resulting lack of experience took its toll. They knew almost nothing about how to run their energy businesses, water businesses, and broadband business, and they failed miserably as a result.[15]

On Creative Thinking
The Importance of Being There

Have you noticed that many people today can't seem to fully focus on what they're presently doing—their present experiences? One of my sons attended a concert where a musician challenged the audience: "For a moment, put down your iPhones and stop texting your friends about this experience. This concert will only happen once. Experience it!" Consider how trying to "be there" more fully can enrich your experiences and result in better ideas.

Keith Reid, lyricist for the '60s' band Procol Harum, was at a party and overheard someone say to a woman, "You've turned a whiter shade of pale." The phrase stuck with him and he used it to title their song, "A Whiter Shade of Pale," which reached number one in several countries and has aged so gracefully that as of 2009, "it was the most played song in the last 75 years in public places in the United Kingdom." It has been recorded by other bands at least 1,000 times.

But Reid would have never overheard or reflected on the conversation had his mind been elsewhere.[16] This is why some educators speak of "the myth of multitasking." We think we can text on our phones and update Facebook while reading a text or listening to a lecture or attending a business meeting. But since we're "not all there," we fail to fully understand or to fully engage our higher level thinking.

Flex Your Neurons!
Pursuing the Point of Know Return

1. Last week, at an auto dealership, I met a salesman from Morocco who was the top Nissan salesman in the country. I pulled him aside, introduced my 20-year-old son and said, "You've been incredibly successful in your field. Give us two minutes of advice. Why are you so successful?" He gave invaluable tips such as looking people in the eye and being totally honest with customers. Who could you interview to learn more about a topic that interests you?

2. At age 58, I help my 83-year-old mother care for my 109-year-old grandmother. Some would consider it a mundane task, but there's so much wisdom to be mined at granny's house! I regularly ask mom (granny's beyond sharing wisdom) for her advice and her recollections. These greatly inform me about how to more wisely live my life. Oh the wisdom we miss by texting friends during supper rather than engaging our parents and siblings in fascinating conversations! How could wisely worded questions help you to learn more from the experiences of your parents, relatives, and friends?

3. My boys have worked in the fields of graphics, restaurants, a pawn shop, auto and motorcycle mechanics, carpentry, building, and veterinary medicine. I love learning from them about their work, and they seem to love talking about it. How could you get your siblings and friends talking more about their lessons from life, so that you're learning from each other?

4. I've heard that people in Taiwan have for generations designated family historians to record family events of their generation. Thus, they can learn from generations past. Would keeping such a family history be of value to you? If you're interested, map out a plan to make it happen in your family.

Making It More Personal
Practical Takeaways

What are one or more ideas provoked by this chapter that you can apply to help you think more critically?

____

____

____

What are one or more ideas that you can apply to help you think more creatively?

____

____

____

What else do you want to make sure you don't forget?

____

____

____

Recommended Trails
For the Incurably Curious and Adventurous

1. Film versions of historical events often play fast and loose with history, in order to make them more entertaining. Take a movie based on real events and try to discover how closely it adhered to accurate history. You might search, for example "fact check Spielberg's Lincoln," or "Apollo 13 accuracy."

2. Do a web search for famous people (entertainers, athletes, etc.) who died broke. What can we learn from them?

3. Find documentaries or books on the histories of people/businesses that might be valuable for your career. Map out a plan to view/read them over time, to keep you inspired and growing in your field.

CHAPTER 19

THEY LEARN THE WRONG LESSONS FROM HISTORY

"Those who don't study history are doomed to repeat it. Yet those who do study history are doomed to stand by helplessly while everyone else repeats it."

— From a cartoon[1]

A Fragile Life; A Fragile History

Superior Court judge Charles McCoy, Jr. watched the bailiff help Tucker make his way to the witness stand on crutches. When comfortable, Tucker recounted the event that permanently changed his life. Once a successful Los Angeles investment banker pulling in $600,000 a year, he competed in marathons in his free time. But on that fateful afternoon, as he walked to lunch from his office, a steel beam broke loose as it was being moved by construction workers, striking Tucker on the head, then crushing a nearby car. The workers had failed to secure the beams with a safety harness.

Now, years later, the former picture of health endured excruciating pain when he simply raised his arm. Although he returned to work after six months of rehabilitation, he could no longer think clearly. As a result, he lost his job.

His doctors, including an expert on brain injury, testified that Tucker's injuries were irreversible, and that his only relief from constant, intense pain, would be powerful, addictive drugs.

Tucker's lawyer rested his case and judge McCoy had the weekend to contemplate the grim facts. The outcome seemed so certain that he began calculating a fair reward for damages—perhaps $9 million?

But Monday morning judge McCoy arrived to find a large TV screen in his courtroom. A private investigator had been filming Tucker, starting a year after his accident. According to McCoy, the film showed Tucker

> "stretching, bending, twisting, sprinting like a gazelle, running effortlessly for miles with an ease only champions achieve—all without the slightest hesitation or grimace, and all at night when Tucker assumed no one would see him."[2]

The last film was taken the very week he shared his testimony. Tucker promptly stomped out of the courtroom, leaving his crutches behind.

Now imagine that the investigator had never uncovered the farce. Further imagine that someone had written a riches to rags biography, based on the testimonies of Tucker and his doctors. The author would have thought he was writing historical fact. The readers would have assumed they were reading historical fact. Perhaps only Tucker would have known the truth.

If it's this easy to be led astray with *recent* history, how much more should readers and writers of *distant* history question the accuracy of their sources?

Why do brilliant people believe nonsense? Because they believe ill-founded history, or accept ill-founded conclusions based upon history.

Verifying History

Fortunately, careful historians have ways to distinguish well-established history from questionable history. For example:

- If a historical claim depends upon extant (presently existing) manuscripts, how many manuscripts do we have, to what extent do they agree, and how far removed are they from the originals?
- If the historical claim depends upon people's reports, how many reports do we have and do we have reason to believe that the reporters were honest, accurate and unbiased? (Tucker's testimony demanded extra scrutiny since the case involved money. He had millions of dollars' worth of reasons to fabricate a clever tale.)
- Do archeological findings or known geographical facts confirm the reports?

Example: Abraham Lincoln's famous Gettysburg Address was delivered Thursday, November 19, 1863, in Gettysburg, Pennsylvania. The event was well established since many people were present to verify it and we see no motive for the reporters to lie.

But we're not so certain about the exact wording of the speech. Obviously, we don't have a recording. We have five extant versions of the speech in Lincoln's handwriting, two apparently written in preparation before the speech; but we know that speakers often veer widely from their notes. We also have the versions he wrote after the speech and the reports from newspaper reporters. Yet, they differ from one another in their exact wording. As a result, we can't say we know for certain every word that Lincoln spoke in his address. But by comparing the reports, we can approximate the exact words and feel confident that we've accurately captured his thoughts.[3]

Historians' Fallacies

In 1970, hordes of historians feverishly read the index to David Fischer's book, *Historians' Fallacies*, and breathed a sigh of relief to realize their works weren't criticized. Unfortunately, scores of respected historians found their names included.

There are many ways to botch history, or to draw ill-founded applications from well-founded history. Fischer detailed over 100 of them. Fortunately, many of these errors can be spotted by familiarizing ourselves with the fallacies and research methods we've discussed in earlier chapters, applying them to historians' works. Let's dissect a few that I often see in popular literature.

1. They draw from poor sources.

The Da Vinci Code: Fact or Fiction?

When Dan Brown's *The Da Vinci Code* hit bookstores in 2003, it quickly circled the globe as a worldwide bestseller, eventually selling over 80 million copies. The film adaptation appeared three years later, starring Tom Hanks.

As pure entertainment, it's a fast and furious read, tantalizing readers with mysterious puzzles, clues, action and compelling characters. But an additional feature added to the intrigue—Brown claimed that it was based on fact.

Now at first this would seem to be a confusion of genres, much like claiming that Bart Simpson and Charlie Brown are great actors. After all, it's fiction, a novel. But according to Brown, he took great pains to insure that the historical artifacts, documents, events, secret societies and rituals that he referred to were all factual. When asked on *The Today Show* about how much of his book was based on reality, Brown replied, "Absolutely all of it."[4]

Since this "factual base" contradicts more mainstream beliefs about Da Vinci, the Catholic Church, the life of Jesus and the early church, it naturally created quite a stir among reviewers.

Some early reviewers took Brown's claims at face value. *Publisher's Weekly* described *The Da Vinci Code* as "an exhaustively researched page-turner."[5] A writer for the *New York Daily News* proclaimed "his research is impeccable."[6]

Fortunately for researchers, Brown listed his main sources on his website.[7] Unfortunately for Brown, his list reads like a who's who of conspiracy theory books, known for playing fast and loose with history.[8] In other words, no matter how many hours Brown spent in research, if he was diligently devouring unreliable sources, it was an exercise in futility. No amount of additional reading in such sources would have brought him closer to the truth.

In reading *The Da Vinci Code*, I was glad I'd recently read a well-researched biography of Leonardo.[9] So when one of the characters, early in the story, claimed that Da Vinci[10] accepted "hundreds of lucrative Vatican commissions," I knew that, far from hundreds, he'd accepted only one such commission.[11] (An error of this magnitude is what professional historians would likely deem "a whopper.") When I fact checked (with respected scholars and historians) Brown's claims concerning early church history, secret societies and claims about paintings and artifacts, one after another revealed that Brown's central "facts" were typically pure speculation.

The curator of European Decorative Arts at the Art Institute of Chicago concluded:

> "...how much does this murder mystery have to do with the real Leonardo? The short answer is not much, and the author's grasp of the historical Leonardo is shaky."[12]

More thorough, book-long debunkings were written by 2004, showing in great detail the lack of historical basis. One authoritative critique of the historical claims took over 300 pages to unravel all the historical nonsense.[13]

In the end, *The Da Vinci Code* was just fiction after all. Yet it's amazing how many intelligent readers and reviewers accepted the author's claims, and perhaps even read some of his sources, convinced that they were onto something big, when in reality they'd done nothing more than naively fallen for revisionist history in the form of a conspiracy theory.

So it's not enough for an author to claim that he's done his research. Neither is it enough for an author to document his sources. Only respected, quality sources can build the foundation for a work that speaks with authority.

So when I choose a biography of an interesting person, or a history of a fascinating business, I first discover whether or not it's written by someone who did first-class research or experienced the events first hand and had no reason to skew the facts. Reading a variety of reviewers can often help in narrowing down the best resources.

2. They assume that they can accurately attribute later events to earlier events.

Well if it isn't our old friend *post hoc ergo propter hoc* ("after this, therefore because of this")! Yes, our logical fallacies come in handy as we try to sift history's facts from nonsense.

What Killed Off So Many Europeans?

Often the connections we make from event to event are well founded. Example: Why did 30 to 60 percent of Europeans suddenly die in the mid-14th century? Well, we're on solid historical ground to blame the "Black Death." The connection is well documented. But when we ask where the Black Death came from, things get more tentative. It *likely* originated in Central Asia, was *perhaps* carried by travelers along the Silk Road, *possibly* spread to Europe by fleas on rats traveling to Europe on cargo ships.[14]

But we can't know its origin for certain. We can't send a physician back in time to examine the travelers, dissect the fleas and interview the rats. Thus good historians take care to distinguish solid historical connections from probabilities and pure speculation.

Who or What Caused America's Great Recession?

Think!

In a paragraph or two, sum up what you've heard about the causes of the recent Great Recession (beginning in 2007-2008).

Our brains naturally look for and prefer simple answers, especially if they involve blaming a rival political party. Ask Republicans (or a Republican sponsored commission) and they'll tend to emphasize factors other than those caused by their party. Ask Democrats (or a Democratic sponsored commission) and they'll likely emphasize Republicans' failures. Look no further than the results of the Federally sponsored *Financial Crisis Inquiry Commission*. After interviews with over 700 witnesses, the six Democrats and four Republicans remained divided along party lines as to which factors contributed to or were most important in precipitating the crisis.[15]

But regardless of party affiliation, we tend to develop simplistic mental narratives to explain the recession.[16] Thus, for a time, many proclaimed that Bush's tax cuts caused the recession.[17]

But surely it's too simple to blame the policies or failures of any one president or party. After all, the recession wasn't an exclusively American event—it was global. Various commissions have studied the crisis and compiled long lists of contributing factors, which must somehow be weighed to determine which factors contributed most heavily.[18]

Since the crisis erupted toward the end of George Bush's presidency, it's tempting to place the blame exclusively on him and his party for the crisis. When we see an effect, we naturally look to the closest historical events to assign causes. But looking at the deeper analyses of economists and commissions shows a more complex picture of contributing factors.

- The housing bubble burst, causing large-scale defaults on subprime mortgages, leading to a banking crisis.[19]
- An unprecedented jump in oil prices clobbered the US auto industry, reverberating through the rest of the economy.[20]
- Americans had borrowed way beyond way their means, then had to curtail spending after the housing bubble burst, which hindered economic recovery.[21]
- Many people unwisely bought houses they couldn't afford, often with risky mortgages that could increase their future payments beyond their means to pay.
- Many blame Fed chairman Ben Bernanke's policies.[22]
- Bernanke blamed it on lack of regulation and oversight.[23]
- The government placed quotas on the loan organizations Freddie Mac and Fannie Mae, which led them to make home loans to people who likely couldn't afford them.
- Many blame former Fed chairman Alan Greenspan for policies such as spurring on the real estate bubble by keeping interest rates low.[24]
- Insufficient regulatory laws, as a result of deregulation, allowed excesses.[25]
- Insufficient enforcement of existing laws allowed banks to hide their risky investments.[26]

- The creation of risky, exotic investment schemes by Wall Street and banks, allowed for dangerous speculation.
- Choosing to shield these exotic investment instruments from regulation made them even riskier.[27]
- Banks hid their true financial state (excessive leverage) behind "off balance sheet entities."
- Government policies designed to help the financially disadvantaged to escape a lifetime of renting, and to experience the advantages of home ownership, lowered lending standards.
- Lenders adopted questionable practices.
- Incompetent rating of mortgage backed securities by trusted rating agencies led investors to think their investments were relatively safe.
- Large-scale investing in real estate by individuals and institutions drove housing prices ever higher.
- Brilliant economists' mathematical formulas assured rating agencies, investors and policy makers that investing in subprime real estate wasn't that risky.[28]

Making Sense of Contributing Factors with Narratives

In order to try to understand and weigh the importance of each of these factors, economic theorists (and the rest of us) develop "narratives"—stories of how these various factors worked together to cause the crisis. Many narratives have been forwarded to try to make sense of this recession. Here's mine, based on my admittedly limited knowledge of the field:

> Respected economists published papers suggesting that deregulating the banking industry would make it more competitive and in the end benefit consumers. Mathematical theorists published papers showing that bundling together thousands of loans would reduce the risk of subprime loans, thus allowing banks to make loans to people with less financial stability.
>
> Those in power (Fed chairman, Congress, presidents, etc.) believed these studies to be credible and saw an opportunity to allow those with smaller incomes to escape the rental trap and experience the benefits of home ownership. Thus, they set quotas for the organizations Fannie Mae and Freddie Mac to grant a large percentage of their loans to low income people. In order to achieve these quotas, these organizations had to lower their standards of lending.
>
> Individual and institutional investors in mutual funds poured more and more money into Real Estate Investment Trusts, since these were getting stellar returns in comparison with other mutual funds and investments, causing real estate investments to increase in value far beyond other investments.

Wall Street developed creative investments, such as derivatives, which enabled investors to try their hand at making money on these bundled loans. The government decided to not regulate the derivatives.

The combination of low interest rates (to spur economic recovery from the bursting of the tech bubble) and easy credit helped to fuel a real estate bubble. The banks which invested most heavily in real estate made tons of money, so that they could afford to offer such features as free checking and capture the market share, so that other banks had to join in the real estate frenzy to remain competitive. Some sleazy banks found loopholes in regulations, allowing them to invest more money by hiding how much money they were risking in investments.

Builders got rich building new, expensive neighborhoods, assuming that easy credit and increasing home values would last forever. So they built newer and bigger houses, speculating that people would buy them.

When Dick and Jane saw their friends at work and their apartment neighbors buying nice houses, they wanted a nice house. People with nice houses wanted nicer houses, and banks were happy to lend them money. Dick and Jane failed to notice that they no longer had the safety cushion of former generations who practiced such dull habits as putting away 10 percent of their income into savings. By the 2000s, people were merrily running up credit cards and taking out loans, spending more than they made, seemingly oblivious to the dangers of debt.

Those who were responsible for regulating Wall Street and the banks were apparently too busy to do their regulating stuff. After all, they had fancy dinners and schmoozing events to attend, sponsored by lobbyists for various good causes such as Wall Street investing firms and big banks.

Eventually, the real estate bubble burst, initiated by such factors as people defaulting on their loans, investors getting spooked and pulling out, banks tightening their lending, and people losing jobs.

This is just one of many possible narratives, all of which try to identify the primary causes and connect in a meaningful way the factors that most likely contributed to the Great Recession. So which were the most important factors?

So Who's to Blame?

In some circles, it's fashionable to place the entire blame on the Bush administration. Surely they should shoulder some of the blame, since it happened on their watch, but how much? While our minds love simple solutions, in the end it's not so simple. After all, the *Financial Crisis Inquiry Commission*, with a majority of Democrats, noted that the Clinton administration's decision to shield exotic real estate investment instruments such as derivatives from regulation was a major factor.[29]

Warren Buffett places much of the blame on the economists and mathematicians that government leaders were listening to. Buffett suggests the following lesson from the crisis:

> "Constructed by a nerdy-sounding priesthood using esoteric terms such as beta, gamma, sigma and the like, these models tend to look impressive. Too often, though, investors forget to examine the assumptions behind the symbols. Our advice: Beware of geeks bearing formulas."[30]

A writer for *Newsweek*, exploring causes of the economic crash, concluded with a wise caution about too quickly assigning simplistic causes to this historical event:

> Historians are still debating what caused the Great Depression, so it's not likely this argument will be settled any time soon.[31]

So when respected writers or teachers declare with finality that "Obama wrecked our economy," or "the Reagan administration started this mess," or "greedy bankers caused this recession," don't accept their blanket judgment before asking yourself, "Did they present adequate evidence to connect causes with effects? What about all the other historical factors? Isn't this issue currently dividing even our greatest economic thinkers?"

3. They cherry pick data.

Some writers may get their facts straight, but present only the historical data that supports their views, ignoring the rest. As historians Will and Ariel Durant observed,

> "History is so indifferently rich that a case for almost any conclusion from it can be made by a selection of instances."[32]

Take the writings of Karl Marx and Friedrich Engels.

Through their writings, it could be argued that they impacted the political landscape of the world more significantly than any two people in modern times. Just look at their imprint on the Communist States in the 1900s, including the huge portions of the world represented by the former Soviet Union and China.

In their writings they argued that capitalism was a flawed system which inevitably leads, over time, to capitalists increasingly exploiting the workers. The legitimate way to examine the evidence for this thesis would be to first try to collect sufficient data on the positive and negative impact of capitalism on workers and discover if it has consistently worsened the quality of life for workers over time.

Yet, when scholars have examined Marx and Engle's works, they find them cherry picking events that make capitalism look bad, rather than allowing history to speak for itself.[33]

For example, Marx dug up stories of abuses of workers by factory owners and used them to enrage his readers over the exploitation. Yet his main sources in numerous cases were the reports by government inspectors who were charged with detecting and prosecuting those exploiters. In other words, had Marx revealed his sources, and had his readers understood them in context, they would have seen many of his examples as proof that the capitalist government was *helping* the workers by responsibly correcting many of the abuses Marx was complaining about![34]

Yet such collections of stories wield great power. We remember stories. We identify with them. They engage our emotions. And if we're not careful, we'll believe their conclusions without realizing that we've heard only one side of the story—the side the authors wanted us to hear. In the case of Marx and Engels, their cherry picked stories changed the world. Only an objective study of the positive and negative impact of Marxism can tell us whether they made the world better or worse.

So as you read articles and listen to the news, ask yourself, "Am I hearing an objective report of evidence for both sides, or is the author/broadcaster just cherry picking stories that support his bias?" If articles are promoting a new diet, are they cherry-picking stories of people who successfully lost weight without including stories of people who didn't? If so, you're reading an advertisement, not a serious presentation of the facts.

4. They're enamored with recent history.

Clothing Styles and Recency

Have you ever looked at your parents' yearbooks and laughed out loud at their ridiculous hair styles and clothes? If so, did you stop to think that, to your parents, during their teen years, those ridiculous styles seemed cool? And have you further considered that your own children might one day open *your* yearbook and laugh hysterically at *your* generation's outrageous styles?

My point? Fads seem smart and natural in their time, but can't be fully assessed until we see them in the rear-view mirror.

Intellectual History and Recency

Is it any different with intellectual fads? We find difficulty assessing the supposedly great ideas of our own times, because we absorb them almost without question, just like we absorb current hair styles and clothing trends. We can't imagine that great thinkers of the next generation may look back at many of our generation's "great" ideas with hysterical amusement and wonder.

In 1986, Professor Allan Bloom noted in his thought-provoking book, *The Closing of the American Mind*, that when his students arrived at the University of Chicago, virtually none of them believed in absolute right and wrong. Now certainly many informed, bright people don't believe in moral absolutes, but his point was that these elite students, smart enough to make it into such an elite school, had adopted their position, not by wrestling with the reasoning of history's great thinkers, but apparently by a process more akin to osmosis. In other words, students read popular literature that assumed relativism and their teachers likely preached relativism. The students passively adopted relativism without thinking it through for themselves.

It never seemed to bother them that to be consistent they couldn't say that Hitler was absolutely wrong to kill millions of innocent people.

But such a view dominated the intellectual world in the early and mid-1900's as part of the larger intellectual movement called Modernism.[35]

Modernism, Postmodernism and...What Next?

At each shift in intellectual history, we imagine ourselves standing on the pinnacle of human thought, looking down with a smirk at the ignorant generations past. As evidence for this chronological snobbery, let's reflect upon the naming of modernism. After all, "modern" means "of the present and recent times, not antiquated." So by naming the movement modernism, influential intellects presumably thought that this was the last great intellectual movement that would endure through the rest of human history. "We've reached the pinnacle of human thought," they likely assumed. "Now we're modernists."

But lo and behold many thinkers moved beyond modernist thought, posing a problem in naming the avant-garde manner of thought. So what could the "Committee on Naming Intellectual Movements" call a period following modernism? "Futurism?" No, that wouldn't do, because we're naming what people think *now*, not in the future.

So they began calling it "postmodernism," which of course appears to be a contradiction in terms. How can we possibly live in times that are "beyond modern," if "modern" is by definition "current?" In its favor, the name "postmodern" at least allows us to continue to bask in the arrogance that assumes we're now a part of the last great intellectual movement.

But the current members of the venerable naming committee must by now realize that previous members have painted them into a grammatically induced no win corner. They almost certainly spend their meetings nervously pondering what to call the next intellectual period. "Post-Post Modernism"? Well, that name would saddle the next generation's committee with Post-Post-Postmodernism. I feel for them.

And there are indeed signs that we're moving past postmodernism, a movement which tended to despair of searching for truth, while relishing experience. Today we find influential intellectuals such as Harvard's Michael Sandal arguing that we can indeed find truth, even in morals. His book *Justice: What's the Right Thing to Do?* is wildly popular, widely taught in American universities. (So this guy has the audacity to speak of both "right" and "wrong"? Both Modernists and Postmodernists must be horrified.) He's treated like a rock star when he speaks in Japan or China. If Sandal and those who teach similar ideas end up dominating this intellectual era, I don't envy the job of our current naming committee.[36]

Thus it would seem that our assumption that we live at the pinnacle of intellectual history is ill founded. So don't fall into the trap of believing that the current intellectual fads, any more than our current hair styles, will last indefinitely. More likely, future generations of professors will discuss them with a hearty laugh or a sneer.

My take away? Don't soak up the intellectual fad *du jour* by osmosis. Think for yourself.

The Psychology of Recency

Psychologist have noted the power of "recency"—"the tendency to estimate probabilities not on the basis of long-term experience but rather on a handful of the latest outcomes." This makes sense of the phenomenon of people losing money in the stock market by chasing stocks that are moving up. Typically, they see a stock moving up (recent history) and assume this trend will continue. Yet, they fail to look at the long term history of the stock (and the market in general), which may show that the stock goes up and down at intervals that hardly anyone could predict.[37]

The Impact of Recency

- Surely Karl Marx's conviction of the evils of capitalism was influenced by his own personal history. He was fairly hopeless at managing his money and was often borrowing from lenders and paying off his debts. Since the borrower often finds himself a slave to the lender,[38] he hated those capitalists who hounded him for payment of his debts.[39]

- I have a friend who laments that his business decisions often failed because he consistently bought into "the going thing"—those businesses that were heralded as the smart, blowing and going businesses of the time. Thus, he ended up pouring his time and money into industries at their peak and failed to cash in on the returns that early adopters had seen.

- Enron made tons of money off the deregulation of the natural gas industry (their recent history) and assumed that the same business model would produce similar results in other fields such as electricity, water and high speed Internet. The latter investments left them billions of dollars in debt.[40]

- We've already discussed how recency impacts economic bubbles, causing smart people to invest in the stocks that have been on the rise and are already wildly overvalued. But our brains love those patterns and find difficulty imagining that their profits are the results of a bubble rather than our brilliant knack for investing. As Buffett warns us: "Nobody knows who's been swimming naked until the tide goes out."

- When a busted economic bubble influences us from our recent history, we often make poor decisions as a result. One influential *New York Times* article warned people not to invest in Google's 2004 initial public offering, in part because they compared it to the tech bubble of 1990's. Investors who heeded their warning missed one of the best investments of our time.[41]

According to John Maynard Keynes,

> "...the idea of the future being different from the present [and our recent history] is so

> repugnant to our conventional modes of thought and behavior that we, most of us, offer a great resistance to acting on it in practice."

Therefore, overcome your bias for recent history by comparing it to more distant history, to the histories of other cultures, and by thinking through the line of reasoning that people use to establish cause and effect.

Conclusion

Why do brilliant people believe nonsense? Because they believe ill-founded history or draw invalid applications.

Flex Your Neurons!
Pursuing the Point of Know Return

1. What personal experiences have impacted your beliefs and the course of your life that might need to be examined from a broader perspective?

2. What are some theories or popular ways of thinking that you suspect may be based more upon recency than upon the objective weighing of evidence?

3. Before you read this chapter, what did you believe (or hear) were the main causes of "The Great Recession?" Did this chapter broaden your perspective? In what way?

4. Run imaginary, alternative histories to test the cause-effect relationship. Imagine that the Fed didn't keep the interest rates low after the tech bubble burst, and as a result, we never fully recovered from the busting of the Tech bubble. Would our present economy be better or worse? Let's imagine that taxes were *increased* on large corporations instead of lowered under Bush. Would things be better today, or worse? Might some major corporations have moved to another country to avoid taxation? Might such policies have hindered the rapid rise of Amazon, Google and Apple, which have provided so many jobs?

Making It More Personal
Practical Takeaways

What are one or more ideas provoked by this chapter that you can apply to help you think more critically?

____

____

____

What are one or more ideas that you can apply to help you think more creatively?

____

____

____

What else do you want to make sure you don't forget?

____

____

____

Recommended Trails For the Incurably Curious and Adventurous

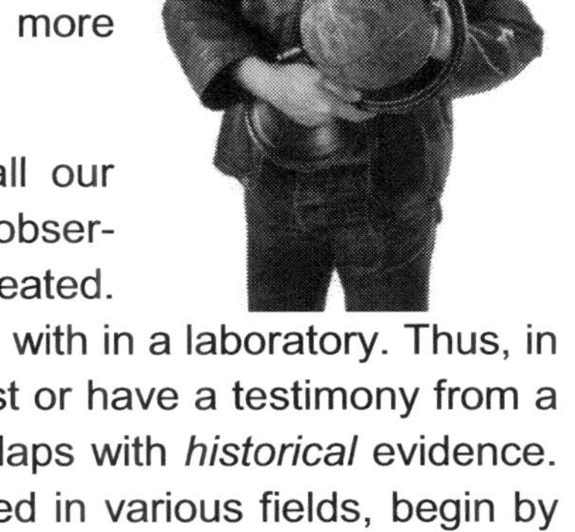

1. In this chapter, I selected a few ways that people botch history. To learn many, many more, read *Historians' Fallacies: Toward a Logic of Historical Thought,* by David Hackett Fischer (New York: Harper & Row Publishers, 1970). Fischer discusses over 100 fallacies that historians are apt to fall for, and shows a seemingly endless number of instances where respected historians did just that. Read it thoughtfully and you'll read history with a more discerning eye.

2. Some people act as if scientific evidence can answer all our questions. Yet, evidence from science typically involves observations of phenomena and experiments that can be repeated. The past can neither be directly observed nor experimented with in a laboratory. Thus, in our courts of law, while we may use an occasional DNA test or have a testimony from a scientist, we typically use *legal* evidence, which often overlaps with *historical* evidence. To understand the differences in the types of evidence used in various fields, begin by searching terms such as "legal evidence," "scientific evidence," and "historical evidence."

SECTION SEVEN

WHY DO BRILLIANT PEOPLE BELIEVE NONSENSE? BECAUSE THEY MISINTERPRET LITERATURE

CHAPTER 20

THEY MISS SUBTLE SHIFTS IN WORD MEANINGS

*"Words are like eggs dropped from great heights;
you can no more call them back than ignore the mess they leave when they fall."*

— Jodi Picoult, *Salem Falls*

"The beginning of wisdom is the definition of terms."

— Socrates

Introduction

In this section, I attack problems in language that lead astray even the brightest among us. I could talk about many issues at the intersection of critical thinking and literature, but I'll confine myself to the most common issues that I've noticed, useful whether you're trying to make sense of a scientific text, a novel, a religious text, a speech, or a song. And since it takes more than linguistic accuracy to produce effective communication, I'll also give some tips at the end of each chapter on using creativity to communicate more clearly, persuasively, and interestingly.

Defining "Smart"

So far in this book, as in the paragraph above and the book title, I've used words such as "smart," "bright," "brilliant," and "genius" in a rather loose, imprecise way. So let's see if we can tidy things up a bit, and in the process explore the importance of, and some difficulties in, defining our words. And since our definitions ultimately impact people, let's begin with a story of a student who was quite obviously *not* very smart.

A Slow Student

I first met Bartle Niesient in my class, *Tomorrow's World Today*. He was a Freshman international student and I desperately wanted to help him succeed. He was likeable enough—content to be his own unique self, seemingly oblivious to what others might think of him. But I quickly realized that academic success would be an uphill battle.

For one thing, he didn't prioritize learning in class. If he didn't like the class, he simply didn't show up very often. When he did drop by, he exhibited a poor rote memory for retaining lectures and often seemed distracted. Since he was also taking first year Physics, I chatted with his professor, who said Bartle was flunking.

Now some people who are slow at academics may make up for it with brilliant relationships, exceptional leadership, or a knack for common sense. But in all three of these, Bartle seemed flawed. In fact, he was so forgetful that he'd frequently lock himself out of his room or forget to take his suitcase on a trip.

I placed a few international calls to talk to his parents and high school principle. They painted the picture of a low achiever. As a child, he began talking much later than other kids. When he finally began to talk, he seemed to have trouble translating his thoughts into words, mumbling sentences to himself before saying them aloud. Thus, the family maid called him "the dopey one." His high school principle called him "dull." His high school faculty said that Bartle didn't fit in with other students and was such a poor student that one teacher told him straight up that he'd never amount to anything, was wasting everyone's time, and should drop out.

So he dropped out of high school.

Yet, he had the presence of mind to take some college prep courses that allowed him to get into college.

Defining "Smart"

From this description of Bartle, let's reflect on the meaning of the word group "bright, brilliant, smart, genius." Below I've listed common characteristics that we associate with "bright" on the left and "dull" (Think: Bartle) on the right. Does it look like I'm on track here? Do you agree with the characteristics I list? Are we getting closer to a definition?

Brilliant	Dull
Strong rote memory for acquiring languages	Weak rote memory for acquiring languages
Amazing memory for facts	Forgetful
Strong at all academics	Some subjects come very slowly
A's come easily	Seldom makes A's
Expresses self well verbally	Not a good conversationist
Understands people and the subtle nuances of their behavior	Often doesn't "get" relationships
Understands time and how to get things done efficiently	Poor at managing time
Can focus on the task at hand	Often unfocused; scatterbrained
Good with directions	Can't find his way home
Can multi-task	Does one thing at a time

Think!

With this introduction in mind, try your hand at writing a definition of "genius" or "smart".

So far, this chapter seems rather duh. We all know what "bright" is. We all know what "dull" is. So why try so hard to define them? Simply because our definitions influence how we size up people, how we treat them, who we choose as friends, who we hire, and what jobs we choose for ourselves. Trust me, this definition is extremely important. So let's press on.

Have We Gone Astray?

In this case, I strongly believe that our discussion has led us far off track.

People seem to define "bright" and "dull" as communicated to them, both subtly and overtly, by their educational experience. When Suzie, still in kindergarten, looks at the ABCs briefly on the blackboard and afterward recites them both backwards and forwards, her astonished teacher refers to her as "very bright." This achievement, and the teacher's reaction, tells her that she's exceptional, one of the elite, securely in that exclusive subset of "very smart students."

Of course, this also sends out a clear message to the other students. Those who take weeks to memorize the ABCs (and could never say them backwards), consider themselves "average." Those who struggle to either remember or write the symbols of our language—either because of poor rote memories, poor visual memories, processing issues, or trouble focusing on a task—begin to see themselves as "slow."

And so it goes throughout our educational experience. We quickly learn to identify the "bright" students as those who easily get A's and master math, reading and writing more quickly than the rest.

So Who Was Bartle Niesient...Really?

The more I study the brain and learning and genius and disabilities, the more I'm convinced that our mental picture of genius and our resulting definitions of genius are somehow misguided. In fact, I purposely led you astray with the story of Bartle Niesient. He actually wasn't my student. I invented his name by shuffling the letters for Albert Einstein, forming an anagram.

Yet, the characteristics I gave "Niesient" are consistent with Einstein. The person that we identified as the poster child for slow—the person we would have likely considered slow had we known him only on the playground and in certain classes—became the very poster child for genius. Somehow, in defining "genius," we've gotten off track. So let's take a closer look at "brilliant/genius" and "dull/stupid."

Here are some characteristics that I culled from Walter Isaacson's excellent biography of Einstein. Add them to your background data for refining your definition of genius:

His childhood through high school

- He was so late beginning to talk that his worried parents consulted a doctor.[1]
- "Every sentence he uttered," recalls his sister, "no matter how routine, he repeated to himself softly, moving his lips" before he said it out loud. "He had such difficulty with language that those around him feared he would never learn."[2]
- The family maid called him "the dopey one." Others in his family considered him "almost backwards."[3]
- "As a young student he never did well with rote learning." He said that he had a "bad memory for words and texts."[4]
- One schoolmaster declared that Einstein would never amount to much. One of his teachers said that she wished he'd leave the school.[5] He dropped out and took some preparatory classes to hopefully prepare him for a technical college.

As a college student and adult

- He flunked his first college physics course.[6]
- He was so absentminded and forgetful that he was always losing stuff, like the keys to his room. If he visited others overnight, he'd often forget his clothes, or even his entire suitcase. One family friend said, "That man will never amount to anything because he can't remember anything."[7]
- His brain was wired to think primarily in pictures. Einstein once said, "I very rarely think in words at all. A thought comes, and I may try to express it in words afterwards."[8]
- His wife watched for him to walk home from the Princeton campus (where he taught) because he'd forget whether he was coming or going, and might start walking back toward the campus.[9]
- He once took public transportation, but forgot to get off at his stop, had to reboard going the other direction, then forgot to get off on his second try.[10]
- In his letters, he'd often close by signing the name of the person he was writing, rather than his own name.[11]
- He couldn't drive. As his wife explained, "It's too complicated for him."[12]
- He admittedly failed miserably at his marriages.[13]

Einstein's Strengths

Yet, he obviously had great strengths. His absentmindedness was probably a result of his ability to concentrate exclusively on whatever he was thinking about. If he's walking home and thinking about how traveling at close to the speed of light alters time, he's probably not thinking about where he's walking.

He excelled early at math (although he'd always need a mathematical "caddy") and enjoyed studying it on his own. He mastered differential and integrated calculus before he turned 15.[14] He was an early lover of philosophy, delighting in Immanuel Kant at age 13.[15] He could obsess on a question for long periods of time until he found a solution. And he put his childlike curiosity and visual brain to good use in formulating and running mental experiments. According to Isaacson,

> "Throughout his life, Albert Einstein would retain the intuition and the awe of a child. He never lost his sense of wonder at the magic of nature's phenomena—magnetic fields, gravity, inertia, acceleration, light beams—which grown-ups find so commonplace."[16]

Eventually of course, people considered him the quintessential genius. In 1999, *Time* magazine crowned him the person of the century, describing him as "the pre-eminent scientist in a century dominated by science."[17]

> **Think!**
>
> With this new data on Einstein's strengths and weaknesses, see if your definition of "genius" or "smart" needs modification.

Was Einstein Odd among Geniuses, Having So Many Mental Weaknesses?

It's not wise to define "genius" by one person. It's too small a sample. Perhaps Einstein doesn't well represent the typical genius. "Surely," some would object, "most people we consider geniuses typically excel at most any intellectual activity they put their minds to. If they're that smart at something, they should be able to master most anything!"

You'd think so. But my study of "really smart people" reveals that those who excel in one area tend to lag behind in other areas.

- Steven Spielberg is a genius at producing movies, but his rote memory was so poor that he couldn't memorize lines for high school plays. He participated by building the sets instead.[18]
- Sam Walton was a genius at understanding and leading the retailing industry, but made so many mistakes with the cash register that an early boss said he would have fired him

if he weren't so good at sales.[19] Once he started Walmart, he missed calendared appointments so often that his secretary refused to schedule them.[20]

- The brilliant, but dyslexic and ADD founder of Kinko's never learned to read and couldn't work his own copying machines.[21]

- Brilliant writer and scholar C.S. Lewis seemed to have a disability with math, getting accepted into Oxford because of a fluke in history. Administrators skipped the math part of the entrance exam due to lacking students because of the war.[22]

- Mel Levine, professor of pediatrics and one of America's top experts on learning, excelled at most academics, but couldn't understand his gym teachers' instructions about physical tasks, couldn't throw or catch balls, and couldn't even operate a manual pencil sharpener.[23]

- Although Leonardo da Vinci is known as a polymath—someone who can do multiple tasks at a genius level—he couldn't do *everything* well. He never excelled at math, seemed to have little natural aptitude for it, and was often inaccurate in his calculations. He also struggled with languages, learning rudimentary Latin but never mastering it.[24]

  Much of his great output in sketches and diagrams was done while he was being paid to do something else. He was great at doing what he wanted to do at the moment, but quite lazy at doing the job at hand, which is characteristic of poor executive functioning of the brain.[25]

- One of today's most successful entrepreneurs in Silicon Valley, Ajit Gupta, once summed up his genius for me: "I'm great at a few things, terrible at hundreds of things."[26]

Redefining "Smart"

If "genius" can be defined by the unique characteristics of those that we all agree are geniuses, then certain standard definitions appear not only imprecise, but misleading. For example, Webster's New College Dictionary defines "smart" as "Characterized by sharp, quick thought: Intelligent." Yet, those who grew up with Einstein certainly didn't consider him "quick." Rather, they described him as "dull" and "slow." I don't get the impression that he was the person who could work a complicated multiplication problem almost instantly in his mind, like a Daniel Tammet.[27] Rather, Einstein had the patience and creativity to work on a math problem until he could find a workable solution.

Merriam-Webster defines "smart" as "very good at learning or thinking about things." This seems much improved in that it doesn't require Webster's characteristic of "quick." But it gives the impression that the "smart" person has the aptitude to learn *most anything* very well. Certainly this wasn't the case for any of the geniuses I mentioned above. They were good at learning certain things, but poor at learning other things.

So allow me to revise Merriam-Webster in crafting my definitions:

> A "smart" person is one who is very good at learning or thinking *about certain things*.

Similarly:

> A "genius" is a person who is extremely good at learning or thinking *about certain things*."

In other words, if I'm on track here, then people aren't geniuses "in general," but are geniuses "at something." People aren't smart "in general," but are smart "at one or more things."

The Vast Implications of our Definitions

"Come on! You're splitting hairs!" some may complain. "This entire discussion resulted in your adding a brief phrase to a definition. Big deal!"

But if I'm right in refining the definition by adding that phrase, the practical implications are quite revolutionary.

Revolutionizing Education

As I write, secondary education in America has a strong focus on general mastery of select subjects, which has its strong points. For example, we have the worthy goal that, by high school graduation, every student should be able to read well, write well, and do well at many types of science and math. Not wanting anyone to be "left behind" with an educational deficit, we don't want them to keep moving through the system until they've mastered these skills to a sufficient level.

In other words, by graduation day, we aspire to have produced students who are "smart" in the general sense of the word. As noble as this sounds, it does result in several problems.

1. We myopically focus on academic weaknesses rather than strengths.

Fourth-grader Timmy brings home with an A in Art, A in Music, B in writing, and a D in Math. When the parents meet with the teachers, what do they talk about? Obviously, how to bring up that math grade.

Without passing middle school and high school math, which will build upon elementary math and get increasingly complex, Timmy can't finish high school. Poor or failing grades in math would severely limit his college options. Repeated failures may cause him to get discouraged and drop out before graduation. So the resounding concern for Timmy, expressed by his parents and school counselors becomes, "How can we help Timmy bring up his Math grade?"

Yet, a large body of evidence[28] shows that our greatest potential for academic growth is typically found in our areas of strength. Perhaps Timmy's brain isn't wired for higher math. Perhaps he'll never be able to achieve even a competence level in Algebra II or Geometry. In his case, if a workable fix can't be found, wouldn't it be better to focus on gaining competence in *basic* math rather than pursuing higher levels of algebra, calculus, and trigonometry? Instead, we worry and fret over Timmy's weakness in math, forcing him to take ever more complicated classes in his area of weakness, which makes him feel dumber and dumber. No wonder so many drop out.

But let's imagine that parents and educators agree on our new definition of "smart"—a definition that recognizes that geniuses typically aren't smart "at everything," but have unusual potential "at something." In a possible world where dictionaries and educators accept this definition, the fourth-grade parent/teacher conference with Timmy may look very different.

First, the teacher mentions a couple of strategies for improving at math, which they realize may or may not entirely solve the issue.

> "Perhaps it will always be a weakness and we'll have to limp along as best we can," suggests the school counselor. "But let's focus our time here on why Timmy's doing so well in art and music, and not bad at all in writing. Perhaps we're discovering some of Timmy's strengths, perhaps even areas of genius."
>
> "We simply must insure that Timmy gets the best possible help to develop these areas of innate talent and interest. Perhaps he needs to attend a magnet school for art students. Perhaps administrators need to insure that he gets classes with select teachers who are best equipped to help him develop his talents. My primary concern is that we cannot allow Timmy to finish his secondary education without exploring and developing his areas of strength."

Isn't this essentially what Da Vinci's father did with his son's education? While he got an exposure to a broad education in his bogotá,[29] he was allowed from an early age to concentrate on his areas of strength. Wouldn't it have been a shame if Da Vinci had been forced to concentrate on his weaknesses (math and languages) rather than develop his artistic strengths? Da Vinci's type of education allowed geniuses to blossom in their area of genius, even if they were very weak in other areas.

Some of America's schools offer a concentration on strengths via a "tech track," whereby students can pursue their interests and strengths, such as art, design, programming, etc. But some schools drop the tech track in order to concentrate on trying to help every student achieve competence in every subject. Thus, those who are poor at math may find themselves doubling up on math, concentrating on their weaknesses rather than exploring their strengths. The spotlight daily shines on students' frustrating and embarrassing weaknesses. If our new definition of "smart at something" were adopted, we might bring back the tech track.

2. Many of our brightest (brightest "at something") students aren't allowed continue their education in the schools best suited for their areas of genius.

We typically require general competence, measured as a grade point average (GPA) in order to get into the best schools. But if we're right by adding "at certain things" to our definition of genius, we realize that we're denying many exceptional students the type education they need to fully develop their genius. Surely we all sense that something's amiss in academia when we realize that Steven Spielberg wasn't accepted into a top film school because of his mediocre high school grades (probably due to his poor rote memory). He had been producing movies since he was in middle school and showed obvious, exceptional talent, as well as extraordinary motivation. Yet, because most colleges want people who are generally competent (smart in general) at every school subject, he had to attend a college that had few film classes, some of which he could have probably taught better than his teachers.[30]

Brain scans of bright ("at something") people like Temple Grandin show that her brain is optimally wired for visual tasks. That's why she can look over a property once and sketch it from memory. Years later she retains a detailed visual memory of places, even stop lights on a street, that's astounding. But being wired for visual tasks means that her brain's *not* wired for other tasks. (A brain can't be wired for everything.) In her case, she could never understand Algebra, no matter how hard she tried and how much time her frustrated teacher spent with her. Fortunately, she learned along the way to concentrate on her strengths, so that she produces studies in her areas of competence and teaches on the university level.[31]

3. Many people who would be brilliant at managing people, leading a company, or designing cars are taught by our system to think of themselves as dumb. Some may never find their niches because their areas of strength were never identified, encouraged, and cultivated in school.

My twins are dyslexic, which makes math and reading/writing quite difficult. But each have very high emotional intelligence and get along great with people. They're also creative thinkers and have artistic talent. Unfortunately, educators had no time to help them identify and grow in their areas of strength. Instead, they had to double up on math and English and concentrate on their weaknesses.

Traits like emotional intelligence, people skills, ability to negotiate solutions, analytical thinking and creative thinking, which are in high demand vocationally, are seldom taught, graded, and rewarded in secondary education. Sure, it's difficult to test and standardize such skills. But while the vast majority of managerial positions need people who can motivate and work with people, our secondary schools prepare managers who can do calculus, but may have no clue how to hire, train, retain, and motivate people.

As Howard Gardner, Psychologist at the Harvard School of Education has said:

> "The time has come to broaden our notion of the spectrum of talents. The single most important contribution education can make to a child's development is to help him toward a field where his talents best suit him, where he will be satisfied and competent. We've completely lost sight of that. Instead we subject everyone to an education where, if you succeed, you will be best suited to be a college professor. And we evaluate everyone along the way according to whether they meet that narrow standard of success. We should spend less time ranking children and more time helping them to identify their natural competencies and gifts, and cultivate those."[32]

Gardner and many others would argue that people aren't typically smart *in general*, or geniuses *at everything*. They're smart *at something,* geniuses *at something.*[33] Even IQ tests evaluate a fairly narrow set of potentially useful types of intelligence.[34]

If we're on track with our definition, when little Suzie recites her ABCs forward and backward, her teacher should *not* respond "Suzie, you're so smart!" But more accurately, "Suzie, you're really smart at memorizing letters! I'll be eager to see if you can learn other things with such ease. For those of you who are finding memorizing the ABCs more difficult, don't get discouraged. Over time, you'll find areas of strength, which Suzie may lack. That's why we all need each other."

Clarifying our definition of "smart" has vast implications for education, child-rearing, hiring, and vocational choice. Unfortunately it seems that the *language* of smart hasn't kept pace with the *science* of smart.

My point? Definitions are important. They have vast implications for our understanding of ourselves and how we build our societies. Getting definitions right often means going beyond looking up words in a dictionary, which only tells us how people *use* the word, not how we *should* use the word to better conform with our current scientific understanding.

The Wider Importance of Definitions

Words are thrown around very loosely these days, with many words meaning entirely different things to different people, often spoken or written with the intent of evoking emotions rather than expressing precise ideas. In politics, the words "liberal" and "conservative" and "socialist" and "progressive" often mean entirely different things to different people.

To further confuse, in educational circles the term "liberal education" refers, not to a political ideology, but to an approach to education that is broad in scope but allows students to probe deeply into an area of interest, with an emphasis on developing analytical, communication and problem-solving skills. In other words, with this meaning in mind, a school that leans conservative in its political stance may offer a liberal education.[35]

Failing to clarify what people mean by these terms obviously leads to confusion. Speakers say one thing; audiences hear another.

In medical science, I find professionals using the term "anecdotal" in a variety of confusing ways. Sometimes it refers to evidence that isn't conclusive, other times to worthless hearsay, and still other times to fairly strong evidence which is based solely upon patient reports (such as reporting how well a pain medication works, relying primarily on patient testimonies).

Popular conversations about scientific issues often confuse the *popular* use of the term "theory" with the *scientific* use of the term "theory." The former typically refers to an idea that has no evidential base, such as when one says, "His explanation of why his wife left is all theory and no evidence." Yet scientists use the term to describe everything from a theory that has *some* evidence supporting it, to one that has a *great deal* of evidence supporting it. No wonder people get confused.

Even words in fields that you'd think would be known for their precision—words or phrases like "science" or "the scientific method" are used with vastly different meanings by scientists, depending upon the field and the context.

I hope you see the importance of getting our definitions right. Let's discuss some ways that speakers and writers, as well as those who interpret them, get their definitions wrong.

Common Fallacies in Defining Terms

"The word aerobics comes from two Greek words: aero, meaning 'ability to,' and bics, meaning 'withstand tremendous boredom.'"

— Humorist Dave Barry

1. Overdependence on Etymology (how a word was originally put together and how the meaning changed through history.)

Linguists warn interpreters not to use a term's etymology to derive the meaning in current usage. In our section on fallacies, this was called the "etymological fallacy." Here's an example to demonstrate why it's considered fallacious. Let's divide the word "refrigerate" into its component parts:

"re" = "to do again"
"frigerate" = "to make cold"

So literally, according to its etymology, we derive the definition of refrigerate as "take something that was once cold and make it cold again." Yet, this leads us astray since refrigerators are also used to "make cold" certain items that were never cold before, like leftovers from a warm lunch.

I've repeatedly heard preachers dividing up words into their component parts or giving their history in order to derive their meanings. They might say, "The Greek word *dunamis* became our English word dynamite; therefore, when you read the word "power" as a translation of the word *dunamis*, think dynamite!" Well, that certainly wasn't what a first century Greek reader thought when he heard the word *dunamis*, since dynamite had yet to be invented.

Unfortunately, I could give many other illustrations of definitions gone awry.[36] Thus, make sure that if you use a dictionary that gives the etymology of a word as well as its present usage that you don't draw your definition from that etymology. The only circumstance where it's necessary to derive a word's meaning from its etymology would be in the case of very rare words ("hypoxlegomena" are words that have been found in only one instance), in a text from ages past, which often lack enough context to derive meaning in the ordinary way. In such cases, we go to etymology as a last-ditch effort, knowing that we're still skating on thin ice.

2. Mistranslation.

Literal, word-for-word translations often fall far short because people miss the subtleties of language. Imagine the challenge of translating English into another language, even just considering the one problem of shifts of meaning over time. Before the 1970s "bad" consistently meant "of poor quality; inferior or defective." Then the younger generation began referring to their favorite artists as "bad," meaning the exact opposite: "of excellent quality." This is just one of many exegetical minefields that translators must traverse.

3. Using specialized, insider language.

Your bill at the auto shop often uses insider language. On the surface, it looks pretty straightforward—"Three hours of labor at $60 per hour and $95 for parts." As an outsider to the industry, you take this to mean that they worked on your car for three hours and paid $95 for the parts. Silly customer! They may have done the work in an hour and a half and paid only $50 for the parts. And they don't consider it lying. Here's how each of those terms gets redefined in the world of auto mechanics.

The time it takes to fix your vehicle is typically listed as "book time," which is an industry standard of an average amount of time it *should* take to fix a specific issue, allowing for typical setbacks. A good mechanic can often consistently beat the book time.

Many mechanics charge you *what you would pay* (or more) for parts if you purchased them from a parts store. But they get a pretty hefty discount for being regular customers, so they typically paid much less for the parts, thus making more money off the parts sale.[37]

In the end, I don't see many mechanics getting filthy rich, so if I've got a good mechanic who charges reasonable prices, I don't quibble about the insider meanings of terms in his bill. Yet, by understanding his terminology I know what I'm paying for, how to compare prices, and when to buy the part and try to fix it myself.

4. Equivocation.

This is one of the common logical fallacies we discussed earlier. The meaning of a word subtly shifts during an argument, invalidating the argument.

I saw this recently in a passage by academic neurologist Kevin Nelson, in his book on near-death experiences. In critiquing the research of cardiologist Pim van Lommel, Nelson took him to task on his usage of the word "dead." Van Lommel had stated, in his report in the prestigious medical journal, the *Lancet*, that he interviewed 344 of his patients who had been resuscitated from cardiac arrest. Sixty-two of them had near-death experiences. "All patients had been clinically dead," van Lommel wrote.

Nelson countered that "the brain is nowhere near physically dead during near-death experiences." He goes on to describe brain death as a condition where so many brain cells rupture that they can no longer sustain life. Since this is irreversible, the patient dies and can't return to life.[38]

Yet, this seems to be a clear case of equivocation. Van Lommel had argued, not that his patients were "brain dead," but that they were "clinically dead," a state from which patients are often resuscitated. "Clinical death" has a very specialized definition in medical science. It refers, not to brain death, but to the cessation of heartbeat and respiration. By using the same word in two different ways, but arguing as if they meant the same thing, Nelson argued fallaciously.

How to Avoid (for Writers) and Recognize (for Readers) Problems with Definitions

1. Consult general and specialist dictionaries.

Specialist dictionaries, for example, in philosophy and medicine, give extensive definitions of words as used in their specialty. But remember, dictionaries merely tell us how a word is commonly *used. Is* (the way a dictionary describes its common usage) doesn't necessarily imply *ought*" (how a word *should* be used), as we discussed in trying to define "genius."

2. Beware of the pitfalls of brief summaries.

I've seen this as particularly a problem in the legal sphere. One of my sons has a "hit and run" on his record. This term conjures up images of crashing into a car and fleeing the scene of the accident, perhaps leaving an injured person unattended and trying to get out of paying for damages. In my son's case, the full report shows that my son backed into his brother's parked car in front of our house and left for work because his brother wasn't around to tell. His brother reported it, and thus it's on his record. But the consolidated report, the report that businesses check when they hire people, merely says he was charged with a "hit and run," which can seriously damage a person's reputation.

Paragraph summaries of peer reviewed articles pose the same hazards. Without reading the full study, terms are often misunderstood.

3. Pay special attention to the word's usage in its immediate context.

In defining words, linguists insist that context is king. More important than how a word was originally put together, or what a word meant fifty years ago, or the primary meaning listed in a dictionary, linguists look to a word's *usus loguendi*—its use in context. Of utmost importance is the *immediate* context—the sentence and discussion in the surrounding paragraphs. This is especially important since the same word can take on so many different meanings, and shades of meanings, depending upon the context.

Take the word "run," to see how its meaning totally changes from context to context.

- "Let's run the marathon." (Participate in a foot race)
- "Run to the store and get me a drink!" (Drive your car there)
- "You've got a run in your hose." (an accessory calamity)

- "I've got to run." (leave)
- "I've got the runs." (intestinal issue)

Those examples are easy enough to discern. The immediate context identifies their meaning. But it's easy for even brilliant writers to shift meanings in ways that aren't apparent to the casual reader. When Dudley Shapere at the University of Chicago critiqued Thomas Kuhn's influential book, *The Structure of Scientific Revolutions*, he argued that Kuhn used the term "paradigm" in so many different ways, and often in such a broad way, as to make the term almost void of meaning.[39]

4. Understand the larger context of the chapter, the book, or the author's other writings.

When the Apostle Paul writes "to the saints at Ephesus," he's neither referring to a select subset of Ephesian believers who are unusually upstanding in their conduct (e.g., "saintly"), nor to those few deemed by religious leaders to have special honor and even power (e.g., Catholic saints). Rather, he's referring to the ordinary believers in Ephesus, warts and all. How do exegetes know this? They compare this passage with Paul's use of the same term throughout his writings.

5. Consider the cultural context.

Words shift meaning from time to time and place to place. For definitions of Greek words in the first century, don't think primarily of how we use the words today, but how they used the words in their culture. One authoritative dictionary for the common (koine) Greek of the first century would be Bauer, Arndt and Gingrich's *A Greek-English Lexicon of the New Testament and Other Early Christian Literature*. Authors of resources such as this scour writings of the time period in close geographical proximity to find numerous occurrences of the word in question, determining various meanings from various contexts.

Writers of historical fiction would do well to consult specialized dictionaries for language usage during the time they're writing about.

6. In important conversations, ask people to define their terms.

Often, "what you're hearing" and "what they're saying" are miles apart. If you sense a disconnect, or know that they're using terms that are often convoluted, ask them to define their terms.

Conclusion

Since we express our thoughts in words and interpret the thoughts of others by understanding their words, look closely at their meanings. Subtle shifts in meaning, such as an absent phrase in discussing "smart" or "brilliant," can impact decisions from our children's education to determining our life's work.

Think Different
Tips for Communicating More Creatively
Teaching to Change Lives

Precise definitions make more *accurate* communication. But don't expect audiences to rush the stage for your autograph because of your accuracy. And certainly don't expect them to remember your talk or change their lives in response. Accurate knowledge, in order to impact, must be served up in creative ways that are interesting, helpful, insightful, motivational, and unforgettable. Once again, we see the power of joining the creative with the critical. Thus, I'll close each of the next few chapters with tips on adding more power and creativity to our communications.

How can we take a well-reasoned argument and bring it to life?

One of Steve Jobs' strengths was his ability to inspire. Example: When Apple needed a new CEO, Jobs began to court Pepsi-Cola's president and marketing whiz, John Sculley. Jobs believed Sculley was the man to take Apple to the next level, but Sculley needed convincing. After all, Sculley already had a prestigious and lucrative position at a respected company. Besides, Sculley wasn't that excited about computers. At their first meeting, Sculley told Jobs frankly that most executives didn't find computers to be worth their trouble. But Jobs turned on the charm: "We want to change the way people use computers."

After several meetings, Sculley was still unconvinced, but told Jobs he'd be willing to offer advice from the sidelines. Then, according to Sculley, "Steve's head dropped as he stared at his feet. After a weighty, uncomfortable pause, Jobs issued a challenge that would haunt me for days. 'Do you want to spend the rest of your life selling sugared water, or do you want a chance to change the world?'"

Sculley felt like he'd been punched in the stomach. He *had* to say yes. Scully said of Jobs, "He had an uncanny ability...to size up a person and know exactly what to say to reach a person." Soon, Apple had a new CEO.[40]

Jobs' yearly presentations of new Apple products to stockholders and the media were legendary. Rather than tell audiences in a sterile, grammatically correct manner where the company was going, he motivated and inspired, convincing them that they were not just making new products, but changing the world.

How can we teach and write to change lives?

1. Take your communications seriously.

Most people, in their daily communications, seem to speak rather spontaneously. But if you're speaking/writing to motivate people to take action, make adequate preparation. The best speakers appear to be speaking spontaneously and effortlessly, but from my experience in interviewing great speakers, that effortless manner came as a result of great planning. As one person said of the great speaker Winston Churchill, "Winston has spent the best years of his life composing his impromptu speeches".[41]

Having studied Jobs a bit, I'd guess that he prepared those words for Sculley, down to the body language of dropping his gaze to his feet, the dramatic pause, and the carefully worded, loaded-for-impact sentence.

2. Know your audience.

What motivates them? What turns them off? What's important to them? The more you know about your audience, the better you can tailor your speech/article to them. I often ask my students about their personal interests, vocational interests, etc. Then I can gear my lectures/discussions to speak directly to those interests.

3. Use fascinating illustrations and stories to make your points memorable.

In this chapter, had I restricted the discussion to how to properly define words, without illustrating the concept, you'd have likely yawned through the chapter and remembered nothing. But hopefully you'll remember some of the fascinating details of Einstein's weaknesses, so that the next time you hear a person label someone as dumb because of their forgetfulness, you'll think of Einstein and reflect: "Well, just because she forgets where she's going doesn't necessarily make her dumb." Hopefully, you'll also connect this thought with the importance of and difficulty of defining words.

I'll write more about collecting and using stories at the end of the next chapter.

4. Collect ideas from everywhere.

A large part of creativity (some would argue it's the very essence of creativity) is connecting two ideas from different realms that nobody has yet put together.[42] If true, this might explain in part why so many great ideas come to people while they're not working on the project at hand. Einstein's best ideas often came to him as he played his violin.[43] I get many of my best ideas while driving. One author looked at a filing cabinet with two drawers—one for letters A-N, the next O-Z. He wrote down "Oz", which became the name of his fictional world, which was adapted to film as *The Wizard of Oz*.[44]

When director George Lucas was working on the film *American Graffiti*, someone asked him for Reel 2, Dialogue 2 of the film, abbreviating it to R2-D2. It sounded cool to Lucas, so he jotted it down in his small notebook where he recorded name ideas, plot angles, and "anything that popped into his head." In this way, R2-D2 would become the name of the spunky little droid in *Star Wars*.[45]

For me, this means to never, ever be caught without paper and pen. (Others might prefer to text ideas from a smart phone to a cloud-based app like Evernote, to be accessed and stored later on your desktop computer, iPad, or Netbook.)

5. Find others who offset your weaknesses.

In my opinion, most writers don't have it all, e.g., the ability to spot all grammatical errors, catch inconsistencies, stay on task for months and years, "hear" the rhythm of sentences, see the big picture, use humor, organize tons of details, recognize flaws in logic, make readers laugh, find all factual errors, develop intriguing characters that people care about, do thorough research, write catchy titles, do painstaking research, etc.

For this reason, many writers work closely with a favorite editor, or regularly run chapters or articles by a writers' group. C.S. Lewis and J.R.R. Tolkien did this with their writers' group, the *Inklings*. Many speakers have a person or team they work with at a certain point of their preparation. Many writers for TV and films work as a group, or hand off their version to the next writer for further refining. (Remember Pixar's "Brain Trust.")

6. Distance yourself from the manuscript/talk before revisiting it.

Stephen King locks a completed manuscript in a drawer and waits at least six weeks before pulling it out for personal editing. Why? When we're in the heat of writing, we lose perspective and become blind to our faults. Taking a break and coming back later can help us to see the manuscript through fresh eyes.

7. Add "that little something extra."

When an interviewer asked Johnny Depp about his acting, Depp said that he liked to not only play the part prescribed, but to add "that little something extra." We can certainly see that in his films. Think: Jack Sparrow in *Pirates of the Caribbean*. Steve Jobs added "that little something extra" to his yearly presentations, ending them with "Oh, and one last thing…" so that he could leave his audiences with a bombshell. No wonder one documentary on Jobs was titled, "One Last Thing."

Flex Your Neurons!
Pursuing the Point of Know Return

1. Note this week how people (in personal conversations, in the media, etc.) use words like "smart" and "genius" and "brilliant." What do you think they mean by those terms? Do you think we should use the terms in a different way? Why or why not?

2. What are some of the best online sources for accurate definitions? What are the best dictionary Apps for smart phones?

3. Trace the meaning of the word "cared" in this sentence. Does it shift? If so, how did the meaning change, and what would this fallacy be called?

> Jim: Did you hear about the murder at the gas station? Apparently the murderer had just been fired. He must not care at all about people.
>
> Bob: Oh, I think he cared a lot about people, and that's why he shot up the place. He cared that his boss was so insensitive as to fire him. Why would he have killed him had he not cared?

4. Often, unclear definitions result in unclear reasoning. Take the following two sentences. Does the second sentence logically follow from the first? On what definition does the conclusion hinge?

> "Our proven oil reserves will be depleted by 2080. So we'd better prepare ourselves now to live in a world with no oil."

5. How could you take creativity in your communications to the next level?

6. What speakers and writers inspire you? What do they do that differentiates them from boring communicators? What characteristics of inspiring communicators could you adopt?

Making It More Personal
Practical Takeaways

What are one or more ideas provoked by this chapter that you can apply to help you think more critically?

____

____

____

What are one or more ideas that you can apply to help you think more creatively?

____

____

____

What else do you want to make sure you don't forget?

____

____

____

Recommended Trails For the Incurably Curious and Adventurous

1. Find various types of dictionaries that might be useful to you. Consider which might be the best to consult for the following information:

- How New Yorkers used a certain word in 1920.
- A slang word used by California "valley girls" in the 1980s.
- The history of a word.
- The meaning of a word in the Koran.
- An extensive discussion of the philosophical meaning of, and the history of, "existentialism."

2. If you're interested in pursuing this theme of "What is smart?" and "What is modern brain science and psychology telling us about mental human potential?" read some of the following books:

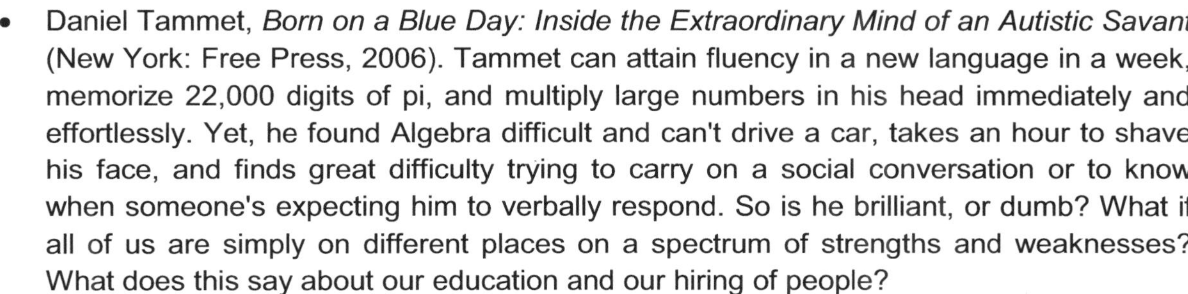

- Daniel Tammet, *Born on a Blue Day: Inside the Extraordinary Mind of an Autistic Savant* (New York: Free Press, 2006). Tammet can attain fluency in a new language in a week, memorize 22,000 digits of pi, and multiply large numbers in his head immediately and effortlessly. Yet, he found Algebra difficult and can't drive a car, takes an hour to shave his face, and finds great difficulty trying to carry on a social conversation or to know when someone's expecting him to verbally respond. So is he brilliant, or dumb? What if all of us are simply on different places on a spectrum of strengths and weaknesses? What does this say about our education and our hiring of people?

- Temple Grandin (with Richard Panek), *The Autistic Brain: Thinking across the Spectrum* (New York: Houghton Mifflin Harcourt, 2013). Another autistic who explains (sometimes by showing her actual brain scans) much about how different brains can be wired, either from birth or from our early years.

- Harvard Psychologist Howard Gardner defends and explains his theory of multiple intelligences in his book, *Frames of Mind* (New York: BasicBooks, 1983). If Gardner is on target, then there are many kinds of minds, each of which has a different set of strengths and weaknesses. This would imply that a person might be considered a genius in a specific field of thought, such as "spatial intelligence," but not so smart at "linguistic intelligence."

- In 1995, Daniel Goleman published *Emotional Intelligence: Why It Can Matter More than IQ* (New York: Bantam Books, latest edition in 2010). This is a good book to take one type of intelligence—that which makes one smart at people skills—and show how it works. Although Goleman says that emotional intelligence can be developed, we can see from Tammet and Grandin that for some people it will come much easier than others. But again, this shows why a person might be a genius at math, but clueless about relationships.

3. Many good books have been written on effective communications. For a brief but powerful book to complement my points above, read *Teaching to Change Lives: Seven Proven Ways to Make Your Teaching Come Alive,* by Howard Hendricks (Multnomah Books, reprint, 2003).

4. A popular classic on persuasion is *Influence: The Psychology of Persuasion*, by Robert B. Cialdini (New York: Collins, revised edition, 2007).

CHAPTER 21

THEY MISINTERPRET PHRASES AND SENTENCES

"It's dreadful what little things lead people to misunderstand each other."

— L.M. Montgomery, *Emily's Quest*

A Grammatical Insight Ignites a Reformation and Changes History

In July of 1505 a German law student named Martin Luther travelled alone, by foot, on a road outside the Saxon village of Stotternheim. As he approached the village, the sky darkened and he suddenly found himself caught in a vicious thunderstorm. A bolt of lightning pierced the sky, landing so close that it knocked him to the ground. Terrified, he took it to be a call from heaven and on the spot vowed to become a Catholic monk.[1]

But Luther failed to find peace of mind. The religious instruction he'd received as a child painted the picture of a wrathful, fearsome God who couldn't seem to be pleased no matter how much Luther fasted and prayed and confessed. He never felt good enough for God and struggled with feelings of hate toward God.

Fortunately, almost a decade into Luther's monastic experience, an Augustinian vicar named Johann von Staupitz sympathized with Luther's plight and tried various ways to help him. He decided that Luther should study for his doctor's degree and teach the Bible. (Significantly, during Luther's time, studying the Bible wasn't emphasized by the Catholic church.) His study of Paul's Epistle to the Romans provided the key that unlocked the spiritual and psychological chains that bound his spirit.[2]

The key came in the form of a phrase that he struggled to understand: "the righteousness of God." Luther couldn't fathom why Paul was so excited about "the righteousness of God," since it was precisely God's righteousness that made Luther so depressingly aware of his own *un*righteousness.

Think!

Imagine that you're Martin Luther, reading this text: "For in it the righteousness of God is revealed...." (Luther would have been studying the Latin Vulgate and original Greek texts.) Without the benefit of context, what possible interpretations of this phrase, "righteousness of God" could you imagine?

Suddenly it struck him. This phrase wasn't speaking of "God's righteousness," but rather a "righteousness *from* God"—a righteousness that isn't *earned* by constant fasting and prayer and holy living, but a righteousness that is freely given (imputed) to those who accept the free gift offered by Jesus' payment for sins on the cross.[3]

Finally, Luther found the freedom and joy he'd been missing. He no longer needed to *earn* God's favor and heaven, but to accept a price that had already been paid. Luther was transformed.

The echoes of Luther's insight concerning this tiny phrase reverberated through history. He would risk his life to challenge the church during a particularly bleak period of its history, when power plays, insincerity, and teachings designed to enrich the church often took the forefront. By tacking his famous 95 theses to the Wittenberg door, he sparked a revolution that jump-started Protestantism, reformed Catholicism, changed the shape of Western Civilization, and ultimately impacted the world.

Such is the power of a little phrase, rightly interpreted.

The Problem with Genitive Phrases

In ancient Greek, as well as in English, phrases such as this (English: noun + "of" + noun; Greek: the genitive case of a noun) can be legitimately read in several ways.

- "The *love of Cherie* (meaning "Cherie's love") insured that the orphans were well cared for."
- "For the *love of Cherie* (meaning "my love *for* Cherie"), I've sacrificed all other loves."
- "The *counsel of my professors* (meaning the counsel I received *from* my professors), helped me choose a suitable vocation."

So if similarly (or exactly) structured phrases can have entirely different meanings, how can we interpret them correctly?

Building on the last chapter, context once again reigns as king. In the case of Paul in his letter to the Romans, his explanation of imputed righteousness in his surrounding chapters and other

Pauline epistles tells us what he meant by the phrase.

But phrases such as this can still pose a quandary for translators. A perhaps more literal translation of Romans 1:17 from the original Greek text into English, as given by the New American Standard Bible, is "the righteousness of God," leaving the interpretation in the hands of the reader. But the most *literal* translation doesn't always communicate the original sense most effectively. Many (perhaps *most*) readers would understand "the righteousness of God" as "God's righteousness" and thus misunderstand its intent. So the New International Version, in a less literal but perhaps more accurate translation, reads "a righteousness from God."

So sentences and their phrases are critical for our understanding, but are often difficult to interpret. How can we understand and use them better?

Tips for Understanding Sentences and Phrases

1. Know your grammar for the language you're reading.

A Greek present tense speaks more of "kind of action" than "time of action." Thus, if the verb is present tense, interpret it as "Seek (and keep on seeking) and ye shall find," as opposed to "Seek once..." when the verb is in the present tense.

2. Don't trust titles to be accurately descriptive of the article.

We've already talked about titles under the subject of media bias, but I'll just remind readers that titles often serve several purposes to editors, such as spinning a story to agree with their political bias or sensationalizing it to attract readers, both of which compromise accuracy.

3. Ask "What was the intended meaning of the author(s)?" before asking "What does it mean to me today?"

While some art, poetry, or songs are created to provoke different meanings in different people, other expressions have a particular meaning in mind. But finding that meaning isn't always easy. For example, one duty of our courts is to interpret the meaning of our founding documents as applied to specific cases.

Recently, The Supreme Court ruled on a case which questioned the right of a city council to begin its meetings with prayer. Some people felt that the prayer violated the phrase "Congress shall make no law respecting an establishment of religion..." in the First Amendment to the U.S. Constitution. Others felt that since the counsel was open to include prayers from diverse faiths, that they did nothing to "establish" a particular religion.

Decisions in such cases are often made, in part, by trying to determine the intentions of those who originally drafted and adopted the First Amendment. If you want to wrestle with this phrase and the Supreme Court decision on this case, I include more specifics under "Flex Your Neurons!"

4. When interpreting important historical documents, from the founding documents of your country to the Bible to the Koran to Plato's Republic, consult commentaries by respected scholars.

Often, they reveal cultural or linguistic nuances unknown to those who aren't scholars in those fields of study.

5. Consider the cultural context.

This is important for interpreting the First Amendment. What were the concerns of the early drafters and adopters about church and state relations they'd observed in Europe? What were they trying to protect or promote in America?

I've heard people quote Jesus' teaching that God "sends rain on the righteous and the unrighteous," as meaning that he sends hard times on both good and evil people. After all, we speak of "rainy days" as bad days, and say "Don't rain on my parade!" Yet, Jesus spoke these words in a dry, agrarian culture, so that early hearers almost certainly took it to mean that God gives good gifts, such as rain, to both the deserving and undeserving.

An acquaintance who works with a pharmaceutical company often interacts with people from other countries. When explaining a procedure to a Japanese contact, she asked several times whether the person understood, and she kept replying "Yes." Yet, it became apparent later that she didn't understand at all. The problem? Japanese resist admitting that they don't understand something. Perhaps they're embarrassed; or perhaps they think it reflects poorly on the person who's doing the explaining.

6. Beware of deceptive phrases in advertising.

Grocery store products contain enough misleading phrases to warrant a handbook to interpret them. So this juice "contains 100 percent fruit juice." But it doesn't actually say that 100 percent of the content is fruit juice. It just "contains" *some* "100 percent fruit juice." Look to the ingredients to find how much is actually fruit juice. The same goes for any bread that "*contains* 100 percent whole wheat flour."

7. Look for all possible antecedents.

I'm colorblind, which often gets me into embarrassing situations. One day my wife noticed a wild, strange, collarless cat wandering the neighborhood. She asked me to call animal control, since she was concerned for the safety of our small children. When I called, they asked some questions about the neighborhood and our house, then asked about the color of the cat. I asked my wife, "What color is it?"

Now she thought I was still describing the house, and responded "Sawmill green with yellow trim." So I relayed to animal control that they should look for a green cat with yellow trim. After I hung up, I said, "Honey, are you sure that cat was green?" She said, "I was talking about the house! They'll never show up!"

The problem was the antecedent of "it." I was thinking "cat"; she was thinking "house."

Unclear antecedents often confuse communication, both in writing and speaking. I may review my own manuscript multiple times and never notice the unclear antecedents, since I already know what I'm referring to. This is where multiple early readers and editors come to the rescue.

8. Be alert for unclear punctuation.

Writers, make sure that your punctuation clarifies your meaning. While all the nitpicky punctuation rules in *Elements of Style* are often helpful, remember that the primary purpose of punctuation is to make sure people can understand what the heck you're writing about. Review your sentences with several different inflections and emphases to see if they can be misread. If it's even remotely possible to misread a sentence, somebody will certainly read it that way.

9. Learn the most common phrases that often confuse people in the language you're interpreting.

Once you're made aware of, for example, the problems with unclear antecedents and genitive phrases, it's much easier to spot potential problems with multiple meanings. Again, consult *Elements of Style* for the bare basics of English grammar. Serious writers should consult the latest edition of *The Chicago Manual of Style*.

Conclusion

Sentences and their phrases can be confusing, but deciphering them can open up new worlds of understanding. In some cases it can change human history. Learn to recognize the common issues, and you're more likely to spot them and avoid misinterpretations.

Think Different!
Tips for Communicating More Creatively
Finding, Collecting and Using Stories

Making your sentences and phrases clear isn't enough. How do we make them interesting and impactful? Typically, when I hear truly impactful speakers, it's the quality of their stories that make the biggest impact.

From this book, you'll probably remember my stories before you recall my principles. Fortunately the stories often connect our minds to the principles they illustrate. No wonder great speakers are typically great story tellers.

Stories also provoke critical thinking. By positioning them *before* the point I wish to make, readers are challenged to use their higher level reasoning to try to draw out a life lesson.

I find stories everywhere—in my reading, in conversations, in the news. When I find a great story, I put it in a physical file or digital folder, categorized by popular topics. If I find great stories in a book, I write the location in the back of the book, for example, "p. 154, story on motivation for learning."

If I'm writing an article or book, and want to put one of the stories into my own words, I may do further research to confirm and collect important details. Thus I consulted a respected biography of Martin Luther to write the story that opened this chapter.

I also intentionally collect a *variety* of stories—business leaders, religious leaders, thinkers, sports heroes, writers, musicians, scientists—so that I can impact a variety of people.

Thus, when I plan a talk or write a book, I've got wealth of stories to pull from. Many of the stories simply come to mind as I write, so that all I have to do is pull the appropriate book off the shelf and look in my hand-written index, or pull something from my physical or digital collections.

Similarly, I keep research, jokes, great visuals, and other ideas in the same topical files for later use. It's a practice I started in college that has paid off richly through my decades of speaking and writing.

Flex Your Neurons!
Pursuing the Point of Know Return

1. Above, we introduced a case where the Supreme Court ruled on an issue of public prayer in the context of a city council, which some deemed to be in violation of the Establishment of Religion clause in the First Amendment. This is a good example of interpreting a phrase. Before looking at the specifics of the case, and how the Supreme Court ruled, ask yourself a couple of questions:

- What do you think the authors of the First Amendment meant by "Congress shall make no law respecting an establishment of religion, or prohibiting the free exercise thereof; or abridging the freedom of speech…."?

- Do you believe that opening a city council meeting with prayer in some way establishes a religion?

The First Amendment Center at Vanderbilt University is a good starting point for finding articles on the First Amendment: http://www.firstamendmentcenter.org/about-the-first-amendment.

To gather details on the case, search for the case "Town of Greece v. Galloway." Here are a couple of articles:

- Town Meetings Can Have Prayer, Justices Decide, by Adam Liptakmay, *New York Times*, May 6, 2014 - http://www.nytimes.com/2014/05/06/nyregion/supreme-court-allows-prayers-at-town-meetings.html

- Breaking — Supreme Court upholds legislative prayer in *Town of Greece v.* Galloway, *Washington Post*, by Jonathan H. Adler, May 5, 2014 - http://www.washingtonpost.com/news/volokh-conspiracy/wp/2014/05/05/breaking-supreme-court-upholds-legislative-prayer-in-town-of-greece-v-galloway/?tid=pm_national_pop

2. I wanted to watch the latest installment of "The Hobbit" films, but my son didn't want to see it if it left us hanging to await the final film. Seeing the title, I assumed it must be the final film, since it was titled *The Desolation of Smaug*. I took this to mean that Smaug (the dragon) would be killed, which comes near the end of Tolkien's book. I was wrong. Thinking back to our discussion of genitive phrases, how should I have interpreted "The Desolation of Smaug?"

3. Concerning unclear antecedents, what are several possibilities for what "it" refers to in the following passage?

> "For my brother's bachelor party, we took him on an ill-planned wilderness adventure during the day, and played video games all night. We forgot to set our clocks and almost missed the wedding. It was a disaster."

How could the sentence have been written more clearly?

4. Look at packaged food descriptions and product descriptions in a grocery store. How are many of the descriptions written in a deceptive way? Bring back some instances to class for discussion.

5. Do you like the way the Martin Luther story was told at the beginning of this chapter? If so, what elements made it more interesting? If you were telling the story, what would you change? People who can tell and write interesting stories are often seen as interesting people. How could you improve your story telling skills?

6. Write a brief account of something interesting that happened to you. Have your fellow students critique it to try to make it more clear and interesting.

Making It More Personal
Practical Takeaways

What are one or more ideas provoked by this chapter that you can apply to help you think more critically?

____

____

____

What are one or more ideas that you can apply to help you think more creatively?

____

____

____

What else do you want to make sure you don't forget?

____

____

____

Recommended Trails
For the Incurably Curious and Adventurous

1. As I sought a publisher for my first book, I read the following tip from an acquisitions editor at a respected publisher: "If I were writing a nonfiction book for publication, I'd read Zinsser's *On Writing Well* and do what he says." I read Zinsser and wrote a short list of his suggestions to guide me in revising my manuscript (e.g., "get your subjects moving by substituting active for passive verbs.") Result: A respected publisher offered me a contract! Thus, to improve your writing, I highly recommend *On Writing Well, by* William Zinsser (New York: Harper Perennial). Originally published in 1976, Zinsser updated and added to it through the years.

2. Some writers swear by Strunk and White's *Elements of Style* (New York: Macmillan) as the classic, handy summary of grammatical tips. But for me, it's easy to get bogged down in some of the minutia. In my opinion, Arlene Miller's (no relation to me) more recent *The Best Little Grammar Book Ever* (Petaluma, CA: Bigwords101, 2010) offers much of the same information in a more engaging way.

3. For many professors and professional editors, *The Chicago Manual of Style* (Chicago: University of Chicago Press, latest edition) remains the standard bearer of all things proper in writing. At over 1,000 pages, it's the reference book I keep close at hand for grammatical minutia.

4. For those studying the Bible as literature, a quite comprehensive (over 700 pages) classic in interpretation is *Biblical Hermeneutics: A Treatise on the Interpretation of the Old and New Testaments,* by Milton Terry (Zondervan, 1974 reprint edition). To hone your exegetical skills by examining common exegetical errors, study D.A. Carson's *Exegetical Fallacies* (Baker Academic, second edition, 1996).

5. For a good book on creativity in writing stories, particularly humorous and touching stories from real life, see *Bird by Bird: Some Instructions on Writing and Life,* by Anne Lamott (Anchor: 1995). For writing fiction, see Stephen King, *On Writing: A Memoir of the Craft* (New York: Scribner, 2010, anniversary edition). In fact, if you're pursuing writing, I'd read many books on writing, in order to compare and contrast how writers approach their craft, so that you don't fall into the trap of thinking there's only one way to write. Some write at night, some early morning; some swear by writing long hand, others on their computers. My wife put together a collection of quotes by popular writers on the writing life. See *Writing Conversations: Spend 365 days with your favorite authors, learning the craft of writing,* by Cherie K. Miller (Wisdom Creek Press, 2010).

CHAPTER 22

THEY USE FAULTY PARALLELS AND ANALOGIES

"[Science undergraduates] are inept at those turns of phrase or happy analogy which throw a flying bridge across a chasm of misunderstanding and make contact between mind and mind."

— William Lawrence Bragg

American Education in Crisis

According to authoritative sources, America's secondary education has become so poor that it's in a state of crisis.

- **Comparing our *students* with those in other countries** - According to our Secretary of Education, "We have a real state of crisis" in education. We're scoring so poorly compared to other nations in technology, math and literacy that we're in danger of not being able to compete in the global economy.[1]
- **Comparing our *adults* with those in other countries** - According to the editors of the New York Times, "In a recent survey by the Organization for Economic Cooperation and Development, a global policy organization, adults in the United States scored far below average and better than only two of 12 other developed comparison countries, Italy and Spain."[2]

From these quotes, it appears that we're shortchanging the next generation with an inferior education.

Comparisons with other countries strongly influence our views of both how we're doing and what changes need to be made. But in doing such comparisons, it's vital that we discover the answers to such questions as:

- Are the comparisons accurate?
- Should we try to emulate the top-scoring countries?
- Are the comparisons fair, or are we comparing apples with oranges?

Our answers to these questions have a far-ranging impact on how we raise our children, which schools we send them to (or opt for home schooling), and choosing political leaders (who often push opposing solutions for fixing our education). Ultimately, few doubt that the quality of our education significantly impacts the future of our nation and our world. Since I'm no specialist in educational reform, I don't pretend to solve our problems in this chapter. But at least we can clarify the issues by learning to think beneath the surface when we draw parallels between our own educational system and those of other cultures. In the process, we'll hopefully come to better understand the challenges of making accurate comparisons and analogies.

Think!

Write a hypothesis stating your opinion as to why you think America's education is failing.

Example Hypothesis #1 - Students these days don't really want to get ahead, so they don't take their studies seriously. Thus, there's not much that frustrated teachers can do to motivate them.

Example Hypothesis #2 - Teachers don't treat students as individuals, but try to cram everyone into the same mold, which frustrates everybody to no end.

Your Hypothesis -

____

____

____

____

Recommendations from *The New York Times*

When we argue for changes in education, we must use accurate data and argue correctly from that data. Unfortunately, many if not most discussions suggest parallels with other countries that are far from exact, making their recommendations questionable at best.

Let's take a recent article in *The New York Times* as an example, authored by the NYT editorial board. It's titled *Why Other Countries Teach Better*, subtitled *Three Reasons Students Do Better Overseas.**

***Overseas = "beyond or across the sea" (Merriam-Webster)**

(Digression: Since the article was written by Americans, a population never distinguished for its geographical savvy, let's try to ignore the fact that the NYT used Canada as one of their three examples of "overseas" countries. Since only half of New York city's residents own cars, we should perhaps forgive them for failing to notice that Toronto is easily accessible by land. Alternatively, perhaps this serves to underscore the problems with education in America, making it a perfect segue into the body of this chapter.)[3]

In brief, the article begins by stating that America's education compares poorly to other countries in testing and is in danger of not being able to compete globally. Thus, according to the article, we must make some big changes. They then look to Shanghai, Finland and Canada, which consistently score exceptionally in standardized testing in Math, Science, and Literacy. For each country, they highlight a feature they believe we should adopt to improve America's education.

Clarifying the Line of Argument

Since the authors didn't make their line of argument explicit, let's attempt to formulate it ourselves. How about this?

Implicit Argument That America's Failing at Educating Her Students

Premise One: International comparisons of standardized test scores for Math, Science and Literacy provide an objective way to measure how well America is educating her students.

Premise Two: America is performing poorly in its standardized test scores, compared to many other countries.

Conclusion: America is failing at educating her students.

Implicit Argument That Emulating the Best-Performing Schools Will Make Us Successful

Premise One: By identifying and emulating the factors that caused top-performing countries to lead the pack, we can eventually lead the pack.

Premise Two: We've identified the factors that caused top-scoring countries to lead the pack.

Conclusion: By emulating these factors, we can eventually lead the pack.

I believe that both of these arguments are *valid*, meaning that if you agree with the premises, then you must agree with the conclusions, since they logically follow. But is each argument *sound*, meaning, do you agree with each of the premises? If the premises are wrong, then the conclusion is likely wrong as well.

By the way, the line of argument in this NYT article is typical of the majority of articles I see comparing America's education with that of other countries. So we're not just critiquing an article; we're critiquing a popular and influential way of thinking about our education.

So let's gather more data concerning this issue by spotlighting differences between America and Finland, not only in their education, but also in their culture and demographics. Then, we'll use this data to evaluate comparisons of the two countries.

Think!

To set us up mentally for the next section, allow me to give you a problem to solve. Try to solve it as quickly as possible, as if you are doing a timed test:

> Imagine that you're driving a bus. You start with 30 passengers. At the first stop, 15 get off and three get on. At the second stop, 5 get off and 7 get on. At the third stop, 13 get on and 12 get off. Then, you have an accident at a busy intersection. Nobody is hurt, so you call the insurance claims adjuster. He asks you one question and only one: "Was the driver male or female?" Quickly now, without looking back…what's your answer?

At first reading, the majority of people throw up their hands and declare it was a trick question. "Who knows whether the driver was male or female? You never told us!" But I did indeed tell you. I told you in the first sentence. "You" were driving the bus. But most people get so distracted with the mathematical data that they entirely overlook the most critical data.

My point? In comparing the educational systems of different countries, it's easy to focus on one or two characteristics that jump out to us, while totally ignoring other characteristics that may, upon further reflection, turn out to be much more important.

So while *The New York Times* editors briefly mention a couple of distinctives in Finnish education (like free school lunches for all and a rigorous curriculum) they quickly focus on what they consider the most important distinctive—superior teacher training—suggesting that this is the area we need to focus our efforts on to improve our education. And perhaps they're right.

Yet, for those willing to dig a bit deeper, there are many aspects of Finnish education and culture and demographics which differ from the American system and context. Without considering as many distinctives as we can compile, how can we possibly discern which are 1) the most important to Finnish education and 2) which, if any, should be adopted in America?

Below, I've listed some ways Finland educates differently from America. Imagine that you've been sent to Finland with a delegation of American educators to observe their educational system. You return with the following observations. Try to come up with recommendations, based upon

1) Which you think are the most important.
2) Which you think would transfer best from Finnish culture to American culture.

Finland Versus America: An Apples to Apples Comparison?

I'll organize these observations into sections on demographics, geography, and differences in how Finland educates. Note that although demographics and geography can greatly impact test scores, educators are largely powerless to change them.

Demographic Apples and Oranges

- **America is educating almost three times as many students who were born in foreign countries, compared to Finland.** The high school I attended (Dalton High School) was fairly homogeneous. Surely this contributed to our fairly high SAT scores. Over the years, the demographic changed to almost 50 percent Hispanic. (Today, first generation Mayans are impacting the education in the area as well.)

  Imagine comparing scores between the old Dalton High and the new Dalton High, when so many of today's students have yet to master English. Imagine how absurd it would be for a state official to look at a drop in test scores and, without noting the change in demographics, conclude that the quality of teachers must have dropped significantly, suggesting that we could solve the problem by having the teachers get masters degrees. Is this any different from comparing the USA to Finland, without considering this significant difference?

  "...as of 2010, just 4.6 percent of Finnish residents had been born in another country, compared with 12.7 percent in the United States."[4]

- **Three percent of Finland's students live in poverty, as opposed to twenty percent of American students.**[5] Poverty is strongly correlated with poor test scores. To see the impact of poverty, compare test scores among American schools. While there are exceptions, the wealthier districts exhibit a strong tendency to score significantly better. After all, their homes tend to be more stable. Students get more parental support. They have less problems with violence in their neighborhoods. Their parents have more time to support the teachers and schools as volunteers. They attract better teachers.

  Thus, it's no wonder that there's a strong correlation between the wealth of a district and its scores. According to one observer of Finnish schools, “there is a near absence of poverty.”[6]

- **Fourteen percent of Finnish children live in single parent homes, versus 27 percent in the USA.** We realize the importance of this when Finnish officials tell us how important the early years are to education. The government gives parents books on childrearing at the birth of a child. Yet, single parents in America are often so preoccupied with working multiple jobs that they find difficulty fully engaging with their children's education.[7]

Thus, comparing demographics, it makes little sense to compare Dalton High, with a large number of students in poverty and many learning English as a second language, to a school in Helsinki pulling from an entirely different demographic, and concluding that we'll solve the problem with better teacher training. Can it be purely coincidental that many of the world leaders in test scores are also many of the most homogeneous cultures? For example, Japan and

South Korea are the first and second most homogeneous countries in the world. Their students also consistently score at the top of international testing.

To get closer to an apples to apples comparison with Finland, we might compare Finnish schools to only the American schools that have a similar distribution of wealth, a similar number of students who grew up speaking the language, a similar number of single parent homes, etc. When we do this, a very different statistic emerges:

> "Note that U.S. schools with poverty rates comparable to Finland's (below 10 percent) *outperform* Finland and schools in the 10-24 percent range aren't far behind."[8] (italics mine)

If this statistic holds true, then we should reconsider the assumption that America's schools are doing something terribly wrong. Perhaps our teachers are doing a pretty good job, given the demographics some are working with. Perhaps our schools located in areas with more stable demographics are doing pretty well, even excellent, compared to other countries. Perhaps our mandate shouldn't be figuring out how to overhaul out entire education system, but figuring out how to better educate our socially disadvantaged students, or how to help their families stabilize and escape from poverty.

Geographical Apples and Oranges

Finland is smaller than the state of California, wedged between Norway, Sweden and Russia. Only six million people worldwide speak Finnish, compared to about a billion people who either grew up speaking English or have acquired it. This is very significant when we speak of the Finns doing so much better than Americans at learning other languages.

Imagine that you're growing up in Finland.

- You're extremely motivated to learn other languages, since you'll almost certainly need them to do business in several languages.
- Even within your own country, your next door neighbors and friends may grow up speaking both Swedish and Finnish, since both are national languages.
- Your parents likely speak a couple of additional languages and can help you learn them growing up.
- Your teachers are probably fluent at several languages, so that you're introduced to multiple languages at an early age and it quickly becomes a part of your school life.
- The TV shows and news and video games you play may be in multiple languages, giving you practice from an early age.

No wonder they excel at foreign languages! No wonder it would be difficult, if not impossible, to replicate their success at language acquisition in America.

Differences in How Finland Educates

Comparing our education with that of other countries can provide a wonderful resource for ideas. Yet, the articles we read comparing our education with other countries often pull out a few characteristics of Finnish education and suggest that applying those to our schools will help, while ignoring many other aspects. As you read the below characteristics of Finnish schools, ask yourself, "What would I like to adopt for American education?" Circle your choices and try to rank them for priority.

- Adopt/Not Adopt - **They start academics later than us.** They don't emphasize math or reading till about age seven, when their compulsory education starts, reasoning that before that age, students need to be learning such foundational skills/traits as communication, social awareness, empathy, and self-reflection.[9]
- Adopt/Not Adopt - **They have no mandated, standardized tests, except for one at the end of the 12th grade year (think: SAT or ACT) to decide if they're qualified for college.** Throughout, they deemphasize testing, especially deemphasizing comparing grades between students and between schools.[10]
- Adopt/Not Adopt - **They spend less money on education (about 30 percent less) per student than American schools.**[11]
- Adopt/Not Adopt - **They don't put "gifted" or "special ed" students in different classes. Instead, they stay in the classes with the other students.** Those who are stronger in certain subjects help the weaker. Weak students also get extra help from educational specialists, who have even more training than the regular teachers. Thirty percent of the students receive some kind of special help at some point.[12]
- Adopt/Not Adopt - **The national curriculum consists of broad guidelines rather than specifics of what content must be taught and tested.** Control over policies rests with town councils. Accountability and inspection rest primarily with teachers and principals.[13]
- Adopt/Not Adopt - **Comprehensive (grades 1-9) education is broad, including "four to eleven periods each week taking classes in art, music, cooking, carpentry, metalwork, and textiles."** By contrast, one of my Asian students told me that "all we studied was math and science."[14]
- Adopt/Not Adopt - **They don't emphasize testing in their weekly work.** "We prepare children to learn how to learn, not how to take a test," said Pasi Sahlberg, a former math and physics teacher who is now in Finland's Ministry of Education and Culture."[15]
- Adopt/Not Adopt - **They value play,** allowing 15 minutes of play between lessons in elementary school.[16]
- Adopt/Not Adopt - **Teachers give minimal homework.**[17]

- Adopt/Not Adopt - **Students don't spend as much time in school as other Western nations.** When Dr. Pasi Sahlberg, of Finland's Education Department, was asked what he thought about the many hours Asian students spent in school, he replied,

  > "There's no evidence globally that doing more of the same [instructionally] will improve results. An equally relevant argument would be, let's try to do less. Increasing time comes from the old industrial mindset. The important thing is ensuring school is a place where students can discover who they are and what they can do."[18]

- Adopt/Not Adopt - **Classes are small - typically not more than 20 students.**[19]

- Adopt/Not Adopt - **In schools with more disabilities and poverty, they pay special education specialists a higher salary since they've had to put in more schooling.** Including special education teachers, schools have about one teacher for every seven students. Teachers need to know the students personally.[20]

- Adopt/Not Adopt - **They offer nine years of comprehensive education, then students can choose the college track or tech track.**[21]

- Adopt/Not Adopt - **They start teaching a couple of foreign languages by age nine.**[22]

- Adopt/Not Adopt - **They foster the sense that the entire faculty is responsible for the success of each student, rather than just their individual teachers.** Since the schools are typically smaller than American schools, all teachers feel responsible for little Timmy's success, whether he's in their class or not, and can offer suggestions.[23]

- Adopt/Not Adopt - **They require "that every teacher earn a fifth-year master's degree in "theory and practice" at one of eight state universities—at state expense."**[24]

- Adopt/Not Adopt - **There's much less top-down (federal level) control, so that teachers have more autonomy to choose their own texts, and ways of assessing whether students are getting the material or not.** As a result of their training and autonomy and success (and probably many other factors), teaching has become a much-envied and respected occupation—they look up to teachers much like we look up to physicians or lawyers. This insures that many of the best students compete to become teachers. Thus, "In 2010, some 6,600 applicants vied for 660 primary school training slots."[25]

- Adopt/Not Adopt - **"For residents, school lunches are free, preschool is free, college is free."**[26]

Questionable Premises: The Problems with Parallels

The challenge of comparing education systems (America versus Finland) or businesses (Microsoft versus Apple) or families (mine versus my neighbor's) or musicians (Led Zeppelin versus The Beatles) is that the comparisons are seldom if ever exactly parallel. Thus, we must question the premises of articles and presentations that make such comparisons.

> "Our students perform horribly at math compared to other countries!" an article proclaims. "We've got to get better teachers!"

Oh really? Based on what data? Are the "other countries" educating the same demographics as we are? What would a more apples to apples comparison find?

> "Shanghai is beating our students in standardized tests. We'd better find out what they're doing!"

But Shanghai is educating, not everyone, but their select, most promising students, making it an unfair comparison.[27]

> "Nations such as Singapore are outscoring us in math. Unless we catch up with them, they'll soon overtake us in our global economy!"

But what's our purpose in education? To do well on standardized tests? If so, we may do well to adopt massive rote memory and drills aimed at scoring high on tests, much like Japan and Singapore. But what's the opportunity cost of obsessing on test scores? What if an obsession with rote learning produces people who can do well on Jeopardy, but find difficulty thinking critically or relationally or creatively? Perhaps by having a broader curriculum, allowing for creative and critical thinking, and allowing time after school to explore our talents and interests, we develop more and better entrepreneurs.

Bill Gates spent massive amounts of time outside of high school working at a local tech company, practicing his programming and learning about business. Warren Buffet started and worked at many businesses during his middle school and high school years, helping him to understand businesses and contributing to his ability to know which businesses are more likely to succeed. Could Gates and Buffett and hosts of others have succeeded had they spent all their after school time feverishly memorizing material for tests?

Singapore's students do great on tests, but don't do well in starting new businesses. Perhaps there's a correlation between this problem and their educational methods.

> "Finland outscores us on standardized tests. If we give all our teachers more training, we can match their scores!"

But as we've seen, there are many ways Finnish schools differ from ours. And once we compare apples with apples (in this case schools with a similar socioeconomic mix as their schools), we find that the scores may not differ significantly. If they are indeed offering a better education in certain ways, then we must first decide which differences are the most important and which might work well in Finland, but not at all in America.

The Art of Asking Good Questions

Again, this applies to comparing, not just schools, but businesses and sports and styles of childrearing. So learn the habit of dreaming up the many and varied questions necessary to evaluate comparisons and analogies.

Here are some of the questions we should ask when assessing comparisons of school systems:

1. Are we comparing all relevant aspects, or are we just cherry-picking the aspects that seem important to us?

2. Do we have a way to judge which differences are actually impacting the quality of education, and to what extent? Don't be guilty of *pos hoc ergo propter hoc*, assuming that since certain events (styles of teaching, etc.) took place prior to the testing, that each of these *caused* the superior scores.

3. Have we identified and understood the impact of the demographic and geographical differences?

4. Do we understand the cultural differences that may make a practice work in one culture, but not in another? Example: A practice that works in Walmart may not work in a high end store. A practice that works in Japanese education (extremely high parent involvement, due in part to a culture that emphasizes shame on the family if a student doesn't achieve A's, and a culture where the best jobs are reserved for those with the highest grades), may not work in America (where many parents are content with C's or even passing). This process might be called "contextualization."[28]

5. Are we considering opportunity costs?

- If we implement tougher tests, do we raise drop-out rates?
- If we implement more services, are we willing to pay more taxes or add to the national debt to fund them?
- If we institute high stakes testing, do we produce high anxiety youth, resulting in high suicide rates? (Part of the high suicide rate in Japan is attributed to shiken jigoku—"Examination Hell.")[29]
- If we emphasize rote memory in order to promote high test scores, do we fail to develop creative and critical thinking skills?
- If we require all students to take four years of high school math, do we hold back the students who love and excel in math, since they're often thrown together with students who hate and struggle with math?
- If not all students can excel at math, but we require them to master higher forms of math in order to graduate, doesn't this make teaching math an incredibly discouraging career, since teachers must flunk so many discouraged students?

Conclusion

We dare not stop learning and tweaking our education. Analyzing the best schools and discovering their best practices is a great way to find great ideas. I actually like the NYT article. It revealed some helpful ideas. But if we assume parallels that aren't parallel, we risk discouraging passionate teachers and failing to inspire the next generation of learners.

So the next time someone says, "We ought to do things like ____ does them!" stop and think.

Think Different
More Tips for Creativity in Communication
On Content: Fresh and Counterintuitive in a Style That Communicates

So you want to write an article to inspire your generation to get more exercise. The last thing people want is the same old thing regurgitated by yet another writer. The worst thing students could say about my content is that they already knew it, or that it was intuitively obvious.

To avoid these common maladies, I choose content with these principles in mind:

- Fresh information trumps stale.
- Counterintuitive trumps intuitive.
- Inspiring trumps boring.
- Practical trumps impractical.

Reflect on the nature of some of the concepts we've covered in this book. Our trusted medical sites can't be trusted?! Wikipedia is often a fabulous tool for research?! The experts we confidently quote are often off-the-charts wrong?! That content, and some of the content of each of my chapters, is probably new to most students. I'm trying to keep my content fresh, counterintuitive, practical, and hopefully effective at inspiring readers to think for themselves.

Prioritize the Counterintuitive

In his classic work on creativity—*A Whack on the Side of the Head*—Roger von Oech urges us to experiment with "arguing for the opposite" of received wisdom. So when you hear experts lamenting about the sorry state of education in America, try defending the opposite, even if at first it appears ridiculous.

- How might *lowering* certain educational standards lead to better learning?
- How might *less* testing produce better students?
- If America achieved the top scores in the world, might the required changes in our education *hurt* our innovative edge rather than *help* it?
- What if teachers are doing a pretty good job of teaching, given the demographics they're working with?

- What if an overemphasis on science and math turns students off to the subjects rather than inspiring them to become scientists?

By "arguing for the opposite" we often find counterintuitive data that makes for interesting writing or speaking. Even if we conclude that the standard view was right all along, by trying to argue for the other side, we surely come to a better understanding of the issues.

On Appropriate Style: What is Good Writing and Good Literature?

This is an interesting philosophical issue, roaming into the realm of aesthetics. But before the discussion, read the following passage and imagine that a fellow student handed it to you, asking for your candid input. What would you recommend?

> I said, "Who killed him?" and he said "I don't know who killed him but he's dead all right," and it was dark and there was water standing in the street and no lights and windows broke and boats all up in the town and trees blown down and everything all blown and I got a skiff and went out and found my boat where I had her inside of Mango Key and she was all right only she was full of water."

Critical thinkers might remember a label to slap on this hapless writing and advise the writer: "It's a run-on sentence—an obvious infraction of proper English. If you ran out of periods, here's a quarter. Run down to the corner store and pick up a package of five periods and sprinkle them throughout that 'sentence gone wild.'"

Creative thinkers might be divided: one group arguing that it's a cool way to express the jumble of thoughts that flood our minds when we first encounter a disaster area. Other creatives may despise it, seeing it as proof of the deplorable state of American education.

Actually, I pulled the quote from the short story "After the Storm," by Ernest Hemingway, winner of a Pulitzer, and considered by many one of the greatest writers of the 1900s.

My point? It's difficult to agree on what constitutes good writing. Let me suggest (and many will differ) that good writing can only be judged within a genre, by those who love and appreciate that genre. In other words, good writing is largely in the eye of the reader. If a large number of readers love Hemingway's style, they're probably the best to pass judgment on that passage.

The implication of my view is that communicators need to be in touch with their audiences. You may love William Shakespeare, but if your intended audience hates Shakespearian English and prefers a more colloquial style, you'd be foolish to ignore their preferences. So instead of letting an authority figure tell you what good writing is, why not find the most talented writers who write for your audience, learn from their works, and listen to what they say about writing? While most great authors and musicians don't *end up* with a style that merely mimics their mentors, they often begin there.

Flex Your Neurons!
Pursuing the Point of Know Return

1. After looking at the similarities and dissimilarity's between America's education and Finland's, what elements do you think should be adopted from Finland, if any?

2. In general, what do you think should be done to improve America's education? How would you defend your view if you were a policy maker?

3. Why do you think people often go astray in using analogies, comparing school systems, comparing companies, or comparing products? How could we make more accurate comparisons?

4. With pen and paper in hand, watch a couple of episodes of a well-written TV show, such as "House" or the recent BBC rendition of "Sherlock Holmes." Note the characteristics of the writing that make it work. Note especially House's use of analogies, as related to this chapter. (If you hate these shows, find a show you like.) You'll likely find more elements by viewing with a friend or group of friends. After collecting characteristics, try your hand at writing the dialogue for a portion of an episode.

Making It More Personal
Practical Takeaways

What are one or more ideas provoked by this chapter that you can apply to help you think more critically?

____

____

____

What are one or more ideas that you can apply to help you think more creatively?

____

____

____

What else do you want to make sure you don't forget?

____

____

____

Recommended Trails
For the Incurably Curious and Adventurous

1. If you're passionate about improving our education, continue to read articles that reveal problems and suggest paths for improvement. The more you read, the more you'll likely see how educated people often differ in their analyses and prescriptions. What paths do various professors in academia recommend? What are teachers in the classrooms recommending? What are business leaders saying they need their employees to know? What are students saying? Is there any kind of consensus as to what, if anything, needs to be done?

2. As I mentioned in another context, those who struggle with writers' block often connect with their creative muse by reading *The Artist's Way,* by Julia Cameron (New York: Penguin Putnam, 1992).

3. To foster creative thinking in business, education, writing or whatever, read a classic (translated into 11 languages) on creativity: *A Whack on the Side of the Head: How You Can Be More Creative,* by Roger von Oech (Grand Central Publishing, revised edition, 2008). It's also just plain fun to read. Imagine…a book on creativity that's actually written creatively! It will help you to argue the opposite of what everybody knows, to ask the questions people don't tend to ask, such as the ones we asked in this chapter.

4. To learn more about creative thinking, read books that study creative people to discover what makes them tick. Frank Barron, et. al., edited *Creators on Creating,* offering essays by creative people discussing their creativity, from Ingmar Bergman to Tchaikovsky to Frank Zappa (New York: Penguin, 1997). Denise Shekerjian interviewed 40 people who won the prestigious MacArthur Award for accomplishments demonstrating creative genius. Rather than devote a chapter to each person, she distilled 14 principles of creativity from the interviews, devoted a chapter to each principle, and quoted from the interviews to illustrate and illuminate each principle. *Uncommon Genius: How Great Ideas Are Born* (New York: Penguin Books, 1990). From such books, compile your own list of keys to creativity.

5. Read full biographies (and/or watch documentaries) of creative people you admire in various fields, from music to sports to math to science to politics. From these biographies, add to and revise your list of keys to creativity.

6. If you want to delve into the academic research on creativity, Jon and Ronni Fox wrote an accessible introduction to the subject: *Exploring the Nature of Creativity* (Dubuque, Iowa: Kendall/Hunt Publishing Company, 2000), which will introduce you to much of the relevant research. Next, study the *Handbook of Creativity*, in which Robert J. Sternberg, a Yale professor of psychology and education, attempts to "provide the most

comprehensive, definitive, and authoritative single-volume review available in the field of creativity." Its 22 chapters, covering a wide range of topics related to creativity, are written by scholars in their fields. (Cambridge: Cambridge University Press, 1999.) To update the book by a decade of research, see James C. Kaufman and Robert J. Sternberg, eds., *The Cambridge Handbook of Creativity* (Cambridge University Press, 2010).

CHAPTER 23

THEY FAIL TO CORRECTLY IDENTIFY AND INTERPRET FICTION AND FIGURATIVE LANGUAGE

"No story can be devised by the wit of man which cannot be interpreted allegorically by the wit of some other man."

— C.S. Lewis, *On Stories: And Other Essays on Literature*

"Persons attempting to find a motive in this narrative will be prosecuted; persons attempting to find a moral in it will be banished; persons attempting to find a plot in it will be shot."

— Mark Twain, in his preface to *The Adventures of Huckleberry Finn*

"American Pie": What Does It Mean?

Anyone who listens to 1970's radio stations has heard the song "American Pie." It's one of the all-time great road trip songs. Written and performed by folk rock artist Don McLean and published in 1971, it's one of those elite classic hits that still gets plenty of air time, allowing listeners to nostalgically reflect upon many of the seminal events of the tumultuous '60s.

Listeners often ask, "But what does all its cryptic language refer to, such as...

- "the day the music died"
- "moss grows fat on a rollin' stone"
- "and while the king was looking down, the jester stole his thorny crown."?

Fortunately, a Google search provides some promising answers. The first site Google offered gave a helpful phrase by phrase commentary, revealing that, for example:

- "The day the music died" refers to the tragic death of singer Buddy Holly in a plane crash in 1959.

- "moss grows fat on a rollin' stone" refers to both Bob Dylan (who wrote a song titled "Like a Rolling Stone") and Buddy Holly (who quoted an English proverb in one of his songs: "A rolling stone gathers no moss.")
- "and while the king was looking down" refers to Elvis Presley, who was often referred to as "the king" of rock and roll. "The Jester stole his thorny crown" refers to Bob Dylan becoming more popular than Elvis with the younger generation.[1]

While these interpretations sound reasonable, especially when stated with such assurance, why should I believe them? Is the commenter just guessing? Did he interview McLean? How can we, with any degree of certainty, interpret figurative expressions?

The Importance of Interpreting Literature*: from Chernyshevsky to Ozzy

In exile during his college years, Vladimir Lenin read Chernyshevsky's novel, *What is to be Done?* five times. According to Lenin, "It completely reshaped me. This is a book that changes one for a whole lifetime," showing "what a revolutionary must be like." Unfortunately, the novel showed only contempt for ordinary people, in all likelihood influencing Lenin's contempt for people and his willingness to sacrifice multitudes in pursuit of his political goals.[2] No wonder Martin Amos considered *What is to be Done?* "the most influential novel of all time."

***Literature =** in its broadest sense, any written documents, including fiction, nonfiction, scientific studies, poetry and song lyrics.

"But it was just a novel!" some might object. "Fiction. A made up story." Yet it resonated with Lenin in a way that other writings hadn't, influencing not only the course of his life, but the course of the world.

Literature is important. It impacts us. Thus it's important to understand its deeper meanings and decipher its symbols.

More than one family brought lawsuits (unsuccessfully) against Ozzy Osbourne for a couple of his fans who committed suicide, allegedly while listening to his music and taking his song *Suicide Solution* as an invitation to suicide.[3] It could be argued that they would have killed themselves anyway, regardless of their musical preference, but according to a summary study in the *Journal of the American Medical Association*, while some young people may not be influenced by negative music, those who lack a strong moral compass may identify with the meanings of songs and indeed make behavioral decisions based upon them.[4]

But the word "solution" in the song title can have multiple meanings. While some take the song to mean that suicide is a "final solution" to having to face tomorrow, it can equally be taken to refer metaphorically to alcohol abuse as a type of suicide, resulting from a dangerous chemical "solution" (a blend or compound, a liquid mixture) that mimics the impact of a slow suicide.

According to Ozzy, speaking in the context of the people who committed suicide:

> "(It's) solution as in liquid, not a way out. The song's about the dangers of alcoholism—alcohol will kill you just like any other drug will…it's just a terrible case of misinterpretation…."[5]

So there you have it on the authority of that creator and expositor of great literature, Ozzy Osbourne: It's important to identify and correctly interpret figurative language.

Objective Versus Subjective Interpretations

Literature can be taught and interpreted in many ways. Some professors want students to read primarily with a view to how the novel or poem *impacts them*, emphasizing "what it means to you" rather than "what the author meant." Such an approach can be a profitable exercise—sometimes therapeutic, always creative, helping us to clarify and come to grips with our own feelings.

In fact, some art was never meant to communicate any particular truth. Rather, the artist created it to provoke different meanings in the minds of different viewers or readers. And there's nothing wrong with this approach, whether it's expressed in a sculpture or novel or song.

But in the present chapter, I'm interested in literature that was intended by the author to mean something in itself and to communicate something, like Chernyshevsky's *What is to be Done?* I'm trying to provide direction when we ask "What did Don McLean mean when he wrote those lyrics?"

Here are some principles that might help.

How to Rein in our Flights of Fantasy

1. Discover What the Authors Say about Their Meaning

When McLean was asked what "American Pie" meant, he famously replied, "It means I don't ever have to work again if I don't want to."[6] In an email, he clarified a bit:

> "As you can imagine, over the years I have been asked many times to discuss and explain my song "American Pie." I have never discussed the lyrics, but have admitted to the Holly reference in the opening stanzas. I dedicated the album *American Pie* to Buddy Holly as well in order to connect the entire statement to Holly in hopes of bringing about an interest in him, which subsequently did occur…."
>
> "You will find many 'interpretations' of my lyrics but none of them by me."[7]

So the interpretation of "the day the music died" referring to the day Buddy Holly died in a small aircraft tragedy seems pretty secure. But what of the interpreter's dogmatic statements that "moss grows fat on a rollin' stone" refers to Bob Dylan and "while the king was looking down" to Elvis Presley? Both are certainly possible, but in light of McLean's statement, do we have any reason to take them any more seriously than educated guesses?

The same criticism could be leveled against those who see great symbolism in J.R.R. Tolkien's *Lord of the Rings*. Since Tolkien placed the evil land of Mordor in the East, and since Tolkien, as well as many other British citizens of the time, distrusted the intentions of Soviet Russia, it's tempting to conclude that Mordor symbolized Russia. But fortunately, Tolkien himself cleared this up by stating that he placed Mordor in the East because of "simple narrative and geographical necessity." Tolkien was all about writing great stories that people could "apply" in their own way. In his own words:

> "I cordially dislike allegory in all its manifestations, and always have done so since I grew old and wary enough to detect its presence. I much prefer history, true or feigned, with its varied applicability to the thought and experience of readers. I think that many confuse 'applicability' with 'allegory'; but the one resides in the freedom of the reader, and the other in the purposed domination of the author."[8]

In his introduction to the second edition of *Lord of the Rings*, Tolkien states:

> "As for any inner meaning or 'message', it has in the intention of the author none. It is neither allegorical nor topical."[9]

By way of contrast, other authors, such as Tolkien's good friend C.S. Lewis, had no qualms with writing stories that contained deeper meanings, as in his *Space Trilogy* and his *Chronicles of Narnia*. Lewis was quite open about the spiritual intentions of his works and makes the symbolism quite evident to those who are aware.[10]

The value of discovering the author's intention is demonstrated by the early reviewers of Lewis' *Out of the Silent Planet*, the first book in his *Space Trilogy*, very few of whom noticed the biblical analogies. (Lewis said that only two in 60 reviewers recognized the religious symbolism.)[11]

In studying the Bible as literature, the intent of the author of each book is often stated, or is made obvious by its content. Psalms is a collection of songs, and should be interpreted as such. Proverbs is a collection of wisdom in the form of pithy sayings, not commands and promises that speak authoritatively to every situation. Thus, a proverb stating that wisdom leads to a long life isn't contradicted by the early death of a wise person. We're talking *principles* in Proverbs—the way things *generally* work—rather than the way they *always* work.[12]

The author of Luke, both in his account of Jesus' life (The Gospel of Luke) and history of the early church (The Acts of the Apostles) claims to be writing history based upon his own careful investigation. Thus, to take what was intended as history and to suggest (as is the habit of some writers and pastors with overactive imaginations), that each number and name and incidence has a deeper, symbolic meaning, would seem to be no different from the professors of literature who feel they simply must find deeper meaning in *The Lord of the Rings*. The former was written as history, the latter as a children's story. Obsessively looking for "deeper, symbolic meanings" risks losing all objectivity in flights of fancy that were never intended by the authors.

Surely it's safer to distinguish "what it means" (requiring sufficient reasons) from the equally legitimate "what it means to me," or as Tolkien expressed it, how it "applies" to my situation (requiring introspection and resonance). A helpful first step is to discover the author's stated intention.

2. Study the Historical Context

I fear that the intention of the author didn't take us very far in our journey to comprehend "American Pie." McLean never tells us, as Tolkien did, that it's merely a story with no deeper or symbolic meaning. Quite to the contrary, he tells us that it was inspired by Buddy Holly's death. It certainly appears that the often cryptic phrases mean something, but McLean declines to tell us those meanings. Thus, I feel warranted in continuing my search for those deeper meanings.

Fortunately, those who study the 1960s (or who paid attention while living through them) can identify many phrases in the song that have special meaning. Thus, the historical context can help us to better appreciate almost all of the lyrics and suggest possible meanings.

For example:

- "a generation lost in space" - A popular TV series titled "Lost in Space" aired 83 episodes from 1965-1968. McLean seems to be comparing the TV family that was lost in space to young people losing their moorings in the tumultuous 1960s.
- "And while Lennon read a book of Marx" - The Beatles (with John Lennon as one of the primary song writers) transitioned from singing almost exclusively love songs to political songs and social messages with songs like "Revolution." So it's quite possible that The Beatles were the "quartet playing in the park."

All in all, based on McLean's constant historical references, he seems to be painting a picture of the optimistic, relatively stable 1950s (at the end of which Holly and his music died), followed by the angst and disillusionment of many in the '60s. The impact of drugs, lost faith in the government (and anyone over 30 years old), and even a blatant embracing of evil by some musicians led McLean to a feeling of remorse and loss. (See the passage in "American Pie," evidently about the Rolling Stones playing their song "Sympathy for the Devil" at the outdoor festival at Altamont, while members of Hell's Angels beat a fan to death in front of the stage.)

For me, having grown up in the latter '60s and early '70s, many of these lines hold special meaning—perhaps different meaning, or even *more* meaning, than McLean originally intended. In one interview, he expressed surprise upon hearing about how his song had such deep meanings. So perhaps it's good that he refused to tell the meanings he intended. I'd hate to hear that some of the phrases were just thrown together because they happened to rhyme. In the end, I might like my interpretation better than his.

So whether you're interpreting a song or a religious text or the founding documents of a country, the historical context should be considered.

3. A Check for Reining in Flights of Fancy: Find Other Interpretations.

Had I stopped my "American Pie" search at the first website I encountered, I might have bought into that person's interpretation. After all, the writer sounded very sure of the meanings he set forth, as if they were not his personal take, but the general consensus of what everyone in the know thought. After reading his interpretations, it was easy for me to read them back into the lyrics.

But by extending my search to other sites, I found a variety of interpretations, each of which seemed just as possible as the first. While certain phrases seemed to draw a consensus opinion, others were interpreted in wildly different ways. For example, "moss grows fat on a rolling stone" has been thought to refer to such various people/things as Bob Dylan, Elvis, rockers in general (raking in the money), a stagnating music industry, or the Rolling Stones.[13]

The takeaway? Resist believing the first interpretation that occurs to you, or the first interpretation you hear, no matter how dogmatically the professor or writer presents his or her view. By looking at many interpretations, we can weigh the evidence for each, perhaps in the end determining that one makes more sense than another, or alternatively concluding that the phrase is so vague that we'll likely never know with any degree of certainty what it means.

Yet, living with uncertainty doesn't sit right with many interpreters. Not comfortable with degrees of certitude, they feel that they simply must find *the* definite answer and express it with equal certitude. But in doing so, don't they hinder our search for truth by proclaiming their ill-formed opinions as the final word?

Why does a person give one and only one interpretation of "moss growing thick," present it with an air of finality, and not even reveal to readers that many other equally valid suggestions have been offered? Perhaps they heard this interpretation, believed it implicitly, and passed it on before checking for other interpretations. Perhaps they mask their insecurity by playing the part of the confident authority.

In interpreting "American Pie," such unwarranted dogmatism does little harm. But in other cases, when people make life decisions based upon a person's interpretation, writers and speakers should exercise more care.

In interpreting the Bible or other influential literature, this is where consulting the best commentaries comes in. Experts on the relevant historical context and original languages often help us to see things differently from our first, uninformed perceptions.

Some who teach literature feel that they simply must find deeper meanings everywhere. In the popular text, *How to Read Literature Like a Professor*, Thomas Foster, an English professor, notes that for many professors "everything is a symbol of something, it seems, until proven otherwise."[14]

So if, to your literature professor, every meal represents the Lord's Supper and every Fall season represents death, check out a few other interpretations. If you discover multiple conflicting opinions, with insufficient evidence to indicate which might be right, just keep nodding your head at the appropriate places during your professor's lecture, answering the test questions the way your professor wants you to, while in your own mind assuming that his overactive imagination has taken him for a ride. Just resist allowing him to take *you* along for the ride as well.

4. Apply the Common Rules of Exegesis* and Hermeneutics*.

Two of my favorite college classes were hermeneutics and Greek exegesis—both of which attempt to construct a consistent science of interpretation. For me, they rescued all types of literature from being hopelessly adrift in a sea of subjective opinion.

***Exegesis =** determining the meaning of a text based on a careful, objective analysis.

***Hermeneutics =** the branch of knowledge that deals with properly interpreting texts.

Paying attention to exegetical principles keeps us from arbitrarily interpreting words according to our fancy. Consulting the appropriate dictionaries and lexicons can help. But when multiple meanings of words are possible, we explore the immediate and larger context in which the words are used. Exegesis helps us to understand how grammar influences meaning, as we demonstrated with Martin Luther reflecting on the Greek genitive phrase, "The righteousness of God."

In hermeneutics we explore, for example, abuses in interpreting figurative language. If I tell a fictional story to make a point, like the story of the bus that wrecked in chapter 22, I'm making a single point with the story. My context (what I'm talking about when I introduce the story) told you the meaning of the story (we obsess on certain details while overlooking others). Proper hermeneutics suggests that I call a literary foul if someone tries to interpret this story to mean that I think all buses are dangerous, bus drivers should be more careful, or (*a la* Freud) that the bus driver represents a repressed and resented father figure in my life.

Conclusion

While exegesis and hermeneutics help us to see through much literary nonsense, they may, as in the case of obtuse writing, merely reinforce that a passage is indeed obscure and indecipherable. I fear that the most informed and talented exegete or hermeneut is helpless to tell us with authority what McLean's moss on a rolling stone meant. Fortunately, most literature isn't so obtuse.

Think Different
More Tips for Clear, Lively, Creative Communication
A Helpful List

As we've seen, from an artistic perspective, not all literature is intended to be clear. Sometimes an artist wants the meaning to be obscure, or to leave the meaning "in the eye of the beholder." But when we write to communicate truth, we want to be both clear and creative, keeping our audiences both on track and awake. Here are some final tips (not absolutes):

1. Don't use an obtuse word when a clear, common word works just as well. My skin cream container warns: "Not for ophthalmic use." Surely more people would better understand, without any loss of meaning whatsoever, "Don't put in your eyes!"

2. Omit unnecessary words. This is the bulk of my personal editing—cutting words, sentences and entire sections.

3. Write brief sentences. As a rule, the longer the sentence, the more ways it can be misunderstood.

4. Keep your subjects moving by using active verbs, rather than either passive verbs or verbs of being. Example: Which sentence stimulates more action?

> "Luther was almost hit by a bolt of lightning." (passive verb: the subject receives the action)
>
> "A bolt of lightning pierced the sky, knocking Luther to the ground." (active verb: the subject acts)

5. Make regular divisions (like paragraphs or subheadings) and use any excuse to leave white space. Note how people lay out their blogs, typically using white space to divide thoughts rather than traditionally indented paragraphs. Dyslexics groan when they see a page of nonstop words. In my opinion, added white space helps all readers. This is quite a transition from the longer, sometimes page-long paragraphs of past writers such as C.S. Lewis, but I think it's an upgrade.

6. Get over the academic thing. If you're writing solely to impress your professor and a few nerdy friends, feel free to use specialized, insider, academic language. But if you want people outside academia to read your work, write for a more general audience. Let your research and the quality of your ideas, not your arcane style of writing, make people take you seriously.

7. Learn from various fields of communication. Read the *New York Times* for great journalistic writing. Note how sportscasters find 50 creative ways to say "He's out!" in baseball, to keep their commentary from being monotonous. Learn how literary writers paint vivid scenes and fascinating characters. Study how certain popular fiction writers keep stories moving with sparse prose and minimum description, allowing readers more latitude in creating their own mental versions of scenes and characters. Study standup comedians, who've mastered one of the most difficult forms of communication—their expressions, their pauses, their motions, their content, how they interact with their audiences.

8. Get candid input from teachers, from friends, from family, from anyone who's willing to share a tip. In classes, I solicit regular input on the effectiveness of my teaching, asking students to evaluate me both mid semester and at semester's end.

9. KEEP HONING YOUR CRAFT! Whether you're teaching a class, leading a seminar, managing an office meeting, coaching a baseball team, or writing an article, there's always more to learn. Although I've been studying communication all my life, I still take classes on teaching and constantly get ideas from my fellow teachers and students.

Flex Your Neurons!
Pursuing the Point of Know Return

1. Go ahead, use this as an excuse to find the song "American Pie" and listen to it in its entirety. What do you make of it?

2. Think of a song that you've never completely understood. Do some research (as I did with "American Pie") to try to find

    a. if it has an intended meaning and

    b. if so, what it is.

3. When your teachers (present or past) wax eloquent on the "hidden meanings" of various pieces of literature, do you ever question their confident assertions? If so, how might you determine whether there's sufficient evidence for their claims?

4. Would people describe your verbal communications (formal and informal) as clear and lively? What are one or two ways you might improve your speaking so as to be a more interesting person?

5. How could you hone your writing to make it more clear, lively, and interesting?

Making It More Personal
Practical Takeaways

What are one or more ideas provoked by this chapter that you can apply to help you think more critically?

____

____

____

What are one or more ideas that you can apply to help you think more creatively?

____

____

____

What else do you want to make sure you don't forget?

____

____

____

Recommended Trails
For the Incurably Curious and Adventurous

1. If you're pursuing writing or (more broadly) communications, consider joining a writers' group or speakers' group (e.g., Toastmasters) or communication group (e.g., a Meetup group—www.meetup.com—or campus organization for communicators) to learn from one another.

2. To find the most useful articles and books on understanding literature, ask a couple of English professors or search such terms as "understanding literature," "interpreting literature," "exegesis," "hermeneutics."

3. On clear and lively writing, find articles by your favorite authors (authors who write in a style you wish to emulate) on how they write. And don't forget to study screenwriters. They seem to be more likely to write in groups or give mutual input. Do their processes tend to differ from that of journalists and authors? If so, what elements of their writing would you like to incorporate?

4. On clear and lively communications (beyond writing), find articles by your favorite communicators and discover ways to improve your own communications.

SECTION EIGHT

WHY DO BRILLIANT PEOPLE BELIEVE NONSENSE? BECAUSE THEY FAIL TO HARNESS THEIR PASSIONS

CHAPTER 24

THEY'RE OVERWHELMED BY THEIR EMOTIONS AND PASSIONS

"When dealing with people, remember you are not dealing with creatures of logic, but creatures of emotion."

— Dale Carnegie

Emotions and the Teen Mind

As I write this chapter, I'm reeling from the senseless death of a vibrant, promising young lady who meant a lot to me. She didn't make it to age 25.

Haley had everything going for her—bright, attractive, personable, ever radiating an infectious energy. If I could bend time, I'd go back to that first day she was offered heroin and ask, "What's going through your mind?" I want to know what hijacked her decision-making skills, making one of the most addictive, destructive drugs known to humans look like a great idea.

Since I can't bend time, I'll never know for certain. But I can discover some of the common ways that people allow their emotions to hijack their reasoning. I can also learn strategies for more clear-headed thinking. To find the answers, I turned to some experts in psychology.

The Teen Brain: A Work in Progress

According to the National Institute of Mental Health, teen brains haven't fully matured. They're still under construction. This could, in part, explain the teen years (and early 20s) being fraught with dangers, including high rates of drug and alcohol abuse, crime, and death by injury.

To better understand brain development, scientists scanned the brains of children and followed up with scans as they matured. Their conclusion? Until we're in our early 20s (some develop later and some earlier) we're not working with a fully developed brain.

Significantly, the parts of the brain that mature last are those that allow us to control our impulses and plan ahead. The connection of these functions with making rational decisions is obvious. To a teen mind—on an impulse and with little or no thought for the future—heroin or burglary or a motorcycle race on a busy Los Angeles street might seem like great ideas for an evening of fun with friends.

Think!

If you're in your teens or early 20s, what implications might this have for making better decisions?

To the high school teen or young college student who's reading this, a couple of implications for life stand out:

- Watch who you hang around.
- Run some of your ideas by responsible adults.

As many success gurus have recommended, "You can't soar with eagles if you hang out with turkeys." Or as basketball great Kareem Abdul Jabaar put it, "Don't let those who are going nowhere influence your opinions."

If you're with your friends one night when they all decide on a whim to try heroin ("Come on, don't be a wuss!"), the emotional, thrill-seeking part of your brain may overwhelm your not-yet-fully-developed impulse inhibitor and your life may take a dramatic turn for the worse.[1]

Concerning running ideas by respected adults, Solomon suggested that "in an abundance of counselors there is safety." Even if you don't consult them, just thinking "What would my parents (or adults I look up to) think about this decision?" can help you to think more rationally, beyond the emotion of the moment. Until your brain's clicking on all cylinders (or until all the cylinders are fully developed), don't fully trust what it's telling you.

Below, we'll talk about other strategies for keeping our emotions and impulses from overriding our reason; but first, let's explore the *adult* brain, which is often hijacked by emotions as well.

Emotions and the Adult Mind

America's Most Innovative Company

If you were a high achieving college graduate in the 1990s, looking for a growing, exciting, respected company to work for, Enron would have likely made your short list. And if you were an investor, buying Enron stock seemed to be a no brainer. An innovator in selling natural gas and energy, their stock grew by 311 percent from 1990 to 1998. But that was just the warm-up. As they kept diversifying into other industries, in 1999 their stock skyrocketed by an astounding 56 percent, then 87 percent in 2000. The top three agencies that rate companies assured the public of their credibility by giving Enron glowing ratings as a reputable, safe investment, well into 2001.[2]

For six consecutive years, from 1996 to 2001, Enron was crowned "America's Most Innovative

Company" by *Fortune Magazine*. In the year 2000, Enron made *Fortune's* list of best companies to work for in America. It had become our nation's seventh largest corporation and was the darling of business publications and investors.

No wonder the world stood aghast when in December of 2001, the same year it was declared "America's Most Innovative Company," it declared bankruptcy. Its stock dropped from its former high of $90 per share to 26 cents a share. Careers died. Leaders were sentenced to prison. Those heavily invested lost their life savings. Their vice chairman committed suicide.[3]

What went wrong?

Enron's leaders had no lack of academic brilliance and education. Just look at the intellectual credentials of three of the highest ranking officials, who were later sentenced to prison:

- **Ken Lay,** founder, chairman and CEO - PhD in economics.
- **Jeff Skilling,** president and chief operating officer - MBA from Harvard Business School, graduated in the top five percent of his class. Skilling said that in his admissions interview to Harvard he was asked, "Are you smart?" To which he replied, "I'm f****** smart."[4]
- **Andrew Fastow,** chief financial officer – MA degree in business administration from Northwestern University.

Both within Enron and to the watching world, they were the smartest of the smart—intimidatingly smart.

But if you read various accounts of Enron's fall, certain words and phrases keep turning up, such as in a review in a respected accounting journal: "greed," caught up in "market euphoria," "arrogance," "intensely competitive."[5]

Those are interesting words for an accounting journal—words that are more emotional than intellectual. In fact, I never saw a study of Enron calling their leaders "intellectually incompetent" or "dumb." One of the most respected accounts of Enron is titled "The Smartest Guys in the Room." So how did such smart guys end up in jail? Why did they fail so miserably? Somehow, they allowed their emotions to highjack their brains and as a result commit crimes so audacious that any level-headed person should have known better. Their greed and arrogance brought them down.

True, Enron exploited accounting loopholes and outright lied and deceived the world about their true activities and financial state. But look deeper. *Why* did they exploit and lie and deceive? Perhaps constructing a brief narrative would clarify the impact of emotions and make their journey to the dark side more understandable.

Their arrogance and overconfidence led them to believe that they were so smart and talented that they could pull Enron out of any mess, no matter how bad things got. Since some of their acquisitions and projects were hemorrhaging hundreds of millions of dollars, they desperately needed to hide this from the public until they got it under control. After all, as long as their stock kept growing in value, they could leverage it to offset their losses. But if the public saw their great losses and lost faith in them, their stock would take a dive, potentially pulling them under. Since desperate times call for desperate measures, their leaders felt that creative accounting for the short haul could be justified, just until things got back on track.

Unfortunately for Enron, the leaders were not only deceiving the public, but appear to have been deceiving themselves. Skilling once told *BusinessWeek* that he'd "never not been successful at work or business, ever."[6] No wonder he was overconfident and felt he could fix anything that was wrong with Enron, even till the very end. As researchers McLean and Elkind reported, "It is difficult to find any evidence that Skilling...has ever admitted that he failed at Enron. Not even to himself."[7]

From Enron to Us

Today we look with disgust at leaders such as Lay, Skilling and Fastow, the poster children for corporate greed. But seen apart from their positions of unique power and influence, perhaps they're not that different from the rest of us. After all, these are men who took vacations with their children and involved themselves in the community. Fastow, when he wasn't cooking accounting books or awarding himself millions of dollars in bonuses, seemed to be "the picture of a devoted family man." He regularly left work to spend long lunches with his wife, whom he adored. Each week, he calendared a couple of hours for "dad's night with the boys."[8] They are people, more like you and me than we'd like to imagine.

So shouldn't we admit that we're all tempted by the same drives and emotions that brought down Enron and caused Haley to try heroin?

Most of us are at least a bit overconfident; we tend to assume that we'll never fail at business or become alcoholics or drug addicts. We have a strong tendency to explain away our failures as due to other people's failures—a sorry teacher or inept boss or clueless coach. Yet, while studies find that most of us are about average (obviously), we like to think of ourselves as above average, resulting in emotions that lead us to imagine we can get away with things that average people can't, like:

- turning in a paper for class that's partly stolen from another student or author.
- obtaining a copy of the exam from a friend who has the same professor in an earlier class.
- not reporting under the table cash payments to the IRS.
- finding creative ways to bolster profits on paper to keep our stock strong.

I recall one of my college English professors who admitted to us that she wanted so badly to be valedictorian of her class at Ohio State that she dated her closest rival, solely for the purpose of distracting him from studying for tests.

Why do we succumb to the strong emotions that accompany lying, cheating and stealing? I suppose that, like the Enron guys, many of us think the ends justify the means. Like the Enron guys, we're not planning to be corrupt for the rest of our lives; we just need to bend the rules a bit to get through this class. We're just competitive enough to justify it by imagining that everybody's doing it. We're arrogant enough to believe we can get away with it. And we're greedy enough to think we deserve to graduate with honors, even if we had to lie and cheat and steal to get there. "After college," we tell ourselves, "we'll put the unethical shortcuts behind us and make decisions on the basis of pure reason and upstanding motives."

But isn't that the way the Enron leaders probably thought during their college years?[9] I doubt they planned from the start to allow their baser emotions to cloud their reason. Cutting corners was supposed to be just a temporary thing. But with practice, it became their character.

Beyond succeeding in business and resisting drugs, controlling emotions is essential to our everyday success—realizing that envy is hurting your relationship with that star athlete on your team, realizing that your uber competitive nature is leading you to run over people, understanding that your out-of-control temper is impacting your decisions and your relationships with family, realizing that your arrogance often leads you to take irrational risks.

So how can we rein in our emotions? Here are some ideas.

How to Keep Emotions from Clouding our Thinking

1. Don't imagine that "smart" protects you from letting emotions run away with you.

In the case of Enron, "smart" merely enabled leaders to justify their emotions and corrupt methods, using their skills to deceive. So keep your ego in check.[10]

2. Recognize the vulnerabilities of your stage of life.

Having a not-quite-adult mind can lead to stupid decisions, if you trust it implicitly and fail to get objective input.

3. Recognize your emotions and passions.

Skilling and Lay never seemed to realize that their overconfidence was deceiving them. In late October of 2001, a bit over a month from declaring bankruptcy, Lay spoke at a meeting open to all employees. He insisted that Enron had consistently done the right thing and promised that they'd make it through fine. By this time, his employees knew better. A few minutes into the Q & A period, someone handed Lay a written question, which he read aloud:

> "I would like to know if you are on crack. If so that would explain a lot. If not, you may want to start because it's going to be a long time before we trust you again."[11]

As seemed to be the case with Skilling and Lay, we're often blind to how far our emotions have taken our reasoning for a ride. As we'll see below, we simply must open ourselves to the candid criticism of others if we ever hope to discover our emotional shortcomings.

When I was involved in rehabbing foreclosure properties, experts in the field warned me that rule number one for succeeding in this business was: "Don't fall in love with your properties!" Real estate investors who allow their emotions to run wild end up spending so much money beautifying a property that they end up losing money.

Critical thinking guru Edward De Bono helps people to separate out emotions from facts by asking them to imagine that they're putting on various thinking hats, one at a time. Let's say you're trying to decide whether to accept a new position in Denver, which would involve moving your family from Los Angeles. First, suggests De Bono, put on your white hat, which represents purely facts and figures—no emotions allowed! Later, emotions will be considered, but asking all interested parties to start with listing facts and figures can help us to be more objective. If you absolutely love the Rocky Mountains and Denver Broncos, it might be difficult to stay objective!

4. If you're inflamed, calm down.

Surely you've heard reports of people killing each other over a road rage incident.

Just imagine: road construction and two accidents have turned your hour commute to college into two hours. You're late for your midterm. You finally see a clearing, but someone cuts you off, almost causing an accident. Enraged, you lay on your horn and yell "Moron!" The other driver pulls off the road and waves you over.

This is exactly how fist fights and homicides break out between otherwise intelligent people. Days later, perhaps in jail with a black eye and an act of violence on your record, you can't believe what happened.

So if you're discussing an important issue and you feel the anger building, take a break. Count to 10. Leave the room till you can regain control. Table the discussion for a better day when everyone's more rested. Nobody can make wise decisions when anger has hijacked your thinking faculties.[12]

5. Open yourself to other views.

Skilling and Lay appeared to be increasingly out of touch with their company. Surrounding themselves with people who thought like they thought and dismissing contrary input, they could increasingly live in a fantasy world of their own making.[13]

Although they were billions of dollars in debt, they'd tell themselves and the world, "We're doing great! I've never been more optimistic about Enron's future!" As long as they ignored contrary opinion, they could believe what they desperately wanted to believe.

Astoundingly, Ken Lay conducted his personal investments eerily similar to the way he conducted Enron's finances. As a result, although he had made millions of dollars over the years through Enron, he had also massively borrowed in order to make various investments, many of which were tied to the health of Enron's stock. He ignored his advisors, who strongly encouraged him to diversity. By January of 2001, he owed $95 million, and was struggling to pay his creditors.

"Other views" are what we get from respected colleagues and friends. When I resist getting input, I sometimes discover that it's because I really, really want to take a certain path, but suspect that if I get counsel, they'll warn me against that path.

6. Establish formal accountability.

This makes the last point—"getting other views"—a formal, regular part of your life and business.

Coach Joe Gibbs was one of the most successful professional football coaches ever. But even as his team competed in a Super Bowl, he agonized over his millions of dollars of debt. His personal finances were in shambles as a result of investments gone awry. The investments seemed wise when people presented them—building racquetball complexes when the sport was very popular, developing neighborhoods in an oil rich area while oil was booming. But they blew up on him.

To dig his way out and to make better decisions, people counseled him to run future decisions by his wife and a board of wise counselors. Establishing formal accountability turned his life around.[14]

7. Note when you're attacking people rather than their ideas.

Profitable discussions stick to the data and the reasoning. But people issues provoke emotions that can deflect from the real issues.

At Enron, rather than listening to naysayers, the leadership dismissed them. They would rationalize negative input:

- "They're just short sellers out to make us look bad!"
- "That accountant just has it in for us!"

Rather than look seriously into the negative data people were uncovering, they labeled naysayers as enemies and ignored them.

One of my favorite college presidents used to say, "I consider my enemies as my best friends." He knew that if he couldn't answer their objections, he might be wrong. They were often more willing to point out his faults than his friends.[15]

8. Develop cultures of clear thinking and integrity, rather than ruthless competition.

Enron's leaders were competitive risk takers, and they developed a culture of high competition among their employees. According to one reflective article,

> "Enron's corporate culture encouraged rampant, ruthless internal competition, driving otherwise decent human beings to take risks of a kind they knew were dangerous and wrong. Asked to choose between losing face and losing shareholder's money, self-image won out—as it always will. If companies foster internal competition, they can and should expect to see even the finest employees' values fall by the wayside."[16]

Many of their employees were rated on a scale of one to five. "One" meant they were making serious money for Enron. They were showered with benefits and honor. "Five" meant they were close to being fired. Such an environment promotes, not teamwork and camaraderie and open learning, but hiding your best ideas, jealousy of the big winners, and winning at all costs. This generated a culture of fierce competition, whereby "immediate gratification was prized above long-term potential."[17]

9. Recognize (or flee from!) situations that prey on your emotions.

Public auctions can prey on the emotions associated with winning and losing and competition. Offers of big money can corrupt. (Enron was paying Arthur Anderson, one of our nation's most trusted accounting firms, over a million dollars a month. No wonder they were willing to bend the rules. As a result of the scandal, the firm no longer exists.) The promise of money, power and prestige has turned many a great mind to mush. Lack of sleep increases our susceptibility to impulsive behavior.[18]

My wife and I determined to never make a purchase the day of a presentation, since it was typically a high pressure sell. This little practice saved us from many poor decisions.

Drinking and certain drugs (such as Meth) make people overconfident. Perhaps Haley was influenced by a drug or alcohol when she was first offered heroin. Under the influence of meth, she might have felt invulnerable.

10. Don't be intimidated.

Have you ever been in a conversation where you really didn't understand what someone was talking about it, but in order to save face, you had to act like you understood? I have. Let's call it "intellectual intimidation," or "intellectual bullying." Enron used fancy language and vague terminology to hide the fact that they were billions of dollars in debt. Thus, their public accounting disclosures were described as "mind numbingly complex."[19]

So why did the banks that were lending them money, the rating agencies, and the stockholders, all of whom had the duty to analyze the company, put their faith in Enron when they couldn't have possibly understood how Enron was actually making money?

I'd suggest that, in part, they were intimidated by "the smartest guys in the room" and were influenced by not wanting to appear ignorant. It would be more than a bit humbling for a great investment company like Merrill Lynch to send someone to Enron and confess, "I've read your accounting sheets, but I still can't for the life of me understand how you're making money. Show me in simple language your profits and losses on a sheet of paper."

Of course, the smart guys at Enron would respond that it can't be put that simply. "After all, we're dealing here with cutting edge deals that involve cutting edge accounting." Then, they'd launch into a discussion that nobody could fully understand. No wonder they could intimidate and appear to be "the smartest guys in the room."[20]

Warren Buffett became the world's greatest investor in part by making sure he understood how the companies he bought were generating their income, and assessing whether or not their approach was sustainable. Although Enron's stock was flying high, although the ratings agencies gave it the highest ratings, although banks were willing to lend them money, although they were audited by one of the top accounting firms in the country, none of this would matter in the least to Warren Buffett if he couldn't clearly understand how Enron was making the money it was claiming to make.

Thus, a Stanford document on Enron references Buffett:

> When asked about why he didn't invest in dot-com companies, Warren Buffett responded, "I have an old-fashioned belief that I should only expect to make money in things I understand. And when I say understand, I mean understand what the economics of the business are likely to look like 10 years from now."[21]

If all investors followed Buffett's advice, companies that failed to provide sufficient information for investors to understand their financial position would find it very difficult to raise money from the investing public.

Buffett's mentor, Benjamin Graham, deserves quoting again in this context: "You are neither right nor wrong because the crowd disagrees with you. You are right because your data and reasoning are right."[22]

Conclusion

Whether we're making personal or business decisions, our passions and emotions can hijack our thinking. Those who are unaware of their influence, or allow them to take charge, will often find themselves making foolish and destructive decisions.

Think Different

So far this chapter has been largely negative—how people screw up by letting emotions get out of control. But there's a positive side to our emotional states. Let's explore how some of these potentially negative emotions can have a positive side.

First, the developmental state of the teen brain offers advantages as well as dangers. As the National Institutes of Health explains:

> "Scientists emphasize that the fact that the teen brain is in transition doesn't mean it is somehow not up to par. It is different from both a child's and an adult's in ways that may equip youth to make the transition from dependence to independence. The capacity for

> learning at this age, an expanding social life, and a taste for exploration and limit testing may all, to some extent, be reflections of age-related biology."
>
> "Research findings on the brain may also serve to help adults understand the importance of creating an environment in which teens can explore and experiment while helping them avoid behavior that is destructive to themselves and others."[23]

So getting input from young people, if adults will only listen, could be of great value to innovation, precisely because they're thinking differently at that age.[24]

Second, the hyper-competitive bent of Enron's leaders wasn't all bad. Competition can be a great motivation to success! They simply needed to understand the dangers of competition, provide for themselves checks and balances, and straighten out their moral compasses. We need each other, not just for keeping ourselves in line, but to maximize the creative flow of ideas. But we'll explore more on the positive side of emotions in the next chapter.

Flex Your Neurons!
Pursuing the Point of Know Return

1. Imagine that you worked at Enron. Do you think you'd have likely recognized early on that something was awry, or do you think you'd have been blinded by the heady euphoria of working for such a successful, smart company? Why?

2. Do you consider yourself more *objective*, or more *subjective*, in making decisions? How would your friends and family answer this question regarding you? How might this help or hinder your decision-making?

3. Think of an acquaintance or family member who you believe is overly ruled by emotions. Is there anything that anyone could say or do to help this person make more reasonable decisions? List your best ideas.

4. Think in the realm of your career interest or your current realm of influence. How can you keep from making overly emotional decisions in these realms?

5. If it's a common human tendency, as certainly was the case with Enron, to be "blind to how far our emotions have taken us for a ride," what steps can we take to offset this tendency?

6. If you were about to make a poor decision, is there someone currently in your life (like a close friend or accountability partner) who would challenge you on the decision? If not, how could you take steps to bring such a person into your life?

7. How can we do a better job of harnessing the positive aspects of the teen brain? Many teens are too shy or insecure to share their ideas. How could classes and office meetings be better arranged to encourage a better flow of ideas? (Examples: Meet in smaller groups, like Google? Meet around round tables, rather than lecture-style rooms?)[25]

Making It More Personal
Practical Takeaways

What are one or more ideas provoked by this chapter that you can apply to help you think more critically?

____

____

____

What are one or more ideas that you can apply to help you think more creatively?

____

____

____

What else do you want to make sure you don't forget?

____

____

____

Recommended Trails
For the Incurably Curious and Adventurous

1. Do you need a track to run on when making decisions—a method that helps you to consider (not ignore) your emotions, but keeps you from being ruled by them? A leading authority on conceptual thinking, Dr. Edward de Bono, has written a very accessible and practical book to answer this question: *Six Thinking Hats: An essential approach to business management from the creator of lateral thinking*." (New York: Little, Brown and Company, 1985)

Although he's writing for business leaders, the approach is simple enough to be used by individuals making important decisions. In brief, he recommends thinking through a problem in this sequence:

- **Put on your white hat**, which represents facts, figures and objective information.
- **Put on your red hat**, considering your emotions and feelings.
- **Put on your black hat**, looking at your logical negative thoughts.
- **Put on your yellow hat**, considering only positive, constructive thoughts.
- **Put on your green hat**, incorporating your creativity and new ideas.
- **Put on your blue hat** to organize your thought process, using metacognition to think through the best way to use the information gleaned from donning the other hats.

Read the book to see in more detail how to put this method into practice.

2. Enron certainly failed to think straight in the moral domain. In making good decisions, balancing emotion with reason, it's not only necessary to think through the most *practical* thing to do, but to ask "What's the *right* thing to do?" Harvard professor Michael Sandel helps us to answer that question in his popular book *Justice: What's the Right Thing to Do?* (Farrar, Straus and Giroux, reprint edition, 2010).

3. To understand better what went wrong at Enron and to explore this fascinating study in how emotions and reason can go awry in leading a company, read *The Smartest Guys in the Room: The Amazing Rise and Scandalous Fall of Enron*, by Bethany McLean and Peter Elkind (New York: Penguin, updated edition, 2004).

4. Search terms/phrases such as "Dialectical Behavior Therapy" (DBT) and the related concept of "Wise Mind." These approaches to counseling are often studied/employed in connection with helping people with Borderline Personality Disorder (BPD) to control their emotions in order to make wiser decisions. But the principles can be used by anyone to make wiser decisions. Also search "Cognitive Behavior Therapy" (CBT), which seeks to counterbalance the tendency of some to make decisions based upon overly emotional factors.[26]

CHAPTER 25

THEY FAIL TO EMPLOY EMOTIONAL INTELLIGENCE AND COMMON SENSE

Warren Buffett on what to look for in choosing a business partner:

"I think you'll probably start looking for the person that you can always depend on; the person whose ego does not get in his way; the person who's perfectly willing to let someone else take the credit for an idea as long as it worked; the person who essentially won't let you down, who thought straight as opposed to brilliantly."

— quoted from *Of Permanent Value*

As we near the end of the book, I feel a bit closer to you, since we've travelled so far and explored so many ideas together. So I might as well come out into the open about one of my darker secrets.

I'm a bit of a Trekkie.... There, I said it.

Star Trek began as a 1960's sci-fi TV show, inspiring five subsequent Star Trek TV series, twelve films, and scores of video games. Today, interest in the Star Trek saga continues to grow. The latest (2013) film, *Into Darkness*, earned over $467 million worldwide, making it the highest-grossing Star Trek film ever.

While I don't attend Star Trek conventions or own a phaser autographed by Sulu or Scottie, I do occasionally find myself asking, "What would First Officer Spock or Captain Kirk do in this situation?" My reasons are very practical and will soon become apparent.

What's Your Image of the Supremely Logical, Critical Thinker?

Spock—the stoic, analytical character played by Leonard Nimoy in the original series—would win any vote by first generation trekkies. He's Mr. Logic. His Vulcan heritage bestowed upon him a mind of rare mathematical and logical genius. If you need a cold, calculated assessment of the data, ask Spock.

In this picture, Spock stands to the left—no smile, no relational warmth, clueless that the photographer is a beautiful woman who thinks he's cute. Perhaps the camera reminded him of the history of photography, and he's reorganizing that mental file of data as he poses.

"If Spock had been running Enron," some might suggest, "he could have avoided all the emotional nonsense that blinded the leadership—the greed and arrogance and childlike competition. With Spock at the helm, it might be a viable company to this day."

Perhaps that's true, but I fear that those who deprecate all emotions and assume that the most accurate logic is that which most effectively bars emotion from each equation, may find themselves face to face with contrary data of the most troubling sort—Why was *Kirk* the captain of the Starship Enterprise rather than *Spock*?

Spock's Limitations

A part of people's fascination with *Star Trek* was the diverse, yet complimentary personalities that triggered fascinating interactions. Take McCoy, the physician (far right in the picture). He had deep feelings and thought very relationally—the polar opposite of Spock. (Look at his exuberant smile. He just realized that the photographer is a great friend of his sister.)

Naturally, Spock and McCoy often butted heads in either serious or light-hearted conflict. But Kirk (at center in the picture) had that rare talent for leadership which enabled him to consider the advice of his crew and blend the best of both worlds—logic and emotions—to make wise decisions.

The great value of Spock was that he could evaluate circumstances with pure logic, unclouded by emotional considerations. But his greatest strength was also his greatest weakness. He had no emotional intelligence—a severe deficit in understanding how emotions could and should inform his logic.

How Emotional Intelligence* Can Enhance Logic

***Emotional Intelligence** = the ability to understand, recognize and deal with emotions, both personally and interpersonally.

So imagine that a Klingon warship stands between the Starship Enterprise and a colony of people they desperately need to rescue. Listen carefully to a possible exchange:

> **Spock:** "Our firepower far exceeds theirs. Logically, their only option is to allow us through without a fight."
>
> **McCoy:** "Your logic fails to consider that the captain of this particular Klingon vessel has never lost a fight and takes great pride in that he never backs down to anyone. I fully expect that he'd rather die than let us through."
>
> **Kirk:** "If McCoy is right, perhaps we can negotiate a pass in a way that allows the Klingon captain to save face with his crew and continue feeling superior to us."

Note: *Both Spock and McCoy are arguing rationally.* They weren't pitting logic against emotions. Rather, McCoy, because of his emotional intelligence, was able to add data to the line of argument that proved crucial to Kirk's handling of the standoff.

Put in a syllogism, Spock argued:

> **Premise 1:** If a Klingon warship captain realizes he's outgunned, he'll back off.
> **Premise 2:** The captain realizes he's outgunned.
> **Therefore:** He'll back off.

Conversely, McCoy argued:

> **Premise 1:** If a Klingon warship captain is overconfident and filled with pride, he'll put up a fight even though he's outgunned.
> **Premise 2:** This captain is overconfident and filled with pride.
> **Conclusion:** He'll put up a fight even though he's outgunned.

Note that both are equally valid arguments—the conclusions logically follow from the premises. Yet McCoy's argument is superior in that he takes into account data provided by emotional intelligence. His argument, if both sound and valid, demonstrates that Spock's first premise errs in that it fails to take into account the Klingon captain's pride. It doesn't mean that McCoy is smarter *in general* than Spock. McCoy is smarter than Spock *at evaluating emotional/relational data.* Spock is smarter *at insuring that any given argument is argued in a valid way.* Both are valuable skills and a good leader understands and draws upon those strengths.

So could Spock have saved Enron? Perhaps. But in a sense, Enron already had its Spock-like mind in Jeff Skilling. People never referred to Skilling as simply "smart." They called him "incandescently brilliant" or "the smartest person I ever met."[1] Here's how his high bandwidth mental processing was described:

> "He could process information and conceptualize new ideas with blazing speed. He could instantly simplify highly complex issues into a sparkling, compelling image."

But for all his brilliance, the same authors noted one of his "dangerous blind spots":

> "...he didn't really understand people. He expected people to behave according to the imperatives of pure intellectual logic, but of course nobody does that...."

So in Skilling we have high academic intelligence, but low emotional and relational intelligence. From my reading of Enron, that was one of the key factors in its fall.[2]

So let's look at some real life examples of what happens when emotional intelligence is lacking—in business decisions, in science, in arguing for our points of view, and in evaluating the views of others. Reflecting on these, brainstorm some practical ideas for how to add emotional intelligence to your decisions.

When Emotional Intelligence is Left Out of the Equation

Lack of Emotional Intelligence Hinders Research and Development

At New York's 1964 World's Fair, Bell Labs' Picturephones were a hit. Visitors could sit in booths and talk to one another while seeing each other, much like we do on Skype today. But in the 1960's such technology was extraordinary, seemingly capturing the essence of future communications.

To most, it seemed obvious that Bell Labs should commit the millions of dollars necessary to develop this technology. After all, businesses could conduct meetings long distance without making people travel. People could see their loved ones when they were far from home. It might even relieve congested cities by allowing people to work from the country.

So they conducted market research, which indicated that most people saw a need for Picturephones in their businesses and almost half perceived a need in their homes. The conclusion of the study? Many people wanted to see who they were talking to.

Unfortunately, researchers apparently failed to clarify whether they wanted others *to see them* as well.[3] Perhaps people, if they were asked a couple of further questions, would consider it preferable to communicate without a visual, such as being able to talk to the boss from home in your pajamas, or without fixing your hair, or without worrying about the baby food splattered on your blouse.

After mega dollars and thousands of hours of people power were spent in development, the Picturephone made its debut in Pittsburgh and Chicago. Astonishingly, after a "vigorous sales campaign" over an 18 month period, Chicago had only 46 customers and Pittsburgh had eight. What happened?

After evaluating the colossal failure, topping their list was the insight that people liked the impersonal aspects of phone calls and didn't think the visual aspect added that much to the conversation. Apparently, the market research had failed to ask questions that sufficiently considered such drawbacks.

Surely it's significant that predicting such human behavior and thinking to ask the most relevant questions in surveys require large doses of emotional intelligence. Perhaps their team of researchers failed to include enough relational thinkers in designing their surveys.[4]

Thus emotional intelligence is critical for helping companies make wise decisions.

Emotional Intelligence Can Help Determine Which Companies Will Likely Succeed

At a technology conference, I heard an investor and advisor to Silicon Valley start-ups share an insight he'd gleaned from years of consulting and observing which entrepreneurs succeed.

> "If someone tells me in essence, 'I've got an idea that's gonna make tons of money!' I don't pay them much attention. But if someone says, 'I've got an idea that's gonna help a lot of people,' I'm all ears. Those startups tend to make it."[5]

If this insight is on target, it's not the kind of insight that's typically highlighted in accounting spreadsheets. Those who know accounting but have no social intelligence might have never noticed this characteristic of successful companies.

The more I read about Enron, I look in vain for the leadership obsessing about how their business plan is going to help so many customers. Instead, I find them obsessing over stock valuations and company growth and slick deals that are likely to make millions of dollars. Customers appear to be viewed, not as people, but as potential sources of revenue. Perhaps, in the final analysis, those who focus obsessively and exclusively on profits fail to realize those profits over the long-haul, since they long ago lost sight of their customers.

Enron wasn't killed by letting *all* emotions and passions influence them. The *right* passions—passions for integrity and passions to serve and passionate concern for people—can greatly enhance the bottom line. Enron was killed by promoting *destructive* passions and emotions (brutal competition, greed, vanity). No wonder the leadership lost all respect and employees began to openly ask of their supposedly brilliant leaders, "Are you on crack?"

Why do bright people—even "The Smartest Guys in the Room"—believe nonsense? Because they fail to reason with emotional intelligence.

When Emotional Intelligence Runs Short among Great Thinkers

Many picture those who've impacted the history of human thought as brilliant individuals who were passionately driven by a pure and sincere quest for truth. But when we look more closely at their written works and peek into their lives, we often find those whose emotional intelligence, or lack thereof, influenced their opinions at least as much as their research and logic.

Bertrand Russell

In the history of philosophy, Russell symbolizes for many a modern day Spock. One of the most prominent and influential philosophers of the 20th century, he was widely considered a great and innovative logician.[6] "For the masses of people all over the world," according to writer Paul Johnston, Russell became "the quintessence, the archetype of the abstract philosopher."[7]

Thus, the article on Russell in the venerable *Encyclopedia of Philosophy* paints a picture of a truly great thinker and humanitarian who often got into trouble for fearlessly standing for the truth as he saw it. The committee for the Nobel Prize for Literature described him, in presenting Russell with the award in 1950, as "one of our time's most brilliant spokesmen of rationality and humanity…."[8]

But does an aptitude for abstract logic necessarily lead a person to a purely logical assessment of issues that impact us in real life? Beyond logic and math, Russell pontificated on an astonishing variety of subjects, including politics, religion, justice, sex, marriage, philosophy, history, education science, peace, and disarmament. Interestingly, some historians and philosophers note that although he possessed a keen understanding of logic, when he wrote his popular essays and books, he seemed to by and large write opinion pieces, without evidence of dispassionately reading and comparing the most studied opinions on the subjects, or of objectively sifting the relevant facts and rigorously testing his conclusions with logic.[9]

Historian Will Durant observed that once Russell came down to earth from his earlier obsession with math and logic, he would "never once make use of the impeccable formulae piled like Pelion upon Ossa in his *Principia Mathematica*."[9.5]

For all his great genius in abstract logic, Russell seemed to lack emotional intelligence. Thus, although he viewed his writings as purely reasonable and factual, he seemed oblivious to how his passions impacted both his reasoning and his choice of data. As one student of Russell summed up his emotional life:

> "Russell was not a man who ever acquired extensive experience of the lives most people lead or who took much interest in the view and feelings of the multitude."[10]

According to Russell's daughter, he "always found people difficult."[11] He once said, "I like mathematics because it is *not* human."[12]

He loved theory, but often found difficulty navigating the real stuff of life. According to Paul Johnson,

> "no one was more detached from physical reality than Russell. He could not work the simplest mechanical device or perform any of the routine tasks which even the most pampered man does without thinking."[13]

For example, he never could seem to figure out how to make a cup of tea, a skill surely of great practical import for any English gentleman. When his third wife went out of town, she wrote him a few simple steps for making tea.

- Put the kettle of water on a hot plate.
- Wait for it to boil.
- Pour the water into a teapot.
- Add tea leaves.

Simple for most people, but apparently not for Russell. Somehow, even with these simple instructions, he managed to fail miserably at making his cup of tea.[14]

Thus armed with a logic whose premises often failed to take into account common sense and human emotions, he often drew conclusions that more practical and people-oriented folks might roll their eyes at. For example, he saw marriage vows that promised fidelity as a potentially harmful convention of a superstitious age. Modern marriages, thought Russell, should be "open," allowing people the freedom to "love the one you're with," as songwriter Stephen Stills put it.

Putting this philosophy into practice, he went from wife to wife and affair to affair, seemingly oblivious to the tremendous emotional toll he was exacting from all involved. His unstable home often positioned his children as pawns of the adult parent figures, who tried to pull them over to their side of the squabble *du jour*.

So why couldn't such a brilliant man have predicted the emotional and relational toll that such a lifestyle would exact?[15] Russell's own reflection is telling. All seemed well to him when *he* slept around. But when *his wife* cashed in on the open relationship agreement, he was amazed at how hurt and jealous and unforgiving he became. He didn't like her any more. Astoundingly to Russell, he couldn't get past the strong feelings. In Russell's on words, admitting his lack of emotional intelligence, "Anyone else could have told me this in advance, but I was blinded by theory."[16]

"Blinded by theory."

That would be an interesting thread to follow through Russell's life. His "tragic flaw," said one of his wives as he left her for another, was that he could betray someone he'd loved and apparently show "so little regret." For all his supposed great love and concern for mankind in general (which he expressed in his theories and writings), he seemed to find difficulty loving any specific human (excepting his children) over time.[17]

(An interesting study on emotional intelligence and its impact on intellectuals would be to read Bertrand Russell's autobiography, then read his life as seen through the eyes of his daughter [*My Father, Bertrand Russell*, by Katharine Tait], who was also well educated and a great writer and thinker in her own right, but showed more emotional intelligence than her father.)

How Lack of Emotional Intelligence Led Russell Astray

Let's look at some specifics, each of which demonstrates the problems caused by lack of emotional intelligence. Do you see some of these characteristics in your own thinking?

1. An either/or mentality.

An intellectual with emotional intelligence might ask herself, "If I'm so absolutely certain of my position on this controversial belief, how come so many intelligent, informed people disagree with me? Have I honestly taken the time to fully understand their position and how they arrived at it?" Such an approach assumes enough emotional intelligence to get inside the head of another person—the ability to empathize.

But Russell, in his popular writings, shows little sign of understanding the strongest arguments against his position. Instead, he excelled at setting up and knocking down straw men.

One commentator, speaking of Russell's railings against religion, observes,

> "But for the most part he contents himself with shying at Aunt Sallies*. The serious reader who wants a balanced statement of the pros and cons is best advised to look elsewhere."[18]

***Shying at Aunt Sallies =** a British phrase for knocking down straw men.

By ignoring the strongest arguments of the other side, he could argue his position as the only sensible position. Yet, seeing only one side of an argument leads to dogmatic, either/or thinking. As his daughter observed:

> "He needed certainty, he loved clarity with a passion, and he could not bear any kind of muddled thinking. "Either/or" was much more congenial to him than "both/and" (my favorite); "it is" was better than "it may be"; "the truth is" was preferable to "perhaps."[19] (Parentheses by Russell's daughter)

Thus, Russell was "always an absolutist."[20]

Also impacting this either/or thinking was his temperament, which included a relish for holding contrarian positions. Again according to his daughter Katherine, "he was so used to considering the majority wrong that he felt comfortable only in opposition."[21] Obviously, this emotional tendency would prejudice him against majority views.

2. Arrogance.

Rather than listening to and learning from people, Russell saw himself as an intellectually superior aristocrat. According to Katherine, "He was an aristocrat, who had been taught to think himself superior...."[22] This characteristic would allow him to explain away why so many people disagreed with him. In his view, if they were as smart and educated as him, they'd certainly see it his way.

Along this line, it's interesting to note the difference between how he saw himself and how others saw him. In the first paragraph of his autobiography, he notes that one of the "overwhelmingly strong" passions that governed his life was an "unbearable pity for the suffering of mankind," which he longed to alleviate. But later in his autobiography he relates how he, in spending a day with a woman, decided that he wanted her, no matter how it impacted anyone else.

> "...I did not care what might be involved. I wanted to leave Alys [his wife], and to have her leave Philip [her husband]. *What Philip might think or feel was a matter of indifference to me*." (Italics and brackets mine.)

While I appreciate his candor, this "indifference" shows a troubling lack of compassion for a fellow human being. Neither did he apparently care how this would impact his devoted wife. (She was understandably devastated.) This wasn't a singular event; it would be his pattern throughout life—pursuing new intimacies with no apparent regard for how this would impact those closest to him.

My point? Although he was academically brilliant, his lack of emotional intelligence seemed to make him oblivious to the disconnect between his opening autobiographical comments on being driven to alleviate human suffering, and his later comments about his significant contributions to, and lack of concern for, the suffering of those closest to him. His "me first" attitude in relationships showed arrogance and self-centeredness of the highest order.[23]

3. Lack of serious, objective research.

According to scholars Edwards, Alston and Prior, "For those whose philosophy is shaped not by a respect for facts but by their wishes Russell has always been scathing in his contempt."[24] In a letter, Russell said, "...I care much less about my opinions than about their being true."[25]

But his life and writings speak otherwise.

In his popular writings, he shows a strong tendency to cherry pick facts that support his feelings, rather than doing objective research.[26]

Thus, his essays don't typically exhibit thorough endnotes or fresh research, but rather include wildly speculative and errant data that he finds consistent with his prejudices.[27]

So where do we find his passionate "respect for facts?" Certainly not in his essays. If he were so concerned about truth, why didn't he rigorously engage the strongest arguments of those who held opposing opinions? Why didn't his essays exhibit honest and thorough research? Why did he make huge blanket statements on issues he's not prepared to back up with evidence?

I'd suggest that Russell saw no contradiction between his stated passion for truth and his lack of rigorous research. After all, having a dogmatic personality that saw only black and white, he knew he was right. He knew the relevant facts were on his side, whether he took the time to unearth them or not. So why look seriously at the best opposing arguments or data that might count against his convictions?[28]

Which leads us to our next point.

4. Dogmatism on less-than-conclusive points.

Those with emotional intelligence can put themselves in the intellectual and emotional shoes of those who hold different positions on controversial issues, which often leads them to soften their stance to "it seems to me" or "while other fine thinkers amass data and come to a different position, I hold that...."

But Russell saw black and white. Colin Brown speaks of the "cocksure confidence of his generalizations."[29] Typically this is a fault ascribed to those we label fundamentalists, not academic philosophers. Yet once again, we see him failing to practice what he preached. In his essay on Voltaire, he wrote,

> "No opinion should be held with fervour. No one holds with fervour that seven times eight is fifty-six, because it can be known that this is the case. Fervour is only necessary in

commending an opinion which is doubtful or demonstrably false."[30]

Perhaps he demonstrates the truth of this passage, thereby condemning himself as he rants about ("holds with fervour") his opinions on issues that have more than one defensible position.

- Paul Johnson speaks of Russell's "mounting anger, accompanied by a lack of concern for the objective facts, the attribution of the vilest motives to those holding different views, and signs of paranoia…."[31]
- In a speech in Birmingham, Russell said, "We used to think Hitler was wicked when he wanted to kill all the Jews. But [United States President] Kennedy and [British Prime Minister] Macmillan not only want to kill all the Jews but all the rest of us too. They're much more wicked than Hitler…. I will not pretend to obey a government which is organizing the massacre of the whole of mankind…They are the wickedest people that ever lived in the history of man."[32]
- "Children should be sent to boarding schools to get them away from mother love."[33]
- "The scientific attitude to life can scarcely be learned from women."[34]

5. Unexamined acceptance of authorities who agreed with him.

Emotionally intelligent scholars understand that the opinions and research of others can be motivated by and impacted by their desires and prejudices. Thus, they think through received opinions independently. But Russell seemed to blindly accept the opinions of social scientists if they agreed with his views.

According to his daughter,

> "My father's respect for science, coupled with his rejection of all old-fashioned orthodoxy, led him into absurdities that a greater confidence in his own good sense might have avoided."

Thus, he followed what his daughter described as a "crude behaviorism," which assumed that if we just apply the latest science in raising our children, we can raise a generation of children "almost wholly free from disease, malevolence and stupidity," and free from irrational fears.[35]

To accomplish this, Russell felt that children should be left to cry in their cribs, unless they are in physical distress. We should care for their physical needs "without excessive expressions of sympathy."[36] Otherwise, reasoned Russell, children will learn to manipulate others with their cries and we'll raise tyrants. While it seems harsh, according to Russell and the authorities he followed, ignoring their cries for emotional comfort is the best way to produce a healthy and happy child.

But his daughter, with greater emotional intelligence, begs to differ. Looking back as an adult on her childhood, she's appalled at the reasoning that led to these decisions. If this view of childrearing was based upon someone's experience, "whose experience?" she asks. Certainly not *her* experience. Who really understands what's going on inside an infant's mind? What if she's truly scared and needs affection? How do we know that more cuddling and comforting in such a situation will produce a tyrant?

But being "mesmerized by the authorities," he held confidently to this "crude behaviorism," seemingly without asking himself such pertinent questions as: "Since this isn't the way your mom and I were raised from infancy, how did we end up so smart, confident and fearless?"[37]

His confidence in his childrearing methods eventually evaporated when he realized that his own children had grown up full of fears and anxieties. He sadly admitted that he "failed as a parent."[38]

6. He failed to realize how his own upbringing and emotions influenced his positions.

People with emotional intelligence can better assess how their own background and emotions are influencing their conclusions. Russell seemed largely oblivious to these influences, imagining himself to be purely reasonable and logical. According to Johnson,

> "Russell was not merely ignorant of how most people actually behave; he had a profound lack of self-awareness too.... Even more seriously he did not perceive that he himself was exposed to the forces of unreason and emotion that he deplored in common people."[39]

His parents, both of whom died when he was young, were atheists and relished challenging prevailing views, which Russell apparently internalized. After their death Russell was raised by stern, rigid, joyless, but religious grandparents. Grandmother Russell believed that "plain food, uncomfortable living and unceasing moral exhortation mixed with reproach were good for boys."[40] Surely this impacted his rejection of religion at age 15 and at least partially explains his internalizing his father's "arbitrary taste for radical ideas."[41] I heard one intellectual say that Russell's radical views were better explained by his autobiography than his books and essays.[42] I'd tend to agree.

In reacting against his own austere childhood, Russell eagerly embraced an equally extreme position that children would be fine if we simply gave them enough freedom in their school environment. Let them decide if they want to go to class or not. Let them use any foul language they desire. Why inhibit their expression and interfere with their natural quest for enlightenment?

But implementing this in his supposedly progressive and enlightened school, he failed to provide enough secure boundaries to keep physical and emotional bullying at bay. Surely children need a certain amount of direction and boundaries. And his children needed emotionally available parents with a stable relationship. His daughter Katherine claims that her parents didn't understand these needs. Reacting against his own dysfunctional upbringing, he implemented an equally dysfunctional extreme in raising his own. It's hard to see balance when we're blinded by our own background and emotions.

Conclusion on Russell

Why would a man who seemed emotionally clueless and so out of touch with real life that he couldn't figure out how to fix his own tea, imagine that he was imminently qualified to fix society? Russell makes a good example of lack of emotional intelligence because the world considered his great strength to be his extremely intelligent, supremely logical mind.

Yet, a closer examination finds that his opinions were often influenced by his upbringing and personal passions, of which he seemed to be largely unaware because of his emotional ignorance. Perhaps the most dangerous influencers among business leaders and academics are those who don't have enough emotional intelligence to realize how their passions are impacting their reasoning.

So whenever you read a supposedly great intellect or great researcher or brilliant businessman, look beyond the argumentation and facts they present. Consider what passions may be influencing their choice of data, methods, and reasoning.

Why do brilliant people believe nonsense? Because they often fail to include emotional intelligence in their reasoning.

Think!

We just looked at what can happen when we leave emotional intelligence out of our decision making. We may make poor and costly business decisions (Bell Labs developing the picture phone), or promote ideas we think are brilliant, but are strongly influenced by our personalities and desires (Bertrand Russell).

So before I list some practical ways to plug emotional intelligence into our decision making, contrive your own list, based on the above discussions and your personal reflections and experiences. You may come up with some better ideas than I share below!

Think Different!

So how can we plug emotional intelligence into our arguments and research and life decisions?

1. When examining a proposal or line of argument, make sure you're giving all intelligent views a chance.

As we saw with Russell, sometimes lack of empathy and emotional intelligence can lead us to dismiss the views of others before we give them a fighting chance. Make sure to understand the best arguments of the opposition before assuming all who disagree are morons.

2. Intentionally reflect upon your emotions.

I tend to doubt and question my emotions, since I've seen emotions lead so many astray. How many people do you know who've fallen in love and allow their emotions to blind them to a person's faults? "She's perfect!" declares the person who's infatuated. But nobody's perfect. Blinded by emotions, we see things the way we want to see them and make illogical decisions.

But *ignoring* emotions can be just as dangerous as being *ruled* by them. For this reason, conceptual thinking guru Edward de Bono recommends that when grappling with a complicated issue, after examining the relevant cold, hard data, we proceed to examine our emotions and feelings about the issue. Both are important.[43]

Had Enron leaders intentionally asked key employees about their *feelings* concerning various company policies, putting aside for the moment their brilliant theories and the facts that supported them, they would have surely uncovered much relevant data.

For example, drawing on relevant emotions, they might have asked their employees,

- If our stockholders understood our accounting methods, whether we can justify them or not as legitimate in the world of accounting, would this enhance or detract from their trust? Might they feel betrayed? If so, how might this impact our business?
- When we encourage Darwinian competition, how does that impact our feelings toward coworkers and leadership? Could this result in a lack of camaraderie and sharing of information, resulting in poor decisions?
- How do you feel when you see cutthroat behavior rewarded monetarily? Does it inspire you to try harder, or demoralize you and make you want to join a competing company instead?

Howard Behar's insights at Starbucks seem to have been perceived emotionally. They weren't the type of insights that Spock would have likely made. While the earlier leadership obsessed about replicating the Italian experience and focused obsessively on the quality of the coffee, Behar asked the deeper question: Why are people coming to Starbucks? He concluded it wasn't all about the coffee. "We're not filling bellies; we're filling souls." That one insight, along with empathizing more with the customers, impacted the decisions at Starbucks and took them to the next level of success.[44]

So don't deprecate emotions. They're often used in the higher levels of critical thinking, such as those described by Bloom's Taxonomy. So embrace them. Get them out in the open. Examine them. Separate them out and include them in your reasoning.

3. Don't rule out intuitions and first impressions.

My first response is typically to question my intuitions and first impressions. After all, as we saw in earlier chapters, we're often led astray by them.

Yet, to ignore them would be to set aside important data. Surely we should ask ourselves, "Why is my intuition or first impression of the argument so negative?" Perhaps our brains collected data through the years that resulted in this intuition. The intuition may indeed be wrong, but again it may be right, taking into account data that we've long since forgotten.[45]

Einstein would say that his intuitions impacted his path to formulating his theory of relativity. "A new idea comes suddenly and in a rather intuitive way," Einstein said, "but is nothing but the outcome of earlier intellectual experience."[46] In this case, his intuitions led to his greatest discoveries. But his intuitions could also lead him astray. He once stated, "Quantum mechanics is certainly imposing, but an inner voice tells me that it is not yet the real thing."[47] He would spend the rest of his life resisting the discoveries of quantum physics.

4. Draw on your understanding of people.

An important part of the success of the Mayo Clinic is that leadership went far beyond coldly analytical thinking. Their mantra "Patients first!" took them beyond the clinical question of how to diagnose an illness. It put them in touch with their patients on multiple levels, so that desk ladies, building designers, janitors, schedulers and systems analysts all looked at their work through the lens of how patients were being impacted. To do this, they had to understand and empathize with people.

Mayo Clinic president Dr. Denis Cortese once expressed this in an essay:

> The best physicians and healthcare providers are part engineers and part artists. The engineer sees the problem and applies technology to fix it….
>
> The artist knows when the patient needs a warm smile, reassuring words or a gentle hug. It's the artists who make every patient feel welcome, comfortable, secure, hopeful. The artist sees the anxiety and reassures the new mother that her baby's fever is nothing to worry about. The artist listens to the middle-aged patient unloading his frustration over failed attempts to quit smoking. The artist knows when there's nothing more the engineer can do and helps the patient and family cope at the end of life. What the artist does is why I became a physician."[48]

As a writer, I must empathize with those who don't think like me. Some readers are motivated by things that don't motivate me. Others don't share the same judgments on what is interesting and what is boring. The best communicators understand this and take pains to try to see things as others see them, to get inside their heads.

In writing this book, I've tried to repeatedly ask myself, not just "Is this paragraph relevant to critical and critical thinking?", but additionally,

- Is it relevant to my *readers*?
- Is it *interesting* to my *readers*?

- Does it *motivate* my readers, making them want to know more?

Sometimes I answer these questions by drawing from my own understanding of people; but additionally I run sections by others to see how they respond. Answering these questions correctly makes the difference between an interesting and boring book, between a motivator and a yawner, between lightning and a lightning bug.

Which leads to the next suggestion...

5. Beware of creating simplistic profiles of emotionally intelligent people.

So you want to add someone with more emotional intelligence to your group of advisors. Although psychologists have done a fine job discovering the incredible variety among people's thought processes, emotions and personalities, it's notoriously difficult to assemble a profile of an emotionally intelligent person. Perhaps it's more accurate to say that certain people have strong emotional intelligence in one area, others in another.

While Kenneth Lay, president of Enron, demonstrated lack of emotional intelligence on several levels, he could show great emotional intelligence on other levels. Had you flown in one of Enron's jets with Lay, he'd have likely personally served you snacks at some point during the flight. He could be very likeable and personable. Had you only observed him in this context, you'd have likely assumed that he was an incredibly humble, socially intelligent guy.[49]

Bertrand Russell, for all his ranting, raving and caustic comments, could be remarkably self-effacing and humble in other circumstances. His daughter said he was the perfect grandfather to her children, and he gave substantial financial support to enable her husband to attend seminary in preparation to serve as missionaries to Uganda.[50]

Thus, rather than thinking, "we need both a Spock and a McCoy on our board," think more in terms of people being somewhere on the social intelligence spectrum. People come packaged in fascinatingly unique personalities which defy all attempts to simplify, categorize, and label them.

6. Think beyond "success" to "happiness," both regarding ourselves and others.

This practice often engages our emotional intelligence. For Enron, the bottom line consideration for decision-making seemed to be how much money a deal would generate. But what if the leadership thought a bit deeper and asked, "Why do people want money?"

Typically, people think that more money will make them happier. Yet, psychologists have found that after we've climbed above the poverty line, making an additional $10,000 or $100,000 or even $1 million doesn't do much for our happiness.

So if producing happiness for the most people (employees, customers, etc.) were a priority, how might that influence our decisions? On many levels, Enron failed to implement a satisfying work environment or produce happy people. Enron Executive Cliff Baxter took home his millions, but became so disgusted with what he'd become that he committed suicide.[51]

7. Allow your presentations to tap into emotions.

Great writers and speakers go beyond presenting cold facts and figures. While their ideas are hopefully firmly grounded in sound research, their presentations are typically filled with delightful and memorable stories that engage people on an emotional level.

So ask yourself when you read a great book or watch a great movie or view a great TED Talk, "What not only *informed* me, but *moved* me about that presentation?" Typically, great novelists create characters we care about and share stories we identify with.

If you want to change people's lives, study how to impact them on both an intellectual *and* emotional level.

8. Enhance your people skills.

Whether you consider yourself emotionally intelligent or an emotional idiot, there's much more you can learn. (Remember, your greatest potential for improvement just might be in an area you consider yourself strong.) Read articles on relationships. Study emotions. Read classic works like Dale Carnegie's *How to Win Friends and Influence People.* The more we sharpen our relational and emotional skills, the better we can use emotional intelligence in our reasoning.

9. Ask if it's the right thing to do.

Many intellectuals shied away from asking this question through much of the 20th century. Influenced by modernism, they denied that objective right and wrong had much meaning in a relativistic age.

Thus, for me it's intellectually invigorating to see intellectuals such as Harvard political philosopher Michael Sandal teaching an extremely popular class and writing a popular book with the title *Justice: What's the Right Thing to Do?* When good people think only in utilitarian terms, their bottom line question is "what's good for the greatest number of people?" The problem with such thinking is that Nazi's could (and did) use it to justify atrocities: "By getting rid of all these undesirables in death camps, we can produce a better society where more people will be happy." Enron leaders could justify cheating and lying by assuring themselves that keeping the stock values high made the employees and stockholders happy.

Sandal, as well as many other contemporary intellectuals, argue that some things are just plain wrong, no matter how many people we imagine will be benefitted from our wrong deeds.[52] Since the book you're reading isn't a book on moral philosophy, rather than argue for objective right and wrong I'll merely say that I think it's helpful to ask, in any decision, "Is it right?" Whether you're basing your morals on your conscience, your religious convictions, reasoning with scientific data, or a combination of these, surely asking the moral questions helps us tap into emotionally intelligent thinking.[53]

10. Celebrate plain old, down to earth common sense.

I've often reflected back to an evening meeting of a campus organization while studying at the University of Georgia. A respected academic from another university presented his ideas on a controversial issue and invited questions. Several students raised decent objections that he either evaded or gave unsatisfactory answers to. Finally, one young lady raised her hand and, with a thick southern drawl that gave the impression she'd recently arrived in Athens from a provincial upbringing in the mountains, said, "Sometimes people get so smart that they're just loony...just loony."

At first, I was rather embarrassed for her. But the more I thought about it, I felt she was right. In the intellectual's presentation, his salient points did seem odd, and ill supported by the evidence he presented. Perhaps most of the attendees were thinking her thoughts, but feared to express them. Her practical, seemingly backwoods intelligence cut straight through all the intellectual trappings and, like the little boy in *The Emperor's New Clothes,* expressed a practical gut instinct that may have very well hit the target.

All of which takes me back to this chapter's opening statement by Warren Buffet on what to look for in a business partner:

> *"I think you'll probably start looking for the person that you can always depend on; the person whose ego does not get in his way; the person who's perfectly willing to let someone else take the credit for an idea as long as it worked; the person who essentially won't let you down, who thought straight as opposed to brilliantly."*

Intellectual brilliance can often obscure a lack of common sense. As I mentioned in an earlier chapter, Buffet blames "geeks with calculators" in part for the recent real estate crisis. Their theories of reducing the impact of bad loans by bundling them in huge packages failed to take into account human nature and the way reducing the standards for loans could be taken advantage of.

No wonder Buffet would prefer hiring someone who "thought straight" rather than "brilliantly." In my opinion, the girl from the country, by thinking "straight," came to a more reasonable conclusion than the professor who reasoned "brilliantly."

"The Smartest Guys in the Room" at Enron thought brilliantly, but not straight. Those with common sense and emotional intelligence could see Enron's fatal flaws early on, had the leadership only been willing to listen to them.

Bertrand Russell's daughter could have told her father about the problems with his "progressive" school, had he only thought to ask. But the self-perceived "brilliance" of Russell's thinking blinded him to the value of those who thought straight.

Which leads me to my final point.

11. Get input intentionally from those others wouldn't consider.

Why should I take Bertrand Russell more seriously than anyone else when he speaks on marriage, sex and family? Think back to our discussion where we tried to define "smart." Those who agreed with my data and reasoning in that section might note that Russell was smart "at certain things." He could reflect brilliantly upon the relationship of math with logic, but not so well upon the relationship of open marriages to a stable family or society.

But people are lured into thinking that someone talented at abstract logic is probably talented at anything. He obviously wasn't. When it came to understanding mechanical devices, fixing tea, or fixing schools, he appeared to be much worse than average. He was a mechanical and relational cripple. Why would we expect him to be above average in understanding ethics and fixing the world's problems?

Was he a trained family counselor? No. Had he studied for years the results of surveys and studies of the best families and societies and how they operate? No. Did his four marriages and numerous sexual escapades make him an expert on marriage? Hardly.

Russell would have done well to consult with his children, his wives and girlfriends, his next door neighbors, and particularly those who disagreed with his views. Rather, he tended to despise those "beneath" him or those who disagreed with him. "Everybody is a genius," someone suggested, "but if you judge a fish by its ability to climb a tree, it will live its whole life believing that it is stupid."

To truly test our conclusions, we'd typically do well to listen to a wider range of people, including people who come to the table with a different set of experiences and different ways of thinking.

Conclusion

I'll close this chapter with an extended quote that's almost certainly extreme. But please understand the data that the author's trying to sum up. Paul Johnson wrote a book titled "Intellectuals," which delves into the lives of select people who've significantly shaped the way we think and make political and personal decisions in modern times, including Rousseau, Shelley, Marx, Tolstoy, Hemingway, Russell, Sartre, and Chomsky.

What Johnson reveals, in his well-researched and well-documented expose, are the petty rivalries, pathetic research, flawed reasoning, selfish and vain motives that often shaped the lives and writings of these highly influential intellectuals.

Granted, perhaps Johnson cherry-picked the influential intellectuals with the most obvious flaws. (I don't see these flagrant flaws in intellectuals such as Frederick Coppleston, or Will and Ariel Durant. But Johnson would probably argue that these were primarily historians as opposed to peddlers of new and influential ways of thinking.)

Yet Johnson's main point is clear. Intellectuals are people. And like most people, their likes and dislikes and passions inform their methods of research, the data they choose, and their conclusions. And granted, it's improper to argue that since these intellectuals and their ideas were often driven by less-than-honorable motives, that we'd be better off without any intellectuals. After all, Johnson himself was educated at Oxford and is a respected intellectual in his own right. But when so many leaders and ordinary citizens have been influenced by the intellectuals he examines, he believes it pays to reflect more deeply upon them, as we reflected upon Bertrand Russell, to better evaluate the sources of their views and to determine if they're worthy of their following.

With this in mind, listen carefully to Johnson's conclusion after studying the above intellectuals:

> "A dozen people picked at random on the street are at least as likely to offer sensible views on moral and political matters as a cross-section of the intelligentsia. But I would go further. One of the principal lessons of our tragic century, which has seen so many millions of innocent lives sacrificed in schemes to improve the lot of humanity, is—beware intellectuals. Not merely should they be kept well away from the levers of power, they should also be objects of particular suspicion when they seek to offer collective advice. Beware committees, conferences and leagues of intellectuals. Distrust public statements issued from their serried ranks. Discount their verdicts on political leaders and important events. For intellectuals, far from being highly individualistic and non-conformist people, follow certain regular patterns of behavior. Taken as a group, they are often ultra-conformist within the circles formed by those whose approval they seek and value. That is what makes them, *en masse*, so dangerous, for it enables them to create climates of opinion and prevailing orthodoxies, which themselves often generate irrational and destructive courses of action. Above all, we must at all times remember what intellectuals habitually forget: that people matter more than concepts and must come first. The worst of all despotisms is the heartless tyranny of ideas."[54]

To bring balance to this assessment, I'd suggest that while consulting respected intellectuals is often wise, don't assume they're the final arbiters of truth. And while it may be prudent to have a data-driven logician like Spock on your board, balance him out with a McCoy, Ohura, Scotty, Sulu, and Kirk, all of whom could blend logical and emotional intelligence to improve decision-making.

Why do brilliant people believe nonsense? Because they often fail to allow empathy, emotional intelligence, and common sense to shape their thinking.

Flex Your Neurons!
Pursuing the Point of Know Return

1. Are your intellectual strengths more like Spock, McCoy, or Kirk? In light of your strengths/weaknesses, what kinds of people do you need to balance you out?

2. How do our prior discussions on "strengths" and "multiple intelligences" dovetail with the main lessons of this chapter?

3. How could Russell or Skilling have made better decisions by recognizing and learning from people with intellectual strengths different from their own?

4. How can we take into account intuitions and feelings without allowing them to dominate our decision-making?

Making It More Personal
Practical Takeaways

What are one or more ideas provoked by this chapter that you can apply to help you think more critically?

____

____

____

What are one or more ideas that you can apply to help you think more creatively?

____

____

____

What else do you want to make sure you don't forget?

____

____

____

Recommended Trails
For the Incurably Curious and Adventurous

1. To grow in understanding, empathizing with, and working with people, see *Emotional Intelligence*, by Daniel Goleman (New York: Bantam Books, 1995). Then read the classic on relationships, *How to Win Friends and Influence People*, by Dale Carnegie (New York: Simon & Schuster, first published in 1936).

2. To understand the profound limitations and prejudices of some of history's most influential intellectuals, read *Intellectuals*, by Paul Johnson (New York: Harper Perennial, 1988). To try to understand Bertrand Russell and his mental quirks, read Johnson's chapter on Russell and *The Autobiography of Bertrand Russell* (New York: Simon & Schuster, first printed in 1951). Also read Russell's life through the eyes of his daughter: Katherine Tait, *My Father Bertrand Russell* (New York: Harcourt Brace Jovanovich, 1975).

3. Reinforcing Johnson's warning about intellectuals, Berkeley professor Philip Tetlock brings together a wealth of research to argue that the foxes (who know many little things) tend to predict better than the hedgehogs (those who know one big thing), although the latter are considered the experts and everybody wants to hear their opinions. Also significant: Tetlock found those speaking in more tentative terms like "perhaps," and "possibly" are far better predictors than the dogmatic, assured experts. Philip E. Tetlock, *Expert Political Judgment: How Good is It? How Can We Know?* (Princeton: Princeton University Press, 2006).

4. As with the last chapter, Debono's Six Thinking Hats helps solve some of the problems encountered in this chapter. If you tend toward a Spock personality type, consciously put on each of Debono's "Hats" to make sure you consider emotions, feelings, and creativity in your decisions.

5. Read this recent article, which references much research in emotional intelligence and applies it to business: Harvey Deutschendorf, "Why Emotionally Intelligent People Are More Successful: Research shows that people with strong emotional intelligence are more likely to succeed than those with high IQs or relevant experience," *Fast Company* (June 22, 2015).

CONCLUSION

On a Passion for Seeking Truth

"...a candidate who demonstrates capabilities in critical thinking, creative problem-solving and communication has a far greater chance of being employed today than his or her counterpart without those skills."

— Norman Augustine, former chairman and CEO of Lockheed-Martin, which employs over 80,000 engineers[1]

"If a man can write a better book, preach a better sermon, or make a better mousetrap than his neighbor, though he build his house in the woods, the world will make a beaten path to his door."

— Saying on display at the Mayo Clinic[2]

The Black Mamba

Yesterday my wife and I heard a world-class speaker. It was generally great stuff—potentially life changing. Yet one of his illustrations seemed a bit extreme. He spoke of teaching in an African country inhabited by deadly snakes, including the Black Mamba. According to the speaker, two characteristics make it especially dangerous: its speed and its poison. As the fastest of all snakes, slithering up to 40 mph, we can't outrun it. As the most venomous of all snakes, a strike can kill you within three steps.

To me, these claims seemed rather incredible. I couldn't imagine a snake keeping up with me in my car at 40 mph, so I fact-checked him. According to my sources, while the Black Mamba is indeed the world's fastest snake; it maxes out at about four mph, a far cry from 40 mph. True, it's the world's most poisonous snake, but its bite takes about 30 minutes to kill, much longer than it takes to walk three steps.

"Insignificant details!" some may argue. "Communicator's license!" justifies another. But for me, when I hear exaggerated claims and sloppy research, I ask myself, "If he's mistaken on these details, which he stated with such assurance, why should I trust his accuracy in the rest of his message?" He could have easily introduced the information with, "According to some natives I spoke to in Africa..." and I might have let it go.

But after those statements, a question mark hung over the rest of his message, ruining its impact.

My point? Truth is important.

Beyond Cynicism: Empowered to Seek Truth

I vividly recall a formative experience from my college days, over three decades ago. On the same day of classes, two professors, both of whom I respected for their integrity and scholarship, taught contradictory truths with equal enthusiasm and authority. Yet, either one or both of them were dead wrong.

The experience plunged me into a period of cynicism and pessimism in my quest for truth. I reasoned,

> "I'm not likely to ever be as well informed as these two professors are in their field. Yet, they came to diametrically opposed conclusions. How can I ever hope to achieve any degree of certitude in seeking the truth of such important matters?"

Fortunately, I'd later take courses in exegesis and hermeneutics and research and logic. The tools I acquired helped me to distinguish fact from fiction, well-supported statements from bogus claims. Of course, I often had to settle for degrees of certitude rather than "the truth" on many issues, but at least I had ways to evaluate the contradictory claims made by supposed experts. My newfound tools set me free in my search for truth. I wrote this book to pass on those tools. Practice and expand upon them and I hope you'll feel set free as well.

Truth Is Important

Why search for truth? Because missing it brings heartache and embracing it can lead to success.

By missing the truth...

- Professionals in the recording industry rejected The Beatles because they believed that recent trends (a temporary demise in electric guitars and full bands) would continue into the future.
- Savvy Dutch businessmen lost everything by speculating on tulip bulbs.
- Bright students trained for overcrowded fields because they were led astray by questionable statistics.
- People destroyed their health by following medical advice based upon poor science.
- Skewed research by intellectuals, resulting in dangerous political theories, created 20th century political movements that killed tens of millions of innocent people.

By finding and embracing the truth…

- The Mayo Clinic revolutionized medical care by institutionalizing learning from one another and listening more attentively to their patients.
- Starbucks succeeded by learning to listen to their customers and balancing their original vision with innovation.
- Google tapped into creativity by allowing their employees to spend 20 percent of their time pursuing pet projects and making their insights available for input from all their colleagues.
- Martin Luther King Jr., Nelson Mandela, and Mahatma Gandhi found ways to bring about social change without instigating bloody revolutions.

Thus, it pays to develop a passion for truth, utilizing our tools to both see through nonsense and positively pursue innovation and truth.

Wanted: Passionate, Sincere, Seekers of Truth

From Chapter Two, I can still picture Julie, passionately seeking to protect her daughter Jade from catching a cold, which had in the past developed into a serious bout with pneumonia. Driven by concern for her daughter, she plunged into a couple of hours of intense research. She wasn't trying to get published or enhance her platform or impress her teachers or colleagues. Her motives were pure. Driven by concern for her daughter, she passionately sought the truth.

That mental picture of Julie researching at her dining room table with Jade by her side motivates me.

So perhaps it's best to end this book with mental pictures—images that can motivate us to a life of passionate learning.

Can you picture teenager Bill Gates going to the C-Squared company after school (and sneaking out of his bedroom at night) to test software and passionately pursue any opportunity to learn programming? Can you see the Mayo brothers taking vacations from their medical practice to traverse America and Europe, learning from the most innovative and successful surgeons? I like to picture Will and Ariel Durant spending their lives researching and writing a history of civilization, Frederick Coppleston dedicating his life to writing an unparalleled history of philosophy.

I can see Steve Jobs obsessing over how to make a computer or iPhone or iPad more user friendly, so that a child in another country, with no instructions, could figure them out. I can see young Albert Einstein trouncing through the mountains with his friends, trying to unravel the mysteries of time and space. I also see him, lost in some thought experiment, forgetting whether he was walking home or walking to work. I see Yngwie Malmsteen and Tommy Emmanuel relentlessly practicing their guitars and continuously learning from other great guitarists.

I can picture Sam Walton snooping through other people's stores to learn what they're doing right, and sharing donuts with his truck drivers early Saturday mornings, to pick their brains on how his stores are doing. I see the CEO of Starbucks bursting out of his "Italian Experience" paradigm by observing the young lady who left his shop to find one that offered non-fat milk. I see Soichiro Honda relentlessly tinkering with his engines, taking non-credit classes that would one day help him revolutionize both the motorcycle and automobile industries.

By way of contrast, I picture the person who reflects over his life thus far, only to realize that it was mostly spent watching TV shows and playing video games, paying just enough attention to lectures and homework to pass tests and one day hold a piece of paper in his hands that supposedly signifies that he knows something.

It's largely up to you and me as to how we choose to live our lives. Let me recommend a passionate search for Wisdom and Truth, motivated by a concern for others.

I'll end with the words of Solomon, calling out to us from millennia past. Don't just read his words. Catch his passion!

How blessed is the man (person) who finds wisdom,
And the man who gains understanding.
For its profit is better than the profit of silver,
And its gain than fine gold."
She is more precious than jewels;
And nothing you desire compares with her.
Long life is in her right hand;
In her left hand are riches and honor.
Her ways are pleasant ways,
And all her paths are peace.
She is a tree of life to those who take hold of her,
And happy are all who hold her fast."

—Proverbs 3:13-18

(Personal request by the authors: Please consider writing a review of this book on Amazon.com or another review site or mentioning it on social media or recommending it to a friend. If you found value in the book, or even if you were disappointed with the book, an honest review could help others decide whether or not this book could benefit them. The best gift you can give an author is a helpful review!**)**

Consolidate Your Wisdom

Are you serious about pursuing truth through honing your critical and creative thinking skills? A great next step would be to glance back at the takeaways you wrote at the end of each chapter. Narrow down your list to ten practical insights which, if put into practice, could set a course for a lifetime of chasing wisdom. Write them below. Perhaps you could state them as goals and put them on your refrigerator or bulletin board.

1.

2.

3.

4.

5.

6.

7.

8.

9.

10.

Appendix 1
A Great Big List of Fallacies

To avoid falling for the "Intrinsic Value of Senseless Hard Work Fallacy" (see also "Reinventing the Wheel"), I began with Wikipedia's helpful divisions, list, and descriptions as a base (since Wikipedia articles aren't subject to copyright restrictions), but felt free to add new fallacies, and tweak a bit here and there if I felt further explanation was needed. If you don't understand a fallacy from the brief description below, consider Googling the name of the fallacy, or finding an article dedicated to the fallacy in Wikipedia.

Consider the list representative rather than exhaustive.

Informal fallacies

These arguments are fallacious for reasons other than their structure or form (formal = the "form" of the argument). Thus, informal fallacies typically require an examination of the argument's content.

- Argument from (personal) incredulity (aka - divine fallacy, appeal to common sense) – I cannot imagine how this could be true, therefore it must be false.
- Argument from repetition (*argumentum ad nauseam*) – signifies that it has been discussed so extensively that nobody cares to discuss it anymore.
- Argument from silence (*argumentum e silentio*) – the conclusion is based on the absence of evidence, rather than the existence of evidence.
- Argument to moderation (false compromise, middle ground, fallacy of the mean, *argumentum ad temperantiam*) – assuming that the compromise between two positions is always correct.
- *Argumentum verbosium* – See proof by verbosity, below.
- (Shifting the) burden of proof (see – *onus probandi*) – I need not prove my claim, you must prove it is false.
- Circular reasoning (*circulus in demonstrando*) – when the reasoner begins with (or assumes) what he or she is trying to end up with; sometimes called *assuming the conclusion*.
- Circular cause and consequence – where the consequence of the phenomenon is claimed to be its root cause.
- Continuum fallacy (fallacy of the beard, line-drawing fallacy, sorites fallacy, fallacy of the heap, bald man fallacy) – improperly rejecting a claim for being imprecise.
- Correlative-based fallacies
    - Correlation proves causation (*cum hoc ergo propter hoc*) – a faulty assumption that correlation between two variables implies that one causes the other.
    - Suppressed correlative – where a correlative is redefined so that one alternative is made impossible.
- Ambiguous middle term – a common ambiguity in syllogisms in which the middle term is equivocated.
- Ecological fallacy – inferences about the nature of specific individuals are based solely upon aggregate statistics collected for the group to which those individuals belong.
- Etymological fallacy – reasons that the original or historical meaning of a word or phrase is necessarily similar to its actual present-day meaning.
- Fallacy of composition – assuming that something true of part of a whole must also be true of the whole.
- Fallacy of division – assuming that something true of a thing must also be true of all or some of its parts.
- Fallacy of many questions (complex question, fallacy of presupposition, loaded question, *plurium interrogationum*) – someone asks a question that presupposes something that has not been

proven or accepted by all the people involved. This fallacy is often used rhetorically, so that the question limits direct replies to those that serve the questioner's agenda.

- Fallacy of the single cause (causal oversimplification) – it is assumed that there is one, simple cause of an outcome when in reality it may have been caused by multiple causes.
- False attribution – an advocate appeals to an irrelevant, unqualified, unidentified, biased or fabricated source in support of an argument.
- Fallacy of quoting out of context (contextomy) – refers to the selective excerpting of words from their original context in a way that distorts the source's intended meaning.
- False authority (single authority) – using an expert of dubious credentials and/or using only one opinion to sell a product or idea. Related to the appeal to authority fallacy.
- Gambler's fallacy – the incorrect belief that separate, independent events can affect the likelihood of another random event. If a coin lands on heads ten times in a row, the belief that it is "due to the number of times it had previously landed on tails" is incorrect.
- Hedging – using words with ambiguous meanings, then changing the meaning of them later.
- Historian's fallacy – occurs when one assumes that decision makers of the past viewed events from the same perspective and having the same information as those subsequently analyzing the decision. (Not to be confused with presentism, which is a mode of historical analysis in which present-day ideas, such as moral standards, are projected into the past.)
- Homunculus fallacy – where a "middle-man" is used for explanation, this sometimes leads to regressive middle-men. Explains without actually explaining the real nature of a function or a process. Instead, it explains the concept in terms of the concept itself, without first defining or explaining the original concept. Explaining thought as something produced by a little thinker, a sort of homunculus inside the head, merely explains it as another kind of thinking (as different but the same).
- Inflation of conflict – The experts of a field of knowledge disagree on a certain point, so the scholars must know nothing, and therefore the legitimacy of their entire field is put to question.
- If-by-whiskey – an argument that supports both sides of an issue by using terms that are selectively emotionally sensitive.
- Incomplete comparison – in which insufficient information is provided to make a complete comparison.
- Inconsistent comparison – where different methods of comparison are used, leaving one with a false impression of the whole comparison.
- *Ignoratio elenchi* (irrelevant conclusion, missing the point) – an argument that may in itself be valid, but does not address the issue in question.
- Kettle logic – using multiple inconsistent arguments to defend a position.
- Ludic fallacy – the belief that the outcomes of non-regulated random occurrences can be encapsulated by a statistic; a failure to take into account unknowns in determining the probability of events taking place.
- Mind projection fallacy – when one considers the way one sees the world as the way the world really is.
- Moral high ground fallacy – one assumes a "holier-than-thou" attitude in an attempt to make oneself look good to win an argument.
- Moralistic fallacy – inferring factual conclusions from purely evaluative premises in violation of fact–value distinction. For instance, inferring *is* from *ought* is an instance of moralistic fallacy. Moralistic fallacy is the inverse of the naturalistic fallacy defined below.
- Moving the goalposts (raising the bar) – argument in which evidence presented in response to a specific claim is dismissed and some other (often greater) evidence is demanded.
- Naturalistic fallacy – inferring evaluative conclusions from purely factual premises in violation of fact–value distinction. For instance, inferring *ought* from *is* (sometimes referred to as the *is-ought fallacy*) is an instance of naturalistic fallacy. Also the naturalistic fallacy in a stricter sense as defined in the section "Conditional or questionable fallacies" below is an instance of the naturalistic fallacy. The naturalistic fallacy is the inverse of moralistic fallacy.

- Nirvana fallacy (perfect solution fallacy) – when solutions to problems are rejected because they are not perfect.
- *Onus probandi* – from Latin "*onus probandi incumbit ei qui dicit, non ei qui negat*" the burden of proof is on the person who makes the claim, not on the person who denies (or questions the claim). It is a particular case of the "*argumentum ad ignorantiam*" fallacy; here the burden is shifted on the person defending against the assertion.
- Proof by verbosity (*argumentum verbosium*, proof by intimidation) – submission of others to an argument too complex and verbose to reasonably deal with in all its intimate details.
- Prosecutor's fallacy – a low probability of false matches does not mean a low probability of *some* false match being found.
- Proving too much – using a form of argument that, if it were valid, could be used more generally to reach an absurd conclusion.
- Psychologist's fallacy – an observer presupposes the objectivity of his own perspective when analyzing a behavioral event.
- Referential fallacy – assuming all words refer to existing things and that the meaning of words reside within the things they refer to, as opposed to words possibly referring to no real object or that the meaning of words often comes from how we use them.
- Regression fallacy – ascribes cause where none exists. The flaw is failing to account for natural fluctuations. It is frequently a special kind of the *post hoc* fallacy.
- Reification (hypostatization) – a fallacy of ambiguity, when an abstraction (abstract belief or hypothetical construct) is treated as if it were a concrete, real event or physical entity. In other words, it is the error of treating as a "real thing" something that is not a real thing, but merely an idea.
- Retrospective determinism – the argument that because some event has occurred, its occurrence must have been inevitable beforehand.
- Shotgun argumentation – the arguer offers such a large number of arguments for their position that the opponent can't possibly respond to all of them. (See "Argument by verbosity" above.)
- Special pleading – where a proponent of a position attempts to cite something as an exemption to a generally accepted rule or principle without justifying the exemption.
- Wrong direction – cause and effect are reversed. The cause is said to be the effect and vice versa.

Faulty Generalizations

These reach a conclusion from weak premises. Unlike fallacies of relevance, in fallacies of defective induction, the premises are related to the conclusions yet only weakly buttress the conclusions. A faulty generalization is thus produced.

- Accident – an exception to a generalization is ignored.
    - No true Scotsman – when a generalization is made true only when a counterexample is ruled out on shaky grounds.
- Cherry picking (suppressed evidence, incomplete evidence) – the act of pointing at individual cases or data that seem to confirm a particular position, while ignoring a significant portion of related cases or data that may contradict that position.
- Inductive fallacy – a more general name for fallacies such as hasty generalization. A conclusion is made from premises that only lightly support the conclusion.
- Misleading vividness – involves describing an occurrence in vivid detail, even if it is an exceptional occurrence, to convince someone that it is a problem.
- Overwhelming exception – an accurate generalization that comes with qualifications that eliminate so many cases that what remains is much less impressive than the initial statement might have led one to assume.
- Pathetic fallacy – when an inanimate object is declared to have characteristics of animate objects.

- Thought-terminating cliché – a commonly used phrase, sometimes passing as folk wisdom, used to quell cognitive dissonance, conceal lack of thought-entertainment, move onto other topics, etc.

Red Herring Fallacies

These are errors in logic where a proposition is, or is intended to be, misleading in order to make irrelevant or false inferences. In the general case any logical inference based on fake arguments, intended to replace the lack of real arguments or to replace implicitly the subject of the discussion.

- *Ad hominem* – attacking the arguer instead of the argument.
  - Poisoning the well – a type of *ad hominem* where adverse information about a target is presented with the intention of discrediting everything that the target person says.
  - Abusive fallacy – a subtype of "ad hominem" when it turns into verbal abuse of the opponent rather than arguing about the originally proposed argument.
  - *Ad Hominem Tu Quoque* - (personal inconsistency, aka "you too" fallacy) - "This fallacy is committed when it is concluded that a person's claim is false because 1) it is inconsistent with something else a person has said or 2) what a person says is inconsistent with her actions."

- *Argumentum ad baculum* (appeal to the stick, appeal to force, appeal to threat) – an argument made through coercion or threats of force to support a position.
- Appeal to equality – where an assertion is deemed true or false based on an assumed pretense of equality.
- Association fallacy (guilt by association) – arguing that because two things share a property they are the same.
- Appeal to consequences (*argumentum ad consequentiam*) – the conclusion is supported by a premise that asserts positive or negative consequences from some course of action in an attempt to distract from the initial discussion.
- Appeal to emotion – where an argument is made due to the manipulation of emotions, rather than the use of valid reasoning.
  - Appeal to fear – (*Ad Baculum*, or *Ad Metum*?) a specific type of appeal to emotion where an argument is made by increasing fear and prejudice towards the opposing side.
  - Appeal to flattery – a specific type of appeal to emotion where an argument is made due to the use of flattery to gather support.
  - Appeal to pity (*argumentum ad misericordiam*) – an argument attempts to induce pity to sway opponents.
  - Appeal to ridicule – an argument is made by presenting the opponent's argument in a way that makes it appear ridiculous.
  - Appeal to spite – a specific type of appeal to emotion where an argument is made through exploiting people's bitterness or spite towards an opposing party.
  - Wishful thinking – a specific type of appeal to emotion where a decision is made according to what might be pleasing to imagine, rather than according to evidence or reason.
- Appeal to motive – a premise is dismissed by calling into question the motives of its proposer.
- Appeal to novelty (*argumentum novitatis/antiquitatis, ad novitam*) – a proposal is claimed to be superior or better solely because it is new or modern.
- Appeal to poverty (*argumentum ad Lazarum*) – supporting a conclusion because the arguer is poor (or refuting because the arguer is wealthy). (Opposite of appeal to wealth.)
- Appeal to tradition (*argumentum ad antiquitam*) – a conclusion supported solely because it has long been held to be true.
- Appeal to nature – wherein judgment is based solely on whether the subject of judgment is 'natural' or 'unnatural'.

- Appeal to wealth (*argumentum ad crumenam*) – supporting a conclusion because the arguer is wealthy (or refuting because the arguer is poor). (Sometimes taken together with the appeal to poverty as a general appeal to the arguer's financial situation.)
- Argument from silence (*argumentum ex silentio*) – a conclusion based on silence or lack of contrary evidence.
- Bulverism (Psychogenetic Fallacy) – inferring why an argument is being used, associating it to some psychological reason, then assuming it is invalid as a result. It is wrong to assume that if the origin of an idea comes from a biased mind, then the idea itself must also be a false.
- Chronological snobbery – a thesis is deemed incorrect because it was commonly held when something else, clearly false, was also commonly held.
- Fallacy of relative privation – dismissing an argument due to the existence of more important, but unrelated, problems in the world.
- Genetic fallacy – a conclusion is suggested based solely on something or someone's origin rather than its current meaning or context.
- Judgmental language – insulting or pejorative language to influence the recipient's judgment.
- Naturalistic fallacy (is–ought fallacy, naturalistic fallacy) – claims about what ought to be on the basis of statements about what is.
- *Reductio ad Hitlerum* (playing the Nazi card) – comparing an opponent or their argument to Hitler or Nazism in an attempt to associate a position with one that is universally reviled. (See also – Godwin's law)
- Texas sharpshooter fallacy – improperly asserting a cause to explain a cluster of data.
- *Tu quoque* ("you too", appeal to hypocrisy, I'm rubber and you're glue) – the argument states that a certain position is false or wrong and/or should be disregarded because its proponent fails to act consistently in accordance with that position.
- Two wrongs make a right – occurs when it is assumed that if one wrong is committed, another wrong will cancel it out.

Conditional or Questionable Fallacies

- Broken window fallacy – an argument that disregards lost opportunity costs (typically non-obvious, difficult to determine or otherwise hidden) associated with destroying property of others, or other ways of externalizing costs onto others. For example, an argument that states breaking a window generates income for a window fitter, but disregards the fact that the money spent on the new window cannot now be spent on new shoes.
- Definist fallacy – involves the confusion between two notions by defining one in terms of the other.
- Naturalistic fallacy – attempts to prove a claim about ethics by appealing to a definition of the term "good" in terms of either one or more claims about natural properties (sometimes also taken to mean the appeal to nature) or God's will.

Formal Fallacies

These are errors in logic that can be seen in the argument's form. All formal fallacies are specific types of *non sequiturs*.

- Appeal to probability – is a statement that takes something for granted because it would probably be the case (or might be the case).
- Argument from fallacy – assumes that if an argument for some conclusion is fallacious, then the conclusion *itself* is false.
- Base rate fallacy – making a probability judgment based on conditional probabilities, without taking into account the effect of prior probabilities.

- Conjunction fallacy – assumption that an outcome simultaneously satisfying multiple conditions is more probable than an outcome satisfying a single one of them.
- Masked man fallacy (illicit substitution of identicals) – the substitution of identical designators in a true statement can lead to a false one.

Propositional Fallacies

A propositional fallacy is an error in logic that concerns compound propositions. For a compound proposition to be true, the truth values of its constituent parts must satisfy the relevant logical connectives that occur in it (most commonly: <and>, <or>, <not>, <only if>, <if and only if>). The following fallacies involve inferences whose correctness is not guaranteed by the behavior of those logical connectives, and hence, which are not logically guaranteed to yield true conclusions.

Types of Propositional fallacies:

- Affirming a disjunct – concluding that one disjunct of a logical disjunction must be false because the other disjunct is true; *A or B; A; therefore not B*. For this to be fallacious, the word "or" must be used in an inclusive rather than exclusive sense. Example:

  Premise 1: To be on the cover of Vogue Magazine, one must be a celebrity or very beautiful.
  Premise 2: This month's cover was a celebrity.
  Therefore, this celebrity is not very beautiful.

- Affirming the consequent – the antecedent in an indicative conditional is claimed to be true because the consequent is true; *if A, then B; B, therefore A*.
- Denying the antecedent – the consequent in an indicative conditional is claimed to be false because the antecedent is false; *if A, then B; not A, therefore not B*.

Quantification Fallacies

A quantification fallacy is an error in logic where the quantifiers of the premises are in contradiction to the quantifier of the conclusion.

Example: The existential fallacy – an argument has a universal premise and a particular conclusion.

Formal Syllogistic Fallacies

Syllogistic fallacies – logical fallacies that occur in syllogisms.

- Affirmative conclusion from a negative premise (illicit negative) – when a categorical syllogism has a positive conclusion, but at least one negative premise.
- Fallacy of exclusive premises – a categorical syllogism that is invalid because both of its premises are negative.
- Fallacy of four terms (*quaternio terminorum*) – a categorical syllogism that has four terms.
- Illicit major – a categorical syllogism that is invalid because its major term is not distributed in the major premise but distributed in the conclusion.
- Illicit minor – a categorical syllogism that is invalid because its minor term is not distributed in the minor premise but distributed in the conclusion.

- Negative conclusion from affirmative premises (illicit affirmative) – when a categorical syllogism has a negative conclusion but affirmative premises.
- Fallacy of the undistributed middle – the middle term in a categorical syllogism is not distributed.

Index

Endnotes

Introduction

1. Walter Isaacson, *Steve Jobs* (New York: Simon & Schuster, 2011), pp. 535,536.
2. Philip Norman, *Shout! The Beatles in Their Generation* (New York: Touchstone, 2005) p. 152.
3. Ibid., pp. 144,146. Perhaps industry people should have heard them in concert rather than in their studios. Members of *The Beatles* didn't feel well about their performance at the audition, perhaps because of the pressure (pp. 143,144).
4. Dorothy Sayers, "The Lost Tools of Learning" (published at Oxford, 1947).
5. A 2011 survey of over 1,000 people who hire for a wide range of industries found less than 10 percent reporting that colleges did an excellent job of preparing students for the workplace. Applicants performed below employer's expectations on such skills as critical thinking. Survey by the Accrediting Council for Independent Colleges and Universities (ACICS), "Panel Discussion: Workforce Skills Reality Check," http://www.acics.org/events/content.aspx?id=4718.

6) John Baldoni, "How Leaders Should Think Critically," *Harvard Business Review*, Jan. 20, 2010. When *The Wall Street Journal* interviewed 2191 people who recruit from the top business schools, attributes they looked for included analytical and problem solving skills, which are clearly in the domain of critical thinking. Ronald Alsop, "The Top Business Schools" (A Special Report), *The Wall Street Journal*, Sept., 2003.
7) Richard Florida and Jim Goodnight, "Managing for Creativity," *Harvard Business Review*, July 2005.
8) *Op. cit.*, "Workforce Skills Reality Check."
9) A study of students in Taiwan found a class combining critical and creative thinking scoring better at both critical thinking *and* originality than a class that discussed only critical thinking. *Yulin Changa, Bei-Di Lib, Hsueh-Chih Chena, Fa-Chung Chiuc,* "Investigating the synergy of critical thinking and creative thinking in the course of integrated activity," *Taiwan Educational Psychology: An International Journal of Experimental Educational Psychology,* 2014. http://www.tandfonline.com/doi/abs/10.1080/01443410.2014.920079#.VGTC0slPKmU. Significantly, the University of Massachusetts, Boston offers an MA combining Critical and Creative Thinking. http://www.umb.edu/academics/caps/degree/creative-thinking.

Chapter 1: They're Overconfident

1. James B. Stewart, *Disney War* (New York: Simon & Schuster, 2005), pp. 486, 487.
2. Ibid., p. 527.
3. Plato, *The Republic*, from *Plato in Twelve Volumes*, translated by Paul Shorey (Cambridge: Harvard University Press, 20c-24a) 1969.
4. In Socrates' words (as placed in his mouth by Plato, translated from the original Greek), "For I certainly do not yet know myself, but whithersoever the wind, as it were, of the argument blows, there lies our course." *The Republic, op. cit.*
5. Sam Walton with John Huey, *Sam Walton: Made in America* (New York: Doubleday, 1992) p. 212.
6. Ibid., pp. 56,57,60-62,228,229. They would evaluate one another's strengths and weaknesses, report their bestselling item, and compete for the best volume producing item.
7. Ibid., p. 63. According to associate Charlie Cate, "I remember him saying over and over again: go in and check our competition. Check *everyone* who is our competition. And don't look for the bad. Look for the good.... Everyone is doing something right."
8. Ibid., pp. 81,82.
9. Ibid., pp. 22,23.
10. Ibid., p. 211.
11. Ibid., p. 230.
12. Jack Welch and Suzie Welch, *Winning* (New York: HarperCollins, 2005), pp. 25ff. See also Jack Welch, with John A. Byrne, *Jack: Straight from the Gut* (Warner Business Books: New York, 2001), pp. 162ff. On being idea-driven, he speaks of "candid feedback at every level." Welch gave a warning notice to a manufacturing leader who was "not open to ideas from others" (p. 163). Related comments by Welch: "Not being an open thinker would be a killer." "Treat people with dignity and give them a voice." Also see p. 176 on Welch as a facilitator. He would ask, "What would you change if you were in my shoes?" (p. 180)
13. *Straight from the Gut*, *op. cit.*, pp. 182, 183.
14. Ibid., p. 183. Note also: "...the people closest to the work know it best. Almost every good thing that has happened in the company can be traced to the liberation of some business, some team, or some individual." Welch created "a culture where everyone began playing a part, where everyone's ideas began to count, and where leaders led rather than controlled." (p. 184)
15. Another great example of organizing a company to create and implement a steady flow of ideas would be the SAS Institute in Cary, NC. It has made the top 20 of Forbes' list of best companies to work for every year since Forbes began compiling the list. Its employee turnover rate is an astounding three percent to five percent, compared to the industry average of 20 percent. Revenues have grown for 28 years straight. The secret to their success? According to writers for the *Harvard Business Review*, "SAS has learned how to harness the creative energies of *all* its stakeholders, including its customers, software developers, managers, and support staff." They manage their creativity according to three guiding principles: "Help employees do their best work by keeping them intellectually engaged and by removing distractions. Make managers responsible for sparking creativity and eliminate arbitrary distinctions between "suits" and "creatives." And engage customers as creative partners so you can deliver superior products." Concerning candor at SAS, "it's not in keeping with the corporate culture to withhold constructive

criticism of higher-ups or hide problems from them; doing so would just result in an inferior product. In fact, most of SAS's leaders have an open-door policy. People are free to pop in to talk over an issue or pitch a new product idea. And the CEO might stop by your office to ask you questions about the project you're working on." Richard Florida and Jim Goodnight, "Managing for Creativity," *Harvard Business Review*, July 2005.
16. Concerning the importance of humility in getting the best jobs, it's instructive that when *The Wall Street Journal* interviewed 2191 people who recruit from the top business schools, two of the schools were criticized by certain recruiters because they found their graduates to be arrogant, which was a big turnoff to the recruiters. Ronald Alsop, "The Top Business Schools" (A Special Report), *The Wall Street Journal*, Sept., 2003.
17. This fictional town was created by "Garrison" Keillor for the radio show *A Prairie Home Companion*. "The Lake Wobegon Effect" refers to the observed phenomenon that large portions of groups see themselves as above average in such areas as leadership or driving skills.
18. O. Svenson, "Are we all less risky and more skillful than our fellow drivers?" *Acta Psychologica* 47 (2), 1981: p. 143.
19. Richard L. Brandt, *The Google Guys* (New York: The Penguin Group, 2009, 2011), p. 61.
20. Novelist Terry Kay shared this illustration in a talk he gave at the Georgia Writers Association at Kennesaw State University.
21. Here's how Drew Barrymore describes director Steven Spielberg's relationship with her as a child actor in the hit film *E.T.*: "All of us were free to offer input, but he especially seemed to like the silly things the kids came up with. Like in the scene where Henry, Robert, and I are hiding E.T. in the closet from our mother, Henry tells me that only kids can see E.T. There wasn't a line to go with that, and Steven told me to just make something up. So when we did the scene again, I just shrugged and said, 'Gimme a break!'" "He'd often take me aside and say something like, 'You're talking to me now. Do you really like this? Or do you have a different idea? Do you think it could be done a different way?' Eventually I'd add something and Steven would smile and say, 'Good, let's combine ideas.' It made me feel so good. For once I didn't feel like some stupid little kid trying to make people love me. I felt important and useful.'" Drew Barrymore, with Todd Gold, *Little Girl Lost* (Pocket Books: New York, 1990), p. 58.
22. In Dr. Philip Tetlock's brilliant and painstakingly researched analysis of why experts are so often wrong in their forecasting, he concludes that "The dominant danger remains hubris, the...vice of closed-mindedness, of dismissing dissonant possibilities too quickly." This is why Tetlock concludes that often a group of generally informed people may do better at political forecasting than a team of experts; thus the value of getting input from many diverse people, rather than automatically going with the advice of a team of experts. Philip E. Tetlock, *Expert Political Judgment: How Good Is It? How Can We Know?* (Princeton, NJ: Princeton University Press, 2005), p. 23.
23. Personal interview with Ajit Gupta, 2014. These articles tell a bit more about his many accomplishments: http://en.wikipedia.org/wiki/Ajit_Gupta, http://www.forbes.com/sites/brucerogers/2012/11/19/how-ajit-guptas-aryaka-is-disrupting-the-wide-area-network-business/.

Chapter 2: They're Under Confident

1. This wasn't just an off-the-cuff remark by Einstein in the heat of argument. At the time of his remark, in 1901, he was engaged in a series of squabbles with academic authorities. According to Isaacson, in his biography of Einstein, this quote "would prove a worthy credo, one suitable for being carved on his coat of arms if he had ever wanted such a thing." Walter Isaacson, *Einstein: His Life and Universe* (New York: Simon & Schuster, 2007), p. 67.
2. People react to experts in a variety of ways. One researcher identified *Simplifiers* (those who make a decision based on simple premises and hold to it forever), *Delegators* (who have an authority they trust), and *Questioners* (those who look for pros and cons and evidence). The following article claims that the Questioner group has grown in recent times. For example, rather than trusting a doctor implicitly, Questioners want to know the doctor's rationale and to be involved in the process. For more on cognitive styles of decision making, see http://en.wikipedia.org/wiki/Decision-making#Cognitive_styles. Note also the response below this blog post: http://www.brendan-nyhan.com/blog/2014/03/new-study-on-vaccine-messaging.html.
3. Christopher Cerf and Victor Navasky, *The Experts Speak* (New York: Pantheon Books, 1984 edition), p. 183. From *Elvis, We Love You Tender* (New York: Delacorte Press, 1979). Cerf and Navasky suggest that current media relies to an unhealthy measure on parading experts before their audiences. "...the mainstream media, and particularly television, have as their principal narrative convention the citation, quotation, and interviewing of experts.... In the mass media, where anchors and reporters are not permitted to have opinions of their own, expert opinion is all that is left.... If the Institute of Expertology is right, then, TV is a medium where a person who is wrong at least half the time is interviewed by another person whose chief qualification is that he has no opinion on the subject. From this encounter the truth is supposed to emerge." *The Experts Speak*, 1998 edition, p. xxv.
4. Ibid., 1984 edition, p. 183, quoting from Atyeo and Green, *Don't Quote Me* (Bounty Books, 1994), p. 54.
5. *The Experts Speak* (1979 edition), p. 182, quoting from Jeff Greenfield, *No Peace, No Place* (Garden City, NY: Doubleday, 1973).
6. Ibid., p. 177, Johann Adolph Scheibe, quoted from Max Graf, *Composer and Critic* (New York: W.W. Norton, 1946).
7. Ibid., p. 177, citing Joseph Schmidt-Gorg and Hans Schmidt, eds., *Ludwig van Beethoven* (Hamburg:Deutsche Grammophon Gesselshaft, 1970), p. 36.
8. He was reviewing the first performance in Vienna. *The Experts Speak*, p. 178, quoting from Louis Spohr, *Selbstbiographie* (Kassel: Barenreiter, 1861).
9. Ibid., p. 152, citing Henri Peyre, *Writers and Their Critics* (Ithaca, NY: Cornell University Press, 1944).
10. Ibid., p. 153, citing Clifton Fadiman's review of *Absalom, Absalom* in *The New Yorker*, Oct. 31, 1936.
11. Ibid., p. 157. Citing Harry Thompson Peck, in *The Bookman*, January 1901.
12. Ibid., p. 157. Citing Nicolas Slonimsky, *A Lexicon of Musical Invective* (New York: Coleman-Ross, 1953).
13. Ibid., p. 159. Citing David Frost and Michael Deakin, *David Frost's Book of the World's Worst Decisions* (New York: Crown,

1983), p. ix.
14. Ibid., p. 173. Citing Larry Swindell, *The Last Hero: A Biography of Gary Cooper* (Garden City, NY: Doubleday, 1980).
15. Ibid., p. 173. Citing Christopher Finch and Linda Rosenkrantz, *Gone Hollywood* (Garden City, NY: Doubleday, 1979), p. 335. See also Bernard Rosenberg and Harry Silverman, eds., *The Real Tinsel* (New York: Macmillan, 1970), p. 187.
16. Ibid., p. 175. Quoted by Barbara Walters on an ABC TV special, December 2, 1980.
17. Ibid., p. 203. Citing Arthur C. Clarke, *Profiles of the Future*, Revised Edition (London: Victor Gollancz, 1974).
18. Ibid., p. 203. Citing A.M. Low, *What's the World Coming To? Science Looks at the Future* (Philadelphia: J.B. Lippincott, 1951).
19. Ibid., p. 204. Citing Robert Conot, *A Streak of Luck: The Life and Legend of Thomas Alva Edison* (New York: Seaview Books, 1979), p. 245.
20. Ibid., p. 207. Citing Robert Conot, *op. cit.*
21. Ibid., p. 207. Citing Morgan and Langford, *Facts and Fallacies* (London Corgi, 1982), p. 20.
22. Ibid., p. 208. Citing Gabe Essoe, *The Book of Movie Lists* (Westport, Conn.: Arlington House, 1981), p. 222.
23. Ibid., p. 208. Citing Sir George Bidell Airy, *The Autobiography of George Bidell Airy* (Cambridge, England: Cambridge University Press, 1896), p. 152.
24. Ibid., p. 209. Citing Rochester and Gantz, *The Naked Computer* (Arlington Books Publishers Ltd., 1984).
25. Ibid., p. 209. Citing David H. Ahl, in an interview with Cerf and Navasky, 1982.
26. James W. Finney, in the introduction to *Hiroshima Plus 20*, prepared by *The New York Times* (New York: Delacorte Press, 1965), p. 16. Unfortunately, Finney doesn't document where this quote was originally spoken or published.
27. Cerf and Navasky, *op. cit.*, p. 35.
28. Ibid., p. 47.
29. Ibid., p. 50. Gordon Thomas and Max Morgan-Witts, *The Day the Bubble Burst: A Social History of the Wall Street Crash of 1929* (New York: Doubleday & Company, 1979), p. 410.
30. Ibid., p. 203. Chris Morgan and David Langford, *Facts and Fallacies* (Exeter, England: Webb & Bower, 1981), p. 64.
31. "Common Cold," National Institute of Allergy and Infectious Diseases (November 27, 2006, retrieved 11 June 2007; A.M. Fendrick, A.S. Monto, B. Nightengale, M. Sarnes, "The economic burden of non-influenza-related viral respiratory tract infection in the United States," *Arch. Intern. Med.* 163 (4), 2003, 487–94.
32. http://www.webmd.com/cold-and-flu/features/cold-and-flu-iq - searched 1/12/2014.
33. http://www.medicalnewstoday.com/articles/166606.php - January, 2014.
34. http://www.everydayhealth.com/cold-and-flu/colds-and-the-weather.aspx - January, 2014.
35. http://www.merckmanuals.com/professional/infectious_diseases/respiratory_viruses/ common_cold.html - - January, 2014.
36. http://www.mayoclinic.org/diseases-conditions/common-cold/basics/risk-factors/con-20019062 - January, 2014.
37. http://www.niaid.nih.gov/topics/commoncold/pages/cause.aspx, last updated May, 2011 - January, 2014.
38. Ibid.
39. http://www.cdc.gov/getsmart/antibiotic-use/URI/colds.html - January, 2014.
40. http://www.nhs.uk/Livewell/coldsandflu/Pages/Preventionandcure.aspx - January, 2014.
41. http://www.cardiff.ac.uk/biosi/subsites/cold/commoncold.html - January, 2014.
http://www.nhs.uk/Livewell/coldsandflu/Pages/Preventionandcure.aspx. See primary document here: Johnson C, Eccles R. (2005) "Acute cooling of the feet and the onset of common cold symptoms." *Family Practice* 22: 608-613.
42. http://www.cardiff.ac.uk/biosi/subsites/cold/recent.html - January, 2014.
43. Sources include:

a - Johnson C., Eccles R. (2005), *op. cit.*
b - Eccles R. *Acta Otolaryngol* 2002; 122: 183–191 "An Explanation for the Seasonality of Acute Upper Respiratory Tract Viral Infections"; from the Common Cold Centre, Cardiff School of Biosciences, Cardiff University, Cardiff, UK.
c - Mourtzoukou E.G., Falagas M.E., *Int J Tuberc Lung Dis.* 2007 Sep;11(9):938-43. "...most of the available evidence from laboratory and clinical studies suggests that inhaled cold air, cooling of the body surface and cold stress induced by lowering the core body temperature cause pathophysiological responses such as vasoconstriction in the respiratory tract mucosa and suppression of immune responses, which are responsible for increased susceptibility to infections."
d - Eccles, R. (2007). "Mechanisms of symptoms of the common cold and influenza." *British Journal of Hospital Medicine (London, England), 68* (2), 71-75.
e - Eccles, R. (2005). "Cold feet, cystitis and common cold: parallels between respiratory and urinary tract infections." *Family Practice, 22*(6), e letters 608-613.

44. According to the World Health Organization, "The case definition of the common cold is symptoms of a runny and/or stuffy nose, sneezing, with or without symptoms of headache and cough." (http://www.who.int/maternal_child_adolescent/documents/fch_cah_01_02/en/).
45. Their article on the common cold is too brief to even mention prevention. Since it provides no endnotes, it's no help for finding primary sources. http://www.britannica.com/EBchecked/topic/128201/common-cold.
46. http://en.wikipedia.org/wiki/Common_cold.

47. http://rarediseases.info.nih.gov/news-and-events/pages/28/rare-disease-day.
48. http://en.wikipedia.org/wiki/Wikipedia:Size_of_Wikipedia.
49. See the psychology of under confidence and bias in this regard: http://www.spring.org.uk/2012/06/the-dunning-kruger-effect-why-the-incompetent-dont-know-theyre-incompetent.php.
50. For example, they write, "Keep sharing your written work with peers. Indeed, sharing runs through the entire process of research and writing." Peter J. Taylor and Jeremy Szteiter, *Taking Yourself Seriously: Processes of Research and Engagement* (Arlington, Massachusetts: The Pumping Station, 2012), p. 13. In the sharing experience, they emphasize such attitudes/practices as listening, respecting, and encouraging candid input. See especially their example of how the CARE project succeeded once they began listening to the people they were trying to help, rather than assuming they were the experts with all the answers. (pp. 262ff.)

Chapter 3: They're Married to Brands

1. James R. Healey, "J.D. Power: Most Reliable 3-year Old Cars," USA Today, Feb. 12, 2014.
2. Adam Fisher, "Toyota and Lexus: A Tale of Twin Brands," CBS Money Watch, March 12, 2010.
3. Aaron Crowe, "Doctors, Lawyers in Luxury Cars Hurt Worst by Recession," Nov. 29, 2010. http://jobs.aol.com/articles/2010/11/29/doctors-lawyers-in-luxury-cars-hurt-worst-by-recession/.
4. Actually, more could be saved, if he could purchase the Toyota outright to avoid making payments. But we'll let the money saved in interest be offset by higher repair expenses for purchasing an older vehicle.
5. Jerry Edgerton, Report: Which Cars Cost Least to Repair?, *CBS Money Watch*, Nov. 14, 2011. http://www.cbsnews.com/news/report-which-cars-cost-least-to-repair/. The top-ranked model, the 2009 Toyota Corolla, had not only infrequent trips to the shop but an average repair cost of just $45.84. Note how this differs from the study of owners, and consider why it might differ.
6. For Sam Walton's life, read Sam Walton with John Huey, *Made in America: My Story* (New York: Doubleday1992). For more on Thomas Stanley's studies of self-made millionaires, read Thomas Stanley and William D. Danko, *The Millionaire Next Door: The Surprising Secrets of America's Wealthy* (New York: Pocket Books, 1996) and Thomas Stanley, *The Millionaire Mind* (Kansas City: Andrews McMeel, 2000).
7. Gary Smith, *Introduction to Statistical Reasoning* (Boston: WCB McGraw-Hill, 1998), pp. 186–87. For the original sources see Betsy Morris, "In This Taste Test, the Loser Is the Taste Test," *The Wall Street Journal*, June 3, 1987 and Michael J. McCarthy, "New Coke Gets a New Look, New Chance," *The Wall Street Journal*, March 7, 1990.
8. Mary E. Woolfolk, William Castellan, Charles I. Brooks, *Psychological Reports*, Vol. 52 (1), Feb., 1983, 185-186.
9. I published this research in J. Steve Miller, *Publish a Book! Compare over 50 Publishing Companies* (Acworth, GA: Wisdom Creek Press, 2012).
10. http://answers.yahoo.com/question/index?qid=20111101081305AAHo67b. This lawyer did an informal survey and found people differing greatly in their opinions: http://thenutmeglawyer.blogspot.com/2013/01/does-it-matter-what-type-of-car-your.html.
11. Two excellent biographies of Warren Buffett document the frugality of his early years and how his passion to accumulate wealth eclipsed any childhood need to seek self-esteem from wearing the right clothes or owning the right things. See the early chapters of Roger Lowenstein, *Buffett: The Making of an American Capitalist* (New York: Main Street Books, 1995) and the more recent Alice Schroeder, *The Snowball: Warren Buffett and the Business of Life* (New York: Bantam Books, 2008). One of Buffett's classmates, Norma Jean Thurston, noted how his fellow students joked about how he wore the same tennis shoes year-round, coming across like a country bumpkin. According to Thurston, "Most of us were trying to be like everyone else. ...I think he liked being different. ...He was what he was and he never tried to be anything else." (Lowenstein, p. 26.) What a motivating example for overcoming the peer pressure that leads us to worship brands!

Chapter 4: They're Blinded by Prejudices, Preconceptions, and Biases

1. Greg Kot, "How the Isley Brothers Became – and Stayed – the First Family of R & B," *Chicago Tribune*, November 4, 2001, Sec. 7, p. 1. http://en.wikipedia.org/wiki/List_of_best-selling_music_artists http://en.wikipedia.org/wiki/Elton_John
2. Walter Isaacson, *Einstein: His Life and Universe* (New York: Simon & Schuster, 2007), 284-289.
3. Ibid., p. 447.
4. Ibid., pp. 283ff.
5. Ibid., pp. 282,283.
6. Ibid., p. 298.
7. Joseph McBride, *Steven Spielberg* (New York: Simon & Schuster, 1997), p. 27.
8. Celia Popovic and David Green, *Understanding Undergraduates: Challenging our preconceptions of student success* (Routledge, 2012), pp. 7,202,203.
9. Lecture by David Green at Kennesaw State University, Feb., 2013.
10. T.F. Pettigrew, "The Ultimate Attribution Error: Extending Allport's cognitive analysis of prejudice," *Personality and Social Psychology Bulletin* 5 (4) 1979: pp. 461–476.
11. http://www.nbclosangeles.com/news/local/Women-are-Better-Drivers-Than-Men-Study-137202638.html It appears that the question, "Are men drivers better than women drivers?" is a separate question from the one we considered.
12. T. F. Pettigrew, L. R. Tropp, "A Meta-analytic Test of Intergroup Contact Theory," *Journal of Personality and Social Psychology*, 90 (2006), 751–783.

13. T. T. Pettigrew and L. R. Tropp, "How Does Intergroup Contact Reduce Prejudice? Meta-analytic tests of three mediators," *Eur. J. Soc. Psychol.*, 2008, 38: 922–934. doi: 10.1002/ejsp.504. "We test meta-analytically the three most studied mediators: contact reduces prejudice by (1) enhancing knowledge about the out group, (2) reducing anxiety about intergroup contact, and (3) increasing empathy and perspective taking. Our tests reveal mediational effects for all three of these mediators."
14. http://www.songwritershalloffame.org/index.php/exhibits/bio/C181. See also http://en.wikipedia.org/wiki/Bernie_Taupin#Personal_life.
15. I've not been able to trace down the president who said this. I'm thinking it was Theodore Roosevelt, but so far have failed to find it. If it wasn't Roosevelt's words, he certainly lived it. Trace the references to Roosevelt in *How to Win Friends and Influence People* (consult the index) and you'll find him studying up on people's interests before he met them, so that he could talk intelligently about their interests, remembering the names of people of the lowest status, and taking a sincere interest in their lives.
16. http://blogs.ajc.com/atlanta-forward/2013/08/27/robust-exports-in-georgia/.

Chapter 5: They Believe What They Want to Believe

1. Found in Alice Schroeder, *The Snowball: Warren Buffett and the Business of Life* (New York: Bantam Books, 2008), p. xi.
2. Walter Isaacson, *Steve Jobs* (New York: Simon & Schuster, 2011), pp. 83,123,131,132,151.
3. Ibid., pp. 36,38,77,79.
4. Ibid., pp. 75,78.
5. Ibid., pp. 73,343,344,372,383,377-389,497,498.
6. Ibid., p. 19.
7. Ibid., pp. 117-124.
8. Ibid., p. 82.
9. Ibid., pp. 119,452ff.
10. A more recent study found that parents resistant to having their children vaccinated actually became *more* resistant after given factual information about the vaccination. Brendan Nyham, Jason Reifler, Sean Richey, and Gary L. Freed, "Effective Messages in Vaccine Promotion: A Randomized Trial," *Pediatrics.* Note especially the insightful comment below a blog post summary of this study, distinguishing three kinds of thinkers ("questioners," "delegators," and "simplifiers") and why they wouldn't be positively impacted by the scare tactics/authoritative approach. Karen Crisalli Winter, March 7, 2014 (3:07 p.m.), comment on Brendan Nyhan, "New Study in Pediatrics on Vaccine Messaging" (March 3, 2014), http://www.brendan-nyhan.com/blog/2014/03/new-study-on-vaccine-messaging.html.
11. David P. Redlawsk, Andrew J.W. Civettini, Karen M. Emmerson, "The Affective Tipping Point: Do Motivated Reasoners Ever 'Get It'?" *Political Psychology*, August, 2010, Vol. 31 Issue 4, pp. 563, 31.
12. Philip Norman, *Shout! The Beatles in Their Generation* (New York: MJF Books, 1981), p. 35.
13. "The Foxification of News," *The Economist*, July 7, 2011, http://www.economist.com/node/18904112.
14. Mark Jurkowitz, et. al., of The Pew Research Center, "The State of the News Media 2013," http://www.stateofthemedia.org/2013/special-reports-landing-page/the-changing-tv-news-landscape/.
15. But Fox, according to the Columbia Journalism Review, has more diversity than MSNBC. Fox hires sharp liberals to have real debates with conservatives, http://www.cjr.org/feature/and_from_the_leftfox_news.php, http://www.politico.com/blogs/media/2013/12/is-msnbc-worse-than-fox-news-179175.html.
16. "During the late stages of the 2012 presidential campaign, a Pew Research analysis found that Barack Obama received far more negative coverage than positive on the Fox News Channel. Yet Fox found its ideological mirror image in MSNBC. In the final stretch of the campaign, nearly half (46%) of Obama's coverage on Fox was negative, while just 6% was positive in tone. But MSNBC produced an even harsher narrative about the Republican in the race: 71% of Romney's coverage was negative, versus 3% positive," http://www.pewresearch.org/fact-tank/2014/01/14/five-facts-about-fox-news/. If you watched the 2012 election on MSNBC during the final week, according to the Pew Research Center's *Project for Excellence in Journalism*, there were no positive articles about the Republican candidate, Mitt Romney. None. http://en.wikipedia.org/wiki/MSNBC#Negative_Romney_coverage_in_2012_presidential_election. Also from this article: In the Pew Research Center's 2013 "State of the News Media" report, MSNBC was found to be the most opinionated news network, with 85% of the content being commentary or opinions, and only 15% of the content being factual reporting.
17. According to a NYT article by their first public editor, the NYT does indeed represent a certain worldview. "...readers with a different worldview will find The Times an alien beast." He is himself liberal, and unabashedly says that the NYT is overwhelmingly liberal in each relevant section of the paper. He then goes through to show examples of what's reported and what's not reported, then justifies its liberal bias by saying that it's representing the residents of NYC, who tend to believe the same way. Daniel Okrent, "The Public Editor: Is The New York Times a Liberal Newspaper?," July 25, 2004, http://www.nytimes.com/2004/07/25/opinion/the-public-editor-is-the-new-york-times-a-liberal-newspaper.html.
18. On media bias in popular media: http://newsroom.ucla.edu/portal/ucla/Media-Bias-Is-Real-Finds-UCLA-6664.aspx The original research, from which the article was drawn, is Tim Groseclose and Jeffrey Milyo, "A Measure of Media Bias," *The Quarterly Journal of Economics* , Vol. 120, No. 4 (Nov., 2005), pp. 1191-1237. The study was of news content, not editorials. *USA Today* was closest to the center for newspapers; the NYT was far to the left (p. 1191). It found the *Washington Post* leaning

to the right. As for *Wall Street Journal*, the researchers were surprised to find that its news section was the most liberal of the 20 popular news outlets studied, yet the editorial section (opinion pieces) was quite conservative (p. 1213). The WSJ was farthest from center, with NYT next. While the UCLA study found Fox News to have a conservative bias, it found Fox News Special Report with Brit Hume to be one of the most centrist news outlets.
19. "The Public Editor," *op. cit.*
20. Media Matters for America, another self-described progressive media watch group, dedicates itself to "monitoring, analyzing, and correcting conservative misinformation in the U.S. media." Shouldn't reporters, when they quote these watch groups, tell the group's agenda? Conservative organizations Accuracy In Media and Media Research Center argue that the media has a liberal bias, and are dedicated to publicizing the issue. The Media Research Center was founded with the specific intention to "prove ... that liberal bias in the media does exist and undermines traditional American values," http://en.wikipedia.org/wiki/Media_bias_in_the_United_States.
21. For a helpful list of types of media bias to watch for, with helpful examples, comments and questions for teachers, see: http://www.studentnewsdaily.com/example-of-media-bias/news-headline-or-opinion/.
22. "...partisans perceive *less* bias in news coverage slanted to support their view than their opponents on the other side of the issue."
23. "In a range of studies, when news audiences who hew to opposing sides on an issue are given the same news coverage of the topic to evaluate, both view it as biased in favor of the other side." It's called the "hostile media effect." "Researchers believe that the explanation for this hostile media effect is selective categorization: opposing partisans attend to, process, and recall identical content from a news presentation but mentally categorize and label the same aspects of a story differently – as hostile to their own position." Matthew C. Nisbet, "Why Partisans View Mainstream Media as Biased and Ideological Media as Objective," http://bigthink.com/age-of-engagement/why-partisans-view-mainstream-media-as-biased-and-ideological-media-as-objective. In sum, "partisans perceive *less* bias in news coverage slanted to support their view than their opponents on the other side of the issue."
24. William Lane Craig, *On Guard* (Colorado Springs: David C. Cook, 2010), pp. 36,46ff.
25. Thomas Nagel, *The Last Word* (Oxford University Press, 1997), pp. 130-131.
26. Sarah Boseley, "Statins for people at low risk of heart disease needs rethink, says top doctors," *The Guardian*, June 10, 2014, http://www.theguardian.com/society/2014/jun/10/statins-low-risk-heart-disease-rethink-doctors-nice.
27. Nina Teicholz, "The Questionable Link between Saturated Fat and Heart Disease," *Wall Street Journal* Online, May 6, 2014, http://online.wsj.com/news/article_email/SB10001424052702303678404579533760760481486-lMyQjAxMTA0MDEwMzExNDMyWj.

Chapter 6: They're Trapped in Traditions

1. Edward S. Ninde, *The Story of the American Hymn* (Nashville: Abingdon, 1921), pp. 94-97.
2. Steve Miller, *The Contemporary Christian Music Debate* (Carol Stream, Illinois: Tyndale House, 1993), pp. 139-147.
3. Of course, it's been more complicated and convoluted than this brief summary presents, with both denominational and nondenominational churches and organizations wrestling with issues of new musical forms, both nationally and internationally.
4. http://www.starbucks.com/about-us/our-heritage.
5. Schultz, Howard and Dori Jones Yang, *Pour Your Heart Into It: How Starbucks Built a Company One Cup at a Time* (New York: Hyperion, 1997), p. 35.
6. Ibid., p. 87.
7. Ibid., pp. 166, 167.
8. Ibid., pp. 166-169.
9. Ibid., p. 169.
10. Ibid., p. 206.
11. Ibid., p. 209.
12. Sam Walton with John Huey, *Sam Walton: Made in America* (New York: Doubleday, 1992), p. 34.
13. Ibid., p. 63.
14. David Burkus, *The Myths of Creativity* (San Francisco: Josey-Bass, 2014), p. 21. Psychologist Mihaly Csikszentmihalyi studied 91 prominent people to find their perspective on the process that led to their creative moments. Almost all went through five stages: preparation, incubation, insight, evaluation, and elaboration.
15. Ibid., pp. 18-20.
16. For example, in Edison's work to invent a light bulb, he followed his usual course of collecting all the information he could find on the subject. He assumed that the light would best glow in an environment of a gas, so he bought all the transactions of the gas engineering societies, and all the back volumes of gas journals. William M. Meadowcroft and Charles Henry Meadowcroft, *The Boys' Life of Edison* (Harper and Brothers, 1911) p. 136.
17. Gene N. Landrum, *Profiles of Genius* (Buffalo, New York: Prometheus Books, 1993), p. 185.
18. Ibid., pp. 79-81.
19. Walter Isaacson, *Steve Jobs* (New York: Simon & Schuster), p. 329.

Chapter 7: They Fail to Identify Hidden Assumptions

1. David McCullough, *1776* (New York: Simon & Schuster, 2005), pp. 58-60,111.
2. Ibid., p. 25.
3. Ibid., p. 76.
4. Ibid., p. 72.
5. Ibid., p. 74.
6. Ibid., p. 81.
7. Ibid., pp. 24,79.
8. Ibid., pp. 82-85.
9. Ibid., p. 78.
10. Ibid., pp. 86, 87.
11. Ibid.
12. Ibid., pp. 88,89.
13. Ibid., pp. 90,91-93.
14. Ibid., pp. 88,89.
15. Ibid., p. 95.
16. Ibid., pp. 99-105.
17. Ibid., pp. 148, 158,161,191,197.
18. Ibid., p. 148.
19. Ibid., pp. 225,254,269.
20. Ibid., p. 270.
21. Ibid., p. 256.
22. Ibid., p. 270.
23. Ibid., pp. 260,261.
24. Ibid., p. 276.
25. Ibid., p. 284.
26. Ibid., pp. 280,281,283.
27. Ibid., pp. 283, 290-293.
28. Ibid., p. 73.
29. Richard L. Brandt, *The Google Guys* (New York: The Penguin Group, 2011), pp. 5,6,46.
30. Ibid., p. 76.
31. "The World's Most Valuable Brands," *Forbes*, http://www.forbes.com/powerful-brands/list/.
32. "Google Inc. Announces Fourth Quarter and Fiscal Year 2013 Results," Google.com, https://investor.google.com/earnings/2013/Q4_google_earnings.html, See also https://www.trefis.com/company#/GOOG.
33. According to Gates' biographers, "Rule Number One" of dealing with Bill Gates was to stand up to him. According to Gates' personal assistant, "He [Gates] liked it when you stood up to him.... If you backed down from Bill, he wouldn't have respect for you." Stephen Manes and Paul Andrews, *Gates* (New York: Simon & Schuster, 1994), pp. 200, 259. See also p. 179 on Paul Allen and Bill Gates coming to good decisions at Microsoft by hashing through their disagreements. Note that some people manage to enjoy their arguments rather escalating to screaming fits and ending in animosity. Albert Einstein didn't agree with Neils Bohr's views on quantum physics, but he found their many discussions a great delight. Einstein wrote to Bohr after one of their visits: "Not often in life has a human being caused me such joy by his mere presence as you did...." Walter Isaacson, *Einstein* (New York: Simon & Schuster, 2007), p. 325.
34. Example of Jobs' associates arguing against his ideas: Jobs thought of the computer as "a bicycle for the mind" and insisted on changing the name of their "Macintosh" computer to "Bicycle." His colleagues thought it was stupid and refused to use the name. Eventually, Jobs relented. Walter Isaacson, *Steve Jobs* (New York: Simon & Schuster, 2011), p. 115. See also how they argued on pp. 145-147,460,468,498,499,569.
35. Schultz, Howard and Dori Jones Yang, *Pour Your Heart Into It: How Starbucks Built a Company One Cup at a Time* (New York: Hyperion, 1997), p. 156.
36. Ibid., pp. 156ff.
37. Ibid., p. 60.
38. Ibid., pp. 101-109.
39. "Skunkworks® Origin Story," Lockheedmartin.com, http://www.lockheedmartin.com/us/aeronautics/skunkworks/origin.html. They would distill 14 practices and rules for their future skunkworks® groups. See "Kelly's 14 Rules and Practices" here: http://www.lockheedmartin.com/us/aeronautics/skunkworks/14rules.html.
40. John Gertner, *The Idea Factory: Bell Labs and the Great Age of American Innovation* (New York: The Penguin Press, 2012), p. 4.
41. Ibid., p. 222.
42. Ibid. For example, see p. 56 on Shockley, others on p. 194. Bell labs allowed tremendous personal freedom to conduct new research (p. 355).
43. Ibid., p. 177.
44. Ibid., p. 354. The author of *The Idea Factory* says that Google's 20% rule was picked up from an old Bell Labs tradition.
45. *The Google Guys*, *op. cit.*, pp. 57-59; 176-178.
46. Robert Spector, *Amazon.com: Get Big Fast* (London: Random House, 2000), p. 85.
47. Ibid., p. 215.

Chapter 8: They Underestimate the Power of the Paradigm

1. Walter Isaacson, *Einstein: His Life and Universe,* (New York: Simon & Schuster, 2007), p. 163, quoting from "Einstein to Maurice Solovine, Apr. 10, 1938" in Maurice Solovine, *Albert Einstein: Letters to Solovine* (New York: Philosophical Library, 1987), p. 85.
2. *Einstein*, pp. 323, 324. If energy were introduced to a gas of atoms, photons would be emitted. Yet (and this is what would bother Einstein), "*there was no way to determine which direction an emitted photon might go*. In addition, *there was no way to determine when it would happen*." In classical physics (*a la* Newton), "if you knew all the positions and velocities in a system you could determine its future." Einstein's theory of relativity was indeed radical, but it didn't violate Newton's strict rule of cause-and-effect. Yet, the indeterminacy of either the time or direction of a photon's emission (or particles such as electrons) undermined cause-and-effect, since the resulting states couldn't be determined beforehand. Einstein's strict determinism would also lead him to believe in an impersonal rather than personal God. A personal God could make free decisions and make changes in the universe, thus disrupting a strict sequence of natural cause and effect. Also due to his determinism, he didn't believe in the freedom of people to make choices. (p. 391)
3. Ibid., p. 323.
4. Ibid. See primary source on p. 609.
5. Ibid., p. 333.
6. Ibid., p. 95.
7. Ibid., p. 100. For primary sources, see p. 320 on Einstein's transition from a revolutionary (on relativity theory) to a conservative (on quantum theory). See 330ff for more developments in quantum physics and Einstein's problems with it. According to Heisenberg, "When one wishes to calculate 'the future' from 'the present' one can only get statistical results, since one can never discover every detail of the present." (p. 333) Who knows? In the end Einstein might get the last laugh, if a "theory of everything" could establish a cause-effect relation that has hitherto remained undiscovered.
8. Ibid., pp. 254,255.
9. John Farrell, *The Day Without Yesterday* (New York: Thunder's Mouth Press, 2005), pp. 10,11.
10. Ibid., p. 13 and others as well.
11. Ibid., pp. 254,255. Could Gamow have been exaggerating? Perhaps. See Farrell's endnote, p. 225. Yet, the comment is consistent with what we know of Einstein's feelings about his decision. It must have been extremely disappointing. In a letter to Lemaitre, Einstein admitted that "since I have introduced the term [the cosmological constant] I had always a bad conscious." (*Einstein*, pp. 169,353-356). Concerning Einstein's resistance to quantum physics, the tables had seemingly turned. While he had once stood against authority, now the one who tossed aside Newton's idea of absolute time couldn't part with the idea of the static universe. (p. 254) But while some viewed Einstein as becoming more conservative concerning science in his later years, Einstein viewed himself as the revolutionary who was still in the business of bucking scientific fads, with the recent fad being quantum physics. (p. 463)
12. Farrell, *op. cit.*, p. 149.
13. Ibid., p. 13.
14. Quote from Robert Jastrow, *God and the Astronomers* (New York: W.W. Norton & Company, 1978) p. 112. See similar quote in Farrell, *op. cit.*, pp. 105,106.
15. Ibid., p. 112.
16. Helge Kragh, *Cosmology and Controversy: The Historical Development of Two Theories of the Universe* (Princeton, New Jersey: Princeton University Press, 1996), p. 253. Hoyle was an atheist and felt like a beginning of the universe implied a God, so his emotional preference was for a static universe which had no beginning. According to Farrell, Hoyle "did not hesitate to associate his atheism with the steady state model." (Farrell, *op. cit.*, pp. 153,205.) He wasn't alone. "...many scientists admittedly resisted the big bang theory because for them it seemed to imply the moment of creation." (206)
17. Jastrow, *op. cit.*, p. 16.
18. Nicholas Wade, in *Science,* called it "A landmark in intellectual history."
19. The way Plank originally put it: "A new scientific truth does not triumph by convincing its opponents and making them see the light, but rather because its opponents eventually die, and a new generation grows up that is familiar with it." *Wissenschaftliche Selbstbiographie. Mit einem Bildnis und der von Max von Laue gehaltenen Traueransprache.* Johann Ambrosius Barth, Verlag (Leipzig 1948), p. 22, as translated in *Scientific Autobiography and Other Papers,* trans. F. Gaynor (New York, 1949), pp. 33–34, as cited by Thomas Kuhn, *The Structure of Scientific Revolutions,* second edition (Chicago: The University of Chicago Press, 1962, 1970).
20. See Farrell, *op. cit.*, pp. 39,40.
21. See critiques and evaluations such as Ian Barbour, *Myths, Models and Paradigms* (New York: HarperCollins, 2013). See also Dudley Shapere, University of Chicago, *Philosophical Review*, vol. 73, 1964, pp. 383ff.
22. Reflect on his personality. The same traits that may have contributed to his great breakthrough—roguish, dismissing authority, etc. (*Einstein, op. cit.*, pp. 45,49,67,93)—were the same traits that may have kept him from accepting evidence for quantum physics or the Big Bang.
23. Here I'm reformulating a sentence people have used in reference to paradigms captivating church leaders, something to the effect of "Those who are most resistant to the present move of God are often those who were involved in the last move of God."

24. *Einstein*, *op. cit*., pp. 62,122,123.
25. *Einstein*, pp. 61,62,123. They would exchange 229 letters over their lifetimes and would die within weeks of each other. Besso lacked focus, drive and diligence, but had "an extraordinarily fine mind" that was nevertheless "disorderly". His boss called him "completely useless and almost unbalanced." On Einstein's relationship with Besso, see pp. 27,61,62,122,123,136,137. Einstein's big breakthrough on relativity came while discussing it with Besso, which Einstein acknowledged in his breakthrough paper.
26. Einstein carried on conversations all his life with Neils Bohr, who was also a great friend. So to Einstein's great credit, he held his position on quantum physics with his eyes wide open to the other side, rather than isolating himself in his office and refusing to interact. See *Einstein*, pp. 192,193 on working through the math for his relativity theory with Grossman. See p. 222 on Hilbert's assessment of Einstein's lack of understanding of four-dimensional geometry. On p. 215 Isaacson described Grossman as Einstein's "mathematical caddy." Einstein continued to use mathematical caddies throughout his life (pp. 368,397,450,537).
27. Lain Carter, "Tiger Wood's Former Caddie Apologizes for Race Remarks," BBC.com, Nov. 5, 2011, http://www.bbc.com/sport/0/golf/15605113.
28. Alice Schroeder gives a delightful description of the similarities and differences that make Buffett and Munger such a successful twosome in pp. 24-30 of *The Snowball* (New York: Bantam, 2008).
29. David Packard, *The HP Way: How Bill Hewlett and I Built our Company* (New York: Harper Business, 1996). They met as college freshmen (p. 18), and established the "next bench" syndrome (p. 97). If your idea appeals to the worker at the next bench, then you might be onto something. The weakness of running it by only one person, in my opinion, is that this person may not represent the interests/needs of a large segment of humanity. But the "next bench" is certainly a good place to start.
30. Richard L. Brandt, *The Google Guys* (New York: The Penguin Group, 2011). Note how Brin and Page argue through the details of important issues. Surely it helps that they share a long history together. They met when Brin volunteered to show a new contingent of students around Stanford; Page was one of them. They subsequently became close friends. http://en.wikipedia.org/wiki/History_of_Google. How do you find such people? Many successful teams met in high school or college.
31. David Berlinski, *Newton's Gift: How Sir Isaac Newton Unlocked the System of the World* (New York: Free Press, 2002), pp. 21,22.
32. Masaaki Sato, *The Honda Myth* (Vertical, 2006).
33. Humphrey Carpenter, *J.R.R. Tolkien* (New York: Houghton Mifflin Company, 1977), p. 152.
34. Ed Catmull, *Creativity, Inc*. (New York: Random House, 2014), p. 67.
35. Ibid., p. 68.
36. Ibid., p. 68, 65-74.
37. *The Google Guys*, op. cit., pp. 59,60.
38. *Einstein: His Life and Universe*, *op. cit*., pp. 79-84. "Ernst Mach...lambasted Newton's notion of absolute time as a 'useless metaphysical concept' that 'cannot be produced in experience.'" (p. 125)
39. Benjamin Franklin, *The Autobiography of Benjamin Franklin* (New York: Dover Publications, 1996 edition) pp. 28,29,45-46. See also Walter Isaacson, *Benjamin Franklin* (New York: Simon & Schuster, 2003), pp. 55-60.
40. *J.R.R. Tolkien*, *op. cit*., pp. 152-154. Much has been written about *The Inklings*. Those wanting to know more should consider reading *The Inklings*, by Humphrey Carpenter. Although I've not read *The Inklings*, Carpenter's biography of Tolkien was quite good and I'd assume *The Inklings* would be of similar quality. Other groups include Steve Wozniak and Steve Jobs meeting with the Homebrew Computer Club before launching Apple. Walter Isaacson, *Steve Jobs* (New York: Simon & Schuster, 2011), pp. 58-63.
41. *The Day without Yesterday*, *op. cit*., pp. 12,13,52,53.

Chapter 9: They Fail to Account for World Views

1. Some of my main sources for these leaders were *The Communist Manifesto*, by Marx and Engels, ed. Samuel H. Beer (Northbrook, Illinois: AHM Publishing Corporation, 1955); Paul Johnson, *Intellectuals* (New York: Harper Perennial, 1988); Martin Amis, *Koba the Dread* (New York, Vintage Books, 2003); Janet Caulkins, *Joseph Stalin* (New York: Franklin Watts, 1990).
2. *Koba the Dread*, *op. cit*., p. 57.
3. Ibid., p. 35.
4. As Alain Brossat put it. Ibid., p. 34.
5. Helge Kragh, *Cosmology and Controversy*: *The Historical Development of Two Theories of the Universe* (Princeton, New Jersey: Princeton University Press, 1996), p. 260.
6. Ibid., p. 260. Soviet chief ideologue Andrei Zhdanov said, "Falsifiers of science want to revive the fairy tale of the origin of the world from nothing...." (p. 260)
7. Ibid., p. 260. Whereas early Russian leaders resisted certain scientific theories because of their Marxism, Einstein resisted certain theories because of his determinism. For Einstein, a God who intervenes in history (such as in a creation) would disrupt the determinism that he believed was a necessary base for science. "Lemaitre recalled how Einstein had complained in one of their meetings that Lemaitre's expanding cosmic nucleus was unacceptable because of its metaphysical implications." Einstein had responded to Lemaitre, "No, not that, that suggests too much the creation." John Farrell, *The Day Without Yesterday* (New

York: Thunder's Mouth Press, 2005), p. 100.
8. Helge Kragh, *Entropic Creation* (Burlington, Vermont: Ashgate Publishing, 2008), p. 230, quoting Paul Davies, *God and the New Physics* (New York: Simon & Schuster, 1983), p. 11.
9. Friedrich Engels fought the second law of thermodynamics because of his atheistic dialectical materialism, which taught that material can have neither a beginning nor an end. (Helge Kragh, *op. cit.*, p. 134). He considered entropy dangerous "because of its association with creation, miracles and theism." (p. 136) For those who want to further explore the history of the laws of thermodynamics, *Entropic Creation* exhibits academic scholarship at its best. The author, Helge Kragh, seems to be familiar with every scientist of any note who considered the laws of thermodynamics and their implications to cosmology. It's not only thorough, but well organized and well written.
10. Ibid., p. 223.
11. Ibid., p. 226, quoted by Kragh, from an East German textbook, Fromm, et al., 1974, p. 137, Einfuhrung in deu dialektischen und historischen Materialismus, Berlin: Dietz Verlag. Note also Chinese scientists fighting against the Big Bang theory. One Chinese scientist who published a paper on Big Bang cosmology had to take refuge in 1989 in the American Embassy to avoid arrest as a traitor. (p. 227)
12. *Koba the Dread*, *op. cit.*, p. 43.
13. Ibid., p. 29. As Lenin said, "We must now give the most decisive and merciless battle to the [clergy] and subdue its resistance with such brutality that they will not forget it for decades to come.... The greater the number of the representatives of the reactionary bourgeoisie and reactionary clergy that we will manage to execute in this affair, the better." (p. 29)
14. Ibid., pp. 63,64.
15. This is found in the introduction to *The Black Book of Communism,* by Jean-Louis Panné, Andrzej Paczkowski, Karel Bartosek, et. al., translated from the original French version by Harvard University Press, 1999, p. x. In this book, six French scholars took up the task of consulting the best sources available to estimate the human death toll of Communism in the 1900s.
16. Janet Caulkins, *Joseph Stalin* (New York: Franklin Watts, 1990), p. 80.
17. Since people made the same wages no matter how hard they worked, there was little incentive to get ahead, make superior products, or put customers first. One waiter in a Bratislava, Slovakia restaurant told me, "You'll probably get better service in the restaurant down the street." From a Communist perspective, this attitude makes sense. Why try to be the best restaurant in town if that would result in more customers and more work, but no more pay? Also, because of the fear of government leaders and their lack of accountability to a higher law of ethics, people tried hard to not stand out. If your grades and work were outstanding, you might provoke jealousy or fear in the leaders, who were the gatekeepers for higher education, better jobs, etc.
18. Alex Rosenberg, *The Atheists' Guide to Reality* (New York: W. W. Norton & Company, 2012), pp. 272-274.
19. Ibid., p. 288.
20. Ibid., p. 19. Rosenberg states these conclusions on pp. 2 and 3, then spends the rest of the book arguing for them.
21. *Koba the Dread*, *op. cit.*, pp. 14,15, 20. This was from his childhood friend.
22. *Intellectuals*, *op. cit.*, pp. 69ff.
23. Mandela modeled his practice of listening to all sides from his early experience in the Thembu tribe, where a regent and his counselors listened to people speak their minds about issues before coming to conclusions. According to Mandela, "It was democracy in its purest form." Nelson Mandela, *Long Walk to Freedom* (New York: Little, Brown and Company, 1994,1995), pp. 20-22.
24. Edited by Clayborne Carson, *The Autobiography of Martin Luther King, Jr.*, (New York: Warner Books, 1998), pp. 19-22.
25. See their autobiographies in this regard.
26. http://www.enterstageright.com/archive/articles/0105/0105churchilldem.htm.
27. This is a variant expression of a sentiment which is often attributed to Tocqueville or Alexander Fraser Tytler, but the earliest known occurrence is as an unsourced attribution to Tytler in "This is the Hard Core of Freedom" by Elmer T. Peterson in *The Daily Oklahoman* (December 9, 1951) http://en.wikiquote.org/wiki/Alexis_de_Tocqueville.

Intermission

1. Walter Isaacson, *Einstein: His Life and Universe* (New York: Simon & Schuster, 2007), p. 299.
2. Benjamin Graham, *The Intelligent Investor*, revised edition, with commentary by Jason Zweig (New York: HarperCollins, 2003), p. 524.

Chapter 10: They Contradict, Leave Out Valid Options, and Knock Down Straw Men

1. Analytical philosopher Alvin Plantinga argues that this line of reasoning is consistent with, and even demanded by, philosophical naturalism. http://www.nybooks.com/articles/archives/2012/sep/27/philosopher-defends-religion/.
2. Susan Blackmore and Alex Rosenberg argue that since our brains were constructed solely through naturalistic evolutionary processes—for survival than for finding truth—our brains build mental models that we can't control (there is no "I" or "self" directing the brain, in the view of both authors) and they can't be trusted to lead us to truth. Susan Blackmore, *Dying to Live* (Buffalo, New York: Prometheus Books, 1993), pp149-164; 221-225; Alex Rosenberg, *The Atheist's Guide to Reality* (New York: W. W. Norton & Company, 2011).
3. For example, Hume's radical empiricism led him to deny that we can establish cause/effect relationships—a belief which would

obviously wreak havoc in science.
4. Richard Dawkins, *The God Delusion* (New York: Mariner Books, 2008), p. 187.
5. Ibid., p. 52.
6. Ibid., p. 136.
7. Ibid., p. 187.
8. Ibid., see also pp. 186-188.
9. Academic biologist H. Allen Orr suggests that Dawkins failed to consider that, rather than ending in an infinite regress ("Who made God?" "Who made the being that made God," etc.), God could be a brute fact, like subatomic particles or matter. "It could, after all, be a brute fact of the universe that it derives from some transcendent mind...." H. Allen Orr, "A Mission to Convert," *The New York Review of Books*, January 11, 2007. http://www.nybooks.com/articles/archives/2007/jan/11/a-mission-to-convert/
10. In *The God Delusion*, Dawkins doesn't even mention the option of God being eternal, much less argue against it. In one of his earlier books, *The Blind Watchmaker*, he least acknowledges that some would argue that God exists eternally, but brushes this option off (rather than forward an opposing argument) with a sentence: "You have to say something like 'God was always there', and if you allow yourself that kind of lazy way out, you might as well just say 'DNA was always there', or 'Life was always there', and be done with it." Richard Dawkins, *The Blind Watchmaker* (New York: W. W. Norton & Company, 1996), p. 200. But why does Dawkins consider "something was always there" an invalid option? After all, prior to the 20th century, the majority opinion of scientists was that the universe was always there, extending into eternity past. Was that "lazy" on their part? In fact, when we consider ultimate origins, we'd seem to be left with two options: either there was nothing prior to the Bang (the standard scientific view of the Big Bang, according to Dawkins), so that something appeared out of nothing, with nothing to cause it, (that's absolutely nothing—no empty space, no vacuum), or that the beginning of the universe was caused by something that existed in some non-material form outside of time and space, existing from eternity past. Is the latter option really stranger than something coming from nothing on its own accord? If not, then why does Dawkins think it so inconceivable (or lazy) that God could have existed eternally? He fails to address this question.
11. Gary Gutting, Does Evolution Explain Religious Beliefs? *The New York Times* (July 8, 2014) http://opinionator.blogs.nytimes.com/2014/07/08/does-evolution-explain-religious-beliefs/?_php=true&_type=blogs&_php=true&_type=blogs&_r=1&
12. C.S. Lewis, *The Screwtape Letters* (New York: HarperOne reprint edition, 2009), p. 1.
13. Alex Rosenberg, *The Atheist's Guide to Reality* (New York: W.W. Norton & Company, 2011), pp. 2,3.
14. Ibid., pp. 164-193.
15. Ibid., p. 16.
16. Ibid., pp. 2,3,310,311.
17. Ibid., pp. 313-315.
18. Ibid., p. 311.
19. Ibid., for example, pp. viii, 304-306. For a helpful critique of this book, see James N. Anderson, *Analogical Thoughts* (blog), August 13, 2013, http://www.proginosko.com/2013/08/the-atheists-guide-to-reality/.
20. "Minus logical positivists, tremendously influential outside philosophy, especially in psychology and social sciences, intellectual life of the 20th century would be unrecognizable." Yet, "By the late 1960s, the neopositivist movement had clearly run its course. Interviewed in the late 1970s, A. J. Ayer supposed that "the most important 'defect' was that nearly all of it was false." http://en.wikipedia.org/wiki/Logical_positivism#Critics. For a brief history of Logical Positivism, see articles such as "Logical Empiricism" or "Theism" in *The Stanford Encyclopedia of Philosophy,* Edward N. Zalta (ed.). It's a wonderful (free!) resource for all things philosophical.
21. H. Allen Orr, op. cit. Dawkins would seem to be a master of the straw man. Perhaps he gives us a clue as to why in his introduction to *The Divine Watchmaker,* where he states his opinion that Darwin's first edition of *Origin of the Species* was more persuasive than the last edition, because in the first edition Darwin didn't deal with all the objections. Apparently, in Dawkins' mind, Darwin's stating other people's objections took away from his argument. So perhaps Dawkins knows many of the objections people would give to his arguments, but is afraid that if he presents the strongest arguments for all sides of his statements, that this will take away from his persuasiveness. Thus, he presents straw men, which are much more easily knocked down. Example: if you look carefully at his arguments against the existence of God in chapter three of *The God Delusion*, he doesn't present the arguments as his strongest opponents present them. In the form he presents them, they're easily destroyed. For example, on Dawkins' critique of the Cosmological Argument for God's existence, see philosopher Edward Feser's critique at http://edwardfeser.blogspot.com/2011/07/so-you-think-you-understand.html. Also, view Dr. William Craig's presentation at Oxford on the same topic at https://www.youtube.com/watch?v=fP9CwDTRoOE.
22. Ed. by Paul Copan, William Lane Craig, *Contending with Christianity's Critics* (Nashville: B&H Academic), p. 5.
23. H. Allen Orr, replying to Dennett's response in the *New York Review of Books,* http://www.nybooks.com/articles/archives/2007/mar/01/the-god-delusion/.
24. See Michael Ruse's response in Does Evolution Explain Religious Beliefs?, op. cit.
25. Note other objections to this argument:

> 1. Going along with our argument concerning the mining operation on the moon, philosophers argue that an immediate explanation doesn't require an ultimate explanation. Example: William Craig suggests that if we found artifacts of a lost civilization, that's sufficient evidence that the civilization actually existed, even if we have no ultimate explanation of where the civilization came from. *Contending with Christianity's Critics*, op. cit., p. 4.
> 2. From a purely naturalistic perspective, we have no *ultimate* explanation of anything. For example, you may ask why this cat is sitting on my desk looking at me? I may respond, "It wants to lick the milk out of my bowl of cereal." But what if you counter, "That's no explanation, where did the cat come from?" I may say, "Its mom." And you may complain, "Yes, of course. But if you can't give me the ultimate explanation of where the cat came from, I refuse to believe that it even exists." Yet, from a naturalistic perspective, all scientific explanations end with the Big Bang, a place at which physics as we know it breaks down and at which scientists tell us all scientific questions stop. All reductionist scientific explanations end with the Big Bang, and if we ask one more "Why?" beyond the Big Bang, science lets us down,

because the Big Bang is a singularity. Thus, if all arguments about the existence of this or that must answer the ultimate question of origins to be meaningful, aren't we stuck with no meaningful arguments at all? Thus, from a naturalistic perspective we can't ultimately answer the question, "Where did this cat come from?" But would Dawkins thus concede that we therefore can't argue for its existence? Surely not.

26. Jack Andraka, A Promising Test for Pancreatic Cancer...from a Teenager?, A TED talk, (Filmed Feb., 2013) http://www.ted.com/talks/jack_andraka_a_promising_test_for_pancreatic_cancer_from_a_teenager?language=enhttp://www.ted.com/talks/jack_andraka_a_promising_test_for_pancreatic_cancer_from_a_teenager.
27. For the story of the development of Starbucks' instant coffee, see Schultz, Howard and Dori Jones Yang, *Pour Your Heart Into It: How Starbucks Built a Company One Cup at a Time* (New York: Hyperion, 1997), pp. 216-218.

Chapter 11: They Fall for Other Common Fallacies

1. I compared lists from 1) the writing center at the University of North Carolina, Chapel Hill, which includes tips for spotting fallacies http://writingcenter.unc.edu/handouts/fallacies/ 2) the University of Idaho http://www.webpages.uidaho.edu/eng207-td/Logic%20and%20Analysis/most_common_logical_fallacies.htm 3) California State, Fullerton, includes nice, down home examples - http://commfaculty.fullerton.edu/rgass/fallacy3211.htm 4) from Purdue University - https://owl.english.purdue.edu/owl/resource/659/03/ 5) the University of Texas, El Paso - http://utminers.utep.edu/omwilliamson/ENGL1311/fallacies.htm 5) Carson Newman, helpful for its division by categories - http://web.cn.edu/kwheeler/fallacies_list.html 6) the University of Louisiana, Lafayette, gives documented examples - http://www.ucs.louisiana.edu/~kak7409/Fallacies.html 7) Mesa Community College - http://www.mesacc.edu/~paoih30491/ArgumentsFallaciesQ.html 8) California State - http://www.csus.edu/indiv/g/gaskilld/criticalthinking/Six%20Common%20Fallacies.htm 9) Sacramento State University 9) the University of Wisconsin, Eau Claire http://www.uwec.edu/ranowlan/logical%20fallacies.html 10) St. Lawrence University 11) the University of Oklahoma 12) North Kentucky University. It's interesting that some of these universities use contradictory definitions of various fallacies.
2. Bertrand Russell demonstrated this tendency. He seemed to relish standing against the majority opinion. A person with his disposition should strongly consider that his assessment of evidence might be skewed by this character trait. See chapter 25 for an analysis of the passions that drove Russell.
3. http://traveltips.usatoday.com/air-travel-safer-car-travel-1581.html.

Chapter 12: They Either Fail to Recognize Fallacies, or Misapply The Ones They Know

1. Aristotle was the first I'm aware of to discuss examples. Apparently, back in 350 BCE, Greek predecessors to today's trolls strolled about annoying the great philosophers, imagining that they were spouting profundities. Thus, Aristotle wrote a work about "Sophistical Refutations," which he defined as "what appear to be refutations but are really fallacies instead." While mainly writing about logical fallacies, he also spoke of assigning fallacies incorrectly. See Aristotle, *Sophistical Refutations,* written c. 350 B.C.E., translated by W. A. Pickard-Cambridge, available digitally here: http://classics.mit.edu/Aristotle/sophist_refut.1.1.html.
2. Aristotle describes this issue: "By a sophistical refutation and syllogism I mean not only a syllogism or refutation which appears to be valid but is not, but also one which, *though it is valid, only appears to be appropriate to the thing in question.*" (Italics mine, Part Eight, *Sophistical Refutations.*)
3. Benjamin Franklin, *The Autobiography of Benjamin Franklin* (New York: Dover Publications, 1996), p. 13.
4. Tetlock, in his respected work, *Expert Political Judgment*, suggests that those who use more temperate language tend to be more accurate in their predictions. He brings together a wealth of research showing that the foxes (who know many little things) predict better than the hedgehogs (who know one niche area in depth), although the latter are typically considered the experts and practically everyone (e.g., news sources) wants to hear from them. Those who speak in terms of "perhaps," and "possibly" are far better predictors than the dogmatic, assured experts. Philip E. Tetlock, *Expert Political Judgment* (Princeton, New Jersey: Princeton University Press, 2005, 2006).
5. Many such schemes of categorization have been proposed through the centuries. For example, John Stewart Mill proposed five general categories: Fallacies of Simple Inspection (or *A Priori* Fallacies), of Observation, of Generalization, of Ratiocination, of Confusion. *A System Of Logic, Ratiocinative And Inductive* (New York: Harper & Brothers, Publishers, 1882, available digitally

at Project Gutenberg). According to Mackie, "Of other classifications of fallacies in general the most famous are those of Francis Bacon and J.S. Mill." See "Fallacies" in *The Encyclopedia of Philosophy* (Vol. 3), pp. 169-179.

6. *Encyclopaedia Brittanica*, 1910 edition, see the article entitled *Fallacy*.

7. From his article "Fallacies," op. cit.

8. David Hackett Fischer, *Historians' Fallacies* (New York: Harper & Row, 1970).

Chapter 13: They Draw Conclusions from Inadequate Evidence

1. Leonard L. Berry, Kent D. Seltman, *Management Lessons from Mayo Clinic* (New York: McGraw Hill, 2008), p. 16.
2. I don't want to point to my sources for this article, since it might falsely incriminate the innocent. At present we don't know all the facts about this case (which is my point in recounting this story), so I don't want to influence people's opinions.
3. A good starting place for studying Black Swans would be here: http://en.wikipedia.org/wiki/Black_swan_theory.
4. http://www.sfgate.com/art/article/Tom-Griscom-The-10-000-hour-rule-3564307.php. Read this article in *Wired*: http://www.wired.com/2013/05/so-you-know-that-10000-hours-makes-an-expert-rule-bunk/.
5. Malcolm Gladwell, *Outliers* (New York: Little, Brown & Company, 2007), pp. 35-37, 41-47.
6. Ibid., p. 47.
7. Ibid., pp. 37-40.
8. Ibid., pp. 39,40.
9. Ibid., pp. 38, 41.
10. Ibid., p. 40, quoting Daniel J. Levitin, *This Is Your Brain on Music: The Science of a Human Obsession* (New York: Dutton, 2006), p. 197.
11. Ibid., p. 41.
12. Ibid., p. 38.
13. Ibid., p. 41.
14. Another potential differentiator would be their love for playing their instruments. If some love it more than others, they understandably practice more and probably get more out of their practice, since they're so fascinated with their instrument and into their music. Some simply lose interest over time. So we can't assume that if we take those who've lost interest and force them to practice as much as the obsessed ones that they'd get just as much out of their practices and would be able to progress at the rate of those with more raw talent.
15. http://www.hfm-berlin.de/en/studies/courses-offered/junior-scholars.
16. Philip Norman, *Shout! The Beatles in Their Generation* (New York: Touchstone, 2005), pp. 157,159. Consider also the successful Barcelona soccer team, which practices much less than others would assume. http://thetalentcode.com/2013/06/07/forget-10000-hours-instead-aim-for-10-minutes/
17. Joshua Foer, *Moonwalking with Einstein* (New York: The Penguin Group, 2011), p. 13.
18. Two good books on strengths are Marcus Buckingham and Curt Coffman, *First, Break All the Rules* (New York: Simon & Schuster, 1999) and Marcus Buckingham and Donald Clifton, *Next, Discover Your Strengths* (New York: The Free Press, 2001).
19. For example, see Temple Grandin and Richard Panek, *The Autistic Brain: Thinking Across the Spectrum* (New York: Houghton Mifflin Harcourt, 2013); Mel Levine, *All Kinds of Minds* (Educators Publishing Service, 1992); Daniel Tammet, *Born on a Blue Day* (New York: Free Press, 2006).
20. See *Moonwalking with Einstein*, opt cit. See also https://www.youtube.com/watch?v=gWI4liX4PNw.

Chapter 14: They're Snowed by Success Bias

1. Wikipedia on the California Gold Rush.
2. http://www.statisticbrain.com/startup-failure-by-industry/.
3. "Are there any losers?" Self-help speakers typically make a point and then give examples of people who've applied this point with profit. [See Gary Collins, *Helping People Grow* (Santa Anna, California: Vision House, pp. 268,276).] Yet, success stories could be given to back up any number of competing theories.
4. Richard Cole and Richard Trubo, *Stairway to Heaven* (New York: Pocket Books, 2004), p. 40.
5. Temple Grandin and Richard Panek, *The Autistic Brain: Thinking Across the Spectrum* (New York: Houghton Mifflin Harcourt, 2013).
6. Malcolm Gladwell, *Outliers* (New York: Little, Brown & Company, 2007), pp. 55-68.
7. For example, see Sam Walton with John Huey, *Sam Walton: Made in America* (New York: Doubleday, 1992) and *From Lucky to Smart: Leadership Lessons from QuikTrip* (Mullerhaus Publishing Group, 2008).
8. http://www.chrisbrogan.com/how-much-time-should-i-spend-on-social-media.
9. http://gigaom.com/collaboration/how-much-time-does-social-media-marketing-take.
10. http://www.millerfinchmedia.com/2012/02/the-time-it-takes-to-do-social-media-not-10-mins-a-day.
11. http://beth.typepad.com/beths_blog/2008/10/how-much-time-d.html.
12. See J. Steve Miller and Cherie K. Miller, *Sell More Books (Acworth, GA: Wisdom Creek Press, 2011)* and J. Steve Miller,

Social Media Frenzy (Acworth, GA: Wisdom Creek Press, 2013).

Chapter 15: They "Discover" Meaningless Patterns

1. Joseph Bulgatz, *Ponzi Schemes, Invaders from Mars and More Extraordinary Popular Delusions and the Madness of Crowds* (New York: Harmony Books, 1992), p. 87.
2. Ibid., p. 91.
3. From the Bureau of Labor http://www.bls.gov/ooh/construction-and-extraction/carpenters.htm.
4. Bulgatz, op. cit., p. 100.
5. Ibid., pp.79,80.
6. Ibid., p. 108.
7. Ibid., p. 109.
8. Ibid., p. 108.
9. Wikipedia has a good article on economic bubbles. Note especially the psychology of bubbles and examples: http://en.wikipedia.org/wiki/Economic_bubbles.
10. Eric Goldschein, "The Complete History of U.S. Real Estate Bubbles Since 1800," *Business Insider* (June 10, 2012). http://www.businessinsider.com/the-economic-crash-repeated-every-generation-1800-2012-1?op=1
11. Jason Zweig, *Your Money and Your Brain,* early promo copy (New York: Simon & Schuster, 2010), p. 6.
12. Ibid., p. 6.
13. Ibid., pp. 44-45.
14. Zweig, op. cit., pp. 90,91.
15. L.J. Davis, "Buffett Takes Stock," *The New York Times Magazine*, April 1, 1990, p. 16. As cited in Janet Lowe, *Warren Buffett Speaks* (Hoboken, NJ: John Wiley & Sons, 2007), p. 97.
16. Jason Zweig, in Benjamin Graham, *The Intelligent Investor*, revised edition, with commentary by Jason Zweig (New York: HarperCollins, 2003), p. 245.
17. Bulgatz, op. cit., p. 98.
18. J. Steve Miller, *Enjoy Your Money*! (Wisdom Creek Press, 2009) pp. 46,47.
19. *Your Money and Brain*, op. cit., p. 80.
20. *The Intelligent Investor*, op. cit., p. 45.
21. Ibid., p. 45 - the "dividing the dividend by"..." technique was touted for a time by some influential investors. On chimps and investing, see p. 70.
22. See *Your Money and Your Brain*, op. cit., p. 184. Perhaps it's best to be agnostic about the future of the economy.
23. 2001 Chairman's Letter for Berkshire Hathaway.
24. Zweig, op. cit., p. 86.
25. Ibid., pp. 85-87. See the entire Chapter Five in Zweig (pp. 85ff.) on "Confidence."
26. I find part of this quote in Benjamin Graham, *The Intelligent Investor* (New York: HarperCollins, 2003 edition with commentary by Jason Zweig), p. 524. I failed to find the entire quote.
27. Walter Isaacson, *Steve Jobs* (New York: Simon & Schuster, 2011), pp. 64,65.
28. *Steve Jobs*, op. cit., p. 10. ; Stephen Manes and Paul Andrews, *Gates* (New York: Simon & Schuster, 1994), pp. 94,127,191,365,375,399,437.

Chapter 16: They Fail to Closely Examine Statistics

1. U.S. Department of Education, Science, Technology, Engineering and Math: Education for Global Leadership, http://www.ed.gov/stem.
2. Ibid.
3. "Best Jobs in America," *CNN Money* (Oct. 29, 2012), http://money.cnn.com/pf/best-jobs/2012/snapshots/. They apparently weighted their choice highly on the industry growth statistic of 61.7 percent, which they say they got from the Bureau of Labor Statistics.
4. U.S. Department of Labor, Department of Labor Statistics, Occupational Outlook Handbook, "Biomedical Engineers," http://www.bls.gov/ooh/architecture-and-engineering/biomedical-engineers.htm#tab-6. This report has downgraded the growth to 27 percent for the decade 2012 to 2022, which is a huge change, unless someone can show that from 2010 to 2011 biomed grew by a whopping 34 percent! Reports cited below certainly don't show such growth.
5. I gathered this stat by counting the US biomed related programs listed at www.gradschools.com.
6. InfoPlease, Number of U.S. Colleges and Universities and Degrees Awarded, http://www.infoplease.com/ipa/A0908742.html.
7. Department for Professional Employees, "The STEM Workforce: An Occupational Overview," Fact Sheet 2014, pdf found here http://www.google.com/url?sa=t&rct=j&q=&esrc=s&source=web&cd=2&ved=0CCYQFjAB&url=http%3A%2F%2Fdpeaflcio.org%2Fwp-content%2Fuploads%2FSTEM-Workforce-2014.pdf&ei=GAhaVfqsDIKfoQSq04HYAQ&usg=AFQjCNHQzWz6LjG7NuDQe9aARj5DUJXqdQ&sig2=HruuWRCc5GkHyDUtxFEfWw&bvm=bv.93564037,d.cGU.
8. Ibid. According to this 2014 Fact Sheet, "Although the unemployment rate for life, physical, and social science occupations is similar to other STEM occupations, in the last four years these occupations have shed 102,000 jobs and total employment has *declined* by 7.2 percent." (Italics mine.) Of course, biotech would be a subset of these occupations and would need to be

considered separately. Compare this to their statement that "Employment in professional and related occupations *increased* 3.6 percent from 2010 to 2013. (Italics mine.) They gathered their stats from here: http://nces.ed.gov/programs/digest/d13/tables/dt13_318.20.asp.
9. Interestingly, physicians and nurses aren't considered STEM careers. http://www.teachhub.com/should-stem-include-medical-field.
10. Brian Vastag, "U.S. Pushes for More Scientists, but the Jobs Aren't There," *The Washington Post*, (July 7, 2012) http://www.washingtonpost.com/national/health-science/us-pushes-for-more-scientists-but-the-jobs-arent-there/2012/07/07/gJQAZJpQUW_story.html.
11. Ibid.
12. Ibid.
13. Jocelyn Kaiser, "NIH Panel Urges Steps to Control Growth in Biomedical Research Trainees," *Science* (June 14, 2012). http://news.sciencemag.org/2012/06/nih-panel-urges-steps-control-growth-biomedical-research-trainees.
14. "U.S Pushes for More Scientists," op. cit.
15. Ibid. See also Robert N. Charette, "The Stem Crisis is a Myth," *IEEE* (Institute of Electrical and Electronics Engineers) *Spectrum* (Aug. 30, 2013). http://spectrum.ieee.org/at-work/education/the-stem-crisis-is-a-myth.
16. National Science Foundation, *Science and Engineering Indicators, 2012*, "Projected Growth of Employment in S&E Careers" (science and engineering), http://www.nsf.gov/statistics/seind12/c3/c3s.htm.
17. Ibid.
18. Bureau of Labor Statistics, U.S. Department of Labor, *Occupational Outlook Handbook, 2014-15 Edition*, Biomedical Engineers,
http://www.bls.gov/ooh/architecture-and-engineering/biomedical-engineers.htm (visited May 18, 2015). A 2014 report by the National Science Foundation now predicts that the biological sciences will grow 20 percent from 2010-2020. But it's still not referencing any data to back it up. It will be interesting to see how all this plays out over time. According to a couple of studies, "the future labor-market demand for scientific workers is infamously hard to predict." For a great pro and con debate on this, fully documented with authoritative sources, see Jeffrey R. Sharom, "The Scientific Workforce Policy Debate: Do We Produce too Many Biomedical Trainees?" *Hypothesis Journal,* Sept., 2008, Vol.6 No.1, H.H. Garrison and S.A. Gerbi, (1998). See also "Education and employment patterns of U.S. Ph.D.'s in the biomedical sciences," Faseb J 12, 139-148; J. Mervis, J. (2003); "Scientific workforce. Down for the count?" Science 300, 1070-1074; http://www.nsf.gov/nsb/sei/edTool/data/workforce-03.html; http://www.hopkinsmedicine.org/institute_basic_biomedical_sciences/news_events/articles_and_stories/employment/2012_09_Biomed_Workforce.html
19. Percentage of All Professional Workers in STEM Occupations, from the Bureau of Labor Statistics, http://dpeaflcio.org/wp-content/uploads/Percentage-of-all-Professional-Workers-in-STEM-Occupations.jpg.
20. Ron Hira, "Boom-Bust Cycles: A New Paradigm for Electrical Engineering Employment," Center for Science, Policy, and Outcomes,
Columbia University.
http://www.google.com/url?sa=t&rct=j&q=&esrc=s&source=web&cd=2&ved=0CCcQFjAB&url=http%3A%2F%2Farchive.cspo.org%2Fproducts%2Farticles%2FUnemployment.pdf&ei=gytbVeChGMfToASR_IHABw&usg=AFQjCNH2bTTfR0_glF0-n0VSCrF5zN6vIA&sig2=UBZbLr2j_XCNkSRyMi71EA&bvm=bv.93756505,d.cGU

Chapter 17: They Make Common Statistical Blunders

1. The Planned Parenthood Survey (1986) was reported in *Psychology Today*, May 1989.
2. Alan Guttmacher Institute, *Sex and America's Teenagers* (1994) p. 4.
3. In the early 1990's I pulled these statistics from the US Department of Health and Human Services, the Centers for Disease Control, and the Alan Guttmacher Institute (the latter of which is often used by the CDC).
4. Josh McDowell, *Why Wait?* (Nashville: Thomas Nelson, 1994), p. 22.
5. Research by Dr. Marion Howard, *Atlanta Journal*, Jan 18, 1996, p. G1.
6. National Science Foundation, "Science Indicators," 1974, Washington: General Accounting Office, 1976, p. 15, as quoted by Gary Smith, *Introduction to Statistical Reasoning*, pp. 52-54,615.
7. Design & Teach a Course, Carnegie Mellon, Eberly Center,
http://www.cmu.edu/teaching/designteach/design/instructionalstrategies/lectures.html.
8. Donald A. Bligh, *What's the Use of Lectures?* (San Francisco: Jossey Bass, 2000).
9. Bligh, op. cit., p. 56.
10. Ibid., p. 61.
11. D.H. Lloyd, "A Concept of Improvement of Learning Response in the Taught Lesson" (Oct., 1968), p. 24.
12. Maryellen Weimer, "A New Look at Student Attention Spans," *Faculty Focus* (Dec. 4, 2009), http://www.facultyfocus.com/articles/instructional-design/student-attention-spans/.
13. Washington University, "Are You With Me? Measuring Student Attention in the Classroom," *The Teaching Center Journal*, (May 23, 2013), http://teachingcenter.wustl.edu/Journal/Reviews/Pages/student-attention.aspx#.U6GHWChwVgk. It mostly was a minute or less, with the first spike about 30 seconds into the lecture, then at five minutes, eight minutes, etc. Basically, they waxed and waned throughout the lecture—with more attention lapses as time went on—about every two minutes by the end. When active learning was used, students were more engaged and their attention span was longer.
14. http://cfe.unc.edu/publications/fyc6.html.
15. Ibid.
16. Statistics (after the first chart) from the National Science Foundation. "How Do U.S. 15-year-olds Compare with Students from other Countries in Math and Science?" Stem Education Data (2012) http://www.nsf.gov/nsb/sei/edTool/data/highschool-08.html.
17. The NYT editorial board, Why Other Countries Teach Better: Three Reasons Students Do Better Overseas, *The New York Times* (Dec. 17, 2013), http://www.nytimes.com/2013/12/18/opinion/why-students-do-better-

overseas.html?pagewanted=all&_r=1&. The early paragraphs show America comparing poorly to other countries in much the same manner as we discussed.
18. *Introduction to Statistical Reasoning*, op. cit., p. 58.
19. This chart from Wikipedia Commons.
20. J. Mathews, "The Myth of Declining U.S. Schools," *The Washington Post* (02/11/2011), http://voices.washingtonpost.com/class-struggle/2011/02/myth_of_declining_us_schools.html.
21. Ibid.
22. Ibid.

Chapter 18: They Fail to Learn from History

1. Georg Wilhelm Friedrich Hegel, John Sibree, translator, *Introduction to the Philosophy of History* (first published in 1837, now the text is under common domain), Introduction.
2. While philosopher Alex Rosenberg claims that we can learn nothing from history (pp. 242ff); elsewhere, in the same book, he wants to teach us from history. For example, on p. viii he writes of science having been "vindicated beyond reasonable doubt." But isn't that vindication based upon the pattern of success in the history of science? On p. 321 he pontificates from the history of ethics. On p. 315 he recommends that the depressed take Prozac; but isn't that recommendation based upon the medical histories of those who've taken Prozac? *The Atheists' Guide to Reality* (New York: W. W. Norton & Company, 2012).
3. Rousseau fathered four children by Therese, all of whom he abandoned at birth, giving them to an overcrowded hospital, where they in all likelihood either died or became beggars. Paul Johnson, *Intellectuals* (New York: Harper & Row), pp. 21,22.
4. Ibid., 212-219.
5. Ibid., 115-121.
6. Science Museum, Brought to Life: Exploring the History of Medicine, "Keeping It Zipped: Controlling Sexually Transmitted Infections," http://www.sciencemuseum.org.uk/broughttolife/themes/publichealth/sti.aspx.
7. Beezy Marsh, "Syphilis, The Scourge of Kings and Dictators of Old, Is Surging Back," *Daily Mail,* Dec. 5, 2009, http://www.dailymail.co.uk/news/article-1233310/Syphilis-scourge-kings-dictators-old-surging-back.html.
8. From a 2007 personal discussion with accountant and money counselor Larry Winter. He uses an analogy to warn clients about risky ventures and investments. To start a fire, you need three ingredients: air, fuel and something to ignite the fuel. In the same way three things lead to disaster in investing: 1) Do it in a hurry, 2) in an area you know nothing about, 3) with borrowed money.
9. For example, they had no experience running electricity businesses, technology businesses, or water utilities. Over time, this took its toll.
10. For example, see this fact check of the film "Lincoln" on Harvard Press's blog: http://harvardpress.typepad.com/hup_publicity/2012/11/historians-respond-to-spielbergs-lincoln.html.
11. Buffett is perfectly content to spend his days pouring over the financial reports of companies that he either owns or might acquire.
12. See Madeleine L'Engle and Carole F. Chase, *Madeleine L'Engle Herself: Reflections on a Writing Life* (Shaw Books, 2001).
13. Fannie Flagg, who wrote the novel *Fried Green Tomatoes*, once said, "I'm dyslexic. I write the end, then middle, then some of the beginning. I write scenes, then hang them on a clothesline down my great-big, long hallway. It just helps me to see the story visually in sequence. The hardest part is putting it all together at the end. It's like piecing together a quilt. And if I drop it, I have a totally different book. (Found in Cherie K. Miller, *Writing Conversations* (Wisdom Creek Press, 2010), p. 28.
14. Peter Han, *Nobodies to Somebodies* (New York: Penguin Group, 2005), pp. 64-66. A part of the reason they moved on from their first jobs was for professional growth—to keep learning new things and to be stretched.
15. At Enron, leaders such as Jeff Skilling and Rebecca Mark "believed that talent outweighed experience, and in Enron's world, talent meant thirty-somethings with MBAs from all the best business schools. What did it matter that they didn't know a thing about water. They were smart; they would figure it out." Bethany McLean and Peter Elkind, *The Smartest Guys in the Room* (New York: Penguin Group), p. 251. Skilling was so ignorant of the computer industry that he couldn't even send and receive email or turn on his computer, but he thought he could make a killing off broadband. Enron leaders made fun of businesses that concentrated on the day-to-day task of running a business. Thus, they purchased businesses with little concern with how they'd be running them ten years down the road. (pp. 120,182-184,186)
16. http://en.wikipedia.org/wiki/A_Whiter_Shade_of_Pale.

Chapter 19: They Learn the Wrong Lessons from History

1. The name of the artist, on the cartoon, appears to be "Torn" or "Jorn".
2. Charles W. McCoy, Jr., *Why Didn't I Think of That?* (Paramus, New Jersey: Prentice Hall Press, 2002), p. 3.
3. http://en.wikipedia.org/wiki/Gettysburg_Address, see also http://www.abrahamlincolnonline.org/lincoln/speeches/gettysburg.htm.
4. Carl E. Olson and Sandra Miesel, *The Da Vinci Hoax* (San Francisco: Ignatius Press, 2004), p. 242.
5. From Amazon.com.
6. Olson and Miesel, op. cit., p. 21, quoting from Brown's site.
7. I checked his site more recently, and someone seems to have taken the sources down.
8. Olson and Miesel (pp. 223-239) provide a good critique of Brown's primary sources, such as *Holy Blood, Holy Grail*, *The Templar Revelation*, and *The Messianic Legacy.* After in depth research of Brown's historical claims in *The Da Vinci Code*, Olson and Miesel conclude that "Brown's vaunted research largely involved reading Picknett and Prince's book." (p. 263)

9. Michael White, *Leonardo: The First Scientist* (New York: St. Martin's Press, 2000).
10. As he's referred to in popular writing, I'll call him "Da Vinci," although technically that's not his last name, but a reference to where he was from. He should be properly referred to as Leonardo.
11. Dan Brown, *The Da Vinci Code* (New York: Anchor Books, 2003), p. 50. *The Da Vinci Hoax*, op. cit., p. 243.
12. Bruce Boucher, "Does *The Da Vinci Code* Crack Leonardo?," *New York Times*, Aug. 3, 2003.
13. I'm speaking here of *The Da Vinci Hoax*, op. cit.
14. http://en.wikipedia.org/wiki/Black_Death#Origins_of_the_disease.
15. Sewell Chan, "Financial Crisis Was Avoidable, Inquiry Finds," *The New York Times* (Jan. 25, 2011), http://www.nytimes.com/2011/01/26/business/economy/26inquiry.html.
16. James Pethokoukis, "Again, Which Bush Policies Caused the Great Recession? And Which of Obama's Ended It?" American Enterprise Institute, at aei.org, Sept. 4, 2012.
17. "Obama's Claim That The Bush Tax Cuts Led to The Economic Crisis," Fact Checker, *The Washington Post*, Sept. 30, 2012, http://www.washingtonpost.com/blogs/fact-checker/post/obamas-claim-that-the-bush-tax-cuts-led-to-the-economic-crisis/2012/09/30/06e8f578-0a6e-11e2-afff-d6c7f20a83bf_blog.html.
18. http://en.wikipedia.org/wiki/The_great_recession#Panel_reports.
19. Jacob Weisberg, "What Caused the Crash? Let the Bickering Begin," *Newsweek*, 1/8/10, http://www.newsweek.com/what-caused-crash-let-bickering-begin-70921.
20. From a paper by economist James Hamilton. Keith Johnson, "Oil Shock: Did High Oil Prices Cause the Recession?" *Wall Street Journal*, April 22, 2009, WSJ Blogs, http://blogs.wsj.com/environmentalcapital/2009/04/22/oil-shock-did-high-oil-prices-cause-the-recession/.
21. Amir Sufi, Chicago Board of Trade Professor of Finance, University of Chicago Booth School of Business, http://www.thechicagocouncil.org/files/Event/FY14_Events/05_May/House_of_Debt.aspx.
22. Richard M. Salsman, "How Bernanke's Fed Triggered the Great Recession," *Forbes*, 7/17/2011, http://www.forbes.com/sites/richardsalsman/2011/07/17/how-bernankes-fed-triggered-the-great-recession/.
23. Ibid.
24. "What Caused the Crash?" op. cit.
25. Sewell Chan, "Financial Crisis Was Avoidable, Inquiry Finds," *The New York Times*, Jan. 25, 2011, http://www.nytimes.com/2011/01/26/business/economy/26inquiry.html.
26. Ibid.
27. Ibid. See also Ryan Chittum, "Bill Clinton on Deregulation: 'The Republicans Made Me Do It!': The Ex-President Seriously Mischaracterizes His Record", Oct. 1, 2013, *Columbia Journalism Review* - http://www.cjr.org/the_audit/bill_clinton_the_republicans_m.php?page=all.
28. Note Warren Buffett's 2008 Letter to Shareholders of Birkshire Hathaway: "These parties looked at loss experience over periods when home prices rose only moderately and speculation in houses was negligible. They then made this experience a yardstick for evaluating future losses. They blissfully ignored the fact that house prices had recently skyrocketed, loan practices had deteriorated, and many buyers had opted for houses they couldn't afford. In short, universe "past" and universe "current" had very different characteristics. But lenders, government and media largely failed to recognize this all-important fact. Investors should be skeptical of history-based models. Constructed by a nerdy-sounding priesthood using esoteric terms such as beta, gamma, sigma and the like, these models tend to look impressive. Too often, though, investors forget to examine the assumptions behind the symbols. Our advice: Beware of geeks bearing formulas."

http://www.google.com/url?sa=t&rct=j&q=&esrc=s&source=web&cd=2&ved=0CC0QFjAB&url=http%3A%2F%2Fwww.berkshirehathaway.com%2Fletters%2F2008ltr.pdf&ei=vWTmU8ujBeed8gH9_oGwBw&usg=AFQjCNGqn0pEA357hTUi2N3KQ9H8kdJJSQ&sig2=9Otxci58e0je9oGYqp83kQ&bvm=bv.72676100,d.b2U.

"Three hundred million Americans, their lending institutions, their government, their media, all believed that house prices were going to go up consistently," he said. (Quoting Buffett) "Lending was done based on it, and everybody did a lot of foolish things." Steve Lohr, "Like J.P. Morgan, Warren E. Buffett Braves a Crisis," *The New York Times*, Oct. 5, 2008, http://www.nytimes.com/2008/10/06/business/06buffett.html?%3Cem%3Er=0
29. According to the commission, "We conclude over-the-counter derivatives contributed significantly to this crisis. The enactment of legislation in 2000 to ban the regulation by both the federal and state governments of over-the-counter (OTC) derivatives was a key turning point in the march toward the financial crisis." (http://fcic.law.stanford.edu/report/conclusions) While then President Bill Clinton claims the Republican majority in Congress made him do it, the historical data, as summarized in this *Columbia Journalism Review* article, don't seem to support his contention: "Bill Clinton on Deregulation," op.cit.
31. "What Caused the Crash?" op. cit.
32. Will and Ariel Durant, *The Lessons of History* (New York: Simon & Schuster, 1968), p. 97.
33. W.O. Henderson and W.H. Challoner checked the sources for Engle's *Condition of the Working Class in England* (Oxford, 1958). Two Cambridge scholars wrote a paper, "Comments on the use and the Blue Books by Karl Marx in Chapter XV of Le Capital" (1885). Besides cherry picking, Marx and Engles often improperly used their quoted material, putting capitalism in the worst possible light. See discussion in *Intellectuals*, op. cit., pp. 62ff.
34. According to Paul Johnson, "Virtually all Marx's facts, selectively deployed (and sometimes falsified) as they were, came from

the efforts of the State (inspectors, courts, Justices of the Peace) to improve conditions, which necessarily involved exposing and punishing those responsible...." *Intellectuals*, op. cit., pp. 68,69.
35. Allan Bloom, *The Closing of the American Mind* (New York: Simon & Schuster, 1987). On our tendency to allow the current intellectual trends to shape their views, it's interesting to read the intellectual journey of a modern philosopher who decided that today's philosophers tend to take for granted that earlier views (such as Aquinas) have been demolished, without giving the historic arguments a serious look. http://edwardfeser.blogspot.com/2012/07/road-from-atheism.html.
36. Thomas L. Friedman, "Justice Goes Global," *The New York Times*, June 14, 2011.
37. Jason Zweig, *Your Money and Your Brain,* early promo copy (New York: Simon & Schuster, 2010), pp 72,73.
38. Proverbs 22:7.
39. Paul Johnson traces four aspects of Marx's personal history that impacted his writings: "his taste for violence, his appetite for power, his inability to handle money and, above all, his tendency to exploit those around him." *Intellectuals*, op. cit., pp. 69-81.
40. Bethany McLean and Peter Elkind, *The Smartest Guys in the Room* (New York: Penguin Group, 2004).
41. Richard L. Brandt, *The Google Guys* (New York: The Penguin Group, 2009, 2011), p. 113ff.

Chapter 20: They Miss Subtle Shifts in Word Meanings

1. *Einstein: His Life and Universe*, by Walter Isaacson (New York: Simon & Schuster, 2007) p. 8.
2. Ibid.
3. Ibid. In German, they called him "der Depperte."
4. Ibid., pp. 7,16.
5. Ibid., pp. 9,23.
6. Ibid., p. 34.
7. Ibid., p. 39.
8. Ibid., p. 9.
9. Ibid., pp. 438,439. Once a secretary at Princeton received a call from someone asking for Einstein's home address. When she replied that she couldn't give it out, the caller whispered, "Please don't tell anybody, but I *am* Dr. Einstein, I'm on my way home, and I've forgotten where my house is."
10. Ibid., p. 325. Einstein and quantum physicist Niels Bohr were travelling from the train station in Copenhagen by streetcar. Engrossed in conversation, they "rode to and fro," according to Bohr, "and I can well imagine what the people thought about us."
11. Ibid., p. 227.
12. Ibid., p. 438.
13. Ibid., p. 540.
14. Ibid., p. 16.
15. Ibid., p. 20.
16. Ibid., p. 14.
17. *Time Magazine*, Dec. 31, 1999, see cover story.
18. Joseph McBride, *Steven Spielberg* (New York: Simon & Schuster, 1997), p. 98.
19. Sam Walton with John Huey, *Sam Walton: Made in America* (New York: Doubleday, 1992) pp. 17,18. Walton would "screw up the sales slips and generally mishandle the cash register part of things." One man who evaluated personnel for J. C. Penney told Walton, "I'd fire you if you weren't such a good salesman. Maybe you're just not cut out for retail." (p. 18)
20. Ibid., p. 116. According to Walton, "...if you asked me am I an organized person, I would have to say flat out no, not at all." "My style is pretty haphazard."
21. Paul Orphalea, *Copy This!* (New York: Workman Publishing, 2007).
22. C.S. Lewis, *Surprised by Joy* (New York: A Harvest Book, 1955), pp. 12,137,186,187.
23. Mel Levine, *A Mind at a Time* (New York: Simon & Schuster, 2002, p. 25.
24. Michael White, *Leonardo: The First Scientist* (New York: St. Martin's Press, 2000), pp. 160,161, 326.
25. Ibid., pp. 91,152,153.
26. Personal interview with Gupta, 2014.
27. Daniel Tammett, *Born on a Blue Day* (New York: Free Press, 2006), pp. 4,5.
28. Strength advocates such as Marcus Buckingham point to research on over two million people in the workplace by the Gallup organization, showing that people in the workplace are often miscast in their roles. Rather than concentrating on strengthening our weaknesses (which most schools emphasize), strengths advocates argue that our greatest potential improvement is in our areas of strength. See Marcus Buckingham and Curt Coffman, *First, Break All the Rules: What the World's Greatest Managers Do Differently* (New York: Simon & Schuster, 1999).
29. *Leonardo*, op. cit., pp. 28,29,55-70. Leonardo probably began this apprenticeship experience at age twelve or thirteen.
30. Spielberg applied to two prestigious film schools, but was rejected because of his "mediocre academic record." McBride, op. cit., p. 131.
31. Temple Grandin and Richard Panek, *The Autistic Brain: Thinking Across the Spectrum* (New York: Houghton Mifflin Harcourt, 2013).
32. Daniel Goleman, *Emotional Intelligence* (New York: Bantam Books), p. 40. To expand upon Gardner's thesis, see Howard

Gardner, *Frames of Mind: The Theory of Multiple Intelligences* (New York: Harper/Collins, 1985).
33. Bethany McLean and Peter Elkind, *The Smartest Guys in the Room* (New York: Penguin Group), pp 120ff. Note how this impacted Skilling's hiring for Enron. Rather than hire people with experience in the field (such as natural gas or electricity), he hired people who were outstanding students in an academic context, assuming that if they're "smart," they can learn anything (managerial skills, judgment, etc.). Skilling considered himself, in his own words, "f...ing smart," but seemed clueless about his lack of judgment in many matters. For example, businesses can't consistently grow by merely trading. Surely this was part of what led to Enron's downfall. Compare Skilling at Enron to Jack Welch at G.E. At first, Welch loved hiring PhDs, but later realized that some of them couldn't execute business plans.
34. Here's a good place to begin a study of criticisms of IQ tests:
http://en.wikipedia.org/wiki/Intelligence_quotient#Criticism_and_views.
35. Liberal Education is an approach to learning that empowers individuals and prepares them to deal with complexity, diversity, and change. It provides students with broad knowledge of the wider world (e.g. science, culture, and society) as well as in-depth study in a specific area of interest. A liberal education helps students develop a sense of social responsibility, as well as strong and transferable intellectual and practical skills such as communication, analytical and problem-solving skills, and a demonstrated ability to apply knowledge and skills in real-world settings.
http://www.aacu.org/leap/what_is_liberal_education.cfm.
36. Let's take the etymology of the English word *nice*. It comes from the Latin word *nescius*, which meant 'ignorant.' Obviously, the word has significantly shifted meaning over time and the one who appeals to its history to understand its current usage will likely find himself far off course. Yet, I often hear preachers and writers appealing to the etymology of biblical words to derive questionable meanings. See Moises Silva, *Biblical Words & Their Meaning: An Introduction to Lexical Semantics* (Grand Rapids: Zondervan, 1983), p. 38. Note also Silva's entire chapter devoted to etymology (pp. 35-52). See also D. A. Carson, *Exegetical Fallacies* (Grand Rapids: Baker Academic, 1996), pp. 27ff. Even standard reference works can suffer from overdependence upon, or misuse of etymology, a criticism James Barr brought against the most exhaustive lexicon of New Testament words, the *Theological Dictionary of the New Testament*. Surely de Moor's statement concerning Ugaritic lexicography could be applied more broadly to other languages: "An explanation which rests on the sole basis of etymology can never be anything more than a plausible hypothesis." (From de Moor's "Ugaritic Lexicography," p. 85, as quoted by Silva, op. cit., p. 44.)
37. http://community.cartalk.com/discussion/805209/what-should-a-mechanic-charge-for-auto-parts.
38. Kevin Nelson, *The Spiritual Doorway in the Brain* (New York: Penguin Group, 2011) p. 132.
39. See Dudley Shapere, University of Chicago, *Philosophical Review*, vol. 73, 1964, p. 383ff. "The term 'paradigm' thus covers a range of factors in scientific development including or somehow involving laws and theories, models, standards, and methods (both theoretical and instrumental), vague intuitions, explicit or implicit metaphysical beliefs (or prejudices). In short, anything that allows science to accomplish anything can be a part of (or somehow involved in) a paradigm. ... At the very outset, the explanatory value of the notion of a paradigm is suspect: for the truth of the thesis that shared paradigms are (or are behind) the common factors guiding scientific research appears to be guaranteed, not so much by a close examination of actual historical cases, however scholarly, as by the breadth of definition of the term 'paradigm.'" (p. 385)
40. For Jobs' romancing of Sculley for Apple, see Walter Isaacson, *Steve Jobs* (New York: Simon & Schuster, 2011), pp. 148-154. When Jobs showed Sculley the first Macintosh computer, Scully noted that "He seemed more a showman than a businessman. Every move seemed calculated, as if it was rehearsed, to create an occasion of the moment." (p. 152)
41. On the toil Churchill put into his speeches, see http://www.winstonchurchill.org/resources/in-the-media/churchill-in-the-news/sweat-and-tears-made-winston-churchills-name.
42. Denise Shekerjian, *Uncommon Genius* (New York: Penguin Books), pp. 6,7.
43. *Einstein*, op. cit., p. 14.
44. At least 11 screenwriters contributed to *The Wizard of Oz*. Research many of your favorite movies and you'll likely discover that several writers contributed.
45. Dale Pollock, *Skywalking: The Life and Films of George Lucas* (Harmony Books, 1983), p. 141.

Chapter 21: They Misinterpret Phrases and Sentences.

1. Roland Bainton, *Here I Stand: A Life of Martin Luther* (Nashville: Abingdon Press, 1950), pp 15,25.
2. Ibid., pp. 39-50.
3. According to Luther, "I hated that word, 'justice of God,' which, by the use and custom of all my teachers, I had been taught to understand philosophically as referring to formal or active justice, as they call it, i.e., that justice by which God is just and by which he punishes sinners and the unjust.... I couldn't be sure that God was appeased by my satisfaction. I did not love, no, rather I hated the just God who punishes sinners." But when he deliberated on the context of this phrase, he "began to understand that this verse means that the justice of God...is a passive justice, i.e. that by which the merciful God justifies us by faith." ["Justice" is an alternative translation for "righteousness."] Dr. Martin Luther, *Preface to the Complete Edition of Luther's Latin Works* (1545), translated by Andrew Thornton from the "Vorrede zu Band I der Opera Latina der Wittenberger Ausgabe. 1545" in vol. 4 of *Luthers Werke in Auswahl*, ed. by Otto Clemen, 6th ed., (Berlin: de Gruyter. 1967), pp. 421-428.

Chapter 22: They Use Faulty Parallels and Analogies

1. "US in a 'real state of crisis,' education secretary says," *NBC News*, World News, Wed., Oct. 22, 2014, http://www.nbcnews.com/news/other/us-real-state-crisis-education-secretary-says-f8C11354527.
2. Later in this chapter, note that I ask, why compare to only 12 other countries? Why these 12? It looks suspiciously like they were cherry-picked, comparing ourselves to largely homogeneous cultures we knew were at the top on testing. Of course, we came out below them. Studies like this appear to be designed to show the United States at the bottom of lists on charts; but at least the article does note that socio-economic factors are a much greater issue in American culture than the other cultures. The Editorial Board, "Why Other Countries Teach Better: Three Reasons Students Do Better Overseas," Dec. 17, 2013, *The New York Times*, http://www.nytimes.com/2013/12/18/opinion/why-students-do-better-overseas.html?pagewanted=all&_r=1&.
3. If they've changed the subtitle by the time you view it, I've saved a screen shot on the accompanying website. http://www.nytimes.com/2013/12/18/opinion/why-students-do-better-overseas.html?pagewanted=all&_r=0.
4. Anu Partanen, "What Americans Keep Ignoring about Finland's School Success," *The Atlantic*, Dec. 29, 2011, http://www.theatlantic.com/national/archive/2011/12/what-americans-keep-ignoring-about-finlands-school-success/250564/. This also impacts comparisons with Shanghai, an extremely wealthy region, which doesn't even offer education to their 9 million migrant workers. Jill Barshay, "Shanghai Likely to Repeat Strong Results on International PISA test in December," Education by the Numbers, pub. by The Hechinger Report, posted Nov. 18, 2013, http://educationbythenumbers.org/content/shanghai-likely-repeat-strong-results-international-pisa-test-december_644/.
5. Rafael Irizarry, "Stratifying PISA scores by poverty rates suggests imitating Finland is not necessarily the way to go for US schools," Simply Statistics, Aug. 23, 2013, http://simplystatistics.org/2013/08/23/stratifying-pisa-scores-by-poverty-rates-suggests-imitating-finland-is-not-necessarily-the-way-to-go-for-us-schools/.
6. Wayne D'Orio, "Finland is #1!: Finland's education success has the rest of the world looking north for answers," Scholastic Administrator, http://www.scholastic.com/browse/article.jsp?id=3749880.http://www.smithsonianmag.com/innovation/why-are-finlands-schools-successful-49859555/#TFWTePOEAQE6Q1cl.99
7. http://www.google.com/url?sa=t&rct=j&q=&esrc=s&source=web&cd=2&ved=0CEQQFjAB&url=http%3A%2F%2F; Timothy Casey and Laurie Maldonado, "Worst Off - Single-Parent Families in the United States," Dec. 2012, Legal Momentum, www.legalmomentum.org%2Fsites%2Fdefault%2Ffiles%2Freports%2Fworst-off-single-parent.pdf&ei=rluEU_7EFpOdqAbnklHoDg&usg=AFQjCNFbWHlsUqURNi_huOVlWsai48Gmzw&sig2=6QatMcr6pWOXF7NfBOpuNQ&bvm=bv.67720277,d.b2k&cad=rjaSingle parent families.
8. Rafael Irizarry, op. cit.

on/why-are-finlands-schools-

mmends that we need to ensure that

ountries.

527.

nericans for the 21st Century,

-successful-

tion/why-are-finlands-schools-

ol students must take one of the most rigorous required curriculums in the world, including physics, chemistry, biology, philosophy, music and at least two foreign languages." It gives the impression of a monolithic, specific curriculum that all have to master. But read this wonderful document. It's not the type of "rigor" that we're used to seeing. It's low on the specifics that Americans are used to (example: asking students to memorize all the terms and methods to understand plate tectonics) and big on helping students find their areas of strengths and assess their own progress rather than taking standardized tests over content. National Core Curriculum for Upper Secondary Schools, 2003, Finnish National Board of Education, http://www.oph.fi/download/47678_core_curricula_upper_secondary_education.pdf. Could this be one of the reasons that so many more Finns graduate than Americans (93%, over 17% more than Americans) In my county, some schools dropped the tech

track, in order to try to give every student a precollege education. Many drop out because of lack of ability or motivation to take many of the academic courses.) "Why are Finland's Schools Successful?", op. cit.
23. Ibid.
24. Ibid.
25. Ibid.
26. Ibid., Comparatively, half of US teachers quit after the first five years, according to the NEA. Lisa Lambert, "Half of Teachers Quit in 5 Years," *The Washington Post*, May 9, 2006, http://www.washingtonpost.com/wp-dyn/content/article/2006/05/08/AR2006050801344.html.
27. "Finland is #1!", op. cit. "Tom Loveless, a senior fellow at the Brookings Institute, asserted that it has 'systems in place to make sure that students who may perform poorly are not allowed into public schools.'" John Fensterwald, "U.S. Scores Stagnant, Other Nations Pass Us by in Latest International Test," EdSource, Dec. 3, 2013, http://edsource.org/2013/u-s-scores-stagnant-other-nations-pass-by-in-latest-international-comparison/52052#.U4CAKSimXsE. So comparing our elite prep schools to Shanghai might be a better comparison.
28. This is a very astute article, attempting to examine the nuances of such international comparisons: Martin Carnoy and Richard Rothstein, "What Do International Tests Really Show about U.S. Student Performance?", Economic Policy Institute, Jan. 28, 2013, http://www.epi.org/publication/us-student-performance-testing/.
29. Iga M., "Suicide of Japanese Youth," *Suicide Life Threat Behav.*, 1981 Spring; 11 (1): 17-30, http://www.ncbi.nlm.nih.gov/pubmed/7233479.

Chapter 23: They Fail to Identify and Interpret Fiction and Figurative Language

1. Genius.com, "American Pie Lyrics," http://rock.rapgenius.com/Don-mclean-american-pie-lyrics#note-519107.
2. Martin Amis, *Koba the Dread* (New York, Vintage Books, 2003), pp. 27.
3. IMDb, Ozzy Osbourne, Biography, http://www.imdb.com/name/nm0005285/bio.
4. Elizabeth F. Brown and William R. Hendee, "Adolescents and their Music," *Journal of the American Medical Association* 262:12 (22-29 Sept. 1989), 1659-1663.
5. Matthew Wilkening, "30 Years Ago: An Ozzy Osbourne Fan Commits Suicide, Leading to 'Suicide Solution' Lawsuit," Ultimate Classic Rock, Oct. 27, 2014, http://ultimateclassicrock.com/ozzy-osbourne-fan-suicide/.
6. Alan Howard, The Don McLean Story: 1970–1976. *http://www.don-mclean.com/?p=32.*
7. Cecil Adams, "What is Don McLean's Song, 'American Pie' All About?", The Straight Dope, May 15, 1993, http://www.straightdope.com/columns/read/908/what-is-don-mcleans-song-american-pie-all-about.
8. Humphrey Carpenter, *J.R.R. Tolkien: A Biography* (New York: Houghton Mifflin Company, 1977), p. 193.
9. J.R.R. Tolkien, *Lord of the Rings*, Second edition, with introduction by J.R.R. Tolkien (New York: Ballantine Books, 1954) p. xxiii.
10. Sherwood Eliot Wirt, "The Final Interview of C.S. Lewis," Assist News Service, http://www.cbn.com/special/narnia/articles/ans_lewislastinterviewa.aspx. In this, his final interview, Lewis answers the question: "Would you say that the aim of Christian writing, including your own writing, is to bring about an encounter of the reader with Jesus Christ?" Lewis responds: "That is not my language, yet it is the purpose I have in view.
11. *The Letters of C.S. Lewis*, ed. by W.H. Lewis, NY, HBJ, 1966, p. 167. This statement was confirmed by an independent study of his reviews. David C. Downing, *Planets in Peril: A Critical Study of C.S. Lewis's Ransom Trilogy* (Amherst: University of Massachusetts Press, 1992) p. 36.
12. See, for example, Proverbs 3:16.
13. ftp://rtfm.mit.edu/pub/faqs/music/american-pie.
14. Thomas C. Foster, *How to Read Literature Like a Professor* (New York: HarperCollins, 2003) p. xv.

Chapter 24: They're Overwhelmed by Their Passions

1. The teen state of brain development impacts "the urgency and intensity of emotional reactions." "Adolescents and adults seem to engage different parts of the brain to different extents during tests requiring calculation and impulse control, or in reaction to emotional content." "One interpretation of all these findings is that in teens, the parts of the brain involved in emotional responses are fully online, or even more active than in adults, while the parts of the brain involved in keeping emotional, impulsive responses in check are still reaching maturity. Such a changing balance might provide clues to a youthful appetite for novelty, and a tendency to act on impulse—without regard for risk." "The Teen Brain: Still Under Construction," National Institute of Mental Health, NIH Publication No. 11-4929, 2011, http://www.nimh.nih.gov/health/publications/the-teen-brain-still-under-construction/index.shtml.
2. The top rating of Enron's stock by Standard and Poors "continued to bless Enron's debt instruments with triple-A ratings until just months before its collapse." Loren Steffy: A Business Blog, "S&P's Trail of Failure, from Enron to America," *Houston Chronicle*, Aug. 9, 2011, http://blog.chron.com/lorensteffy/2011/08/sps-trail-of-failure-from-enron-to-america/. The other two respected credit rating agencies, "...Moody's Investors Service...and Fitch Ratings, maintained high ratings for Enron until a few days before its bankruptcy filing." "Moody's, S&P Say Enron Lied," USA Today, March 20, 2002, http://usatoday30.usatoday.com/money/energy/enron/2002-03-20-sp.htm.
3. Flynn McRoberts and Cam Simpson, "Ex-Enron Exec's Suicide Note Released," *Chicago Tribune*, April 12, 2002,

http://articles.chicagotribune.com/2002-04-12/business/0204120223_1_suicide-note-ex-enron-baxter.
4. Bethany McLean and Peter Elkind, *The Smartest Guys in the Room* (New York: Penguin Group), p. 31.
5. C. William Thomas, *Today's CPA*, March/April 2002.
http://www.journalofaccountancy.com/Issues/2002/Apr/TheRiseAndFallOfEnron.htm.
6. As quoted in *The Smartest Guys in the Room*, op. cit., p. 350.
7. Ibid.
8. Ibid., p. 365.
9. For example, see how Fastow doctored his resume by claiming personal credit for other's accomplishments.
10. Skilling's favorite book was Richard Dawkins' *The Selfish Gene*, which he interpreted to justify selfish, ruthless behavior in getting ahead. Richard Conniff, "Animal Instincts," *The Guardian*, May 26, 2006, http://www.theguardian.com/money/2006/may/27/careers.work5. Sure, Enron's leaders were the smartest guys in the room ("smart" in the sense of educational credentials and ability to influence and persuade). But ruled by egotistic passion for money and power, they made a plethora of unwise business decisions. At one point, they turned off the power to one of the regions of California that they serviced, in order to fake a shortage. And they thought they could get away with that? Really?
11. *The Smartest Guys in the Room*, op. cit., p. 376.
12. In Psychology, "Dialectical Behavior Therapy" and "Wise Mind" approaches seek to help us control our emotions in order to make wiser decisions. They recommend distinguishing the "reasonable mind" from the "emotional mind" and blending them to achieve a "wise mind."
13. *The Smartest Guys in the Room*, op. cit., p. 317. Enron leaders got rid of Bass at Arthur Anderson, because he wouldn't go along with their "creative" accounting. Enron consistently got rid of naysayers and surrounded themselves with "yes men." Again, they ignore contrary counsel (p. 363). See lots of examples from earlier in their history as well; for example, how they had a large group dedicated to risk control, but controlled the group so that it couldn't stop anything.
14. For his story, read Joe Gibbs, *Racing to Win* (Colorado Springs: Multnomah Books, 2003).
15. The college president was Robertson McQuilkin at Columbia International University.
16. Margaret Heffernan, "Lessons of Enron, 10 Years On," CBS Money Watch, Dec. 2, 2011, http://www.cbsnews.com/news/lessons-of-enron-10-years-on/.
17. Ibid.
18. "Studies of children and adolescents have found that sleep deprivation can increase impulsive behavior; some researchers report finding that it is a factor in delinquency. Adequate sleep is central to physical and emotional health." "The Teen Brain," op. cit.
19. *The Smartest Guys in the Room, op. cit.,* p. 330.
20. "In 2003, Fastow was a prominent figure in *24 Days: How Two Wall Street Journal Reporters Uncovered the Lies that Destroyed Faith in Corporate America.* It was created by the reporters who had broken some of the key stories in the saga, Rebecca Smith and John R. Emshwiller. They described Fastow as "a screamer, who negotiated by intimidation and tirade". http://en.wikipedia.org/wiki/Andrew_Fastow.

"Despite their independence and the variance in their techniques, nearly every sell-side analyst reached the same conclusions about Enron in 2001, right up to the brink of its bankruptcy on Dec. 2. As of Oct. 18, all 15 analysts tracked by Thomson Financial/First Call rated Enron a "buy"–12 of the 15 called it a "strong buy."" Dan Ackman, "Enron Analysts: We Was Duped," *Forbes*, Feb. 27, 2002, http://www.forbes.com/2002/02/27/0227analysts.html. "When financial instruments, or the organizations that create them, become too complex for democratic institutions to understand, they successfully evade oversight. A good rule of thumb should be that opacity is a warning sign, not a badge of honor." "Lessons of Enron," op. cit.
21. Frank A. Wolak, Making Sense of the Enron Nonsense, Policy Brief, Stanford Institute for Economic Policy Research, May, 2002,
http://www.google.com/url?sa=t&rct=j&q=&esrc=s&source=web&cd=7&ved=0CG0QFjAG&url=http%3A%2F%2Fwww.stanford.edu%2Fgroup%2Fsiepr%2Fcgi-bin%2Fsiepr%2F%3Fq%3Dsystem%2Ffiles%2Fshared%2Fpubs%2Fpapers%2Fbriefs%2Fpolicybrief_may02.pdf&ei=ogSjU7XKE8-BqgaAroDwAg&usg=AFQjCNEjUYEYdCDjlBk875IMkasdJXq3nw&sig2=GyQ0CiXGDBVKdLfr-rTi6w&bvm=bv.69411363,d.b2k.
22. Benjamin Graham, *The Intelligent Investor*, revised edition, with commentary by Jason Zweig (New York: HarperCollins, 2003), p. 524.
23. "The Teen Brain," op. cit.
24. Some early quantum physicists used to say that if you wanted to discover something revolutionary in their field, do it before you're 30, since most of them made their great discoveries at an early age. Today some argue that while this was true when quantum physics was first breaking on the scene, today the average age may be around age 45. They theorize that quantum physics was such a sharp break from Newtonian physics, that young scientists had an advantage by not being immersed in the old paradigm. Charles Q. Choi, "The Stroke of Genius Strikes Later in Modern Life," *Live Science*, Nov. 7, 2011.
25. Changes in seating structure can make a huge difference in the flow of ideas. At Pixar, the leadership changed from a large rectangular table to a round table, in order to encourage more people to share in their "brain trust" meetings. Also, they wouldn't allow Steve Jobs to attend, because his personality was so strong that it might inhibit sharing. The Harkness method of teaching emphasizes the benefits of teaching smaller groups around round tables. http://en.wikipedia.org/wiki/Harkness_table. One day last semester, I sat down in the back of a classroom to listen to a student presentation and I felt a sharp pain in my back. After the presentation, I told the students that I'd conduct the remaining discussion from the chair. I was amazed at how this changed the entire dynamic of the discussion. I noticed that especially the students closer to me felt more open to share.
26. This recommended trail comes from a conversation with clinical psychologist Dr. Ken Walker.

Chapter 25: They Fail to Reason with Emotional Intelligence

1. Bethany McLean and Peter Elkind, *The Smartest Guys in the Room* (New York: Penguin Group), p. 28.
2. Ibid.
3. Jon Gertner, *The Idea Factory* (New York: The Penguin Press, 2012) p. 231.
4. Ibid., pp. 229, 230, 231, 262-265, 289. Surveys about mobile (cell) phones indicated there wasn't a need for them, but Bell Labs went ahead with them and won big time. One person surmised that surveys such as these aren't effective when dealing with products that have never before been introduced. People often don't know that they need something until they have it.
5. I heard Jeff Haynie, co-founder and CEO of Appcellerator, sharing this at Kennesaw State University's annual social media conference: SoCon.
6. Paul Edwards, William P. Alston and A.N. Prior, Bertrand Arthur William Russell, *The Encyclopedia of Philosophy*, Vol. 7 (New York: Macmillan Publishing Co., Inc., & The Free Press, 1967), p. 239 - "Russell has exercised an influence on the course of Anglo-American philosophy in the twentieth century second to that of no other individual. "Moreover he had a fantastic memory - in his latter 70s he spoke of remembering almost all his lessons from kindergarten in detail. Bertrand Russell, *The Autobiography of Bertrand Russell* (New York: Bantam Books, 1968), p. 19.
7. Paul Johnson, *Intellectuals* (New York: Harper & Row, 1988), p. 199.
8. Edwards, et. al., op. cit., pp. 235ff. While these authors refer to him as a "great and honest man," (p. 238), one must wonder about his grandiose statements in his writing which seem to have little if any support from honest, objective research. Was it "honest" to present material as solid fact, when it wasn't adequately researched? Surely his former wives, and the husbands of the wives he seduced, would size him up differently. Historian Will Durant "trembled" as he recalled Russell pursuing his wife Ariel, and later reading Russell state his view that any man out of town on business for more than three weeks should be temporarily released from monogamous restrictions. Will and Ariel Durant, *A Dual Biography* (New York: Simon & Schuster, 1977), p. 119.
9. For example, Alister McGrath notes that Russell, in his *History of Western Philosophy,* quotes the urban legend rendition of John Calvin versus Copernicus. *The Twilight of Atheism* (New York, Doubleday, 2004), pp. 80,81.
10. *Intellectuals*, op. cit., p. 198.
11. Katherine Tait, *My Father, Bertrand Russell* (New York: Harcourt Brace Jovanovich, 1975), p. 197.
12. *Intellectuals*, op. cit., p. 199.
13. Ibid., p. 202.
14. Ibid., p. 202.
15. Ibid., p. 216.
16. Ibid. Note also Russell's self-evaluation in a statement to his fiancée: "Once for all, G. A. [God Almighty] has made me a theorist, not a practical man; a knowledge of the world is therefore of very little value to me." *The Autobiography of Bertrand Russell*, op. cit., p. 127.
17. Ibid.
18. Colin Brown, *Philosophy and the Christian Faith* (Downers Grove, Illinois: InterVarsity Press, 1968), p. 227.
19. Katherine Tait, op. cit., p. 184.
20. Ibid., p. 98.
21. Ibid., p. 176. She also noted, "Both our parents, however, were born rebels, passionately convinced that everything the government was doing was completely misguided, if not deliberately wicked....", p. 19.
22. Ibid., p. 6.
23. Paul Edwards, et. al., p. 256. On Russell's childlike "me first" attitude, remember in his autobiography when he pursued another woman regardless of how it might hurt her husband (*Bertrand Russell*, op. cit., pp. 274ff.) In one of his affairs with a woman in the USA, he made her big promises to commit to her, then dropped her. His actions reveal arrogance and self-centeredness of grand proportions, underscored by his tendency to gross overstatement with inadequate accompanying evidence and intellectual bullying of all who disagreed with him. Contrast this with his claim, in the first page of his autobiography, to have great concern for the plight of people.
24. Paul Edwards, William P. Alston, A. N. Prior, "Bertrand Arthur William Russell," *The Encyclopedia of Philosophy, Vol. 7* (New York: Macmillan Publishing Co., Inc. & The Free Press, 1967), p. 256.
25. Bertrand Russell, *The Autobiography of Bertrand Russell* (New York: Bantam Books, 1968), p.132. From a letter to his fiancée, Alys.
26. On his lack of objective scholarship and his tendency to quote any story that bolstered his argument, see *Intellectuals*, op. cit., pp. 204-212.
27. For instance, the following essay, which purports to discover if Christianity has been a source for good, virtually ignores all the positive evidence and merely makes grandiose statements. This essay shows an astounding lack of scholarship, misrepresentations of people who believe differently from him, and a tendency toward revisionist history. "Has Religion Made Useful Contributions to Civilization?" http://www.positiveatheism.org/hist/russell2.htm.

In his first paragraph, Russell answers the question posed in his title as follows: "It helped in early days to fix the calendar, and it caused Egyptian priests to chronicle eclipses with such care that in time they became able to predict them. These two services I am prepared to acknowledge, but I do not know of any others." Seriously? Apparently, he never bothered to study history to research the profound contributions made by Christianity in halting legal infanticide in early Rome, starting hospitals, starting the Red Cross, stopping the slave trade in Britain and America, formulating the scientific method, establishing human rights in America's founding documents, feeding the poor, founding colleges and secondary education for all, worldwide literacy, etc. Of the many books that document these contributions, a good place to start might be the well-documented study by sociologist Alvin J. Schmidt, *Under the Influence: How Christianity Transformed Civilization* (Grand Rapids: Zondervan, 2001).

When I read articles such as this one, it's difficult to understand why people revere Russell as such a fearless defender of truth. Rather, he seemed to be a person who fearlessly and vigorously spoke his mind. But often, his opinions weren't based upon any serious research or dialogue with experts in the fields he addresses. In fact, when we look more closely at his essays, we find the very fundamentalist approach that most intellectuals claim to deplore: an appeal to emotions, an intolerance for the opinions of scholars who disagree, and cherry-picked facts rather than objective study.

28. One of the primary steps in any serious research is to ensure that you've read and/or listened to positions that oppose your own. A part of this involves thoroughly acquainting oneself with "background information" on the topic. What have others already researched in the area? What conclusions have they come to? See, for example, Peter J. Taylor and Jeremy Szteiter, *Taking Yourself Seriously*: Processes of Research and Engagement (Arlington, Massachusetts: The Pumping Station, 2012), pp. 9,21.

29. Colin Brown, op. cit., p. 227.

30. Paul Johnson, op. cit., p. 209.

31. Ibid., pp. 208,209.

32. Ibid., pp. 209,210.

33. Ibid., p. 212.

34. Ibid. For more on Russell's extremism, emotionalism, and lack of objectivity, see especially pp. 204-211 of Johnson, op. cit. He would collect and disseminate propaganda with no pretense to partiality, kept changing his view of pacifism, preaching each new view with equal fervency to the ideas he formerly held. He went to extremes, seemingly unable to find reasonable mediating views. Johnson found in him a "Lack of concern for the objective facts, the attribution of the vilest motives to those holding different views…." (pp. 208,209). According to his daughter, he needed certainty; he was an absolutist. Katherine Tait, op. cit, p. 184. In this way, he played the part of the fundamentalist.

35. Katherine Tait, op. cit., p. 58.

36. Ibid., p. 60.

37. Ibid., p. 62.

38. Johnson, op. cit., p. 219. On their children's anxieties, see not only their childrearing methods [he'd later confess that he "failed as a parent" (p. 219)], but how their innovative school, led by Russell and his wife, contributed to the problems. By assuming that children should be given extreme freedom (choose whether to attend classes, express whatever they want in whatever foul language they desired, etc.) the lack of supervision allowed bullying and caused other emotional traumas that his parents didn't notice. On his children's anxieties, see Katherine Tait, op. cit., pp. 58-61, 67,68,118-128,180. The view of the school from his daughter's perspective is enlightening. (p. 215).

39. Johnson, op. cit., p. 202.

40. Tait., op. cit., p. 39.

41. Johnson, op. cit., p. 198.

42. I believe I read this comment in one of John Warwick Montgomery's books.

43. Edward de Bono, *Six Thinking Hats* (New York: Little, Brown & Company, 1985), pp. 34-79.

44. Schultz, Howard and Dori Jones Yang, *Pour Your Heart Into It: How Starbucks Built a Company One Cup at a Time* (New York: Hyperion, 1997), p. 156ff.

45. Malcomb Gladwell explores both the positives and negatives of intuitions and first impressions in his popular book *Blink: The Power of Thinking without Thinking* (New York: Little, Brown and Company, 2005).

46. *Einstein: His Life and Universe*, by Walter Isaacson (New York: Simon & Schuster, 2007), p. 113.

47. Ibid., p. 335.

48. Leonard L. Berry, Kent D. Seltman, *Management Lessons from Mayo Clinic* (New York: McGraw Hill, 2008), pp. 1,2.

49. *The Smartest Guys in the Room*, op. cit., p. 405.

50. Katherine Tait, op. cit., pp. 191,193,195.

51. On studying what makes people happy, see David G. Myers, *The Pursuit of Happiness* (New York: Avon Books, 1992). On Cliff Baxter's suicide, see *The Smartest Guys in the Room*, op. cit., pp. xvii, xviii.

52. Michael J. Sandel, *Justice: What's the Right Thing to Do?* (New York: Farrar, Straus and Giroux, 2009.

53. Thus, Page and Brin at Google have adopted the mantra, "Don't do evil." Many of their decisions along the way sacrificed money in the short haul, for the sake of not doing evil to people. If they fail to hold to this ideal, with all the information and resulting power they hold, we're all in trouble. See "10 Things We Know" - http://www.google.com/about/company/philosophy/. Perhaps De Bono could recommend "Is it right?" as a seventh thinking hat. But he'd probably say that our moral thinking should have come out in one or more of the other thinking hats.

54. *Intellectuals*, op. cit., p. 342.

Conclusion: On a Passion for Seeking Truth

1. Norm Augustine, "The Education Our Economy Needs," *The Wall Street Journal*, Sept. 21, 2011.
2. Leonard L. Berry, Kent D. Seltman, *Management Lessons from Mayo Clinic* (New York: McGraw Hill, 2008), p. 71.

About The Authors

J. Steve Miller is president of Legacy Educational Resources and teaches at Kennesaw State University. He has taught audiences from Atlanta to Moscow and is known for drawing practical wisdom from serious research and communicating it in accessible, unforgettable ways. His award-winning books have been translated into multiple languages. He offers seminars on "Critical and Creative Thinking" (for students and businesses) as well as "Maximizing Critical Thinking in the Classroom," for teachers. Contact him at jstevemiller@gmail.com.

Cherie K. Miller earned a BS in Communication with an emphasis in Media Studies, followed by a Master of Arts in Professional Writing, both from Kennesaw State University. As her thesis, she wrote a memoir entitled *One in a Million: Living Courageously with a Traumatic Brain Injury*. During her time at Kennesaw State, Cherie won several awards, including Best College News Editor, Best Research Thesis and College of Humanities and Social Sciences' Staff Member of the Year. Since graduating, Cherie has published three books and numerous articles. Her research interests include animal studies, disability studies and the art of writing.